Yale Series in Economic History

The Dutch Rural Economy in the
Golden Age, 1500–1700

Jan de Vries

New Haven and London, Yale University Press

Library of Congress catalog card number: 73–86889
International standard book number: 0–300–01608–5

Designed by John O. C. McCrillis
and set in Baskerville type.
Printed in the United States of America by
The Alpine Press, Inc., South Braintree, Massachusetts

Published in Great Britain, Europe, Africa, and
Asia (except Japan) by Yale University Press,
Ltd., London. Distributed in Australia and
New Zealand by Book & Film Services, Artarmon,
N.S.W., Australia; and in Japan by Harper & Row,
Publishers, Tokyo Office.

To my parents

Contents

List of Maps, Graphs, and Tables

Preface

In this volume I examine the rural economy of the northern Netherlands. The Dutch economy grew rapidly to become uniquely powerful and prosperous in the Europe of the sixteenth and seventeenth centuries. A considerable literature celebrates the development of its trade and commercial institutions, but its more prosaic aspects, particularly the rural sector of this highly urbanized economy, have attracted little interest.

If the explanations of Dutch economic expansion which invoke chance factors and specious sociological arguments are to be superseded by modern economic explanations and if Dutch economic history is to contribute to our understanding of economic development, the entire economy, in its many facets, must be viewed as a whole, and the relationships between the major sectors must be brought to the fore. As a crucial part of this large task, the transformation of the rural economy must be described, the origins of this transformation uncovered, and the consequences understood.

Implicit in this study is the belief that some relationship exists between the structure of an agrarian economy and the prospects for growth in the total economy. It is my hope that the cause of both Dutch history and economic development theory will be served by this attempt to apply to the rural sector of the Dutch economy the methods of economic analysis.

The geographical area I have chosen for analysis, which I call the "northern Netherlands," is synonymous with neither the present-day Kingdom of the Netherlands nor the seventeenth-century United Republic. The instability of political units during the sixteenth century makes any single set of political boundaries undesirable as our unit of analysis. There are compelling reasons, in any case, to avoid the use of purely political boundaries in agrarian history. Soil types, settlement patterns, climate, and the diffusion of local political institutions and cultural characteristics all define agrarian society more accurately than do simple political jurisdictions.

The northern Netherlands, for our purposes, is successively a part of three states: the Burgundian Netherlands, the United Republic, and, after an interlude of French domination, the Kingdom of the

Netherlands. It consists of the provinces of Holland (present-day North and South Holland), Friesland, Groningen, and the western half of Utrecht. (Zeeland, which could logically be included in this group, has been excluded from systematic consideration because of a paucity of both primary and secondary sources.) These maritime provinces possess a geographical and economic unity, a fact that makes them a suitable unit for our study. Their economic history can be sharply distinguished from that of the eastern provinces of Drenthe, Overijssel, and Gelderland (also part of the three successive states referred to above), and that of the southern provinces of Brabant, Flanders, and Hainault, which were united with the northern and eastern provinces until the revolt against Spain in the 1570s. Thereafter these and other provinces become known as the southern Netherlands and, after 1830, Belgium.

Here a word of warning is in order. The physical unity of the region and—viewed from a North American perspective—its small size must not mislead us into believing that the region's economy can be quickly understood. The northern Netherlands in the sixteenth century embraced over 1,000 villages and hamlets and over 40 cities. These settlements were organized into a welter of internal subdivisions and grouped into dozens of regional drainage authorities. And, too, when we begin our analysis in the early sixteenth century, we must take cognizance of the long history already behind the region and its inhabitants. This background divided the northern Netherlands yet again into subregions not necessarily coterminous with the administrative subdivisions.

This study formally confines itself to the sixteenth and seventeenth centuries, a period of economic expansion. Eighteenth-century sources are sometimes used when they can illuminate conditions of an earlier period. For instance, the analysis of eighteenth-century demographic data permits us to make better use of the fragmentary seventeenth-century data. Although our primary concern remains the period of economic expansion, the cessation of expansion and the decline of a later period obviously cannot be ignored; understanding the economy's growth requires some speculation on the sources of its later problems. Still, the reader is reminded that these speculations are no more than that; their confirmation would require a separate study.

The effort to apply economic theory to a historical period when statistical records are not numerous requires occasional resort to model building and hypothetical reconstruction. The hazards inherent in these procedures should not render them anathema, for they can be of benefit so long as their use is made explicit and the conclusions drawn from them are clearly identified as the tentative or suggestive statements that they must be.

Agrarian history frequently must draw upon the resources of local history; its nature necessarily demands of the reader a geographical familiarity he is unlikely to possess. It is hoped that the maps preceding the text and others scattered through the text will ease the burden of distinguishing *Barradeel* from *Baarderadeel, Wormer* from *Purmer,* and *Broek in Waterland* from *Broek op Langedijk.*

In writing this study I have striven to make it of use to both economists and historians. If I have in some measure fulfilled this immodest aim, much credit must go to those who instructed me at Yale University, where a version of this study was submitted as a doctoral dissertation. The director of the Economic History Program, William N. Parker, and my advisor, Harry A. Miskimin, taught, encouraged, and advised me at every step of this work.

Research undertaken in the Netherlands was made possible by a Fulbright-Hays fellowship, a grant from the Council on Comparative and European Studies of Yale University, and an appointment to the Humanities Research Center of Michigan State University.

Archivists and librarians in the Netherlands never failed to offer me every assistance; I must thank, especially, Mejuffrouw Drs. A. Stolp of the Economisch-Historisch Bibliotheek. I value highly the advice and hospitality extended by B. H. Slicher van Bath, the director of the Department of Rural History at the Landbouwhogeschool in Wageningen, and by A. M. van der Woude, also of the Department of Rural History. Van der Woude's important new study, *Het Noorderkwartier* (Wageningen, 1972) appeared while this work was being prepared for publication. The interested reader will find it corroborates and elaborates upon many points made in this volume. No effort has been made to incorporate its findings in this work. Throughout this volume, translations from Dutch sources are my own.

Coaxing usable statistics from the raw data left us by sixteenth- and seventeenth-century government officials can be a tedious task. Although it is ungraceful for an author to remind his reader of this fact, it seems appropriate to mention this here, so that I can adequately express my gratitude for the support and assistance lent by my wife, Jeannie, in the preparation of this volume.

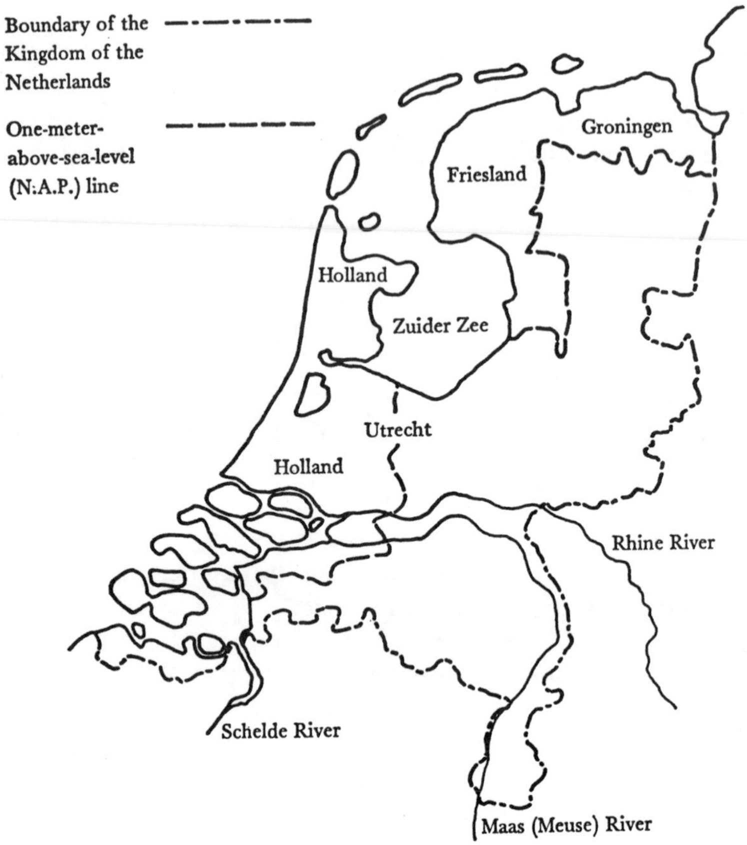
Boundary of the Kingdom of the Netherlands
One-meter-above-sea-level (N.A.P.) line
Groningen
Friesland
Holland
Zuider Zee
Utrecht
Holland
Rhine River
Schelde River
Maas (Meuse) River

The Netherlands, Divided at the One-Meter-above-Sea-Level Line and Showing Principal Rivers

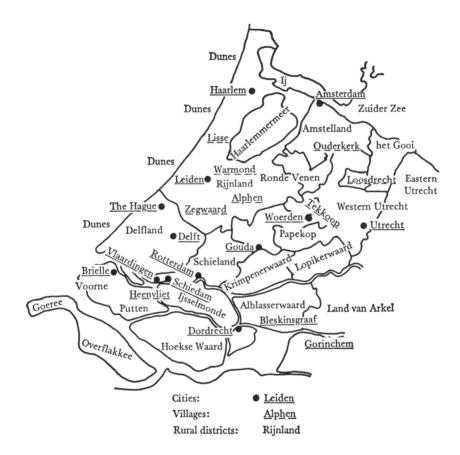

Holland South of the Ij, Showing Principal Cities, Rural Districts, and Certain Villages Mentioned in the Text

Holland North of the Ij, Showing Principal Cities, Rural Districts, and Certain Villages Mentioned in the Text

Friesland, Showing Principal Cities and Certain *Grietenijen* and *Vlekken* Mentioned in the Text. The three major divisions of Friesland—Westergo, Oostergo, and Zevenwouden—are also indicated.

Cities:	●	Groningen
Villages:		Stedum
Rural districts:		Fivelingo

Groningen, Showing Principal Cities, Rural Districts, and Certain Villages Mentioned in the Text

1. Change in Rural Society, 1000–1800

RURAL DEVELOPMENT IN WESTERN EUROPE

Rural society in Europe, until the nineteenth century, was almost everywhere engaged in production for a limited, local market. The medieval manor was seldom an entirely self-sufficient economic unit, but it provided an enduring organizational framework in which a village community could subsist in the absence of well-developed channels of trade. Medieval commerce, which encouraged the remarkable growth of cities, did little to alter the local self-sufficiency of the rural economy, since that commerce remained dominated by long-distance trade in luxury goods. Even the expanding trade of the late fifteenth and sixteenth centuries, which included bulky commodities such as wine, grain, and lumber, touched only a small fraction of total output.

The regime of local self-sufficiency in rural Europe was supported and enforced by two economic facts: first, the high cost of overland transportation, which prevented the development of large market areas in all but a few geographically favored points and which made large-scale trade in most bulky commodities impossible; second, low productivity in agriculture, which prevented the rural economy from generating large surpluses and restrained the development of a nonagricultural class.

Cities with their market areas, which in western Europe ranged from 40 to 85 square miles, were the basic economic units of early modern Europe.[1] The goods traded among such regions comprised but a tiny percentage of the total quantity of goods produced within them, and the nonagricultural population of such a region rarely exceeded one-fifth of the total.

Costly transportation and the small, irregular surpluses from the countryside worked together to limit markets and to keep cities small. Few cities exceeded a population of 20,000 in medieval Europe, and the city of 50,000 was uncommon until the nineteenth century.[2]

Within this pattern of local self-sufficiency, certain cities rose in size above the average. Particularly favorable locations for economic development, access to a scarce resource, or, more commonly, the presence of governmental or religious institutions caused such cities to grow. The large market and investment funds they offered stimulated the development of agriculture in their immediate environs.

Urban demand not only for grains, but also for animal products, vegetables, and industrial crops, encouraged intensive production near the town walls. Here, new techniques arose mainly from the spread of horticultural crops from gardens to farm fields. The German term *intensitätinseln* describes such areas admirably. The intensitätinseln extended but a short distance from the gates of the cities and depended on the cities for both markets and capital. Being so much a creature of the cities, these pockets of advanced techniques and thoroughgoing commercialization were incapable of spreading over the landscape and altering the economic structure of rural society over wide areas. The structure of local self-sufficiency was not altered appreciably by the development of intensitätinseln.

A new production pattern, based on regional specialization and long-distance trade in bulky goods such as grain, cattle, wine, and dairy products, gradually developed in parts of western Europe. Although its antecedents can be traced further back in time, this new pattern developed rapidly only after the late fifteenth century. The new system of regional specialization focused on the numerous population centers of the English Channel–North Sea littoral. Mainly waterborne supply routes connected the central core, composed of the northern and southern Netherlands and southeastern England, with the Baltic, the Bay of Biscay, the Rhine and Maas (Meuse) river valleys, and the northern and western reaches of the British Isles.

From the Elbe eastward along the Baltic coast arose a broad band of grain-exporting lands. Further inland, livestock raising grew to importance, and increasing numbers of oxen were driven westward from Russia, Poland, and Hungary. Another cattle route developed along a north-south axis; from Jutland cattle were driven and transported by sea to be fattened near the urban centers of northwest Europe. A third such flow of cattle was observable in the British Isles. Here cattle bred in Scotland, Wales, and northern England made their way to southern England for fattening and consumption.

Wine produced in France was shipped north from the Atlantic ports; German wine travelled down the Rhine for distribution from Dutch ports. As this trade grew, vineyards in the northern extremities of viticulture fell out of use. Along the North Sea coast intensive dairy production arose, and near the dense net of cities in northwestern Europe dairy output, together with the fattening of oxen and the growing of industrial crops, became increasingly important.[3]

In most areas these growing trade patterns touched the local economy only lightly; at the focus of this diffuse pattern of trade in agrarian products, namely, the Low Countries and southeastern England, the impact was very great. The specialization pattern, which became clearer and more permanent as the volume of trade increased during the late sixteenth and early seventeenth centuries, produced an articulation of the regions of Europe akin to the spatial patterning of agricultural production postulated by the nineteenth-century German economist Henrick von Thünen for the area surrounding a market city. Von Thünen's "rings," which had been significant on a regional—intensitätinseln—basis, now extended outward from a focal point in northwestern Europe to encompass much of the continent. During the sixteenth and seventeenth centuries there took root a structure of agricultural specialization that endures in many ways to the present day.[4]

Still, many regions failed to participate in this growing system of specialization; local self-sufficiency, as described above, continued to characterize their economies. Powerful forces resisting agricultural progress seem to have been operative long after the construction of a framework that permitted such progress through trade-induced specialization.[5] Certain regions, on the other hand, availed themselves of these opportunities, transformed their institutions, and introduced improved techniques.

To explain the pattern of change and stagnation in European rural society the view that urban economic life acted (in the words of Henri Pirenne) to spread "an infection [to the countryside] which roused the peasant from his age-long torpor" [6] has long enjoyed acceptance for want of a more penetrating analysis. But the impulses to economic change do not emanate exclusively from cities. On the contrary, this study affirms the proposition that the historically developed structure of a rural society and the nature of urban-rural economic relationships in a given area crucially affect the course of rural economic development. These factors have influence mainly at the household level. Besides a framework of regional and continental specialization and trade, rural development requires a fundamental transformation of the peasant household economy. To this third, and basic, level of specialization we now turn.

The lack of historical data on the peasant household economy forces the discussion to take the form of "model building." Two models of rural change follow. In these models some basic propositions useful to the historical analysis that forms the bulk of this study will be introduced. The models rest on historical observation as well as economic theory. This information, pressed into rigid models, can be criticized as distorting the reality of rural society, but it should have the redeeming virtue of clarifying basic distinctions of great importance in an effort to determine the nature of that rural social and economic structure which responds readily to opportunities for growth.

Two Models of Rural Development

Consider a self-sufficient society of peasant farmers in which the population and the agricultural techniques employed are stable. Our concern is to understand how this society changes when its social and economic equilibrium is shaken by population growth and the introduction of limited trading opportunities. Our first simplification is to imagine that a society in perfect repose exists; our second simplification is to assume that the disruptive forces arise from a source exogenous to the society upon which they act.

The Peasant Model

There are a variety of imaginable responses to such changes. A common response, which we shall call "the peasant model," consists of peasant families' dividing the land they farm as their numbers increase. This can occur when a farmer divides his lands among his children or through the sale and purchase of land as the techniques employed in agriculture change. This brings us to the second important response. The increasing density of population requires more food production from the land; greater output requires an intensification of land use. Intensification necessarily entails an increase in the labor time expended on each unit of land, which encourages the division of large, extensively utilized holdings into smaller, more intensively cultivated holdings.

It might be considered that the changes outlined thus far set the stage for progress, since new techniques are applied to agriculture in order to increase the productivity of the land. The increased productivity per unit of land is won, however, by the application of techniques that tend to lower the productivity of each hour of labor expended by the farmer. Ester Boserup has shown that decreasing returns to labor time result from adopting progressively more labor-intensive agricultural techniques.* For instance, the effort involved in feeding oneself in a primitive forest-fallow land-use system, where the farmer burns down a forest covering and plants crops on the resulting ash-covered field, is much less than the effort involved in supplying oneself with the same amount of food in a more intensive yearly cropping system, in which careful plowing, harrowing, and weeding are required and the farmer is obliged to gather great quantities of fertilizer and spread them over the fields. Much less land is needed in this latter system than in the former but the total labor time expended to produce a given quantity of grain is far greater.

A growing population that divides its land into smaller holdings must introduce more labor-intensive techniques; these place a downward pressure on labor productivity. During the transition the likelihood of more frequent famine crises is increased and the peasants on the smaller holdings may find, as *morcellement* continues, that they cannot support themselves on their holdings: they enter the labor market periodically as day laborers to supplement their inadequate income from the land.

Now we must break the course of this analysis to examine another factor. Limited trading opportunities with an urban sector arise in this virtually self-sufficient society. The peasants, increasing in number, are unable to produce regular agricultural surpluses to satisfy the new "outside" demand. In fact, increasing numbers of peasants are now entering the grain market as purchasers. These circumstances force grain prices upward relative to other prices. (The demand for grain increases faster than the supply, thereby driving grain prices upward; the high grain prices cause purchasing power to fall, which forces the peasants to curtail purchases of "nonessentials," thereby driving down the relative price of nonfood commodities.)† Without a marketable surplus, the peasants do not have the ability to act as consumers of urban goods, either. In fact, the falling productivity of labor in agriculture as landholdings shrink make labor in home handicrafts a relatively attractive alternative. The result is a rural sector in which most peasants must respond

* See appendix A at the end of this chapter.
† See appendix B at the end of this chapter.

negatively to the new trading opportunity; they strive to avoid market dependence.

The developing crisis situation provides an opportunity for profit to those who can maintain their economic strength through these changing circumstances. Urban capitalists with money to invest and an interest in securing a grain supply for their city and "institutional" landowners such as religious bodies and noblemen, who have kept intact large landholdings in the face of the morcellement process, are in a good position to gain from the economic conditions that bring grief to the peasants. Moneyed men are encouraged to buy land and perhaps to organize production in order to profit from the strong demand for grain. The opportunity to profit is enhanced by the financial embarrassment of the peasants, who cannot resist selling land or submitting to disadvantageous tenurial changes, and by the growth of the day-labor force, which tends to keep wage rates down despite the rise of grain prices.[7]

This model of a rural society responding to two change-provoking factors results in an increased social differentiation of the peasant population. Its chief features are the growth of a marginally employed "cottar" class, the concentration of wealth in the hands of bourgeois, noble, and clerical landowners, and the monopolization of the limited trade opportunities by a few large farms, owned in the main by these rich landowners. Prices, wages, and rents move in such a way as to reinforce the economic strength of the newly dominant large landowners. Income distribution becomes increasingly unequal.[8]

Before developing a second model of rural change we should explore more fully the nature of the rural-urban relationship in the model just described. The rural economy's inability to overcome the basic problem of producing sufficient agricultural output to satisfy the demand of both the growing rural population and the urban population obstructs the development of beneficial trading links between the urban and the rural sectors. The intervention of urban capitalists in the rural economy, however profitable to those capitalists, does not alleviate the basic problem of supply; the rural society's growing income inequality prevents it from acting as a market for urban goods. The growth of rural-urban trade links is frustrated. The city's function in the rural society is simply to serve as an irregular market for surplus goods and to distribute limited quantities of very basic commodities, such as salt, and of luxury goods for the wealthy few. This dearth of trade prevents urban centers from becoming larger or more numerous. Typically, then, only a few cities, with an economic life only loosely integrated with that of the countryside, arise where the rural society answers to a "peasant model" of rural change. Concern over securing a grain supply and interest in profiting from the opportunities in rural areas, as mentioned above, might stimulate urban dwellers to construct a political and economic dominion over the rural society. Such domination, however, is a symptom of the failure of a mutually beneficial relationship to develop rather than an agency of such change.

The Specialization Model

We now return to our basic assumptions of a self-sufficient peasant society with a stable population in order to examine a second model of rural change, which we shall call the "specialization model." Again, the stable initial conditions are disrupted by a rise in population and the opening of the society to trading opportunities with an urban sector. Just as before, the peasants divide their labor time between producing agricultural and nonagricultural commodities.

The response to the changed conditions differs from that in the peasant model in the following way: the peasants do not divide their landholdings; they increase agricultural output on their intact farms by reducing the amount of time spent producing nonagricultural goods and services for their own consumption and applying a much increased proportion of their labor time to agricultural production. The peasant now produces a regular surplus and is able to enter the recently introduced market economy, selling agricultural commodities to the urban market and purchasing nonagricultural goods that had previously been produced, inefficiently, on the farm. The peasant who responds in this manner, by reorganizing the pattern of home production to the exclusion of, or by the reduction of, nonagricultural output, suffers, just as the peasant in our first model, from declining labor productivity in agricultural production. He gains, however, where the peasant in the first model does not, by being able, in economic terms, to capture the static and dynamic gains from internal trade creation and specialization. In other words, the efficiency of labor will increase as the peasant specializes in producing that for which he is best suited, given the factors of production at his disposal and his acquired skills. Goods which he had produced in small quantities, using primitive techniques, he now buys from nonfarm tradesmen whose specialization, as Adam Smith noted, permits them to produce goods with superior techniques and skills.*

The course of prices, wages, and rents observed in the first model recurs in this model, but the disastrous consequences of these price movements upon the peasants do not. In the specialization model the peasant is able regularly to enter the market as a seller of agricultural goods, the price of which is rising relative to other goods. The predatory role of capitalists and noblemen in the peasant model has no counterpart in the specialization model since the peasants themselves reorganize production in response to market opportunities and themselves reap the benefits. Capitalists cannot amass land and revise leases to the detriment of the tenant now, because the peasantry does not experience the growing financial embarrassment which, in the peasant model, provides the opportunity for these developments to occur.

But, one might object, what becomes of the growing population? The peasant population in this model does not expand in proportion to the total population. Some additional labor is required as agricultural intensification spreads and deepens. For instance, a rapid growth of demand for very intensively produced horticultural and industrial crops is likely to occur as urban-rural trade develops. This would require many laborers' working small, commercialized farms. Nonetheless, the bulk of the increased population is not admitted to the peasant sector; it is forced to find nonagricultural employment.

In the first model the population, as it grows, remains attached, however marginally, to the land. Occupational differentiation makes little headway since most households work land and engage in nonagricultural production in a manner calculated to minimize their dependence upon the marketplace. Consequently, neither a demand for goods produced off the farm nor a supply of specialized labor to produce such goods arise in the peasant model. In the specialization model, developing agricultural specialization and rural-urban trade produce an economic framework in which much of the growing nonagricultural labor force can be absorbed. The presence of this growing body of workers expelled from the agricultural sector depresses wages, but while the chief employment opportunities open to the lower strata of the peasant population in the first model was

* See appendix C at the end of this chapter.

casual day labor in agriculture, the rural proletariat in this model has options that raise the prospect of gaining a secure livelihood. Loosened from any ties to the land, these workers can migrate to the cities, which are in a position to grow because of the development of rural-urban trade. In the midst of the farm population, employment opportunities arise, since agriculture requires specialized goods and services—in construction, road and canal building, transportation, marketing, ironmongering—in order to derive full benefit from the specialization process underway on the farm itself.

All these responses to the initial introduction of trade and population growth amount to a restructuring of the rural economic system in which both the use of improved techniques and the development of increased allocational efficiency permit the economy to demonstrate growth, as the word is understood by economists. This restructuring establishes the framework in which investment can expect a good return, producers of both agricultural and nonagricultural goods can expect expanding markets, and a growing population can expect employment opportunities to expand.

The construction of strong trading links between the urban and rural sectors based on rural specialization in agriculture and the concomitant growth of rural demand for manufactured goods is at the heart of economic growth in this model.[9] A large volume of trade flowing between the two sectors affects the nature of the urban sector in two important ways: first, it increases the importance of local trade in an urban economy which otherwise (as in the peasant model, for instance) is mainly concerned with long-distance trade in high-valued commodities intended for the small well-to-do class; second, it increases the number of cities, since the volume of trade warrants more cities and since the frequent market activity of farmers requires a denser network of market sites. The percentage of the total population living in cities is likely to increase under these conditions.

The urban sector's economic interest in the rural sector is more complex in this model than in the first model. In an economy in which agricultural specialization succeeds in increasing production and thereby stimulating trade with the urban sector, the city's chief concern shifts from securing a regular food supply to securing a labor supply at acceptable wage rates. The growth of trade stimulates urban industry for which an expanding labor force must be recruited, and the tendency of densely settled cities to have death rates that exceed their birth rates insures that new workers must be recruited from the rural areas. Clearly, migration to the cities is crucial to the development of the economy in this model.

Just as the concerns of the city differ between the two models, so also do investment opportunities for the urban capitalist. The financial strength of a peasantry, which captures for itself the gains to be made from marketing regular surpluses of agricultural commodities, frustrates the exploitative investment activity typical of the first model. Investment opportunities do arise, however, as a result of the specialization process begun by the peasants themselves; capital is needed if the rural economy is to restructure itself successfully. If trade volume is to grow, transportation facilities must be improved; if output is to increase, capital must be invested in planting orchards and vineyards, acquiring new seed, constructing buildings, and improving drainage and irrigation facilities. All these new capital requirements invite the participation of the urban capitalist.

We need not dwell upon the fact that few rural societies have followed, or will follow, the precise sequence of events outlined in the peasant and specialization models. Although rural change in the real world is more complex than that portrayed in the two models, a discussion of the consequences that emanate from them is useful in isolating two responses of fundamental importance.

In the peasant model the economically undifferentiated peasant society underwent no significant change, as the individual households persisted in a basically self-sufficient production system. The increasingly unfavorable population-resource balance generated social differentiation and increased poverty as the land was divided among a more numerous peasantry.

In the specialization model, the peasantry transformed its self-sufficient household economy to an economy of specialized agricultural producers who were reliant on intersectoral trade for nonagricultural goods. As the population grew, much of the increment found its way into nonagricultural production, either through migration to cities or through the development of crafts and industries in the villages. This response ultimately totally transforms the old peasant society while the response in the former model transforms nothing, but rather enfeebles the intact peasant society.

FACTORS AFFECTING THE COURSE OF RURAL DEVELOPMENT

Now consider the factors, omitted from the models, that contribute to determining a rural society's pattern of response to the pressures of population growth and the introduction of trade with an urban sector. While surely not an exhaustive accounting, the factors considered below form the most important features of the structure of a rural society. Physical, legal, sociological, and economic characteristics will be discussed in turn.

Field patterns and village structure provide the physical framework in which a rural society functions. While it is true that the nature of the physical framework develops in close conjunction with complementary legal institutions, for the sake of clarity we shall discuss these factors separately.

Over the face of Europe spreads a complex pattern of field and village types. For decades historians have been engaged in a remorseless struggle to reduce this bewildering pattern to a finite number of clearly distinguishable categories. The struggle has yet to be crowned with complete success, but a rough schematization will indicate the basic conditions of cultivation. Some basic characteristics that distinguish the field patterns of Europe may be cited. Is the use of the fields subject to communal constraints? Does the cultivator live on his holding or in a nucleated settlement? Are the fields composing a holding few or many, and are they readily divisible? These physical characteristics taken together are sufficient to influence significantly the nature of peasant response in the models discussed above.

The extended and often tedious discussions of field patterns available in many works make another such discourse here unnecessary.[10] The characteristics listed above serve to indicate the significant conditioning role played by the physical structure of the land upon the relative freedom of peasants on different sorts of holdings to organize production to suit changing conditions. It is true that gradual changes have, over the centuries, altered the field patterns in many areas.[11] The stimulus to alter these patterns has very often been the technical requirements of new land-use systems being adopted to accommodate an increased population density. Despite this "flexibility," field and village patterns are a major factor which the peasant must consider when contemplating innovation. In the short run, none of the systems are readily changed and, more significant to our argument, some patterns are more difficult to change than others.

In certain regions the fields became divided into tiny parcels, and farms composed of dozens of widely scattered fragments arose. In other regions large, intact fields and farms have endured for centuries. Although great caution must be exercised in interpreting cartographic data, particularly with regard to the dating of the morcellement process, this feature of the landscape is of great importance to our models. Morcellement is a common feature of nucleated villages with open fields and common wastes. As population increases, the strips in the open fields are subdivided, and cottars carve (assart) small plots from the wastes. Street villages (also known as marsh villages and, in Germany, *Waldhufendörfer*), with long narrow holdings stretching backward from dwellings on the street, exhibit a strong tendency to keep the holdings intact. The pattern in which the waste is brought under cultivation (by clearing at the far end of the holding and thereby extending it into the marsh, or up the slope of a mountain) leaves little opportunity for the carving of cottar holdings. These examples suggest the manner in which field and village patterns can influence peasant response in our models.

The legal system of a region also affects the nature of a rural society's response to stimuli to change. The probability of morcellement, described above with reference to the physical characteristics of a field system, is also affected by inheritance custom. Much has been made of the contrasting rural characteristics of England and France attributed to the former's custom of primogeniture and the latter's custom of division of property among all male heirs. But Thirsk notes that inheritance custom among the English peasantry exhibited no uniformity. The custom of dividing estates ruled in many districts of England. In Germany, Henning notes that *geschlossener Erbfolge* was customary in some, while *Realteilung* ruled in other of the numerous German principalities. He describes no self-evident pattern but notes, just as does Thirsk in England, that the inheritance customs affected the size of landholdings and, hence, the economic structure of rural society.[12]

Little research has been directed to the influence of the custom of property disposition within marriage. Two types were widespread. In one, husband and wife held all property in common. When one died, the survivor had the right to keep half while the other half went to other heirs. In the other type, the property was owned and bequeathed by the husband; the wife's claims were determined in the marriage contract and usually were limited to a cash settlement. Clearly, the tendency toward land fragmentation would be encouraged by the former and retarded by the latter marriage custom.

A combination of partible inheritance and communal property ownership within marriage must have been a potent force compelling morcellement.

While inheritance and property disposition customs obviously shape the physical division of property, they are not likely to be the most important legal factor to influence agrarian change in general. Of greater importance surely is the legal status of the peasantry. Viewing western Europe as a whole, we find that peasant society consisted of a large mass of dependent and a smaller number of "free" peasants. When one examines Europe region by region, the relative proportions of these two legal classes of men are found to vary enormously. In some areas virtually all men could claim freedom from the judicial and economic rule of manorial lords,[13] while in others hardly any could do so. Furthermore, the precise nature of peasant dependency varied from place to place. From the High Middle Ages onward, manumission reduced the ranks of the enserfed, but manorial lords remained as seigneurs to hold judicial and economic power over the formerly enserfed peasantry.

Seigneurial prerogative varied from region to region, but where it was strong, it contributed mightily to lock the subject peasantry into an economic system defined and protected by the power of the seigneur. His powers included the right to levy certain taxes, collect tithes, enjoy unpaid transportation services, enforce privileges such as obligatory use by the peasant of seigneurial mills, winepresses, breweries, and ovens, and, most important, the right to administer justice in, at least, matters of civil justice. This right placed the seigneur in the strategic position of arbiter of village property disputes. Armed with these prerogatives, a powerful seigneur could profoundly affect the economic conduct of the peasant household. The peasant's mobility, the security of his right to work the land and use the common wastes, his right to produce nontithed crops or engage in noncustomary agricultural activities and many other "privileges," all could be restricted in some way by a strong seigneur.

Sociological studies of underdeveloped lands stress the importance of attitudes and household tradition in economic change. A not unreasonable assumption is that in the past sociological factors played an important role in determining how a rural society responded to the stimuli to change examined in the models introduced earlier. We will avoid broad and sweeping sociological factors categorized under "basic attitudes" and "mentality" and instead stress only two specific features of a peasant household that have a direct bearing on our problem.[14]

The family structure of peasant households, whether they are composed of conjugal or extended family groupings, directly influences the specialization process. In the most backward, least commercialized rural districts of the Netherlands, sociologists have noted the survival into the twentieth century of the extended family principle.[15] In a historical study of the Dutch province of Overijssel, Slicher van Bath found that in 1748 the family structure in a commercialized region highly specialized in dairy farming consisted almost exclusively of conjugal families, while in the decidedly more self-sufficient, sandy-soil districts of the province extended families were frequently encountered.[16]

As in so many other matters, we must caution against making too much of the importance of family structure. The findings of the Cambridge Group for the History of Population and Social Structure, as reported by Laslett, show that extended families were not common in seventeenth and eighteenth century England; although evidence is scanty, some demographers hold that most of western Europe has long been populated mainly by conjugal families.[17]

A division of economic responsibilities within the peasant household that excludes men or women from certain tasks can inhibit the specialization response. If, for instance, the labor of women or children is conceived as usable only on specific nonagricultural tasks, such as clothmaking, specialization in agricultural output might be stymied.[18] This sort of cultural barrier can carry over into consumption patterns. If certain goods, available from both home or urban production, are deemed especially desirable when they possess attributes that only home production can impart, the opportunity to specialize household production in agricultural products might be rejected.[19]

Economic characteristics form the final field of inquiry in this discussion. The qualities of the soil often encourage a peasant to produce specific crops, the nature of which can have a bearing on our problem. Crops vary in their bulk, perishability, ability to satisfy directly important human needs, and the distribution of labor time needed through the year for their production. As a consequence, the mix of agricultural output on a farm and the specific crops that soil conditions favor in the event of a move toward specialization will

themselves, by their economic characteristics, influence the response
to new opportunities to produce for the market and specialize. Areas
well suited to dairying, for instance, appear to respond more readily
than many others to such opportunities.

Land tenure rights could shape the economic environment in
which the peasant household operated in a number of ways. Systems
of land tenure, just as field patterns, were numerous and occurred in
such a bewildering variety as to defy categorization. Feudal land-use
systems did not confer exclusive ownership of land but rather conferred certain rights of land use on persons in exchange for obligations to others. The breakdown of this system came hand in hand
with efforts on the part of various social classes to convert their
claims upon the land into actual ownership. No single system replaced the old feudal arrangements; rather, a motley pattern of
compromises arose from centuries of political struggle.[20] Even after
a landlord enjoyed clear title to his land, custom could not be entirely ignored in the terms of a lease. If we cannot generalize about
the distribution over Europe of different sorts of tenure conditions,
some important ways in which they could vary can be mentioned.

The conditions under which peasants held land could allow them
security for generations on end, or for only a year or two. The rental
sum could be levied and payable in money, in which case it was
generally fixed for the duration of the tenure contract, or in kind, in
which case it could be either fixed or expressed as a proportion of
the harvest. If rent was paid in kind, the landowner often specified
the crops and commodities in which payment could be made. In
such leases labor services were often required in addition to commodity payments. This requirement partially tied the lessee to the
production schedule of an estate.

Leases often specified the crop rotation system and agricultural
practices that could be employed on the land. In other cases few
(if any) such stipulations were made. All these possible tenancy conditions together determined in large part whether the entrepreneurial responsibilities on a farm rested in the hands of the owner or
the tenant. They also determined which principal to the lease would
benefit or suffer most from changes in prices and agricultural productivity.

The tenant's response to changing economic conditions depended
in part upon his freedom to exercise entrepreneurial functions and
to invest capital in the farm enterprise with the security that he per-

sonally, rather than the landlord, would be the main beneficiary. Two examples of European tenure systems will illustrate the importance of these observations.

In *métayage* tenure, a form of sharecropping that spread in seventeenth- and eighteenth-century France, the landowner leased fully equipped farms on short terms in return for a large share, perhaps one-half, of the farm's yield.[21] In practice this system amounted to rural slumlordism; there was no scope for capital improvement or technical innovation on the part of the tenant since only the landowner could profit from such efforts. The landowner, for his part, was not encouraged to elaborately equip farms whose tenants possessed no capital of their own and came and went rather frequently.

In *Beklemrecht* tenure (features of which were common all over northwestern Europe, but which is the particular characteristic of seventeenth- and eighteenth-century Groningen), the landowner leased farms on a terminable (usually 6-year) basis, for a permanently fixed money rent. Upon the occasion of a new lease the tenant paid a *geschenk*, or entry fine, of between 0.5 and 2 times the yearly rental. The lessee was responsible for the construction and maintenance of his house and barn. On the other hand, if the owner wished to terminate the relationship, he was obliged to repay the lessee the full value of the farm's buildings. In practice Beklemrecht was a hereditary tenure in which the tenant could freely invest in improvements knowing that he personally would capture the gains to be made from his efforts.[22]

Agricultural specialization and commercialization has now been described on three levels: the regional, the continental, and the household.[23] The long-run success of rural development rests on the successful transformation of the household economy. Therefore, we have presented models of possible household development and have focused particular attention on the physical, legal, sociological, and economic factors that affect the nature of the peasant household's response to changed conditions. The historical basis of this analysis has been kept general but confined chronologically to the period between the High Middle Ages and the Industrial Revolution.

Before initiating our analysis of rural society's role in the development of the northern Netherlands economy in the sixteenth and seventeenth centuries, a description of the medieval legacy of physical and institutional conditions and the agrarian structure at the beginning of the sixteenth century will be of use. This information, when applied to the generalizations made above with reference to the peasant and specialization models of rural change, will aid in understanding the adaptive and responsive capacity of the region's rural economy.

APPENDIX A. THE INTENSIFICATION OF AGRICULTURAL PRODUCTION

See Ester Boserup, *The Conditions of Agricultural Growth*, pp. 23–34. The assertion presented here, that peasants have a variety of production techniques available to them at any given time, requires some explanation. The assertion contradicts the model of agricultural change put forward by Ricardo. He maintained that technological change was the major force in industrial development but that decreasing returns in agriculture would make the problem of food supply bulk increasingly large in the total economy until the time came when the wage bill had become so large (because of increasing food costs) that profits disappeared. At this point, a stable equilibrium condition would rule the economy; population and output would cease growing while rent would have grown large at the expense of profits. Behind this scenario lies the assumption that the land area and the productive techniques of agriculture are fixed.

Empirical observation does not uphold the Richardian view. The inability of land area to grow has not caused rents to absorb income as populations have grown and increased their demand for products of the soil. Instead, increased population has generally brought in its train new productive techniques in agriculture. Boserup's observations of Asian economies have led her to the conclusion that a wide variety of techniques, each with different factor proportions, are available to the peasant. As the population grows, a peasant economy can switch from one to another of these technical systems. The accompanying diagram shows how a society with fixed land resources ($\bar{T}$) and a growing population changes its techniques ($P_1, P_2, \ldots$) to increase its total agricultural output ($Q_1, Q_2, \ldots$).

The lower half of the diagram displays a crucial consequence of movement from less labor-intensive to more labor-intensive land-use systems: the declining marginal productivity of labor (measured by the slope of the total output curve). Increased intensity is generally gained at the expense of the fallow period. A reduced fallow period requires the introduction of some other method of preserving soil fertility. This, in turn, almost inevitably increases the labor input per unit of crop area as well as per unit of output. The tendency for the marginal productivity of labor to fall as the land-use system becomes more intensive accounts for the observed fact that peasants rarely adopt techniques more intensive than required to supply themselves with foodstuffs.

But why, in a peasant society where agricultural production takes up a

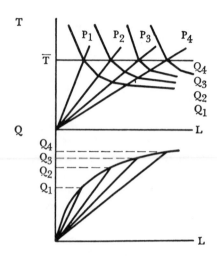

relatively small amount of the peasants' time, would the peasant resist this intensification process until forced into it by growing population pressure? A utility function that places an extremely great value on leisure could explain such conduct, but a more persuasive explanation stresses the large amount of time that must be devoted to the production of non-agricultural goods and the provision of services in an unspecialized peasant economy.

Appendix B. Price and Wage Movement in the Preindustrial Economy

The movement of prices and wages in the two models introduced above can best be understood in the basic framework for the analysis of pre-nineteenth-century economic history developed by B. H. Slicher van Bath in *The Agrarian History of Western Europe, 500–1850*, pp. 98–131, and by Wilhelm Abel in *Agrarkrisen und Agrarkonjunktur*, particularly, pt. 2, chaps. 2–4. Exogenously determined population movements are the main generating factor in this conceptualization. A virtually fixed supply of land and a low price-elasticity of supply for most important commodities is assumed. The income elasticity of demand is zero or negative for grains, and increasingly greater than one for livestock products, industrial crops, and manufactured goods, respectively. This set of conditions is sufficient to explain the general course of prices in the economy under discussion. A change in aggregate demand for grain caused by an increase in population places a strong upward pressure on prices since the supply response to a price increase of grain is only slightly less inelastic than is the elasticity of demand. Since expenditure on basic foodstuffs absorbs a very large percentage of total income, the increase in the price of grain results in a significant reduction in the real income of the population. A change in the consumption mix between two commodities (between grain and all other goods, in this example) as their relative prices change is broken down into a substitution effect and an income effect. Normally, a rise in the price of *A* relative to that of *B* would cause consumers to substitute *B* for *A*, but to decrease consumption of *both A and B* with the decreased real income brought about by the price change. The precise shifts would depend upon the values of the elasticities of demand characteristic of the two goods. In our example, where the demand for basic foodstuffs is totally inelastic, there is no substitution effect away from grain when its price rises. Only an income effect remains, which reduces the consumption of all other goods. (It could very well be that the consumption of grain, as its price increased greatly, would actually increase. This could happen if the falling real income of consumers brought about by the rise of grain prices forced consumers to curtail consumption of luxury foods and rely on a simplified diet of only the most basic foodstuffs. In such a case the demand for grain would increase absolutely.)

When aggregate demand for grain falls, so do grain prices; this occasions an increase in real income that affects chiefly the demand for commodities other than grain. In such a situation the price of livestock products, industrial crops, and manufactured goods would rise—in the order listed—relative to grain prices. The course of prices and wages over a complete cycle of agrarian "growth" and "depression," characterized by rising and then falling, or stagnant, population, can be schematized as in the accompanying diagram.

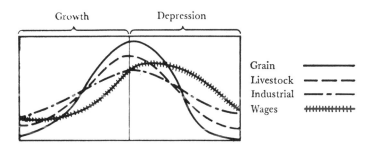

Indices of prices and wages, after Slicher van Bath, *Agrarian History*, graph 9.

APPENDIX C. THE ALLOCATION OF LABOR IN THE PEASANT HOUSEHOLD

In both the peasant model and the specialization model the following assumptions are made: the rural sector produces agricultural commodities

(F) and a variety of nonagricultural goods (Z) according to its production possibility curve.

$$F = F(Z)$$

The rural sector can obtain substitutes for home-produced Z in the form of manufactured goods (M) produced in an urban sector. Since Z is by definition produced and consumed within the household, the trade possibility between the rural and urban sector is expressed by

$$M = P(F - \bar{F})$$

where $\bar{F}$ is the agricultural output consumed by the peasant household and P is the rate of exchange between agricultural and manufactured goods (P_F/P_M). It is clear that in order to substitute M for Z, the peasant household must first transform Z into F and then exchange F for M. The transformation of Z into F consists of redeploying the household's labor time from its initial distribution, which can be expressed as

$$L_T = L_Z + L_F + L_L$$

where L_T is total labor time (best expressed in hours per year), L_Z is labor spent in Z production, L_F is labor spent in F production, and L_L is leisure time (which we shall assume to be a constant). Since most Z activities require little if any land, the expression for Z output can be written as

$$Z = \frac{1}{a} L_Z$$

where a is the labor units required per unit of Z. F output, which uses land (T) (assumed to be fixed in quantity), can be expressed as

$$F = F(L_F, T).$$

The application of labor to land $(\bar{T})$ is subject to diminishing returns.

From the initial distribution described above, the specialization process can be described as concentrating the available household labor in F production. Such a redeployment increases the amount of labor applied per unit of land. The additional labor is subject to strongly decreasing returns if applied to the constellation of techniques appropriate to the factor proportions prevailing before the additional labor is added. Following the analysis of Boserup (see app. A), we observe that the additional labor can be effectively utilized only if a new, more labor-intensive combination of agricultural techniques is adopted. This is necessary because each land-use pattern is characterized by virtually fixed factor proportions. The simple addition of labor to a prevailing land-use pattern would cause the marginal productivity of labor in agriculture (MP_L) to fall to zero very quickly.

If the amount of land at the disposal of the peasant household falls (which is the case in the peasant model), a redeployment of labor from Z to F must occur simply to produce the household food needs ($\bar{F}$). Production for the market, to purchase M for the Z goods that were sacrificed to intensify F production, requires a further redeployment of labor and entails a further fall in the marginal productivity of labor in agriculture. Unless the rate of exchange (P) for the food producer becomes very favorable, he is likely to find that his best strategy is to retain a large portion of the household's labor in Z production. This market avoidance strategy cushions the fall in MP_L in agriculture and gains the equivalent of M goods at a lower labor cost to the household.

In the case of the specialization model, household labor can be absorbed into F production with a less severe fall in MP_L. Specialization occurs more readily and, as a result, the peasant households are put in a position to gain through increased allocational efficiency and by capturing the static and dynamic gains from internal trade creation.

Other factors contribute to determining whether or not a peasant household will shift its production mix toward specialization in F output. Price movements and the utility derived by the peasants from different sorts of commodities play an important role. For a full discussion of these factors, as well as a more complete description of the basic model outlined above, see Stephen Hymer and Stephen Resnick, "A Model of an Agrarian Economy with Nonagricultural Activities." The basic model employed in this chapter relies heavily upon the model presented in this article, and I am indebted to Professor Resnick for a number of discussions about the applicability and consequences of the model.

2. The Structure of Rural Society Around 1500

SOURCES

The core of this work is a description and analysis of economic change. The task of measuring and appreciating the changes that took place in the rural economy of the northern Netherlands during the sixteenth and seventeenth centuries requires that we possess a reasonably comprehensive description of that economy at a point in time. We should want to know what institutional legacy had been left by the medieval era; how the land was controlled, and by whom; how the land was worked, and under what conditions. The relations between social classes and the role of nonagricultural activities must also concern us. In answering these questions we will seek to identify how this rural economy satisfied the conditions of the "peasant" and "specialization" models introduced in chapter 1.

We can hope to answer these questions because of the efforts of rulers in Holland and Friesland, beginning in the late fifteenth century, to compile information needed for the more effective taxation of their subjects.

The most important sources for Holland are, the *Enqueste ende Informatie upt stuck van der Reductie ende Reformatie van den Schiltaelen voertijts getaxeert ende Gestelt Geweest over de landen van Hollant ende Vrieslant, gedaen in den jaere 1494*,[1] known as the *Enqueste*, and the *Informacie up den staet Faculteyt ende Gelegentheyt van de Steden ende Dorpen van Hollant ende Vrieslant om daernae te reguleren de nyeuwe Schiltaele, gedaen in den jaere 1514*,[2] known as the *Informacie*. Both are village-by-village surveys of economic conditions in Holland, the first ordered by the Burgundian duke, Philip the Fair, the second under the future Habsburg emperor, Charles V. Both served to update the information on which was based the principal tax, known as *schiltale* or *Verponding*. The counts of Holland, and their successors, did not tax their subjects directly; they allocated the total tax burden among the villages. The villagers, usually represented by elders, allocated the tax burden among themselves in a manner they deemed appropriate. The ducal tax allocation process, at first based simply on the amount of land in each village, became by the late fifteenth century based on the total wealth of the inhabitants. This new system required periodic revisions of the tax allocation formula to reflect the changing fortunes of villages and their trade.[3]

Both the *Enqueste* and the *Informacie* give the responses to a series of questions put to the elders of every village and the magistrates of every city subject to ducal taxation. The questionnaire of the 1514 *Informacie* asked the following questions: "1) how many hearths does the village number; how does this compare with ten years earlier; 2) how many communicants does the pastor reckon the church has; how does this compare with ten years ago; 3) what excise taxes are levied on the village; has the village contracted debts; 4) how is the tax levy divided among the inhabitants; how many *kerven* or *schotponden* does the entire village pay;[4] 5) how do the inhabitants support themselves, how much money is the land worth in rental and in purchase, how much land used by villagers is owned by monasteries or by religious persons . . . ; 6) how much dike and drainage money is charged to each morgen of land." [5] The questionnaire for the cities varied from this village questionnaire in certain particulars.

The responses given by the village elders were not always clear in meaning; they sometimes referred to now obscure customs or used ambiguous terminology. More seriously, the nature of the inquiry encouraged the respondents to color their economic situation blacker than it was. The poorer their village appeared in the response, the lighter would be their tax burden. A final shortcoming of the *Enqueste* and the *Informacie* is incompleteness. Villages that a seigneur could claim to be his "allodial good" were not surveyed since the ducal government could not tax them. Unity of administration, even within a county or duchy, was still far from complete around 1500.[6]

Among the documents that supplement the *Enqueste* and *Informacie* the most important are the Tiende Penning Cohieren, registers of real property compiled frequently between 1543 and 1561 to facilitate the collection of the onerous property tax on which the Habsburg government relied.[7]

In Friesland, the imposition of the rule of the dukes of Saxony in 1498 soon produced a uniform taxation system. The simpler economic life of this territory permitted the dukes to forego the detailed examination of the rural economy required in Holland and content themselves with a village-by-village list of all landholdings.

These lists stipulated the area, owner, user, and rental value of each parcel of land and in some cases stipulated the use to which the land was put—i.e., arable, pasture, or meadow. This record, the *Register van den Aanbreng van 1511*, together with companion records, the *Aanbreng der Vijf Deelen van 1511 en 1514* and a supplement of 1546, remained the basis of rural taxation until the early nineteenth century. Unfortunately, the *Aanbreng* remains extant for only a minority of the 31 rural jurisdictions, called *grietenijen*, into which Friesland was, and is yet, divided.[8] Further information about economic conditions in early sixteenth-century Friesland can be gained from the *Beneficiaal-boeken van Friesland* of 1543, a compendium of records relating to the extensive church holdings in the province.

THE INTERACTION OF LANDSCAPE AND INSTITUTIONS

The region whose rural economy I wish to describe (the modern provinces of Groningen, Friesland, North Holland, South Holland, and Utrecht) possesses a physical unity that clearly distinguishes it from neighboring territories. A wall of sand dunes, which protects the region from the sea, stretches from southern Holland to that province's northern extremity. From there the dunes stretch in a great arc toward the east but have suffered the sea to break them up into islands as the waters rushed behind the dunes to form a shallow, brackish sea, the Wadden Zee. Maritime clays cover much of the northern seacosts of the region; farther inland, rich river clays have built up along the courses of the numerous rivers which, rising in Germany and northern France, disgorge in a complex and often changing web of channels. Ridges of sandy soil protrude conspicuously in isolated spots, but the predominant alternative to the clay soil is peat (called *laagveen*), a soil consisting of decayed, oxygenstarved plant life, which formed over the centuries in vast, lowlying stretches between the rivers, the dunes, and the clay soils. A tangle of smaller rivers and a profusion of sea arms give the region an amphibious character which, in previous centuries, was reinforced by numerous lakes, the largest of which, the Haarlemmermeer, formed a virtual inland sea.

The broad rivers and extensive marshes that bracket the northern Netherlands long enforced an isolation on the region that had a profound impact on its institutions. Flanders, Brabant, and the other Netherlandish provinces to the south had been important parts of both the Roman and Carolingian empires. As a part of the Roman province of Belgica, this region acquired roads, cities, and *villae,* and in later centuries the Roman *villa* and its associated agricultural regime continued to function. The political and social order associated with feudalism flourished in this region.

The land to the north, on the other hand, was never more than loosely associated with these great empires, which left it alone to function as a marchland.[9] It was a wilderness terrain, either empty or given over to livestock herding. The manorial economy and peasant enserfment, typical of most parts of the Carolingian Empire, were uncommon features here. On a belt of arable land stretching along the dune coast of Holland, some manors arose[10] and in the northernmost districts monasteries proliferated and organized some of their holdings in a manorial form. But serfdom, even where manorialism arose, was rare, and short-lived, leaving few traces past the twelfth century.[11] The Friesian peoples in later centuries, indeed, traced their freedom to a privilege granted by Charlemagne in the ninth century which placed the government directly under the Emperor and imposed only nominal military obligations. It has been proved to be a thirteenth-century falsification; however, it had an important influence on later Friesian consciousness and reflects the thirteenth-century Friesians' pride in their freedom.

The Seigneurie

The presence of a large class of free peasants affected the development of seigneurial institutions in the post-Carolingian period. The decay of imperial power gave noble families the opportunity to elaborate the economic power derived from their manors into a judicial and administrative power as well. But in regions where manors had never existed, where free peasants were numerous, and where vast tracts of land lay still in a state of wilderness, seigneurial institutions existed not at all or in an attenuated form.

Without delving headlong into the thicket of medieval legal history, we can describe the situation with regard to seigneurial development in the northern Netherlands in the late Middle Ages as follows: as one moved north from the southern Netherlands, where seigneurialism was fully developed along lines familiar to students of French medieval society, one moved into regions of increasingly weak seigneurial organization.[12] In the northernmost districts, West Friesland, Friesland, and Groningen, seigneuries were unknown.

There, after about 1100, a system of administration developed in which *grietmannen* (in Friesland) or *redgers* (in Groningen) held judicial power over small districts through election by the citizens. In contrast to the feudal system, where power was nominally derived from above through subinfeudation and the delegation of authority in exchange for fealty, the governmental system of the Friesians, such as it was, based itself on the voting rights of farmers. Friesians held voting rights through the ownership of a certain amount of land or the ownership of a farm invested by tradition with voting rights. Under this custom the bulk of the medieval population was enfranchised.[13]

The northernmost part of Holland was formed by West Friesland, a district conquered from the Friesians. It possessed institutions similar to those described above, with modifications imposed by the rule of the counts of Holland. Immediately south of West Friesland, the districts of Kennemerland and Waterland possessed institutions that may be described as a blend of seigneurial and "free." What distinguished the villages here from those farther south was the presence of a permanent bond of the landowning free men, called *geërfden* or *buren,* who possessed power to counteract that of the village seigneur.[14]

Colonization

Before the twelfth century permanent settlement covered but a limited portion of the northern Netherlands. The maritime clay soils of Friesland, the clay soils that built up along the banks of the rivers, and the sandy soils near the dunes attracted settlers at an early date. The vast tracts of peat bog, called laagveen, which covered most of central Holland, western Utrecht, and central Friesland, required systematic drainage work to prepare them for large-scale settlement; thus, they remained virtually empty until the High Middle Ages, when the counts of Holland, claiming ownership of all empty lands, adopted a policy designed to bring the peat bogs under cultivation.

The timing and method of the colonization of these wilderness expanses directly affected the economic and political character of the northern Netherlands. From the eleventh until the early fourteenth century there occurred an internal colonization movement that spread human settlement over virtually all the peat bogs and reclaimed numerous marshlands along the constantly changing coasts of the Zeeland and South Holland islands. Elsewhere in Europe a similar colonization movement was in progress at this time. In France, England, and western Germany previously unsettled zones were penetrated, and in east-Elbian Germany the drive into thinly settled Slavic lands increased enormously the cultivated area of Europe.[15] The North Netherlands' colonization must be distinguished from other western European reclamation projects. Only in east-Elbian Germany can one find reclamation being carried out in so systematic a manner and over such large tracts as in Holland. Much of fourteenth-century Holland was, in effect, a new country, in contrast to the rest of western Europe, where nearly all areas had long possessed villages or small nuclei around which villages could form.

The success of the counts of Holland in controlling the unsettled land of the country did not signal the advent of their direct exploitation of those vast moors. For whatever reason—perhaps the high cost and time required to make the lands productive—they proceeded to sell portions of it, sometimes to noblemen, sometimes to groups representing prospective settlers, sometimes to men best compared to the *locatores* of the east-Elbian colonization movement.[16] Typically, the counts sold the land together with a tithe right. The purchasers resold the land to colonists but kept the tithe right. This process can be traced rather closely in the sale of a large tract of peat bog adjacent to Holland, in the bishopric of Utrecht. In this case, the bishop gave the land, then unsettled and undeveloped, to a religious foundation, the Capital of Saint Jan, in 1085.[17] The Capital acted as an intermediary in preparing the district for colonization. It constructed basic drainage facilities and roads and determined the pattern of field parcelization. After the construction of an earthen dike and a road thereupon, regular 15-roede (56-meter) intervals were measured to mark the boundaries of the new farms. Settlers could then begin improving their lands extending back from the road some thousands of meters. The Capital imposed upon the colonists a tithe payment of 1 *denier* per farm. The yearly tithe payment bound the colonist to no restrictions on his rights to his land, which he was free to use and dispose of as he saw fit. It simply served as a recognition of the ruling power of the Capital. The Capital acted as seigneur of the villages carved from the lands granted it by the bishop; it administered justice and accumulated over the years certain rights (i.e., rights to collect fees in return for granting privileges to operate ferries and mills, to erect bridges, and to fish). But the seigneuries thus formed presented a different aspect from those ruling over ancient villages. The seigneur's rights were not buttressed by landownership or possession of a manor or of a fortified seat; fear and tradition counted for little. Instead, these new seigneuries were based on businesslike relationships with the colonists, who, in turn, were free men in free possession of their land.[18]

The social structure of these new lands differed considerably from that of older villages. The basic social unit of the new settlements was the peasant farm; the parcelization of land, reflecting this fact, took the form of long and narrow, but continuous, holdings with the farmsteads situated thereupon. The systematic process of colonization left no room for estates or the castellated dwellings of the nobility. In sum, society in the colonized areas offered no significant role for noblemen and did not bind the inhabitants to strong village institutions. The individually settled farmsteads, typically of 16 to 18 hectares in extent, required no cooperative farming practices in their operation.

Hydraulics Organizations

The efforts of the medieval inhabitants to drain their marshy lands and protect themselves from floods raised both a network of dikes and dams and an intricate structure of drainage boards (*waterschappen*) to build and supervise these installations. The origins of the original drainage boards, which encompassed no more than a single village, are shrouded in obscurity. Typically, a representative of the count of Holland, known as a *schout*, shared power with representatives of the inhabitants of the area, known as *heemraden* or *dijkschepennen*. The position of the schout appears to have been quite weak, however, because these drainage boards soon exercised a high degree of autonomy. Their independent authority was heightened in the thirteenth century when many of the waterschappen united into larger organizations to deal with drainage problems of greater scope and complexity. These new regional authorities, known as *hoogheemraadschappen*, consisted of a representative of the count, known as a *dijkgraaf*, and representatives of the citizens, known collectively as the *hoogheemraad*.[19]

In Groningen such institutions arose under the name *zijlvesten*. As an example, Farmsummerzijlvest, dating from at least 1306, was administered by a *zijlrigter* from each of the *eeden* (subdistricts of the zijlvest) and a supervising *schepper*. The zijlrigters were chosen by all owners of at least 30 grazen of land and, since Groningen had no count or his equivalent, the schepper was chosen by the zijlrigters.[20] Throughout the region local inhabitants participated in the drainage boards. This medieval institutional legacy, preserved into the modern era, would distinguish both the economic and political life of the northern Netherlands.

Under the authority of these drainage boards protective barriers were raised to encircle whole districts. To complete such tasks dams were thrown up at the mouths of the smaller rivers (thereby creating the locations and names of many cities—Amsterdam, Rotterdam, Leerdam, Appingadam, etc.). West Friesland, a long-settled, marine-clay district, was one of the first districts cooperatively to raise up an encircling dike, a task completed sometime before 1300. By the mid-fifteenth century dikes protected the entire North Holland peninsula (called the Noorderkwartier).[21] Along the courses of the numerous rivers of South Holland, river dikes were gradually built up. By 1500 they had attained, through continual reinforcement, impressive heights, but, together with the sea dikes, they suffered from structural weaknesses caused by their simple earthen construction. The use of piles, reeds, stones, and tiles was not yet widespread; as a consequence, inundation presented an ever present danger.

In the northernmost provinces, Friesland and Groningen, the early inhabitants of the clay soils protected themselves from the sea by raising up mounds (called *terpen* in Friesland and *weiren* in Groningen) on which they built their hamlets. Over the centuries rising flood levels forced the Friesians to enlarge and heighten their terpen until they rose high (the highest some 38 feet) above the level of the land and covered an area sufficient to accommodate perhaps two dozen farmsteads plus the parish church. Over 500 such terpen scattered over the Friesian clay long formed the only permanently habitable places, remaining even now the focal points of rural settlement in Friesland. After the eleventh century dike construction began, although not until the thirteenth century were any substantial earthen dikes completed.[22] The Leppedike, finished in 1477, completed the basic protective system for the clay soils, although the peat areas remained in a virtually unprotected state.[23]

Drainage installations and windmills played, as yet, but a limited role in most parts of the region. Although the first windmills used for drainage purposes date from 1414, they did not yet form a typical feature of the landscape in 1500.[24] The delay in windmill adoption is accounted for in large part by the fact that rather elaborate drainage installations were needed before windmills could play a productive role. The construction of windmills in the fifteenth century often aroused much opposition, since the lowest lying areas suffered from more frequent flooding when nearby windmills pumped water into overburdened drainage channels.

Dike and drainage installations such as these sought to prevent spring and summer flooding. The inhabitants accepted winter flooding as a matter of course; the drainage authorities were as yet powerless to prevent it.[25] In Waddinxveen, for instance, a windmill erected in the 1490s could keep the fields dry only from mid-March to mid-October. The rest of the year the fields lay flooded.[26] The precarious drainage conditions prevented an intensive use of most of the region's land. In the villages under the jurisdiction of the Hoogheemraadschap van Rijnland, the elders described much land in 1514 as *pro derelicto,* either because it was habitually flooded or boggy, or because peat diggers had exhausted it.[27] The inhabitants of Nieuwveen all owned their own land, the elders noted, because "no one from outside would want any." [28] Half of the village land, they insisted, was of no value at all. In Aarlanderveen over half the 3,550 morgen yielded only a nominal rent, while 500 morgen lay yet in a wild, unused state.[29]

These examples of lands that still lay unused, or marginally used, in the early sixteenth century can easily be multiplied. In Utrecht the peatlands east of the river Vecht were still being cleared for settlement in the 1490s[30] and in the Ronde Venen marginal areas had yet to be taken in hand in 1540.[31] In South Holland the colonization process, which moved eastward from the river Gouwe, reached the village of Moerkapelle around 1400. But in the mid-sixteenth century this area could still be described as "a remote, low morass without decent grass and for the most part unsuitable for either grazing or hay land." [32]

In general, the drainage conditions of the northern Netherlands around 1500 can best be described as defensive. Despite the dike construction of earlier centuries, the threat of inundation had, in fact, become greater, and for three reasons. The last two centuries of the Middle Ages were a period of rising water table and sea level known to geologists as the late medieval transgression, or Dunkirk III. In this period the region experienced a series of catastrophic floods and inundations that far outweighed the efforts of reclamation.

In 1277, for instance, a flood created the Dollart, a submerged area at the mouth of the river Ems. Successive floods enlarged the area of the Dollart until 1525, when it attained its greatest extent.[33] Three lakes in central Holland, which in 1250 covered 9,100 hectares, had merged by 1472 into one large lake, the Haarlemmermeer, covering 11,700 hectares. By 1544 the lake covered 13,220 hectares and storms on its surface threatened even more land.[34]

The greatest disaster of this period was undoubtedly the Saint Elizabeth Day flood of 1421, which inundated the Grote Zuidhollandse Waard, a district covering some 500 square kilometers holding 72 villages. Contemporaries claimed 50,000 persons drowned in the storm—surely an exaggeration; nonetheless, 34 of the inundated villages were lost forever, and the nearby city of Dordrecht, isolated by the flood, never again could maintain the preeminent place it had held until then among the cities of Holland.[35]

The wretched conditions in which many peasants, faced with a steadily encroaching sea, lived are graphically described in a fiscal investigation carried out by the commissioners of the King in the Land van Voorne in 1565. Year by year the fields were crumbling into the sea, a village church had disappeared in this manner, and the commissioners concluded that the growing burden of dike maintenance and the menace of shifting dunes and ravenous rabbits (that lived in the dunes) had "so impoverished [the peasants] that they hardly have the strength to work their lands and pay the rent to their landlords."[36]

The loss of the Grote Zuidhollandse Waard pointed up a second menace to the inhabitants of these maritime provinces: injudicious peat digging, which had weakened the Waard's defenses against flooding. Despite periodic prohibitions on peat digging in places where it would increase the dangers of inundation, the weak governmental apparatus of the fifteenth century could do little to suppress it. By 1494, when information is first available, dozens of peat-bog villages reported that large tracts of land had been destroyed by peat digging and that this impaired their defenses against inundation.[37]

Diepeveen, in a study of the peat-bog villages of Delfland, shows that the taxable value of real property in 6 of 8 such villages had fallen by at least one-half between the "Grote Bede" of 1344–45 and the "Tiende Penning" tax of 1561. This decline he attributed to the destructive impact of peat digging on land values.[38]

A third problem, the natural subsidence of the soil attendant upon settlement and drainage, contributed to the long-term deterioration of land values uncovered by Diepeveen. Numerous village studies attest to the complete change in drainage conditions effected by soil subsidence in this period. In the Utrecht village of Zegveld, for instance, the peatlands originally lay above the level of the river Mije. In the course of the late Middle Ages subsidence caused the level of the land to fall below that of the river. Winter flooding became a regular occurrence, and the construction of levies became a necessity. Only the introduction of windmills, which occurred in 1491, could remedy the deteriorated drainage conditions of this village.[39]

Land-Use Intensity

A large part of the region's land lay, remote and ill drained, as uninhabitable and unfertilized haylands, and inundation was in many ways a more immediate threat than ever before. Despite this, the attention of travelers appears to have been attracted primarily to the better-drained districts, where rich pastures supported herds of fat cattle and small, carefully tended arable plots produced high yields. The Florentine nobleman Ludovico Guicciardini, long a resident of Antwerp and author of a description of all seventeen provinces of the Netherlands, observed of Holland's landscape that "the fields have mainly a very favorable appearance . . . with rich green pastures full of all sorts of grazing cattle, which pastures, according to common opinion, are much greener and richer than in Italy; which is, so I think, because of the plenteous dampness of the earth." [40]

In 1514 the central government required the elders of each village to estimate the rental value of their lands. The responses show that, indeed, the quality of the land varied enormously, from almost worthless hayfields to highly valued, uniquely well drained plots that benefitted from generations of prudent fertilization and careful cultivation. If we exclude a few extreme citations, the highest rents ranged from 2.5 to 4 gulden and the lowest from 4 to 10 stuivers (at 20 stuivers per gulden).[41]

Unused and little-used lands bulked even larger in the provinces of Friesland and Groningen. The clay soils had long been settled, and since the construction of the Vijfdelen and other dikes, their productive qualities had been improved from their natural state. The peat soils and the high moors of Groningen, on the other hand, had hardly been improved at all. In Barradeel and Leeuwarderadeel, two grietenijen on the marine clays, the cultivated land of 1511 comprised 84 percent and 74 percent, respectively, of the cultivated area in 1950. In Idaarderadeel and Achtkarspelen, two grietenijen made up in large part by peat soils, the corresponding percentages were 47 and 46 percent, respectively.[42] No wonder that Albert of Saxony, shortly after his acquisition of Friesland in 1498, considered the province's extensive uncultivated and undiked lands his most important potential source of income. During his short administration, he repeatedly asserted his rights over all uncultivated land and advocated reclamation works.[43]

In Groningen, tax registers of 1520 and 1555 show that less than half the province had been brought under cultivation.[44] Besides the peat fields characteristic of the other provinces, Groningen embraced, in its eastern half, vast high moors (called *hoogveen* to distinguish them from the peat bogs known as laagveen) that lay utterly untouched, save for a few tentative efforts at settlement by inhabitants of neighboring lands who burned the top layer of the moor to create a fertile ash upon which they grew buckwheat and rye crops for several years before abandoning the field for another virgin tract.[45]

Such were the characteristics of the land in the provinces that make up the region under examination. Bordering it lay a broad belt of wooded, sandy-soiled land upon which peasants, clustered in nucleated villages often dominated by a lord, practiced primitive variants of open-field farming.[46] Here in 1500, rental payments in kind and in services were yet firmly entrenched and would remain so until the nineteenth century. In the maritime region under study the land lay divided in enclosed plots that were rented on commercial, usually short-term, leases. A few remnants of common-field organization could still be found in 1500 in the oldest settled districts of Holland; in Friesland and Groningen common pastures and meadows existed in a few places, but they did not last long in this state.

In the village of Oegstgeest, the villagers reduced and restricted common rights from 1456 on, so that by 1500 they had been practically eliminated.[47] The common pastures of Friesland, listed in the *Aanbreng van 1511*, were few and outnumbered by fields whose names betrayed a common-field origin, but which had long since been divided.[48] Only on the Friesian islands in the Wadden Zee and in an isolated sandy-soil district near Amsterdam named het Gooi did common field agriculture persist.[49]

The overwhelming majority of the land was held in fee simple. In 1583 the cities of Friesland wrote to Willem of Orange, describing landownership in Friesland as follows: "There are no feudal goods in the countryside . . . for all the lands are the freely owned lands and goods of those to whom they belong." [50] In the Tiende Penning Cohieren of 1543–61, lands held in feudal tenure, generally identified as *erfpacht,* existed in very few of the dozens of villages whose records have been studied. The structure of the land and the tenure system under which it was worked allow us to answer unambiguously questions about the distribution of landownership. This situation simplifies a study of the landownership characteristics and the related distribution of power in the rural districts of the northern Netherlands.

To summarize, the physical and institutional endowments of the northern Netherlands as it entered the modern era must be distinguished in several important respects from those prevailing elsewhere. Profound historical processes had dictated that this region should escape the full brunt of manorialization and feudalization, which encompassed most of western Europe. This condition, combined with the method of medieval colonization and the region's unique drainage requirements, conspired to produce a free peasantry living in a relatively autonomic society. Yet, the absence in this region of open fields and feudal tenure should not be interpreted to imply the existence of a highly developed economy. While the southern Netherlands had grown to be a great center of European trade and industry with an advanced agricultural sector, the economy of the northern Netherlands in the early sixteenth century can only be described as ancillary to that of the south.

THE SOCIAL STRUCTURE OF DUTCH RURAL SOCIETY

How did the social classes of the northern Netherlands function in the institutional and physical environment whose features I have just sketched? We will consider in turn the nobility, the clergy, the bourgeoisie, and the peasantry to determine what powers each exercised over the other groups and what influence each brought to bear on the agrarian economy. Unfortunately, simple generalizations will not suffice in this subject. The absence of any semblance of political centralization in the Burgundian Netherlands together with the local variations common to any rural society require that, at the very least, we progress on a province-by-province basis.

The Nobility

It is only appropriate to begin with the "virtual representatives" of European rural societies, the nobility. In Holland this class emerged in 1500 from nearly one and a half centuries of factional disputes. Private wars and feuds characterized aristocratic life over much of western Europe in the late fourteenth and fifteenth centuries. In Holland, beginning in 1345, the rather numerous nobility divided itself into two loose coalitions, called the Hoeks and the Kabeljauws. These groups feuded and fought each other over issues that were rooted in disputes over control of important state offices and the rights of patronage which attended them. The disputes also embroiled the patriciate of the cities as well as the bishop and the nobility of Utrecht.[51]

The lesser nobility, goaded by their poverty and the threat of political eclipse posed by the dukes of Burgundy, were also active in these disputes. The death in 1477 of the last of the dukes of Burgundy, Charles the Bold, began one last round of disorders. When it ended definitely in 1492, the number of the lesser nobility had been much reduced. The accredited noble class of sixteenth-century Holland is said to have numbered no more than twelve families. By the eighteenth century their ranks were further reduced to seven families.[52]

The chief sources on which we must depend to determine noble landownership in the early sixteenth century, the *Enqueste* and *Informacie,* are not wholly reliable. Since a nobleman's land enjoyed tax exemption, it served the interests of the villagers (by reducing their village tax assessment) to exaggerate the size of noble holdings. The Tiende Penning Cohieren, first drawn up in 1543, provide a useful supplement to the earlier surveys. To the extent that noblemen can be identified by their names, laborious calculations can coax these fiscal documents to yield accurate landownership statistics.

The chief characteristic of noble landholding that emerges from these sources is a singular lack of pattern. In a few districts—the dune coast and the extreme southeast in particular—noble lands were frequently encountered, while in certain others—the Noorder-kwartier and the central peat bogs, for example—they were virtually nonexistent. But more noteworthy was the tendency of noble land-ownership to be concentrated in certain villages where, for unique reasons, seigneurial rights had been well established and feudal tenure long preserved.

In the Land van Altena the Heer van Baern owned almost half the land of his seigneurie Herpt and the Heer van Zevenbergen owned 70 percent of the 350 morgen that made up Heesbeen.[53] But in the nearby village of Veen no noblemen owned any land at all, and in the other villages for which information is available noble-men appear to have owned rather little land.[54] In 1514 a residue of noble land remained yet in the villages nestled behind the dunes, where numerous ruined castles testified to the power once exercised by the nobility. The seigneur of Lier somehow managed to preserve his claim to almost all the village land—land which was let out in erfpacht (a sort of copyhold) to hereditary tenants.[55] Elsewhere in the district erfpacht was uncommon and the noblemen had to con-tent themselves with a minor part of the land. In nearby Wassenaar, noblemen owned 9 percent of the village lands, in Voorburg 7 per-cent, and in Sluipwijk 25 percent.[56]

An analysis of the Tiende Penning Cohieren in 33 villages scat-tered about Holland provides another view of noble landownership, although their holdings are not in every case clearly distinguishable from those of burghers and the Church. The largest concentration was found in Bleskensgraaf, in the Alblasserwaard, where 73.5 morgen, or 9 percent of the village area, was held by a small num-ber of noblemen.[57] In Alphen aan den Rijn noblemen held 7 per-cent of the land, much of it in erfpacht.[58] On the south Holland islands we again observe great village-by-village contrasts. In Heen-vliet, the seigneur owned a large portion of the village land. 'T Hart's study of the village makes clear, however, that this seigneurie was uniquely ancient and privileged.[59] Neighboring villages, with a different seigneurial development behind them, did not share Heenvliet's characteristics. Thus, in nearby Abbenbroek and West-voorne noblemen owned well under one-tenth of the land.[60]

Over the entire province noblemen owned less, probably much less, than 10 percent of the cultivated land. Their lands were concentrated in villages where they had managed to preserve a measure of their ancient control over rural society. Despite this characteristic noble landholdings were not extensive (the largest, owned by Mevrouwe van Assendelf in Kralingen, consisted of 350 morgen, or 25 percent of the village)[61] nor were they farmed as estates (the *Informacie* makes only one reference to a manor farm, a 60-morgen holding in Ammers operated by the Heer van Liesvelt).[62]

The nobility was not everywhere so weak as we find it in Holland. In neighboring Utrecht the dominant role of the Church and the preservation of aristocratic influence in the eastern, sandy-soil half of the province insured that here the privileged orders would remain firmly in the saddle. In an analysis of landownership as recorded in the Mannuaal van het Oudschildgeld of 1540 we found noblemen owning 34 percent of the land of Kamerick. Similar proportions were in their hands in Breukelen and Maarsden, important villages that bordered the river Vecht. Yet here, as in Holland, there were many other villages—the peat-bog villages of the Ronde Venen and Papekop—where noble landownership was of no consequence.[63]

When we turn to Friesland and Groningen we confront a social structure where noblemen, called *hoofdelingen,* formed no separate class distinguishable by title or legal privilege. Enno van Gelder defined them as "those families who for several generations lived from the proceeds of landownership and offered themselves for employment in government and military offices, or whose relations did, or had done this."[64]

These families had risen from the ranks of the larger farmers; the quantity of land they owned, while generally greater than that of mere farmers, did not invariably distinguish them from the farmers. The possession of one or more *stinzen,* or fortified houses, acted as a more reliable distinguishing characteristic.[65] The historian Winsemius indicated some 200 stinzen in his seventeenth-century maps of Friesland. The hoofdelingen families were numerous (apparently the chronic feuding of the fifteenth century had not decimated their ranks as it had the nobility of Holland) and they were concentrated on the marine clay soils of Westergo and Oostergo.[66]

Syds Tjaerda was probably the wealthiest Friesian nobleman in the early sixteenth century; he owned 3 stinzen and 600 hectares of land. Perhaps 7 other hoofdelingen could be compared with him. In Groningen by far the largest hoofdeling was Christoffel van

Ewsum. In 1491 his family owned 1,899 hectares plus a half-interest in an additional 647 hectares.[67] A few families owned over 200 hectares, but most had to content themselves with much less.

The *Aanbreng van 1511* permits a reconstruction of the land-ownership distribution in certain Friesian grietenijen. But distinguishing hoofdelingen from other landowners is not always possible. Its analysis shows that in Leeuwarderadeel, with 29 stinzen, only 9 persons owned over 100 hectares; in Ferwerderadeel, with 22 stinzen, 5 persons owned over 100 hectares. The majority of hoofdelingen must have owned modest holdings. This deduction is reinforced by the minimum landownership requirement to hold judicial offices in Friesland and Groningen, offices mainly filled by hoofdelingen: 30 grazen, about 15 hectares, sufficed in Groningen while a minimum income of 18 gold gulden per year (equivalent to the rental income of about 20 hectares of good land) sufficed in Friesland.[68]

The modest holdings of these local worthies, when multiplied by their considerable number, gave the hoofdelingen an important position in the northern provinces. If we assume that the lands recorded in the *Aanbreng van 1511* as owned by nonfarmer and non-Church landowners were owned by hoofdelingen, we find 32 percent of the cultivated land of Leeuwarderadeel and 37 percent of the land of Oosterbierum, in Barradeel, in their hands.[69] These figures surely exaggerate hoofdelingen landownership, and we know them to be less numerous in other regions of the province; still, it seems likely that the hoofdelingen owned at least 20 percent of Friesland's land.

The following generalizations about noble landownership in the northern Netherlands appear to be valid: noble holdings were spread very unevenly over the region, tending to concentrate in the districts where noble families had of old been most numerous and in villages where the noblemen still exercised local political power. Nowhere did they monopolize strategic sorts of land (such as commons or forests) or did their land form important estates. Highly unusual, both in Holland and the northern provinces, was a nobleman possessing over a few hundred hectares.

It cannot be said that the noblemen of the northern Netherlands possessed an impressive material base from which to dominate rural society. Their institutional and political base was even less impressive.

In the face of a medieval legacy that undermined the vitality of the basic institutions of noble power, the seigneurie, only a very few northern Netherlands noble families had been able to construct and keep for themselves a firm control over rural society. One of these firmly entrenched seigneurs was the Heer van Heenvliet. His family had held and carefully husbanded the seigneurial rights over this village for centuries. In the early sixteenth century the seigneur possessed the right to exercise not only low (civil) justice—a common right of Dutch seigneurs—but also middle and high (criminal) justice. These powers conferred status upon the seigneurie that exempted the village from ducal taxation. His *banrechten* (rights of ban) were extensive; he held toll rights on the ferries and, later, on the bridges touching his territory. Hunting, fishing, and fowling rights were his to sell. He collected excises on wine and beer and enjoyed the proceeds of the *beestiaal,* the fortieth penny of the selling price of all livestock sold at the weekly market held in the village. He possessed both "great" and "small" tithe rights, which insured that minor and nontraditional crops could not escape his tithe exactions.[70]

Rights such as these, while typical of seigneurial rights in France and the southern Netherlands, were highly unusual in Holland. Many seigneurs enjoyed some of them; few could compare their rights with those of the Heer van Heenvliet. A few tithe and toll rights and the right to place an excise on beer, together with the right to exercise low justice, often exhausted the prerogatives of the seigneur.[71]

Since a nobleman could hardly subsist upon the proceeds from one or two of these meager seigneuries, the rights tended to concentrate in the hands of a few considerable noblemen who resided elsewhere—usually in a large city or in the capital, Brussels. The Heer van Assendelft held 11 seigneuries; Brederode held 23, which embraced 19 villages. Three of the greatest noblemen of the 17 provinces, Orange, Egmond and Hoorne, held seigneuries that together covered 16,000 morgen.[72] This concentration of weak seigneuries in the hands of distant lords engendered a purely business-like relationship between the rural population and the seigneur. To the peasant, the lord's rights were no more than a cost of doing business. In Heenvliet, and a few other villages, on the other hand, the peasant could not so easily ignore the seigneur. Sitting in his castle in the middle of the village, brooding over how he might increase his income and suppress the violations of his rights, the seigneur exerted an influence always to be reckoned with in the economic life of the village.

The accession of Charles V to the Habsburg throne proved to be a blow to the already weak position of Holland's noblemen. Under Charles, the judicial system expanded at the expense of seigneurial courts; in 1515 nobles became liable to taxation on their property, and in 1518 even the lands they held in fief of the monarch became subject to taxation.[73] By 1520 Charles suppressed the nobleman's right to collect tax payments destined for the government in Brussels.[74]

As we have seen, the seigneur's power to appoint priests, sheriffs, and representatives to drainage boards had not always been unencumbered but, such as it was, it became even more restricted in the sixteenth century, as large landowners with urban connections arose in many areas to form a veritable aristocracy of officeholders whom the increasingly isolated nobleman could not ignore.[75]

Since seigneurial institutions had never existed in the northern provinces, the hoofdelingen turned to the offices of grietman in Friesland and redger in Groningen as means of supplementing their incomes. These offices conferred both power and income to the incumbent in much the same way that municipal and county offices enrich their occupants in the twentieth-century United States—through fees and the boundless possibilities for graft and influence peddling. The low property qualification needed to vie for these offices ensured that hoofdelingen did not stand unchallenged, but as the major countervailing power, the monasteries, become progressively weaker, the political power of the hoofdelingen rose.

In Groningen, a new power, that of the city of Groningen, effectively challenged the noblemen of that province. Between 1450 and 1600 the city developed its authority over many districts into a full sovereignty. In het Oldampt, in eastern Groningen, the offices of redger disappeared entirely, and by 1650 the hoofdelingen families had dwindled to one.[76]

Only Friesland experienced a waxing noble power, although there too the growing influence of the cities proved at times worrisome. Nowhere did noblemen exercise a preponderant power or a power based on the widespread subservience of the population. In Friesland, where the offices of grietman in time passed by turns among the owners of the stinzen, the peasant remained in full possession of his property and his personal freedom. The hoofdeling was his de facto superior but nothing more. In the other provinces, the power of the nobleman was in the process of being dismantled as other social classes constructed positions of strength.

The uncommonly weak position of the nobility in the northern Netherlands stands out clearly in a Europe where medieval estates still flourished in testimony to the power of the noble class. In nearby Flanders, for instance, noblemen retained a firm control over the countryside through both extensive landholdings and seigneurial power. Serfdom and feudal dues continued to mold economic relations. The seigneuries were small but profitable, and the numerous nobility formed a powerful class capable of protecting its interests.[77] Noblemen completely dominated Namur and Hainault. Most noblemen who cut a figure at court in Brussels held country seats in these provinces. Their extensive landholdings, reinforced by a monopolization of forestlands, insured their political dominance over the countryside.[78]

The Church

We must next consider the economic importance of the Church and its various institutions which formed, together with the nobility, the privileged classes of preindustrial European societies. The land owned by parish churches to maintain priests, prebendaries, and sextons was generally not abundant. Rare was the parish priest who could be maintained from his church lands. To supplement his income the priest typically charged fees for the performance of official functions and encouraged special offerings at such occasions as saints' days and the death of a parishioner.[79]

More important landowners were the charitable houses, deaneries, and cathedral chapters. Because these were usually urban institutions, income from their lands flowed from the countryside to the cities, there to support the work of hospitals and orphanages and maintain the bureaucracy and aristocracy of the religious establishment. Aside from this transfer of income these institutions played an essentially passive role in the rural economy. Only in Utrecht, the seat of the bishopric, do we find religious bodies that held numerous seigneurial rights.

The largest religious landowners were the monasteries. The Cistercian and Premonstratensian orders in particular acquired great importance in the northern Netherlands by directing medieval land reclamation projects. We are well informed about the size and distribution of monastic lands, since detailed records were made at the time of their confiscation during the revolution against Spain.

The *corpus* lands of the 22 Groningen monasteries averaged about 250 hectares in 1555.[80] The income from approximately 5,000 hectares worked by the monks was supplemented by rents from over 17,000 additional hectares that they leased out. Altogether, the monasteries owned one-seventh of this relatively undeveloped province. Cathedral chapters and parish churches owned considerable tracts as well. Added together, as much as a quarter of the cultivated land of the province, besides large quantities of unused moorland, lay under Church control.[81]

No other province could claim as many monasteries as Friesland, which had 26, plus at least 17 convents, scattered across the countryside. In 1511, 125 of the 140 clay-soil villages for which there are available records included monastic lands within their boundaries.[82] At the time of the reformation 20 percent of the cultivated land lay in the hands of the monasteries.[83]

Holland, well endowed with charitable institutions, had few monasteries. In the vicinity of two ancient and powerful monasteries, Rijnsburg and Egmond, they owned much land but, in general, religious institutions of all types played a much smaller role here than in Friesland and Groningen. An account of the income from religious lands in Holland south of the Ij kept by the new secular owners in 1590, while failing to record the amount of land, cites its total value as 17,753 gulden. This figure is far below the value of Groningen or Friesian monastic lands in that year.[84] Our impression is reinforced by information about all types of Church landowner-ship compiled from the *Informacie* of 1514 and the Tiende Penning Cohieren. They identify only a handful of villages where Church landownership exceeded 20 percent; in most of them, the Church owned under 10 percent.[85]

In the bishopric of Utrecht, as one might suspect, religious bodies, especially capitals and cathedral chapters, held a large share of the land. In 1540 the Mannuaal van het Oudschildgeld recorded all the land of Papendorp in the hands of the Church; in Papekop, 38 percent; in Demmerick, 35 percent; in Kamerick, 31 percent; and in Vinkeveen, 15 percent of the land was owned by the Church.[86]

By the early sixteenth century, religious bodies had ceased to play an aggressive role in the rural society of the northern Netherlands. The "privileged classes," a potent combination in many parts of

Europe, did not here combine to dominate rural society. In Holland neither the nobility nor the Church was a strong landowning power; in Friesland and Groningen the hoofdelingen and monasteries viewed each other with great suspicion. Only in Utrecht could the outlines of the traditional cooperation between these two pillars of European society be detected. The lands owned by religious bodies assume a new importance after the Revolution. Then, the confiscations by provincial government, as shall be seen, fundamentally affect the life of the rural society, particularly in the north.

The Bourgeoisie

Why did burghers own rural land? The extraeconomic benefits accruing to noble and clerical landowners need no further explanation and account for their long-standing interest in land acquisition. But large-scale bourgeois landownership surely requires some explanation. Since in the northern Netherlands noblemen neither operated large estates nor enjoyed a secure power base in the countryside, the phenomenon common to many European countries of bourgeois families' buying land and marrying into noble families to gain power, prestige, and security was here uncommon. Bourgeois families remained in the cities and gained political power and social prestige through cooption into the governing circles of municipal government, the regents.

A portion of bourgeois-owned land directly supported the urban economy. In the first place, urban residents often owned land that they used themselves. The residents of Leeuwarden owned and used a number of large common pastures outside the town walls where they grazed their livestock.[87] This practice was common to many cities of the time, particularly smaller cities, where the inhabitants' break with the land was incomplete. Since no description of a preindustrial European city ever seems complete without an account of the cowsheds and pigsties maintained by the inhabitants in their backyards, this point hardly needs to be emphasized here.

The needs of urban industry accounted for another type of bourgeois land use. Brewers and bakers owned and worked peat bogs, and brickmakers similarly used claylands in the operation of their enterprises. In the mid-sixteenth century 19 Delft brewers owned and directed the exploitation of peatlands in the village of Hogeveen, while in Moerkapelle a large portion of the peatlands had been developed and exploited by consortia of Gouda brewers.[88]

These direct uses can account for only a small portion of the land owned by sixteenth-century *poorters,* as urban "citizens" were known. Most of their land they rented to farmers, almost always on short-term, monetary leases. The absence of feudal landownership principles and hereditary tenure made landownership a relatively liquid form of investment. Profits from trade, the main source of income for the wealthier poorters, could be volatile. The ready availability of land as an alternative investment proved particularly attractive in times of slow trade and also after a sharp rise in trading profits.[89] The social and political irrelevance of landownership notwithstanding, the bourgeoisie bought large quantities of land because it could act as a secure repository for capital.

A few generalizations can be made about the distribution of bourgeois landownership. In the few places where the privileged classes together owned much land, the bourgeoisie held little, since the nobles and the Church characteristically abstained from selling their land unless forced to do so by pressing necessity. The bourgeoisie held little low-valued land; their interest in land apparently stressed income and security rather than speculation. Thus, the low-quality land of Waterland, a district where heavy dike taxes depressed land values and profits were unpredictable, attracted little bourgeois investment capital despite the fact that Waterland lay virtually surrounded by cities.[90] For similar reasons the waterlogged soils of Rijnland attracted little urban interest. The more valuable clay soils along the rivers and in West Friesland, on the other hand, attracted bourgeois capital in large quantities.

A poorter did not confine himself to the immediate environs of his city when seeking a desirable property, nor did he necessarily buy adjacent plots with an eye to rendering more convenient the management of his property. Bourgeois landownership was fragmented and widely scattered, characteristics that reaffirm the purely financial, rather than entrepreneurial or social, role landownership was intended to play. Examination of the Tiende Penning Cohieren of Beets and Alphen shows that the average size of bourgeois-owned parcels was 2 morgen and 6 morgen, respectively. In contrast to religious institutions the bourgeois landowner rarely rented out a complete farm.[91]

The examples in tables 2.1 and 2.2 show that the bourgeoisie owned widely varying portions of the total village lands; on the

TABLE 2.1. Bourgeois Landownership in Selected Villages in Holland, 1514–62
(In morgen, equaling c. 0.85 hectare)

City of Poorter's Residence	Abbekerk 1514	Lamberts-caege 1514	Midwolde 1514	Twisk 1514	Egmond 1514
Alkmaar	55	6	—	9	50
Amsterdam	10	—	—	2	13
Edam	3	—	—	—	—
Enkhuizen	—	2.5	—	—	—
Haarlem	24	2.5	—	—	32
Hoorn	54	—	107	97	—
The Hague	—	—	—	—	—
Leiden	2	—	—	37	—
Medemblik	96	2.5	—	83	—
Monnikendam	—	—	—	—	—
Purmerend	—	—	—	—	—
Other	—	—	—	—	7
Total	244	13.5	107	228	102
Total land	490	75	375	460	280
% owned by Poorters	49.7	18.0	28.5	49.6	36.4

City of Poorter's Residence	Zwaag 1514	Noord Schermer 1514	Ursum 1514	Beets 1558	Opmeer 1514
Alkmaar	—	240	70	7	31
Amsterdam	40	35	80	17	—
Edam	—	—	—	14	—
Enkhuizen	14	—	—	1	—
Haarlem	38	60	74	6	7
Hoorn	217	—	107	53	22
The Hague	11	—	—	—	—
Leiden	—	—	—	—	9
Medemblik	—	—	—	—	14
Monnikendam	—	—	—	5	—
Purmerend	—	—	—	—	—
Other	—	100	—	—	—
Total	320	435	331	103	83
Total land	714	600	680	428	500
% owned by Poorters	44.8	72.5	48.7	24.1	16.6

(*Continued*)

TABLE 2.1—*Continued*

City of Poorter's Residence	Haas-trecht 1514	Alphen 1562	Kralin-gen 1514	Ouder-kerk 1562	Nieuw-koop 1562	Assen-delft 1562
Amsterdam	—	95	—	644	12	150
Dordrecht	79	—	—	—	—	11
The Hague	—	14	96	—	—	11
Haarlem	—	118	—	16	—	108
Hoorn	—	6	—	—	—	—
Gouda	464	44	—	—	2	—
Leiden	—	158	—	—	193	—
Oudewater	214	—	—	—	—	—
Rotterdam	—	18	562	—	—	—
Utrecht	238	49	—	—	—	—
Cities in the Southern Netherlands	—	134	—	—	—	6
Other	—	—	—	50	5	39
Total	995	636	658	710	212	325
Total land	1496	2704	1400	1643	1452	2777
% owned by Poorters	66.5	23.5	47.0	43.2	14.6	11.7

SOURCES: *Informacie*, pp. 123, 603, 87, 140, 116, 391, 483; ARA, Staten van Holland voor 1572, Tiende Penning Cohieren, nos. 1424, 901, 1365, 1391, 1202, 1210.

TABLE 2.2. Bourgeois Landownership as Proportion of Total Land Area in Selected Villages in Holland, 1514–62

Village	Total Land Area in Morgen	Owned by Bourgeoisie	Percentage	Year
Abbenbroek	777	198	25	1562
Amstelveen	2200	660	30	1514
Bleskensgraaf	958	183	20	1558
Hogeveen	257	125	49	1562
Oudshoorn	1674	653	39	1541
Tekkop	480	12	2.5	1562
Ter Aar	2053	72	3.5	1543

SOURCES: ARA, Staten van Holland voor 1572, Tiende Penning Cohieren, nos. 915, 1448, 1539, 1194; *Informacie*, p. 219; RA Brussel, Papiers d'Etat et de l'Audience, Cahiers du X[e], XX[e] et C[e] denier, no. 618–37; Gemeentearchief van Oudshoorn, no. 64; AH Rijnland, Morgenboek van Ter Aar; Diepeveen, p. 63.

whole, their share of the province's land rose considerably above that of either the nobility or the Church.

When we turn from Holland, a province of numerous and populous cities, to the other provinces of our region the importance of bourgeois landownership diminishes. In certain Utrecht villages, the bourgeoisie owned considerable amounts of land, despite the general dominance of the Church and nobility. A very different situation prevailed in the northern provinces of Friesland and Groningen. Friesland's numerous cities were all small, and their trade was as yet little developed. Since they still functioned mainly as limited provisioning centers for the countryside, they possessed few wealthy merchants who might seek real estate to balance their investment portfolios. Aside from fields outside the cities used by the urban dwellers themselves, the Friesian bourgeoisie owned little land in the early sixteenth century.[92]

In Groningen no data are available to shed light on this question. The one large city of the province, Groningen, performed more advanced economic functions than did the Friesian cities. But Groningen's interest in the countryside seems to have expressed itself mainly in fashioning a firm political hegemony over the area. Little mention is made of landownership as a form of investment in the early sixteenth century; in later decades this situation changes fundamentally.

TABLE 2.3.   Bourgeois Landownership in Utrecht, 1540

Village	Total Land Area in Morgen	Owned by Bourgeoisie	Percentage Owned by Bourgeoisie
Kamerick	1365	271	20
Papekop	766	180	23
Papendorp	240	0	0
Vinkeveen	977	50	5

SOURCE: RA Utrecht, Staten van Utrecht, Mannuaal van het Oudschildgeld van het Sticht, nos. 143–1 to 143–4.

The bourgeoisie owned land mainly as a form of capital investment, but, just as the nobility, they possessed a strong interest in developing political power in rural areas. Unlike the nobility, the bourgeoisie desired such power to secure the proper functioning of the urban economy, which was, naturally, their main concern. A durable urban control over the countryside could benefit the bour geoisie in many ways: with exclusive market privileges, they assured themselves of a large, steady volume of farm products; with the right to impose excise taxes in the villages, they assured themselves a market for their beer, wine, and salt; with toll privileges, they could channel trade to routes that led to their city.

Because the northern Netherlands possessed a dense network of cities, conflicting privileges and overlapping rural hinterlands made interurban rivalry endemic. Gaining a stranglehold over rural regions proved impossible for most cities. But the weakness of the nobility and the businesslike character of many seigneuries provided the cities of Holland with a direct way to gain political power in the countryside: the purchase of seigneurial privileges. The rights and privileges of a seigneur, when exercised by a municipal government, did not increase in direct monetary value; the attractiveness of seigneurial rights to the cities lay in the rights to license and control trade and industry—rights of little value to a noble seigneur. The bourgeoisie profited from such power: by prohibiting brewing, spinning, weaving, shipbuilding, and trade in agricultural products in the rural districts, they preserved the prerogatives and the profits of their cities.

In 1529 the city of Amsterdam bought the seigneurial rights of nearby Amstelveen, Osdorp, Slooten, and Slooterdijk from Reinoud van Brederode;[93] Gouda, by the early sixteenth century, had acquired the rights to Bloemendaal, Broek, Thuyl, 't Weegje, Broekhuizen, and Land van Steyn;[94] Leiden, in 1541, bought the rights to nearby Zoeterwoude from the debt-ridden heirs of the seigneur, Cornelis van Swieten.[95] Other cities also participated in this movement and after the Revolution many more seigneuries were purchased. In the early sixteenth century, however, the central government in Brussels frowned on municipal acquisition of seigneurial rights and acted to stop the movement.[96]

The emperor could sometimes be persuaded to bestow privileges upon the cities at the expense of the countryside. Imperial edicts protected the municipal economies by forbidding rural marketplaces in much of Friesland in 1517, banning rural butter markets everywhere in Zeeland, Holland, and Friesland in 1516, and, shortly thereafter, prohibiting rural peddlers from vending a wide array of basic commodities.[97]

The cities' drive to subject the countryside economically through the ordinances of the emperor culminated in 1531. Claiming that depopulation and impoverishment—which threatened the proper maintenance of the city walls and fortifications and the payment of taxes—were at hand, the cities persuaded Charles V to issue the Ordre op de Buiten-nieringe. This edict forbade the establishment of most new industries outside the city walls and forbade new bakeries and taverns within 600 roeden (2.26 kilometers) of all city walls.[98] The cities of Friesland petitioned for a similar edict but were refused.[99] The effectiveness of these imperial edicts varied; the Ordre op de Buiten-nieringe, to judge from continual urban complaints, does not appear to have succeeded in its aim.[100]

The large number of cities in the region placed most rural areas in the fortunate positions of escaping dependence on the markets of a single city. The absence of physical conditions tending toward municipal monopoly and monopsony encouraged the cities to acquire legal privileges to enforce their control over rural areas. In the course of the late fifteenth century two cities acquired such extensive powers over their hinterlands as to distinguish them from the others.[101] Dordrecht, around 1500, enforced a staple privilege (*stapelrechten*), which forced all the inhabitants of the "Kwartier van Zuid Holland" (a region of perhaps 15,000 inhabitants in 1514) to concentrate their buying and selling at the Dordrecht markets.[102] The staple privilege also required most skippers passing by Dordrecht to dock there, unload their cargoes, and allow them to be offered for sale.[103]

The city of Groningen exercised the most far-reaching stapelrechten. Groningen suppressed the market rights of the small city of Appingadam, insisted that all grain, butter, and cheese produced in the province be shipped first to the city, restricted the rural population's beer consumption to that brewed in the city, and forbade most foreign merchants from the rural districts.[104]

Groningen's subjugation of its hinterland is an extreme example of the power that Dutch cities tried to exercise in the rural districts. In most villages farmers remained free to choose which markets they would patronize, and prohibitions of rural trade and industry were never rigorously enforced. But the cities formed a power to be reckoned with in a rural society where the traditional rulers, the nobility and the Church, existed in a precariously weak situation.

The Peasantry

From what has been determined about the rural economic and social strength of the nobility, the clergy, and the bourgeoisie, it is clear that the peasantry owned a substantial part of the land and did not suffer from legal restrictions on their ability to use, buy, and dispose of land.

The extent of peasant proprietorship in Holland can be determined in broad outline from the statistics presented in the *Informacie* of 1514. The limitations of these data (only village land *owned and used* by peasants of that same village was recorded) plus the presumption of untruthfulness that must attach to such information in a document with its purpose render the statistics of little value on the village level. Aggregating these statistics by districts should permit them to show the relative importance of peasant proprietorship in the various parts of Holland, even though the absolute figures will surely understate reality. Peasant landownership ranged from 100 percent on the North Holland islands of Texel and Wieringen and 85 percent in het Gooi (a distinct district of common-field agriculture) to 10 percent around the city of Woerden and 8 percent on the South Holland islands. In the entire province of Holland 42 percent of the land used by peasants was in their possession. We need not accept the exact figures to appreciate that the peasantry as a class owned considerably more land than did the nobility, the Church, or the urban bourgeoisie.[105]

The Tiende Penning Cohieren and Morgenboeken provide more trustworthy statistics on peasant landownership.[106] Maps 2.1 through 2.3 show the village-by-village distribution of peasant proprietorship in central Holland, North Holland, and Utrecht. The most complete information covers some 40 villages of the Hoogheemraadschap van Rijnland. There peasants owned 39,834 of 64,302 morgen, or 62 percent of the land.

The importance of peasant proprietorship varied enormously from village to village. In Rijnland the peasants owned the vast majority of the peatlands but very little of the more valuable soils near the coastal dunes or the productive clays along the Oude Rijn River, which flows through the middle of the vast, central Holland peat bog. Utrecht displays a similar pattern. Peasants owned the vast majority of the Ronde Venen peatlands, while others owned the lands near the rivers and near the city of Utrecht. The fragmentary evidence for North Holland also shows that the peasants in villages near the cities of Alkmaar, Hoorn, and Enkhuizen owned less land than elsewhere. In general, North Holland peasants owned more

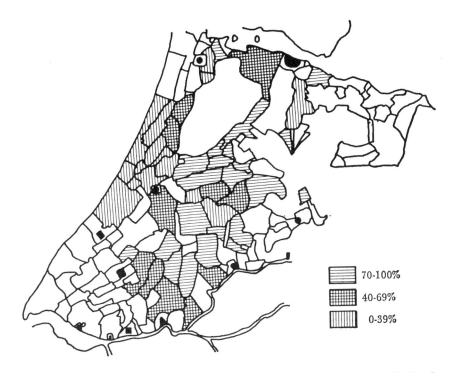

Map 2.1. Percentage of Cultivable Land Owned by the User, Central Holland. Rijnland, 1540–44; Schieland, 1561–62.

SOURCES: Hoogheemraadschap van Rijnland, oude archieven, Morgenboeken; ARA den Haag, Tiende Penning Cohieren.

of the land than did peasants farther south, presumably in reflection of the Friesian peoples' heritage of peasant proprietorship.

When we turn to Friesland itself, peasant proprietorship appears to have been considerably less extensive than in Holland. The difficulty of identifying all the lands of individual proprietors precludes, as it did in Holland, the calculation of total peasant landownership from the data available in the *Aanbreng van 1511*. I have resorted, therefore, to calculating the percentage of farms at least half-owned by their operators. Map 2.4 shows the extent of peasant landownership as calculated by this crude method in 14 of the provinces' 31 grietenijen in 1511. Just as in Holland, the peasants owned much of the poor sand and peat soils and little of the more valuable clay soils. A close examination of the grietenij Barradeel in 1546 reveals that peasants working small holdings (under 10 pondematen, or 3.7

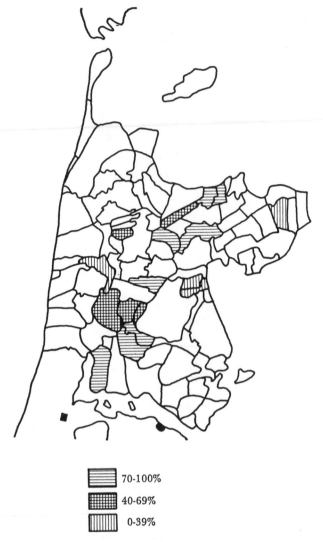

▤	70-100%
▦	40-69%
▥	0-39%

Map 2.2. Percentage of Cultivable Land Owned by the User, North Holland. Noorderkwartier, 1553.

SOURCE: ARA den Haag, Tiende Penning Cohieren.

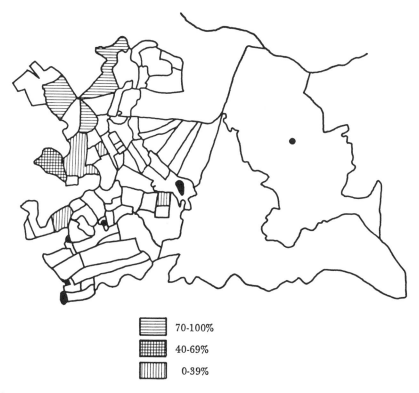

Map 2.3. Percentage of Cultivable Land Owned by the User, Western Utrecht, 1540.

SOURCE: RA Utrecht, Mannuaal van het Oudschildgeld.

hectares) owned over half the land they worked, while those working larger holdings owned under 20 percent.[107] No sources exist to illuminate the question of peasant landownership in Groningen.

In general, peasant landownership was substantial, although it varied greatly from place to place, being particularly widespread on the less desirable lands. Even more widespread was peasant ownership of their houses. Early sixteenth-century dwellings in this region did not represent a large capital investment; even persons altogether without land usually owned their own house.

An effort to acquire a more detailed picture of peasant landownership, by carefully tracing the names of peasants through the village and neighboring village records, shows that the figures presented

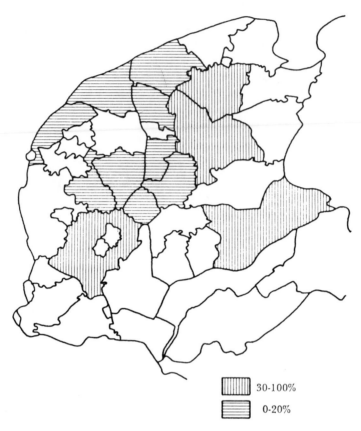

30-100%

0-20%

Map 2.4. Peasant Landownership in Friesland, 1511, Showing Percentage of Farms at Least Half of Which Were Owned by the User.

SOURCE: *Aanbreng van 1511.*

above not only understate its extent but, more important, fail to bring forward the widespread differentiation of the peasantry.

For example, in the central Holland village of Hogeveen peasants owned 26 percent of the land they used, but when the land they owned but did not themselves use is added, they owned 52 percent of the land.[108] In the villages of Opmeer in 1514 and Beets in 1558 the peasants rented nearly a quarter of their land from peasants residing in nearby villages.[109] In the Friesian village of Kornwerd, the *Aanbreng der Buitendijksteren landen* of 1546 reveals that peasant proprietors owned 25 percent of the land they worked and owned a further 20 percent that they rented to others.[110]

The peasantry as a class owned a considerable portion of the land and the privileged classes, as we have seen, rarely possessed the power to hold them in subjugation. Under these conditions cleavages formed within the peasant class and capitalist relations developed in the countryside. Some peasants owned much land, leased it to other peasants, lent money, and engaged in local trade. Other peasants owned nothing and found themselves economically dependent not upon noblemen, churchmen, or their representatives, but upon other peasants.

In contrast, Enno van Gelder's description of rural society in sixteenth-century Flanders and Hainault stresses the cohesiveness of the village community. Here, in a region adjacent to the northern Netherlands, the seigneur and other privileged landowners formed a powerful elite standing opposed to a class of villagers who themselves worked what little land they owned.[111] The distribution of wealth and influence among the peasants paled in comparison with the distinction between the peasants as a whole and their superiors. In open-field villages throughout Europe a peasant cohesiveness based on common rights and responsibilities characterized village society.

In a society with a weak privileged class, without widespread feudal tenure, without open fields and large nucleated villages, any description of peasant society must stress individualism rather than a communal spirit. The customary portrait of rural society in Europe, showing it to be legally divided but socially cohesive, is misleading in many instances but is certainly wrong in the northern Netherlands.[112]

To prepare the way for an analysis of changes in rural class structure in later chapters, we should wish to have a description of the structure of peasant society in the early sixteenth century. This is not a straightforward task. The basic criteria that came to distinguish west European peasants from one another—the right to the common land, the possession or lack of a plough team, and, in the words of Marc Bloch, "the eminence conferred by the power and dignity of service under the lord,"—counted for very little in the northern Netherlands where common land, arable agriculture, and great estates were either absent or of subsidiary importance. The region does not, therefore, yield a terminology to classify the peasantry comparable to that of neighboring countries. In France peasant society divided into two broad groups, the *laboureurs,* who possessed a plough team, and the *manouvriers,* who did not. Within the body of the laboureurs, large tenants of noble-owned farms, *fermiers* or *receveurs de seigneurie,* enjoyed a special status.[113] In northern Germany the operation of a "full farm," a *höfe,* determined one's class: those who did went under the name *bauer, vollbauer,* or *meier;* those who did not were *kossäten, hausler,* or *büdner.* The English stressed legal distinctions by dividing peasants into groups of freeholders, leaseholders, and customary tenants. Often cutting across these categories were the socioeconomic labels of yeoman, husbandman, and cottager.

If the approach used to analyze the structure of peasant society elsewhere in Europe is of little use in the northern Netherlands, how then shall we describe that structure? The beginning point, it would seem, should be to determine the pattern of land use in a sample of subregions and villages.

The systematic colonization of the High Middle Ages endowed much of the northern Netherlands with a remarkably homogeneous rural society. Settlers took up *hoeven,* farms of a standard size deemed suitable to maintain a family. Land developers marked off regular intervals along a road or dike (commonly 30 roeden, or about 110 meters) and permitted the settlers to develop the land between these intervals to a certain depth (commonly 6 voorling, or about 1,250 meters). This process resulted in a series of virtually identical farms, usually of 16 to 18 hectares. Repeated all over the region, thousands of such hoeven structured the rural landscape.[114]

Settlement did not proceed in this orderly, systematic fashion everywhere, but even in districts settled much earlier with irregular field patterns, the hoeve system existed.[115]

Long after the establishment of the hoeve system, the egalitarian, economically undifferentiated rural society appropriate to that field system could still be found in certain areas; in others it had long since been dismantled.

Consider the lush pasture lands of central Friesland, which inspired Euricius Cordus to write:[116]

> Qui laudata aliis, placeat mihi Frisia quaeris
> Non adeò male, si bos vel anas fuerim.

Plough teams and rights to commons could not divide the population here, where arable land was scarce and common fields insignificant. Feudal status distinctions could carry no weight where feudalism never took root. To the Friesians status depended upon one's voting rights, which depended upon possession of a *schotschie-tende huis*. The schotschietende huis referred to a farmstead and its attendant lands (called *ploeggang*) invested with these rights centuries earlier (most authors claim before 1200).

In 1511 the size of farm enterprises in central Friesland reflected the maintenance through the centuries of the schotschietende huis system. The number of rural households in 1511 corresponded very closely to the number of votes (*stemmen*) established centuries earlier. The households operating fewer than 5 hectares were rare; the vast majority disposed of sufficient land to gain a livelihood without being forced to sell their labor to others. A homogeneous peasant society had remained intact (see table 2.4).

But now consider the northern coastal districts of Friesland. Only a few miles distant from the central Friesian district one encounters an entirely different rural society, a society sharply divided between the well-off and the poor. Here, a large proportion of the population held virtually no land while the largest farm size categories engrossed a major portion of the land. The middle categories, representing the average hoeve size of the Friesian farm (about 50 pondematen) were weakly represented (see table 2.5). Graph 2.1 shows the fundamentally different class structures of the two Friesian districts. Graph 2.2 presents this information even more clearly and adds the distribution of land use in a district intermediate to the central and northern districts (see map 2.5).

One might object that farm size alone does not tell us all we need to know about a region's social structure, but in the simple economy of early sixteenth-century Friesland, it can tell us a good deal. In the central district, village craftsmen had not yet made their appearance, nor had rural industry and trade. The peasants performed all manner of economic activity and relied upon the small cities for extraordinary needs. In the northern district a beginning had been made toward economic differentiation. The landless, to judge from their names, were mainly craftsmen. Among the 8 Marrum, Ferwerderadeel, residents who used no land, one encounters a smith, a weaver, and a tavernkeeper. Oosterbierum's 7 landless residents included a merchant, carpenter, roofer, and shoemaker. Economic interdependence distinguished this district from central Friesland. The numerous dwarf holdings in Barradeel, for instance, existed because of the labor demand emanating from the Abbot of

TABLE 2.4. Distribution of Rural Households by Farm Size Categories: Central Friesland, 1511

Size of Farm in Pondematen	Total Number of Households in:					Total	
	Baarderadeel	Hennaarderadeel	Wymbritseradeel	Idaarderadeel	Rauwerderhem	Number	Percentage
(No land)a	17				20	37	2.3
0.1– 9.9	6	9	26	—	6	47	3.0
10 –19.9	15	19	60	2	9	105	6.6
20 –29.9	41	24	96	17	16	194	12.1
30 –39.9	47	32	136	23	25	263	16.5
40 –49.9	50	41	118	48	31	288	18.0
50 –59.9	50	39	91	37	28	245	15.3
60 –69.9	35	37	58	23	14	167	10.5
70 –79.9	13	23	37	10	9	92	5.8
80 –89.9	18	21	27	11	4	81	5.1
90 –99.9	10	13	7	6	3	39	2.4
100 and over	9	8	10	7	5	39	2.4
Total	311	266	666	184	170	1597	100.0

SOURCE: *Aanbreng van 1511.*

NOTE: The stability of this pattern over the centuries preceding 1511 is reflected by the fact that the grietenijen possessed the following number of stemmen, which indicate the number of farms at some time in the High Middle Ages:

Grietenij	Landholding households in 1511	Stemmen
Baarderadeel	294	315
Hennaarderadeel	266	255
Wymbritseradeel	666	577
Idaarderadeel	184	179
Rauwerderhem	150	137
Total	1560	1463

a Only in Rauwerderhem can we be confident that all landless inhabitants were enumerated in the *Aanbreng.* It does not follow, however, that all of the other grietenijen contained landless inhabitants.

TABLE 2.5. Distribution of Rural Households by Farm Size Categories: Northern Friesland, 1511

Size of Farms in Pondematen	Total Number of Households in:				Total	
	Barradeel	Ferwerderadeel	Wonseradeel	Achtkarspelen	Number	Percentage
(No land)	69	18	5	1	93	9.3
0.1– 9.9	43	30	33	115	221	22.2
10 –19.9	38	26	29	70	163	16.4
20 –29.9	17	25	24	70	136	13.7
30 –39.9	23	26	18	45	112	11.3
40 –49.9	18	18	23	25	84	8.4
50 –59.9	14	15	14	25	68	6.8
60 –69.9	13	11	16	25	65	6.5
70 –79.9	5	8	4	5	22	2.2
80 –89.9	3	3	1	5	12	1.2
90 –99.9	1	3	2	0	6	0.6
100 and over	4	4	5	0	13	1.3
Total	248[a]	187[a]	174[a]	386	995	99.9

SOURCES: *Aanbreng van 1511; Aanbreng der Vijf Deelen.*

NOTE: The grietenij that lay between Barradeel and Ferwerderadeel, het Bildt, is excluded from this survey, even though its farm size information is available for the early sixteenth century, because of its completely different history. Drained in 1505, the district was still in the process of being settled during the period under discussion here.

[a] Not all of the villages in these grietenijen are included in the statistics.

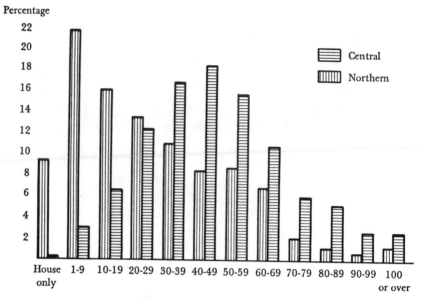

Graph 2.1. Distribution of Rural Households by Farm Size Categories in Central and Northern Friesland, 1511.

SOURCES: See tables 2.4 and 2.5.

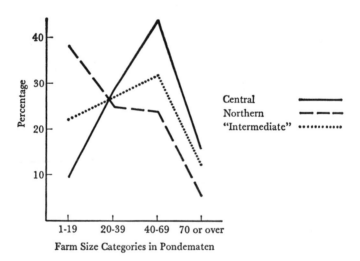

Graph 2.2. Distribution of Rural Households in Central, Northern, and "Intermediate" Zones of Friesland, 1511.

NOTE: The data for the intermediate zone, which comprises Leeuwarderadeel and parts of Dantumadeel and Tietjerksteradeel, cover 825 households and are drawn from the *Aanbreng van 1511*.

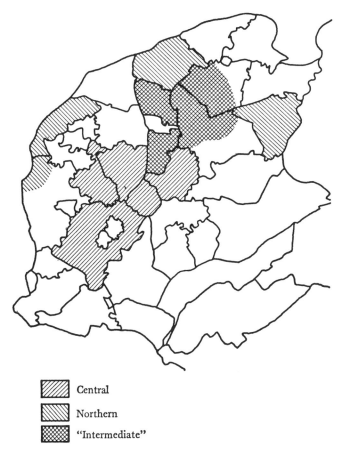

Central

Northern

"Intermediate"

Map 2.5. Central, Northern, and "Intermediate" Zones of Friesland, as Used in Graphs 2.1 and 2.2.

Lidlum's 229-pondematen estate in Oosterbierum, from his 224-pondematen estate in neighboring Tzummarum, and from many other large farms, which, in this arable farming district, required more labor per hectare than did central Friesland farms of comparable size.

In Holland, as in Friesland, no single rural social structure prevailed. The more complex economy of this province with its numerous cities warrants our paying careful attention to its village economic life. Unfortunately, neither the *Enqueste* nor *Informacie* inquired into the size of farms as did the Friesian *Aanbreng*. Not until the compilation of the first Tiende Penning Cohieren and

Morgenboeken in the early 1540s can we describe the distribution of farmholdings in Holland. We will rely on them to analyze the land-use patterns of over a dozen villages scattered about the province, noting especially the extent to which those patterns depart from the medieval hoeve system and possible reasons for such departures. We first consider villages with relatively egalitarian agrarian characteristics and then go on to examine villages which had, by the mid-sixteenth century, evolved a more stratified social structure.

Bleskensgraaf, in the Alblasserwaard, had been settled in the eleventh century. Then it consisted of 42 hoeven, each 22 or 23 morgen in size. In 1515, after enduring the destruction of most of their buildings and houses at the hands of the duke of Gelre's army, 55 households lived there, engaging in agriculture and some fishing and fowling. The women spun yarn and kept cows, but the Gelderland armies had killed a goodly portion of the village livestock.[117]

By 1562, after plenty of time to recover from the destruction suffered in 1514, the village still numbered only 66 households (see table 2.6). All of the households held land, and all except the largest farmers owned some of the land they used. The old 22-morgen hoeve survived intact on only 8 farms. Fourteen peasants operated half-hoeven of 11 morgen, and 10 operated quarter-hoeven of 5.5 morgen. On the other hand, one man, Aert Tomszoon, assembled 2 hoeven, and two other inhabitants had added odd parcels to their full hoeven. Over the course of the centuries a gradual increase in population and the accumulations of a few successful families had considerably altered the old hoeve system, but, for all that, the peasant household of moderate resources remained numerically dominant.

Tekkop, settled sometime before 1200, consisted of thirty-one 16-morgen hoeven. In 1494 and 1514 its 14 households raised cattle and grew some hemp around their farmsteads. All the households continued to be attached to the land in 1561, even though their number had doubled to 28. Seven farmers operated full hoeven and 7 others operated holdings of between 10 and 25 morgen in size. The small and large farmers who flanked this group made up half the village households. Here, as in Bleskensgraaf, the unity of the hoeve system had passed into history, but the community had not yet divided into distinct classes.

In the villages of Mijdrecht, Wilnis, Outhuysen, Demmerick, and

TABLE 2.6. Distribution of Rural Households by Farm Size Categories: Holland and Utrecht, 1540–70

Size of Farms in Morgen	Bleskensgraaf 1562		Tekkop 1561		Ronde Venen 1540		Papekop 1540		Ouderkerk 1561		Alphen aan den Rijn 1562		Westvoorne[b] (Nieuwland) 1570		Warmond 1562		Assendelft 1562		Asperen 1562		Zegwaard 1562	
	no.	%	no.	%	no.	%	no.	%	no.	%	no.	%	no.	%	no.	%	no.	%	no.	%	no.	%
(No land)	0	0	0	0	—[a]		—[a]		44	27.8	92	51.3	0	0	52	46.4	40	12.3	64	50.4	38	19.0
0.1– 4.9	3	4.5	4	14.3	9	4.5	3	6.3	5	3.2	3	1.7	38	57.6			88	27.2			99	49.5
5 – 9.9	20	30.3	4	14.3	31	15.8	10	20.8	16	10.2	9	5.1	14	21.2	9	8.0	56	17.3	30	23.6	34	17.0
10 –14.9	19	28.8	3	10.7	11	5.6	11	22.9	40	25.3	9	5.1	1	1.5	18	16.0	86	26.5	11	8.7	18	9.0
15 –19.9	13	19.6	7	25.0	25	12.7	9	18.7	27	17.1	12	6.7	4	6.1	17	15.2	45	13.9	10	7.9	8	4.0
20 –24.9	8	12.1	4	14.3	22	11.2	10	20.8	21	13.3	11	6.1	3	4.5	6	5.4			6	4.7	3	1.5
25 –29.9	2	3.0	2	7.1	8	4.1	2	4.2	3	1.9	11	6.1	4	6.1	7	6.3	8	2.5			0	
30 –34.9	0	0	1	3.6	23	11.7	3	6.3	2	1.2	8	4.5	2	3.0	2	1.8			3	2.4	0	
35 –39.9	0		1	3.6	18	9.2	0		0		6	3.4	0				1	0.3			0	
40 and over	1	1.5	2	7.1	49	24.9	0		0		18	10.0	0		1	0.9			3	2.4	0	
Total	66	100.0	28	100.0	196	100.0	48	100.0	158	100.0	179	100.0	66	100.0	112	100.0	324	100.0	127	100.1	200	100.0

SOURCES: ARA, Staten van Holland voor 1572, Tiende Penning Cohieren, nos. 1232, 1448, 1391, 1202, 1210, 1495; RA Utrecht, Staten van Utrecht, Mannuaal van het Oudschildegeld van het Sticht, nos. 143-1–143-4; RA Brussel, Papiers d'Etat et de l'Audience, Cahiers du Xe, XXe et Ce denier, no. 618–36; Enno van Gelder, Nederlandse dorpen, p. 32.

[a] Landless households were not recorded. Later evidence suggests they were not numerous.

[b] The land of Westvoorne was recorded in gemet, a unit of land slightly greater than 0.5 morgen. The data have been converted to morgen at the rate of 2 gemet = 1 morgen in this table.

Vinkeveen, which together make up the Ronde Venen of Utrecht, colonizers established hoeven almost double the normal size (33 to 36 morgen) to compensate for the particularly unfavorable drainage conditions that prevailed there in the Middle Ages.[118] As the inhabitants improved drainage and gradually brought the entire area under cultivation, splitting the hoeven became only natural. But this process was still far from complete. Much land still lay totally unused. If we judge from the farm size distribution of 1540, however, the permutation of the original hoeve structure had not yet fundamentally altered the homogeneity of society. The nearby village of Papekop exhibited a similar situation.

Ouderkerk, stretching along the east bank of the Amstel River near Amsterdam, could cite no single colonization scheme as its origin. Older and with more diverse field patterns, the village lands were nonetheless divided among the peasants in a rather egalitarian manner. The 88 households of 1494 fell to 70 in 1514, when the inhabitants' only agricultural activity was cattle raising, which they supplemented by fishing and fowling. The landless hired out as day laborers and as crew members of herring boats.[119] In 1562 the population had grown considerably from its 1514 level to 158 households. Forty-one lived in the village proper as craftsmen, sailors, and day laborers;[120] the remaining population lived from the land as dairy farmers. The land distribution pattern displayed in table 2.6 indicates that the presence of landless villagers and the influence of a nearby city was not incompatible with the preservation of a unitary peasant class.

In the midst of these villages lay many others where the peasantry no longer formed a single socioeconomic group.

In Alphen aan den Rijn, a village of 83 households in 1514, the inhabitants occupied themselves with "agriculture, but mostly with reed cutting, peat digging, day labor, fowling, and fishing." [121] The village grew rapidly to 179 households in 1562. Only 87 could lay claim to any land; among these 87 land users were many who held large holdings; among the 92 landless households, 29 lived outside the village proper in what the tax register referred to as *huisken* (little houses) or "wretched little houses."

Westvoorne, an arable agricultural village on the island of Goeree, exhibits a social stratification akin to that of northern Friesland. Although the village and all those around it escaped the scrutiny of the *Enqueste* and *Informacie,* the special inquiry of 1565, the

Informacie van den Brielle en de Lande van Voorne, permits us to assert that this region relied upon wheat farming and, in the villages, upon fishing for its livelihood. The peasant society here exhibited a polarization between cottars and large farmers; the 9 largest farmers held half the land of this village of 66 households. That this landholding pattern was not confined to a single area is confirmed by the statistics for Warmond, Assendelft, and Asperen in table 2.5. They exhibit a similar pattern despite their differing soils and their distance from one another.

Even sharper class distinctions arose in villages for which Zegwaard may be considered representative. In 1514, 74 households occupied themselves by digging peat, "doing great labor from early morning until late at night in order to earn our costs, and [by] keeping some cows." [122] In 1562 the population stood at 200 households, of which 29 used 10 or more morgen of land, 38 were landless, and the rest labored in the peat bogs, dredging the small plots to earn a meager living. The peat tax records listed only 28 peat diggers active in Zegwaard in 1520; by 1566, 198 were active, of whom 131 were inhabitants of the village.[123] Benthuizen, another peat village, mirrored Zegwaard's situation. Ninety-six of the 149 households used less than 5 morgen and together used less land than the 11 largest land users.[124]

If we turn our attention north of the Ij, we observe yet another pattern of land distribution. Many households were landless, most operated dwarf holdings (which unlike Zegwaard and Benthuizen, were unsuitable for peat digging), and hardly anyone farmed as much as 15 morgen.

In this region, where pastureland predominated, peasants could not subsist on such small holdings, nor could they hope to find employment on the larger farms of neighbors. North of the Ij, peasant society as a whole had turned from agriculture as a primary occupation to other pursuits, which will be discussed in greater detail later.

The *Informacie* of 1514 includes occasional information about the distribution of the tax burden among the villagers that permits us to view peasant society from another angle.[125]

In Noordwijkerhout, near the dune coast, the 300 schotponden, which represented the total village tax burden, were distributed among 2 rich farmers, who paid 15 schotponden each, 7 who paid 11 to 13 each, and 41 others, whose average assessment of 4.5

TABLE 2.7.   Distribution of Rural Households by Farm Size Categories:
North Holland, 1553–58

Total Number of Households in:

Size of Farms in Morgen	Twisk	Opmeer	Beets	Broek op Langedijk	Wormer	
(No land)	12	0	14	0	96	No land
Less than 1	7⎫	73	0	13	218⎬	Under 2 morgen
1– 4.9	38⎭		37	34	⎫	
5– 9.9	21	14	32	7	230 ⎬	
10–14.9	10	8	3	0	⎬	Over 2 morgen
15–19.9	3	5	0	0	⎬	
20 and over	0	2	0	0	⎭	
Total	91	102	86	54	544	

SOURCES: ARA, Staten van Holland voor 1572, Tiende Penning Cohieren, nos. 803, 1385, 901, 843; K. M. Dekker, "De landbouw in Broek op Langedijk in het midden van de 16ᵉ eeuw."

schotponden reflected an average income judged by the village elders to be inadequate to keep them out of debt.[126] A similar situation existed in Wassenaar. The 173 households divided into 3 groups: one, of no more than 25 households, was well-off; a second, numbering at least 100, "have greater debts than assets;" the third, numbering 48 households, relied upon charity and paid no taxes.[127]

In another dune coast village, Lisse, the 18 richest households, which had "thirteen cows, or eleven cows and three horses apiece," paid 100 schotponden each. Together they paid 1,800 of a total 2,260 schotponden. Fifty-nine others paid the remaining 460 schotponden, while 10 were poor and paid no tax.[128] The poor formed a relatively small group in Lisse; in the Oude Rijn River village of Zwammerdam, one-half of the 34 households paid no tax and required community support. Of the remaining 17 households, the 4 richest each owned 12 cows and 4 horses and paid 1.5 schotponden while the remaining 13 paid 0.6 schotpond each.[129]

The economic inequality of Holland's rural society becomes even more apparent when those at the bottom of the social structure are considered. The *Informacie*'s respondents usually took care to mention those households which lived at least in part from alms and could contribute nothing toward paying the village tax assessment.

Throughout Holland south of the Ij, the poor made up 31 percent of the 4,347 rural households for which information was available in 1514. Along the riverbank villages of the Krimpenerwaard, where nonagricultural activities—brickmaking, river transport, and dike maintenance—had attracted many migrants, 40 percent of all households lived in poverty.[130] In nearby districts where agriculture remained the principal means of subsistence, a rural proletariat had fewer opportunities to develop. Correspondingly, in the central villages of the Alblasserwaard poverty afflicted but a quarter and in the Land van Arkel, 28 percent of the households.[131]

In Holland north of the Ij, fewer households suffered under the burdens of poverty: the *Informacie* cited 23 percent of 3,745 households as being in poverty. No great distinction can be drawn between poverty in the countryside and in the cities. The 58,570 communicants in 16 cities included 17,040, or 29 percent, whom the municipal authorities described as impoverished.[132]

The remains of a homogeneous peasant society can be found in the landholding and taxation data just discussed. But it is the pronounced inequality in the distribution of economic resources that impresses itself on the observer.

RURAL ECONOMIC ACTIVITIES

In this era developing socioeconomic class distinctions did not necessarily reflect a growth of occupational differentiation. In a few villages, the elders referred to functional classes, but generally they distinguished between households only on the basis of wealth. In the large villages of Maasland and Schipsluyden, the elders divided the population into farmers (the richest group); fishermen, traders, innkeepers, wagon drivers, etc. (a much poorer group); and the poor, "who have nothing, but live from the holy spirit."[133] The elders of Loosdrecht also divided their 100 households into three (equal) groups: farmers, wool spinners, and common laborers (who made up the one-third of the population in poverty).[134] In Leyderdorp, a village abutting on Leiden's walls, the 50 households in 1514 included 20 farmers, 6 bakers, 4 tavernkeepers (who operated here to escape the excise taxes imposed in Leiden), and 20 impoverished common laborers, who usually migrated elsewhere during the winter.[135]

A much more common description of village economic activity emphasized the unspecialized nature of the peasant's labor. The villagers of Nieuwkoop "collect branches and reed, dig peat, dig ditches and keep a few cows;"[136] those of Alphen, likewise, were not proper farmers, but engaged in reed collecting, peat digging, day labor, fishing, and fowling.[137] And so it went in village after village. The great majority of the rural folk pieced together a livelihood by whatever means were at their disposal. Freshwater fishing and fowling were an important sideline of all and the sustenance of the poorest households in this water-rich region. Spinning occupied the women and, in certain villages near the urban textile centers, the men as well. In het Gooi and in Loosdrecht, Naarden textile factors distributed Westphalian wool to the peasants for spinning; in Rijnland, English wool was spun for Leiden *drapeniers* (textile merchants). The special survey of 1540 revealed that the numerous peasants who spun wool as a subsidiary activity were mainly impoverished inhabitants of rude huts.[138]

Peat, the basic fuel of the entire, forestless region, had long been dug on a casual basis. Beginning around 1500 increased demand from Brabant, accounted for by the rapid growth of Antwerp, induced more people to turn to the peat bogs to supplement their income. In the *Informacie* villages all over South Holland listed peat digging as an occupation, and some complained of fields made useless by excessive peat digging. By mid-century the complaints rose to a crescendo. Edicts prohibited the export of peat—but to no avail. For thousands of rural inhabitants, peat digging had become the primary means of support.[139]

The provision of boat and wagon transportation supplemented the incomes of many peasants. The Leiden inquiry of 1540 found 18 shipmakers in Leyderdorp and Zoeterwoude and a number of men with small farms (with five or six cows) who hired out to transport brick, clay, peat, and farm products in their small boats.[140] All over Holland, in Bergen, Limmen, Wimmenum, Diemen, Zoetermeer, Ijsselmonde, and Scobbelands Ambacht, men sought to supplement their incomes by hiring out their small boats and wagons.[141]

North of the Ij, where the dense network of waterways placed almost every village in direct communication with the sea, ocean sailing and fishing assumed a central role in the rural economy. Here, where the vast majority of farms had dwindled far below the size necessary to support a family, the population was more or less dependent on herring fishing and ocean shipping. The latter activity arose from the former, as the fishermen-farmers sought employment for their fishing craft in the off-season.[142]

A wide variety of other activities supplemented those listed above in the support of the rural household. The respondents to the *Informacie*'s questionnaire listed, among others, shell gathering and lime burning, broommaking, matmaking, sailmaking, ropemaking, roofing, and tree planting.[143]

Why had the peasantry turned to this lengthy array of supplementary employments? In most cases no turning was involved; the rural household's pursuit of numerous employments, agricultural and nonagricultural alike, reflected its nonspecialized nature, which remained unchanging over the centuries. It is an error to think of peasants simply as cultivators. Still, our discussion, which has striven to describe the rural economy at a point in time, has introduced dynamic elements that indicate an intensified pursuit of certain nonagricultural activities in the early sixteenth century. This phenomenon reflected a growing rural population that turned to peat digging and seafaring to earn a living in an economy where agriculture seemed incapable of offering employment opportunities. This last point is of fundamental importance to understand the nonspecialized nature of the rural household. Even peasants working large tracts of land could not fully occupy themselves with agriculture. Except in certain small, geographically favored districts, the low marginal returns to the peasant's labor on the ill-drained, oft-flooded fields forced him to utilize the land in an extensive and extractive manner and to direct a large part of his and his family's labor to other activities.

The consequence of this economic condition can be seen in the number of cattle held by the peasants in this region, where the size of one's herd acted as the premier measure of agricultural wealth. The richest farmers in the villages near Delft and Rotterdam owned a respectable number of cattle. The richest farmer in Bueckelsdijk owned 18 or 19 cows and 2 horses;[144] Jan Goryszoon, the richest farmer in Vrijenbaan, owned 20 to 23 cows, which he grazed on a farm of 40 morgen. The entire village of 14 households owned 217 cows, or 17 per farm, plus 40 horses and 10 hogs.[145] In Overschie, the richest farmer held 16 cows and 2 horses.[146] No subsidiary activities could divert the labors of these villagers, all of whom were undoubtedly prosperous, commercial farmers. Herds of this size, if we can judge from later evidence, required the full-time attention of a peasant household plus a hired milkmaid or two. But these farms were uniquely large; the very largest herds elsewhere in Holland did not exceed 10 to 12 cows.[147]

In Wateringen, where the richest farmer owned 10 cows, the average herd size in 1514 was 3.33 head. Over 4 morgen were required to graze each beast.[148] In Hofwegen, "the richest holds nine or ten cows and two horses, the others hold four or five, or two or three."[149] In Noordwijkerhout, cow ownership was distributed as follows:[150]

    2 held 9 to 10 cows each
    7 held 7 to 8 cows each
   41 held 2 to 6 cows each

In Aarlanderveen and Oudshoorn the peasants held "three, four or five cows at pasture, and some [held] nine or ten, but there aren't many of these."[151]

In Mijnen, herds averaged 6 heads, while the poorest inhabitants contented themselves with 2 cows. In 't Woud and Harnash, herds averaged 5 head, in Limmen, 4 or 5. In Geuderen no one had as many as 4 cows; in Westwoud, the 54 households held 200 cows on 800 morgen, i.e., about 4 head each, with 4 morgen required to graze each cow.[152] Six of the 125 households of Alkemade "have something, the others fish and fowl and hold two or three cows."[153] No one had as many as 4 cows in Zevenhoven and Noorden, while the average herd size in Benthuizen was under 2 and in Hogeveen and Benthoorn under 1.[154]

In North Holland, many households in Zwaag "have but one cow, and some none," while in Ransdorp, where the menfolk all went to sea, "the wives keep a cow or two."[155] From another source we can gain a complete picture of herd size on the farms around Hoorn in 1477:[156]

   149 held 1 or 2 cows each
   127 held 3 or 4 cows each
   144 held 5 to 9 cows each
    42 held 10 to 14 cows each
     4 held 15 to 20 cows each
   Average herd size: under 5

A pattern emerges from this evidence: the very richest peasants held 10 to 12 cows, the average held 4 to 6, and the poorest sort held but 2 or 3. When one takes into account the small size of early six-teenth-century cattle, and their consequently meager milk yields, it becomes clear that the typical herd of 5 or 6 head, which required between 10 and 25 morgen to maintain, could not support a peasant household. The low productivity of the agricultural factors of pro-duction forced even a peasant with a full hoeve at his disposal to cultivate assiduously nonagricultural activities.

Thus far I have ignored arable agriculture. It flourished in a few favored districts where the soil lay relatively high and dry, such as the dune coast of Holland, parts of the islands south of the river Maas, and the coastal clays of Friesland. Elsewhere, arable crops, al-though widely grown in the fourteenth and fifteenth centuries, be-fore the subsidence of the soil, could usually be grown only at the expense of great effort and at great risk. By dredging mud from the drainage ditches and spreading it over the banks, the peasants built up long, narrow, arable strips about 4 to 6 feet wide on which they could grow barley, oats, and buckwheat. In dry years a few other relatively well drained fields could also be successfully put to arable use.[157] In this manner most villages, even in the lowest-lying districts, could grow some grain.[158]

The peasants endured the great expense and risk of arable agri-culture in the northern Netherlands out of physiological necessity. Once the further development of trade could lift from them the necessity of devoting resources to inefficient grain production, they transferred their resources to more productive activities. This fur-ther development of trade occurred during the first two-thirds of the sixteenth century. A description of the important changes that took place is the task of future chapters. Here we can observe that Baltic grain exports, which amounted to some 3,000 last (6 million kilograms) in 1460, rose to 10,000 last (20 million kilograms) in 1500.[159] Not all of this grain found its way to the northern Nether-lands, but even if it had, it could have fed only a small minority of the population. The oft-quoted ordinance of 1501, which asserted that Holland produced grain sufficient for the maintenance of only one-tenth of its population, must be dismissed as a dramatic exag-geration.[160] Sixty years later, when Baltic grain exports attained 5 to 6 times the level of 1500, the Netherlands truly did depend on foreign grain.

As interregional trade links improved and foreign grain imports increased and became more regular, the widespread cultivation of bread grains ceased. Already in the early sixteenth century the elders of some villages failed to mention arable farming where it is known to have been common in earlier years. Once grain could be regularly imported, the peasants began devoting the expensively won, arable strips to the production of industrial crops. By 1514, villages near Leiden grew flax, hemp was produced on and around the Krimpenerwaard, and the villages in southeastern Holland grew considerable quantities of hops.[161]

In the early sixteenth century horticulture had not yet appeared as an important activity.[162] The substitution of industrial crops for bread grains, however, had gone so far by 1529 that Charles V issued a clarifying statement on his tithe policy. He hoped to settle disputes between tithe owners and farmers who had ceased growing wheat, rye, barley, and oats (on which owners of the *decimae magnae* could collect their due) in favor of rapeseed, flax, hemp, hops, and other minor crops (on which only owners of the less common *decimae minutae* could claim a portion).[163]

Rural society in the early sixteenth century was about to embark upon a century-long period of rapid development that would change the face of the countryside, expand trade, increase the productivity of agriculture, and greatly alter relations between the classes. In the first decades of the century some of the harbingers of these changes had already made their appearance; the development of distinct economic classes, superseding the older, more homogeneous peasant society, was well underway. But occupational differentiation, specialization, and production for distant markets did not yet characterize the rural economy. In a few confined districts, dairying, cattle fattening, grain production, herring fishing, or peat digging singly absorbed the bulk of the peasant household's productive labor. But the vast majority of peasant households continued to divide their time between dairying, peat digging, boat and wagon transport, reed gathering, freshwater fishing, fowling, seafaring, spinning, dike and ditch labor, and a wide variety of household activities.

This nonspecialization of the peasant household does not imply self-sufficiency. The numerous and populous cities and the general need, at least occasionally, to purchase grain insured the presence of a substantial local trade. But this trade, trade between non-specialized production units (households) employing primitive productive factors, must be clearly distinguished from the trade that developed later, among specialized production units employing more sophisticated productive factors.[164]

3. Demographic Change

Sources

Population growth played a crucial role in the theoretical models of preindustrial society presented in chapter 1. Before industrialization changing levels of population forced changes in economic structure and social arrangements, and a change in economic fortunes could not fail to affect quickly and directly the size and demographic characteristics of the population. This direct link between economy and population was inevitable in a society where the basic demographic unit, the family household, was also the all-pervading economic unit. In such a situation economic decisions were family decisions and the two could hardly be distinguished.

The fundamental importance of population to the preindustrial economy warrants my beginning the description of the transformation of the Dutch economy with an analysis of demographic change. We must content ourselves with a motley assemblage of evidence, much of which requires various sorts of manipulation before it can serve our purposes. I feel bound, therefore, to begin this chapter with an account of the sources, much as the producer of processed foods must list all the ingredients mixed into his concoctions.

Simple head counts, with little detailed information about the characteristics of the population, exist for Holland in 1622, for Utrecht in 1632, and for Friesland in 1689 (incomplete), 1714, and 1744. In 1795 the revolutionary regime took a nationwide census preliminary to establishing on a rational basis voting rights to a national assembly. An occasional village or municipal census must be added to this list to make it complete.

The list of censuses is rapidly exhausted. We must now turn to various sorts of statistical information initially produced to serve the fiscal needs of the state. In the fifteenth and sixteenth centuries many hearth counts were taken, particularly in the southern Netherlands. In the North we have only the two tax surveys of Holland: The *Enqueste* of 1494 (which also estimated the hearths of 1477) and the *Informacie* of 1514 (which also estimated the number of communicants). An important fiscal device of Holland under the Republic, the Verponding, produced two hearth counts, one in 1632 and the other, one hundred years later. Utrecht, for similar reasons, counted hearths in 1748. A few local hearth counts supplement these data, and the Tiende Penning Cohieren of the mid-sixteenth century often provide sufficient information to serve as hearth registers.

The most vexing problem facing the historian who would use the hearth counts to yield population estimates is what coefficient to apply to the hearth data. In other words, how many people lived in each house? The coefficient, influenced by many factors, varies from place to place as well as from time to time. Historians have used coefficients as low as 4 and as high as 6. Rogier Mols, in his work on European urban demography, made an exhaustive study of the problem, without claiming to find a simple answer.[1] We are aided, however, by the *Informacie* of 1514, which permits us to calculate the number of communicants per house in most cities and villages. The provincial average was 3.7. The percentage of the population made up by noncommunicants depended on the age of first communion, which could vary from twelve to fifteen, and on the age pyramid of the population. Age pyramids for preindustrial Europe and for currently underdeveloped countries indicate that the noncommunicants made up at least a quarter, and very possibly over 35 percent, of the population.[2] Consequently, the number of inhabitants per household must have been over 5. The proximity of Holland's head count of 1622 and the hearth count of 1632 could shed further light on the subject were it not for the unreliability of the Verponding hearth counts.[3] The hearth count of 1732 and mid-eighteenth-century village censuses indicate that a coefficient of 5 would be much too large. By then, for reasons to be discussed, household size had apparently declined considerably.

Lists of men capable of bearing arms, *weerbare mannen,* drawn up from time to time, provide another source of population data. They provide valuable, although difficult to evaluate, information for certain villages in the medieval period, for Friesland in 1552 and for Holland in 1747. In the last case, the lists include all able-bodied men between sixteen and sixty years of age. Population figures can be derived from this information only after calculating a coefficient reflecting the percentage of the total population made up by the men on these lists; for this, one again needs to know the age pyramid of the population.[4]

Contemporary writers provide useful information such as records of town wall expansion and accounts of plagues in their chronicles and descriptive works. One chronicler, Burger van Schoorl, actually went from village to village counting the houses. Of special interest are the works of Nicolaas Struyck and W. Kersseboom, two early demographers, who published studies in the mid-eighteenth century.[5]

I have left until last a discussion of the most important primary sources: parish baptism, burial, and marriage records. The special problems of using such data in a region without a single, all-embracing church and the scarcity of any such data before 1650 limit their utility.[6] The pioneering demographic studies of the French and similar work now being carried out in England have few counterparts in the Netherlands.[7]

The pitfalls that beset the use of Dutch parish records do not exhaust the dangers facing one who uses the sources of Dutch population history. Uncertainties inherent in estimating the coefficients discussed above and the unreliability of many of the raw data themselves must give one pause. Yet, the economic historian must assume the risks because of the great value of historical demographic information: it provides a basis for periodization, an indicator to compare levels of economic activity between periods and regions, and aids in explaining observed economic conduct and interclass relations.

DEMOGRAPHIC MODELS

In the models of rural change introduced in chapter 1 I held population growth to be an exogenous factor. This assumption helped keep the models simple. In the description of the North Netherlands' economy that follows we must discard this simplifying assumption in favor of theories that link economic and demographic change. In the absence of detailed information describing the birth rates, death rates, average completed family size, marriage rates, and age distribution of the population, we cannot truly reconstruct demographic conditions in the Dutch economy. Instead we must consider theoretical models despite the obvious hazards and judge their applicability according to how well they account for the fragmentary information at our disposal.

The Malthusian theory must be the starting point of any analysis of populations before the advent of an industrial economy. Malthus identified positive and preventive checks (the former increase mortality; the latter lower fertility) that singly or together could bring the growth of a population to a standstill in the face of a narrowing gap between output and the subsistence requirements of the population. Should that gap grow (because of new agricultural techniques or additional land) both positive and preventive checks could be temporarily lifted. Historians of preindustrial economies have generally accepted the direct link postulated by Malthus between the (agricultural) economy and the population and the inevitability of tension caused by the capacity of the latter to grow at a faster rate than the former. E. Le Roy Ladurie, in his study of sixteenth- and seventeenth-century Languedoc summarized his findings in a *grand cycle agraire,* the chief components of which were the trend of population growth and of landholding size. Languedoc's population in 1500, small because of medieval development, grew rapidly during the sixteenth century; with it grew the economy, through the simple accumulation of endogenous economic factors. Around 1600 the economy entered a period of "maturity," which was nothing other than the gradual imposition of Malthusian positive and preventive checks to keep the population from surpassing the level that the economy could support. Periodic crises occurred in this period since no cushion existed between the needs of the population and the normal productive capacity of the economy. Only a combination of reduced population and increased agricultural productivity after 1730 permitted Languedoc to embark on another "cycle." [8]

Abel's study of population and price and wage movements in preindustrial Europe shows a strong inverse correlation between population and wages and a positive correlation between population and price trends. This suggests that Malthusian pressures arose regularly when population increased and that the relative balance of population and output accounted for much of the movement in prices and wages.[9]

We need not further belabor the point that an important connection between population and economy existed. But neither Malthus nor the historians cited above tell very much about the nature of this connection. Malthus recognized that the relative importance of positive and preventive checks varied from country to country and that the manner in which population growth was brought to a halt mattered a great deal in determining the standard of living of a population. In graph 3.1 for instance, the stationary population at level *A* is the result of both positive and preventive checks: mortality rose and fertility fell. The smaller stationary population at point *B* is the result almost entirely of a fall in fertility, which checked population growth before growing pressure on the means of

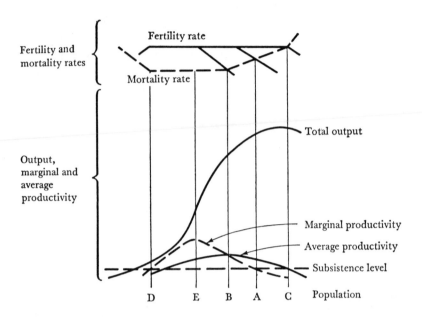

Graph 3.1. The Link between Demographic and Economic Conditions in a Preindustrial Society.

D Physiological minimum population.
E Population level where the marginal productivity of labor is at a peak; i.e., total output grows at its fastest rate. Only after the economy passes this point can we expect an economically induced fall in the fertility rates.
B Population level consonant with the highest per capita income level. If income is equally distributed, a fall in fertility rates could occur only after this point has been surpassed.
A Population level at which "surplus" output (total output minus the subsistence requirements of the population) is greatest. An all-powerful ruler would find this the optimum population level. *Note:* The mortality and fertility curves associated with point *A* are not unique. We can claim only that a combination of positive and preventive checks on population and an autocratically optimum population level must fall between the extremes of *B* and *C.*
C Physiological maximum population.

The graph presents a static portrayal of the model; the units of the abscissa, population, should be understood as population at a given state of technology. Thus, if the economy adopts more productive techniques, the physical numbers of population are increased at each point, and the economy's position on the economic curves is pushed back (to the left).

subsistence forced up the mortality rate. The larger stationary population at point C, on the other hand, is the result of mortality rates
alone rising as the growing population made no effort to reduce fertility rates through the imposition of preventive checks.[10] The standards of living of populations B, A, and C are each different and can
be read from the "average productivity of labor" curve in the lower
half of the graph.

The model displayed in graph 3.1 asserts that the average productivity of labor curve and the mortality rate are directly related. Mortality, in the absence of any overall upward or downward shift (the
result of plague or new health measures), will not rise until the average productivity of labor begins to fall and does not reach the level
of unadjusted fertility rates, thereby bringing population growth to
a halt, until the average productivity of labor falls to the subsistence
level. At this point the feeding of additional persons would place the
entire population in jeopardy. The model also connects the fertility
rate with the economy but not in the clear-cut manner of the mortality rate. The fertility rate depends on the extent of celibacy, the
average age at marriage, the use of birth control techniques, and cultural factors that determine the lactation period and the prevalence
of remarriage after the death of a spouse. The first three factors, in
particular, are sensitive to economic conditions.

So long as total output grows at an ever increasing rate, which occurs until population reaches point E on the graph, no economic
factor can be said to encourage a fall in the fertility rate. Thereafter
total output and the average productivity of labor continue to grow,
but the marginal productivity of labor begins to fall. Unless income
is distributed equally in the society, it is now conceivable that families will begin to sense an economic danger in a continued growth of
their numbers. The graph, while it shows but one mortality curve,
shows three possible fertility curves. These reflect the fact that a fall
(or rise) in fertility is the result of numerous individual decisions.
The decision maker's perception of what is an unacceptable standard
of living and his occupation both influence his response to changing
economic conditions.

The link between the fertility rate and the economy can be summarized as follows: the fertility rate is sensitive to the marginal productivity of labor curve, but the degree of sensitivity varies among
the socioeconomic classes of society. The fertility rate curve in graph
3.1 must be understood as the composite of curves particular to dif-

ferent classes and weighted by the share of each in the total population.

The distinctive demographic characteristics of socioeconomic classes not only affect aggregate figures, as just noted, but also have important consequences in their own right that warrant our attention. Recent findings uphold a division of European society into three basic demographic groups: urban populations, whose high mortality often imposes a negative rate of natural increase; agricultural populations, which frequently impose checks on fertility in the form of delayed marriage and, hence, exhibit low fertility rates; and rural nonagricultural populations, whose early age at marriage and low rural death rates conspire to give them relatively high rates of natural increase.[11] These characteristics make urban growth dependent upon a flow of rural dwellers to the cities. Besides this commonplace they also suggest that a change in occupational structure within rural society is likely to generate profound shifts in and concentrations of population.

The following investigation of demographic change in the northern Netherlands will make use of both the aggregative Malthusian model and the foregoing socioeconomic class analysis. The first requires that we focus attention on changes in the fertility rate. I will argue that mortality rates do not appear to have followed secular trends; population growth must therefore be accounted for by fertility rates that reflect changes in economic opportunity. The class analysis will give direction to our investigation of migration and urbanization, which reflect the location of economic opportunity. Together these ideas should permit the demographic information marshalled below to aid in our understanding not only of the timing of Dutch economic growth but also of the dynamic factors which propelled (and deterred) it.

POPULATION OF THE BURGUNDIAN NETHERLANDS, CIRCA 1500

In western Europe around 1500, a rural population density as high as 40 per square kilometer was unusual. England, France, the Rhineland, and Italy had attained *total* densities of 30 to 35 per square kilometer. Since the urban populations of these countries were, with the exception of Italy, not yet a large portion of the total, we can assume, without the information needed to be precise about the figure, that rural population in much of western Europe exceeded 25 per square kilometer. This figure, of course, can claim validity only over enormous areas; within each country, great differences can be identified between provinces, between valleys and mountains, swamps and fertile plains.

These general characteristics of the rural population density of western Europe are worthy of note to avoid gaining the impression that the rural population density of the Low Countries was uniquely high. Brabant, Flanders, and Hainault, with densities of at least 40 per square kilometer, ranked with the most densely settled regions of Europe. But there were others in their class: Norfolk and Kent in England, the Ile de France and Normandy in France, Jülich and Berg in the Rhineland, and the entire Po valley in Italy.

Almost immediately adjacent to the densely populated provinces of the southern Netherlands lay provinces of extremely sparse settlement. Luxemburg could count no more than 12,585 hearths in 1501, and densely settled Hainault, south of the Sambre River, was more like Luxemburg than like Brabant. In the northern Netherlands no province's rural population density could rank with Brabant's or Flanders'. Holland, with about 28 per square kilometer, was easily the most densely populated northern province. In the Friesian districts the population density stood at 18 per square kilometer while the sandy heathlands of the eastern Netherlands, if Overijssel is typical, supported fewer than 10 persons per square kilometer.

By the standards of western Europe, the rural population density of the northern Netherlands in 1500 was not unusually high. When we turn our attention to urbanization, a very different picture emerges. In most of the Burgundian Netherlands, both north and south, the percentage of the population resident in cities stood at a level far higher than was common in the rest of Europe. For instance, the entire Holy Roman Empire around 1500 contained 3,000 towns with "city rights." Twenty-eight hundred of them were of little significance; their populations did not exceed 1,000. One hundred fifty could claim as many as 2,000 inhabitants, and of the remaining 50 cities only 12 to 15 contained over 10,000 inhabitants.[12]

In the much smaller territory of the Burgundian Netherlands stood 208 "cities," half of which were walled. But at least 20 of these held over 10,000 inhabitants. Holland alone claimed 6 cities of this rank. In Brabant and Flanders at least 8 cities contained over 10,000 inhabitants, and many of them were much larger. In 1526 Antwerp,

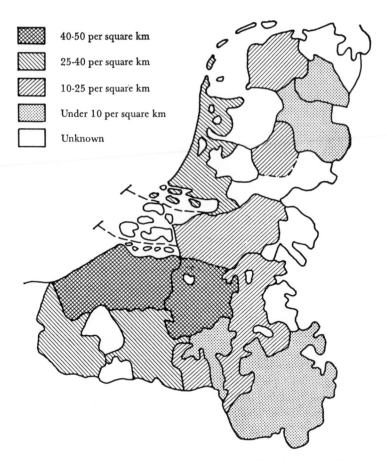

40-50 per square km

25-40 per square km

10-25 per square km

Under 10 per square km

Unknown

Map 3.1. Rural Population Densities in the Burgundian Netherlands, c. 1500.

Province	Date	Rural hearths per square km	Rural population per square km	Percent urban
Friesland	1511	—	18	23
Overijssel	1475	—	8	38
Veluwe (Gelderland)	1526	—	12	32
Holland	1514	5.5	28	50
Brabant (North)	1526	} 6.1	15	16
Brabant (South)	1526		>40	39
Flanders	1469	7.8	>40	40-45
Hainault	1540	7.4	37	29
Namur	1469	1.3	6	<10
Liege	1476	4.5	20	10-20
Luxemburg	1501	0.8	4	<10
Artois	1469	5.7	26	22

NOTE: Maps 3.1 and 3.2 and the discussion that accompanies them are based on the following sources: *Aanbreng van 1511;* Slicher van Bath, *Samenleving onder spanning,* p. 55; H. K. Roessingh, "Het Veluwse inwonertal, 1526–1947"; *Informacie;* J. Cuvelier, *Les dénombrements de foyers en Brabant (XIVᵉ–XVIᵉ siècle),* 2 vols. (Brussels, 1912); J. de

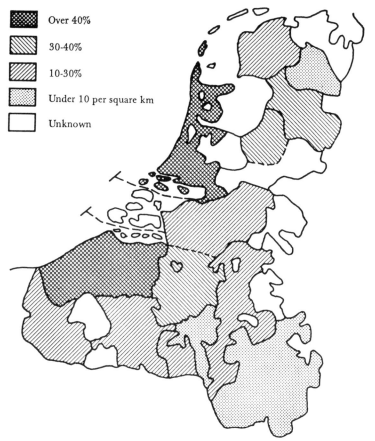

Map 3.2. Urban Population as a Percentage of Total Population in the Burgundian Netherlands, c. 1500.

Smet, "Les dénombrements des foyers en Flandre en 1469," *Bulletin de la Commission Royale d'Histoire* 99 (1935):105–50; M. A. Arnould, *Les dénombrements de foyers dans le comté de Hainaut (XIVᵉ–XVIᵉ siècle)* (Brussels, 1951); D. D. Brouwers, "Les 'Aides' dans le comté de Namur au XVᵉ siècle," *Documents inédits relatifs à l'histoire de la province de Namur* (Namur, 1929); Emile Fairon, "Notes sur la domination bourguignonne dans le pays de Liège," *Bulletin de l'Institut Archéologique liégeois* 42 (1912):1–89; Jacques Grob and Jules Vannerus, *Dénombrements des feux des duché de Luxembourg et comté de Chiny* (Brussels, 1912); André Bocquet, *Recherches sur la population rurale de l'Artois et du Boulonnais* (Arras, 1969). Overviews of this literature are available in: Roger Mols, "De Bevölkerungsgeschichte Belgiens im Lichte der heutigen Forschung"; Faber et al., "Population changes and economic developments," pp. 62–64; Norman J. G. Pounds, "Population and Settlement in the Low Countries and Northern France in the Later Middle Ages," *Revue Belge de Philologie et d'Histoire* 49 (1971):369–402.

about to become one of the largest cities of Europe, could count 50,000 inhabitants while Brugge and Ghent, old trading and textile centers that had seen more prosperous times, still must have numbered at least 30,000 inhabitants each.[13]

It is worth noting that England at this time had but 3 cities of over 10,000 inhabitants; the largest of these, London, contained 60,000 inhabitants in 1534.[14]

The unusual feature of the population of the Burgundian Netherlands in the early sixteenth century was not its size, but its concentration in cities. Only in parts of northern Italy could a counterpart to this phenomenon be found. Another observation that might strike us as unusual is that the rural population density was not necessarily great in regions where a large percentage of the total population lived in cities. In Brabant high density and large urban population went together to be sure, but in Holland the correlation is weaker, and, from all we can tell, this correlation cannot be maintained in Utrecht, Friesland, Groningen, and Overijssel.

These were the characteristics of the northern Netherlands' population around the first decade of the sixteenth century, after more than a century of decline and stagnation.[15] A period of rapid growth was to follow, a period which would leave the region highly urbanized, as before, and would also give it a rural population density much above that of the rest of western Europe. The following province-by-province investigation attempts to present the available data in a framework that will permit our making useful generalizations about the course and character of population growth in the sixteenth and seventeenth centuries.

POPULATION STATISTICS

Holland

Besides charting the overall course of population growth, we wish to uncover changes in the importance of economic classes. By dividing Holland into functional subregions based upon soil types, geographical features, and general economic characteristics, we will be able to localize population growth and urbanization and thereby more fully understand the nature of the economic expansion that occurred during the sixteenth and seventeenth centuries. Map 3.3 shows the basic subregions to which we will have occasion to refer.

The statistical table shows that population growth in Holland, at

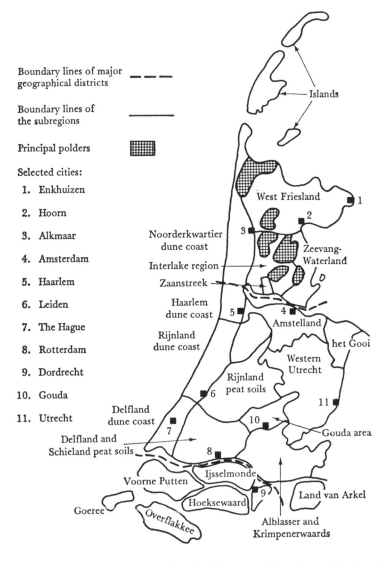

Boundary lines of major
geographical districts

Boundary lines of
the subregions

Principal polders

Selected cities:
1. Enkhuizen
2. Hoorn
3. Alkmaar
4. Amsterdam
5. Haarlem
6. Leiden
7. The Hague
8. Rotterdam
9. Dordrecht
10. Gouda
11. Utrecht

Islands

West Friesland

Noorderkwartier
dune coast

Zeevang-
Waterland

Interlake region

Zaanstreek

Haarlem
dune coast

Amstelland

het Gooi

Rijnland
dune coast

Western
Utrecht

Rijnland
peat soils

Delfland
dune coast

Gouda area

Delfland and
Schieland peat soils

Voorne Putten

Ijsselmonde

Hoeksewaard

Land van Arkel

Goeree

Overflakkee

Alblasser and
Krimpenerwaards

Map 3.3. Holland and Western Utrecht Showing Subregions Mentioned in
Chapter 3.

NOTE: Of the subregions, the following consist mainly of sandy soils: the Dune Coast,
het Gooi, the Islands. The others consist mainly of peat and clay soils.

TABLE 3.1. Population of Holland, 1514, 1622, 1795

	1514	1622	1795
RURAL POPULATION			
Noorderkwartier	*52,070*	*108,246*	*65,712*
Duinstreek	10,100	15,664	9,261
West Friesland	24,850	49,354	26,154
Waterland-Zeevang	7,300	12,326	7,359
Interlake area	2,050	9,388	5,309
Polders	0	3,214	7,947
Islands	7,770	18,300	9,682
Zuiderkwartier	*57,560*	*132,925*	*158,005*
Amstelland	4,400	11,034	15,686
het Gooi	2,100	5,051	8,264
Haarlem Duinstreek	4,800	9,386	9,800
Rijnland: Duinstreek	6,900	13,823	14,735
River area	2,860	9,151	10,514
Peat soils	4,500	26,370	18,521
Delfland: Duinstreek	7,700	10,279	15,216
Peat soils	8,400	16,313	25,315
Gouda peat soils	3,200	12,032	13,719
Krimpener-Alblasserwaard:			
Central areas	5,550	7,758	7,567
Riverbanks	5,700	10,309	16,373
Land van Arkel	1,450	11,419	2,295
Zuid Holland Islands	*[25,000]*	*32,183*	*53,809*
Ijsselmonde:			
Central area	—ª	3,318	4,851
Riverbanks	—	3,933	8,698
Hoeksche Waard	—	8,291	16,060
Dordrecht Island	—	250	1,129
Voorne-Putten	—	8,617	11,705
Goedree-Overflakee	—	7,774	10,666
Total rural population	134,630	273,354	276,826
URBAN POPULATION[b]			
Noorderkwartier	*30,320*	*83,592*	*59,969*
The seven cities	23,320	63,458	34,811
The Zaanstreek	7,000	20,134	25,158
Zuiderkwartier	*95,660*	*291,813*	*425,941*
Amsterdam	13,500	104,932	217,024
Six next largest	64,600	156,953	171,959
Others	17,560	29,928	36,958
Zuid Holland Islands	*14,200*	*21,902*	*21,184*
Total urban population	140,180	397,307	507,094
Cities over 10,000	57,400	327,678	406,997
Total population	274,810	670,661	783,920

SOURCES: *1514: Informacie*; village and city populations were produced by multiplying the number of communicants by 1.5. If the number of communicants and the number of

(*Continued*)

TABLE 3.1—*Continued*

houses displayed a glaring discrepancy, or if the residents belonged to a congregation in another village, the house counts were used as the basis of population estimates. Since 3.7 communicants per house was the province-wide average, 5.5 inhabitants per house was used as the coefficient. The Zuid Holland Islands were only partly enumerated. An estimate based on the proportion of the total chimneys this area claimed in 1552 has been used to estimate a rough figure for its 1514 population. See Naber, p. 18. The only city not enumerated in 1514, Brielle, had 332 hearths in 1523. (K. van Alkemade, *Beschrijvinge van den stad Brielle*, 2:174. *1622:* J. G. van Dillen, "Summiere staat van de in 1622 in de provincie Holland gehouden volkstelling." The total population enumerated in this census exceeds the figure given here because it included areas later detached from the province of Holland. In this study these areas have been excluded from the area of investigation. *1795: Volks-Telling in de Nederlandsche Republiek.*

ᵃ Data for the Zuid Holland Islands in 1514 are incomplete.

ᵇ Urban places are defined as follows: the 18 cities with voting rights in the Staten van Holland (7 in the Noorderkwartier, 9 in the Zuiderkwartier, and 2 on the Zuid Holland Islands), plus Woerden, Weesp, Muiden, Naarden, Oudewater, Vlaardingen, Maassluis, The Hague, and the Zaanstreek.

the rate of 0.84 percent per annum between 1514 and 1622, exhibited a very uneven incidence over the province. In both the cities and the rural districts, the rate of growth varied enormously. The fastest growing rural district, the peat and clay soils of the Zuiderkwartier, experienced an annual rate of growth of 1.3 percent while all rural districts grew at 0.7 percent and some districts grew very little, or not at all.

When we turn to a comparison of the data for 1622 with those for 1795, a period of no overall rural population growth, even greater subregional differences attract our attention. The rural population of the Noorderkwartier fell by 40 percent over the 173 years, while in the Zuiderkwartier, and particularly on the Zuid Holland Islands, the rural population continued to grow. But within these two districts the rates of change varied from a 30 percent decline on the Rijnland peat soils to a 77 percent increase in the riverbank villages of the Krimpenerwaard, Alblasserwaard, and Ijsselmonde.

The growth rates of cities diverged one from another even more than did rural rates. Fully half the population of Holland lived in cities in 1514. This percentage grew to 59 percent in 1622 and 63 percent in 1795. Consequently, the overall rate of growth of urban population surpassed that of the rural population; between 1514 and 1622 it stood at 0.99 percent per annum, between 1622 and 1795 at 0.15 percent. These rates of growth conceal great differences among cities. Amsterdam and Leiden grew furiously; the industrial cities of Haarlem, Delft, and Gouda grew much more slowly; and in the second period, while the port cities continued to grow, the industrial cities fell into headlong decline. In the Noorderkwartier the 7 commercial and port cities grew at a brisk pace until the mid-seventeenth century; thereafter their populations, together with the rural population of this district, fell rapidly. Most dramatic was the fall of Enkhuizen, a city of 21,000 in 1622. By 1795 it had become a tourist attraction of 6,800. In the face of this general decline in the Noorderkwartier, the Zaanstreek, a collection of densely populated industrial villages clustered along the river Zaan, continued to grow.

We must now amass and evaluate additional population data that will permit us to add detail to the broad outlines of population change sketched above. Such detail will hopefully allow us to answer questions about the timing of population growth and the importance of migration.

Graph 3.2 shows the course of population growth of the 5 largest cities of Holland. From this information we can construct a composite of the population of all 5 cities. On the basis of this new series we can extrapolate the total urban population by adding estimates for the remaining smaller cities. Information from various sources permit this for the periods after 1622. (See the note for table 3.2 for details.) Unfortunately we cannot be very confident about the extrapolation of total urban population before 1622.

This statistical trapeze act cannot claim to present exact aggregate population figures for the periods 1565–75, 1660–70, and 1740–50, but the approximation it produces clearly demonstrates the major periods of population change. Before the 1570s the cities grew slowly; Amsterdam accounted for most of the advance. After the Revolution, the urban population veritably exploded. This growth, centered in the largest cities, continued, at gradually falling rates, until the third quarter of the seventeenth century, when it was replaced by a downward movement that reached its nadir in the 1740s. Thereafter urban population slowly revived.

We turn now to fill some gaps in the rural population statistics. Graphs 3.3, 3.4, and 3.5 present the approximate course of population growth in 13 Noorderkwartier villages, 7 Rijnland peat- and clay-soil villages, and 9 villages scattered about Holland, respectively. This information permits the following observations: rural growth tended to be more rapid before the revolutionary years of the 1570s than after. After the mid-seventeenth century the population of the

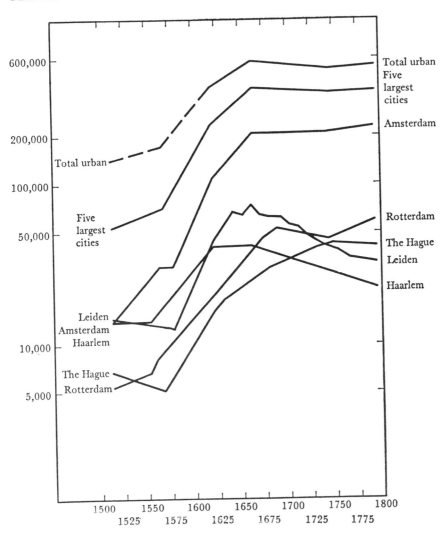

Graph 3.2. Urban Population of Holland, 1514–1795.

SOURCE: See table 3.2.

Noorderkwartier fell rapidly, reaching its low point by the 1740s
if not sooner.[16] The villages of the Zuiderkwartier exhibited no such
uniformity after the mid-seventeenth century; the disparate courses
of population in the 7 Rijnland villages reflected local economic
conditions, such as the state of the peat industry and the presence of
reclamation projects. Data from all these villages taken together produce a course of rural population growth similar to that of the cities

TABLE 3.2. Urban Population of Holland, 1514–1795

	1514	1565–75	1622	1660–70	1740–50	1795
Noorderkwartier						
The seven cities	23,320		63,458	[70,000]		34,811
Zaanstreek	7,000		20,134	[22,000]	28,000	25,158
Zuiderkwartier						
The five largest cities[a]	53,100	69,000	224,489	380,000	352,000	360,851
Others	42,560		67,324			65,090
Zuid Holland Islands					84,600	
Dordrecht	11,200	10,000	18,270			18,014
Brielle	3,000		3,632			3,170
Total	140,180		397,307	[561,000]	[499,000]	507,094
Amsterdam	13,500	30,000	104,932	200,000	200,000	217,024
Index	100	222	779	1481	1481	1607
% of total urban population	9.6		26.4	35.7	40.0	42.8
Maas cities[b]	10,000		33,343		62,000	79,743
Index	100		333		620	797
% of total	7.1		8.4		12.4	15.7
Four industrial cities[c]	51,700		119,323			77,634
Index	100		231			150
% of total	36.9		30.0			15.3

SOURCES: *Amsterdam:* H. Brugmans, *Opkomst en bloei van Amsterdam*; S. Hart, "Bronnen voor de historische demografie van Amsterdam"; idem, "Historisch-demografische notaties betreffende huwelijken en migratie te Amsterdam in de 17ᵉ en 18ᵉ eeuw"; L. van Nierop, "Het zielenaantal van Amsterdam in het midden van de achttiende eeuw"; P. Schraa, "Onderzoekingen naar de bevolkingsomvang van Amsterdam tussen 1550 en 1650"; E. Boekman, "De bevolking van Amsterdam in 1795," *TvG* 45 (1930):278–90. *Leiden:* Posthumus, *Lakenindustrie*, 2:882. *Rotterdam:* L. J. C. J. van Ravesteyn, *Rotterdam tot het einde van de achttiende eeuw; de ontwikkeling der stad* (Rotterdam, 1933), p. 173; van der Woude and Mentink, *Rotterdam*; idem, "Population de Rotterdam." *The Hague:* "Verzameling van nauwkeurige lijsten opgemaakt uit oorspronkelijke registers betreffende sterfde, geboorte en huwelijken in 's Gravenhage: 1755–1773"; *Zeven Eeuwen 's Gravenhage* (The Hague, 1948), pp. 129–31. *Haarlem:* ARA, Staten van Holland voor 1572, no. 1588, Quohieren van het Haardstedegeld (1555); Struyck, pp. 112–13; see also sources for table 3.1. *Hoorn:* Velius, 2: 187–95; C. A. Abbing, *Geschiedenis der stad Hoorn* (Hoorn, 1841). *Gouda:* D. A. Goedewagen, "De geschiedenis van de pijpmakerij te Gouda," in *Goudsche Pijpen* (Gouda, 1942); GA Gouda, no. 2300, Quohier van het Familiegeld; W. Kersseboom, *Derde Verhandeling*, pp. 39–41. *Dordrecht:* ARA, Staten van Holland voor 1572, no. 1587, Quohieren van het Haardstedegeld (1555); no. 1290p, 100ᵈᵉ penning van Dordrecht (1575). *Delft:* J. Rogier, De betekenis van de terugkeer van de Minderbroeders te Delft in 1709," p. 193. *Maassluis:* S. Blom, *Geschiedenis van Maassluis; ontstaan en ontwikkeling der stad* (Utrecht, 1948), p. cxiii. *Zaanstreek:* A. Loosjes, *Beschrijving der Zaanlandsche dorpen*; A. M. van der Woude, "Weerbare mannen," pp. 38–51.

(*Continued*)

TABLE 3.2—*Continued*

NOTE: The estimate for 1660-70 is a conservative one. It assumes that only the 5 largest cities (for which estimates are available) grew after 1622. The remaining cities are set at their 1622 population. The estimate for 1740-50 is based on more independent data. Reasonably good information is available for the 5 largest cities, the Zaanstreek, and several smaller cities. The baptism, burial, and marriage data for the period 1700-39 provided by Kersseboom permit estimates to be put forward for Gouda, Dordrecht, Delft, and Brielle. The cities for which no information exists totaled 55,800 inhabitants in 1795 (about 12 percent of the total urban population). We assume these cities had as many inhabitants in 1740-50 as in 1795. The result is definitely a lower limit estimate.

ª Amsterdam, Rotterdam, Leiden, Haarlem, The Hague.
ᵇ Rotterdam, Delfshaven, Schiedam, Vlaardingen, Maassluis.
ᶜ Haarlem, Leiden, Delft, Gouda.

(with the notable exception of the faster rate of growth before the 1570s), but some villages represented on graph 3.5 appear to have grown very little or not at all in the midst of the general upsurge.

These village data are too sparse to be used in the construction of a more detailed series of rural population. Data sufficient for such a purpose exist only for the mid-eighteenth century. The demographer Nicolaas Struyck, seeking to uncover statistical uniformities in population characteristics, enlisted the aid of village schoolmasters during the early 1740s to compile information concerning over 40 villages in the Noorderkwartier. His work confirms the impression given by graph 3.3 that the sharp drop in population following the mid-seventeenth century was completed by the 1740s. By then, the population of West Friesland and Waterland-Zeevang, the two subregions for which Struyck's figures are most complete, had fallen to 52 percent and 66 percent, respectively, of their 1622 levels.[17]

For Holland south of the Ij, A. M. van der Woude has compiled and analyzed the lists of weerbare mannen (men between the ages of 16 and 60 capable of bearing arms) of 1747. Applying upper- and lower-limit coefficients to these data based on Struyck's study of age distribution, he produced aggregate population estimates which show that the area covered by his analysis, with a population of 122,646 in 1622 and 142,343 in 1795, had between 121,000 and 136,000 in 1747.[18] Rural Holland south of the Ij did not suffer the sharp decline that characterized the Noorderkwartier. On the contrary, its population grew, but the evidence does not permit us to identify positively a single period in which that growth took place.

Can we now construct a more detailed aggregate population curve

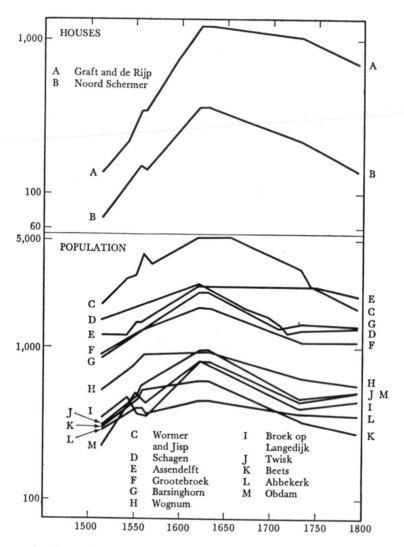

Graph 3.3. Population of Villages in Northern Holland, 1514–1795.

SOURCES: ARA, Staten van Holland voor 1572, Tiende Penning Cohieren, 1543–44, nos. 144–440; 1553, nos. 533–871; 1557–58, nos. 875–1182; 1561–62, nos. 1191–1518; Financie van Holland, Kohier van het Redres-generaal der verponding, 1632, no. 467; Leggers der nieuwe gevormde kohieren, 1732, nos. 485–522; Dirk Burger van Scoorl, *Cronyk van Medenblik*, pp. 289–94, 191–92, 34–38; *Tegenwoordige Staat van Holland*, 8:437–38; C. Mol, *Uit de geschiedenis van Wormer*, pp. 126–28; K. M. Dekker, "De landbouw in Broek op Langedijk"; Gemeentearchief van Twisk, Quohier van alle Familien tot Twisch, 1715, no. 36; van der Woude, "Weerbare mannen."

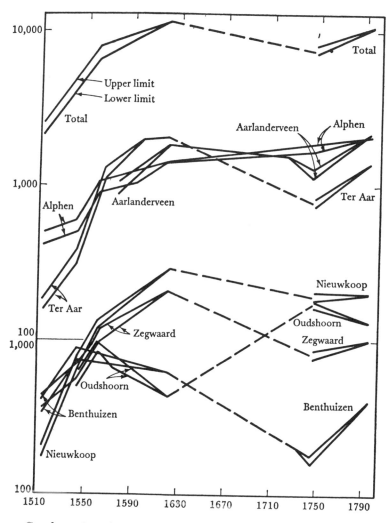

Graph 3.4. Population of Villages in Central Holland, 1514–1795.

SOURCES: AH Rijnland, Morgenboeken; ARA, Staten van Holland voor 1572, Tiende Penning Cohieren; J. Brummelkamp, "Grondgebruik in Aarlanderveen"; Jansen, "Ter Aar"; D. M. Rodenburg, "De Morgenboeken van Benthuizen"; van der Kloot-Meyburg, *Oudshoorn*, p. 10; van der Woude, "Weerbare mannen."

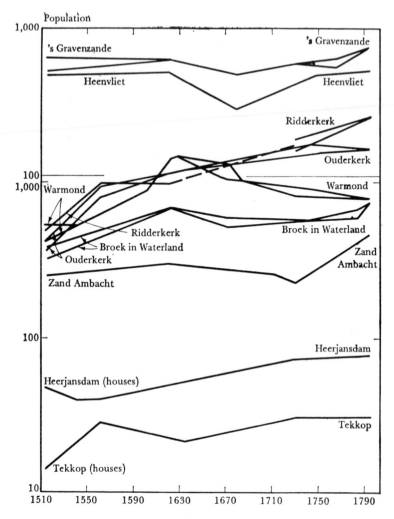

Graph 3.5. Population of Villages in Holland, 1514–1795.

Sources: Archival sources listed for graphs 3.3 and 3.4, plus D. J. Noorden, "De bevolking van 's-Gravenzande en Zand Ambacht, 1680–1795," pp. 73–88; A. G. van der Steur, "Het aantal inwoners van Warmond in de loop der eeuwen"; 't Hart, pp. 49, 252; van Engelenburg, pp. 69, 81, 205; J. W. Regt, *Geschied- en aardrijkskundige beschrijving van Zwijndrechtschenwaard, den Riederwaard en het Land van Putten Over de Maas* (Zwijndrecht, 1848), pp. 86–93, 142–62. See also sources listed for table 3.1.

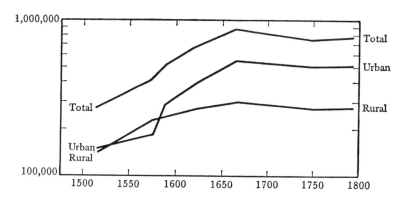

Graph 3.6. Estimated Total Population of Holland, 1514–1795.

for the province of Holland? Graph 3.6 represents such an attempt. The urban population curve represents the data of table 3.2; the rural population curve is based on table 3.1 with a population estimate for the 1740s added and the curve for the period 1622–1740 adjusted to reflect the presumption of continued expansion until the 1660s.[19] Both curves are adjusted for the period 1514–1622 to take into account the concentration of rural growth before and urban growth after the revolt against Spain. A major stimulus to the urban revival at the time of the revolt was the influx of southern Netherlands immigrants. Van Houtte estimated that from 60,000 to 80,000 persons left the south (10 percent of the region's total population) in the period 1570–1600. The majority of these migrants settled in the cities of Holland.[20] The final, adjusted curve of total population cannot claim to give the exact population, but it shows the major periods of urban, rural, and total population change and the rates of change that probably characterized them.

I noted earlier that population growth was not everywhere the same. During the sixteenth-century period of rapid growth people tended to concentrate in certain cities and in certain rural areas. The largest cities, all in the Zuiderkwartier, grew the most rapidly. In the 150 years following 1514 the 5 largest cities grew over sixfold, while the nearly 20 other cities only doubled in size. In the rural areas a similar, if less dramatic, concentration process was at work. Between 1514 and 1622 the sandy-soiled districts of the Zuiderkwartier grew by 79 percent, while the peat- and clay-soil districts more than tripled in population. Both urban and rural population concentrated in the area bounded on the north by the Ij and the south by the river Maas:

here, in 1514, lived 55 percent of the province's population; in 1622, 63 percent; and in 1795, 74 percent.

In rural areas, population grew most rapidly where rural industry thrived; purely agricultural districts grew very little. In the Krimpenerwaard, Alblasserwaard, and Ijsselmonde I have separated the populations of riverbank and interior villages. Shipwharves and brickworks operated in the riverbank villages, and many persons found employment in dike maintenance, transportation, and crafts. In the interior villages, agriculture formed the only important source of employment. The riverbank villages grew rather steadily throughout the 3 centuries after 1514 at an average annual rate of 0.42 percent; the interior villages grew at 0.03 percent per year.

This concentration process is perhaps best seen in rural population density figures. In 1514 none of the Zuiderkwartier subregions for which reliable figures could be compiled had densities far above 50 or below 20 per square kilometer. In 1622 the agricultural subregions exhibited densities around 40 per square kilometer while centers of rural industry such as the dune villages near Haarlem, the peat bogs of Rijnland, and the riverbanks of the Krimpenerwaard and Alblasserwaard now supported at least 100 persons per square kilometer.

This characteristic of Holland's population growth, its highly uneven incidence, is prima facie evidence of large-scale migration. The pattern of migration, in turn, suggests that vigorous economic development acted as the stimulant to this mobility.

By the mid-seventeenth century, when population growth in most areas ceased, Holland could claim to be the most highly urbanized and most densely populated province in western Europe. The other provinces of the northern Netherlands, though less populous, did not fail to contribute to the rapid growth and redistribution of the region's population. To them we now turn.

Western Utrecht

Utrecht, adjacent to Holland on the east, forms a continuation of the peat- and clay-soil district of Holland up to a north-south line that runs through the city of Utrecht and divides the province into two halves. The eastern half, composed of relatively high-lying sandy soil, falls outside the region I am describing. The half of concern to us, called the Nederkwartier, could best have been discussed together with Holland. Unfortunately, a lack of detailed population data for the early sixteenth century prevented this.

TABLE 3.3. Population of Utrecht, 1632, 1748, 1795

| | 1632 | 1748 | | 1795 |
		Houses	Approximate Population	
Rural Population				
Nederkwartier	19,094	4,576	22,880	24,304
Vecht	5,112	1,347	6,735	7,918
Ronde Venen	5,156	994	4,976	4,837
East of Vecht	3,267	973	4,865	4,828
West of Vecht	2,364	475	2,375	2,010
Oude Rijn-Ijssel	3,195	787	3,935	4,711
Lopikerwaard[a]	2,788	592	2,960	3,190
Overkwartier and Eemland	11,185	3,205	16,025	19,186
Total rural population	33,067	8,373	41,865	46,680
Urban Population				
Utrecht	c. 30,000	7,131	25,244	32,294
Amersfoort	c. 8,000	1,700	7,550	8,584
Others[b]	c. 6–9,000	1,208[c]	c. 8,700	8,777
Total urban population	44–47,000	10,039[c]	41,494	49,655
Total population of province	77–80,000	18,451	83,359	96,335

SOURCES: *1632:* P. J. Vermeulen, "Bevolking van het platte land der provincie Utrecht in 1632." *1748: Tegenwoordige Staat van Utrecht*, 12:115–231 passim. Where no population estimate was given, a coefficient of 5 was applied to the house count to produce the population figures. *1795: Volks-Telling.* Population of Utrecht city in 1632 based on van der Woude's burial counts; population of Amersfoort in 1632 based on Johannes Jacobus Herks, *De geschiedenis van de Amersfoortse tabak.*

[a] The portion of the Lopikerwaard in the province of Holland is included in these figures.

[b] Other cities include the 3 other voting cities of Utrecht (Rhenen, Wijk bij Duurstede, and Montfoort) plus 2 "autonomous" cities, Ijsselstein and Vianen.

[c] This figure excludes the houses of Ijsselstein. The *Tegenwoordige Staat van Holland* claimed eighteenth-century Ijsselstein had 3,000 houses. It was a popular residence for tax-avoidance purposes, but this figure is not creditable. I have assumed that its 1748 population was equal to its population in 1795, 2,531 inhabitants.

Table 3.3 presents the available census data. To uncover population trends before 1632 we rely upon the tax records of 1540 and 1600, which list all land-using households. Table 3.4 introduces this information for selected villages. The course of population growth here was similar to that on the adjacent peat and clay lands of Holland. The most rapid growth in the sixteenth century took place on the peat soils (Mijdrecht and Thamen); later growth was confined to the river villages (along the rivers Vecht and Ijssel). The more purely

TABLE 3.4. Population of Selected Villages, 1540, 1600, 1632, 1748, 1795

	1540, Houses	1600, Houses	1632, Population	1748, Houses	1795, Population
Ronde Venen					
Mijdrecht	62	193	2,207	336	1,771
Thamen	20	61	.....	117	640
Wilnis-Westveen	54	68	615	149	785
Outhuysen	21	29	256	50	270
Demmerick	30	52	444	77	384
Vinkeveen	31	47	275	65	329
Subtotals: Houses	218	450	.....	794	.....
Population	...	...	3,797	...	4,179
West of Vecht					
Kamerick	111	144	897	147	948
Papendorp	5	7	43	7	44
Lockhorst	9	9	39	8	44
Papekop-Diemerbroek	48	49	224	35	194
Subtotals: Houses	173	209	.....	197	.....
Population	...	...	1,203	...	1,230
Totals: Houses	391	659	.....	991	.....
Population	...	...	5,000	...	5,409
Per square kilometer: Houses	4.2	7.1	.....	10.7	.....
Population	(21–25)	(36–43)	54.0	(54–64)	58.3

SOURCES: *1540*: RA Utrecht, Staten van Utrecht, nos. 143-1–143-4, Mannuaal van het Oudschildgeld van het Sticht. *1600*: RA Utrecht, Staten van Utrecht, no. 971, Blaffaard van het Oudschildgeld over het Nederquartier, Overkwartier en de steden Wijk, Amersfoort en Rhenen. *1632, 1748, 1795*: See note for table 3.3.

agricultural villages (the second group in table 3.4) grew hardly at all throughout the period 1540–1795.

The population density figures presented in table 3.4 reflect western Utrecht's early sixteenth-century condition as a very lightly settled, ill-drained pastureland. The economic forces that brought rapid change to similar parts of Holland operated here as well.

The province's cities, aside from a few small ones that never amounted to much, consisted of Utrecht, the seat of the bishopric, and Amersfoort, which prospered in the seventeenth century as the center of tobacco cultivation. Reliable population data exist only for 1795, when Utrecht contained over 30,000 and Amersfoort over 8,000 inhabitants. Until the late sixteenth century the city of Utrecht had been the largest city of the northern Netherlands. Ramaer asserts that Utrecht's population in 1562 approached the 30,000 mark.[21] His other figures are often fanciful, but pre-Reformation Utrecht, the seat of both the Church and a lively commerce, surely contained well over 10,000 inhabitants. Van der Woude's burial count confirms that in the 1650s the city's population had definitely attained the 30,000 level.[22] A grandiose, unimplemented plan for the expansion of the city introduced in 1664 was accompanied by reports of a pressing housing shortage in the city, whose last expansion dated from the mid-thirteenth century. No further expansion in fact took place until the mid-nineteenth century.[23]

This single city towered over its province; it alone accounted for nearly half the total population of the province in the mid-seventeenth century, and if we judge from the rapid growth of rural population in the sixteenth century, the city then probably exceeded the rural population.

Before moving on, one last observation should be made about the nature of the cities in the central Holland-Utrecht area. Despite the prominence of the many cities in other parts of our region, this area formed the urban heart of the northern Netherlands. In a great circle, with a radius of about 34 kilometers (21 miles) lay 8 major cities plus a number of smaller ones.

Among these cities, Amsterdam grew more rapidly than the others and attained an international preeminence that has prompted many observers to consider its economy in isolation as the singular successor to Antwerp, as the entrepôt of northern Europe—indeed, as the last of the "city-states" in the European economy.[24]

The population statistics assembled here permit a different description. Amsterdam's rapid growth predated the revolution and fall of Antwerp, and although it attained a population far exceeding that of its neighbor cities, it did not attain the primacy that historical literature has attributed to it. The application of a rank-order formula to Holland's cities shows that in 1622 and 1732 a "normal" distribution of city sizes prevailed.[25] Amsterdam's role can best be described as *primus inter pares.*

The cultural history of the seventeenth century reinforces this conclusion. The flowering of Dutch art and literature did not confine itself to Amsterdam; it did, however, confine itself, to a remarkable degree, to the urban region we have delineated, and which the Dutch now call the "Randstad."[26] Today this urban agglomeration is unique: an enormous population (4.5 million) resides in the ancient cities and their modern suburbs, all strung along the great circle that encompasses an area no larger than greater London or greater New York. And yet, the Randstad cities remain distinct, of manageable size, and endowed with ready access to the countryside.[27] The framework of this metropolitan region of interdependent cities arose in the sixteenth and seventeenth centuries.

Despite the urban particularism and stubborn rivalries which at first characterized intercity relations in the area, a certain specialization of functions took place that contributed, in the course of the two centuries following 1500, to the development of a complex interdependence. During this period of rapid growth the transportation links connecting these cities were much improved; textile production, earlier a feature of each city's economy, was concentrated in Leiden; linen bleaching and finishing became the specialty of Haarlem; ceramics were concentrated in Gouda and Delft; The Hague of course, was the seat of government; and foreign trade focused on Amsterdam and Rotterdam. Utrecht, the religious seat, floundered after the Reformation without a distinct role in the network.

Taken together, as they should be, the later Randstad cities formed an impressive center of economic power. Their rapid growth must certainly have affected even distant rural areas. Economic historians frequently stress London's rapid growth in the development of the English economy.[28] The following comparison (table 3.5) of the population growth of London and the Randstad cities in the sixteenth and seventeenth centuries suggests that a similar role might be attributable to the Dutch cities.[29] Until the late seventeenth century, when London's and the Randstad's population histories diverge, the

TABLE 3.5. Population of London and
the "Randstad," 1514–1800

Year	London	Randstad
1514	. . . .	88,800
1534	60,000	. . . .
1565–75	. . . .	112,000
1582	120,000	. . . .
1603	250,000	. . . .
1622	. . . .	294,000
1625	320,000	. . . .
1660–70	460,000	443,000
1695	530,000	. . . .
1740–50	675,000	413,000
1795	. . . .	438,000
1800	850,000	. . . .

SOURCES: N. G. Brett-James, *The Growth of
Stuart London* (London, 1935), pp. 496–512;
E. A. Wrigley, "London's Importance," pp.
44–45; for Randstad figures see note for table
3.2. Utrecht, for lack of sixteenth-century
data, is excluded from the Randstad totals.
Its inclusion increases the figures from 1622
on by about 30,000.

rates of growth and the magnitudes of population show remarkable
similarities.

Friesland

Friesland's population trends in the eighteenth century are well
known since census figures are available for 1689, 1714, 1744, and
1795. For earlier periods, when the most important demographic
changes occurred, we must resort to the *Aanbreng van 1511,* land-
use records from which we can tally the households of 2 cities and
15.5 of the 30 grietenijen into which rural Friesland is divided. Esti-
mations of the population in the missing grietenijen and of the entire population around 1300 are based on the seventeenth-century
enumerations of schotschietende huizen, the homesteads vested since
at least the thirteenth century with voting rights in this "peasant
republic." In most grietenijen the number of households in 1511
corresponds closely with the number of schotschietende huizen.
Where the households of 1511 were more numerous, in predominantly arable farming districts, the difference was noted and applied
to other grietenijen with the same agricultural characteristics for

which 1511 data are unavailable. Finally, we consider estimates made by Slicher van Bath of the Friesian population circa 900. His estimates are based on the number of terpen (refuge mounds) then in existence multiplied by a coefficient intended to reflect the average population of these settlements.

The customary division of Friesland into four administrative units permits an effortless distinction of urban and rural population. One unit embraces the 11 cities of the province. Though they all possessed city rights, some were very small. The remaining 3 units divide Friesland into 3 rural districts—Westergo, Oostergo, and Zevenwouden. Each district consisted of 10 or 11 grietenijen.

We would present a misleading picture of population developments in Friesland if we assumed that the 3 districts included only rural inhabitants. The rapidly growing population and the concomitant transformation of the Dutch economy generated many new settlements which, despite their lack of "city rights" and walls, displayed an urban economic character. The Zaanstreek of Holland fits this model; in Friesland such settlements, called *vlekken,* or "spots," were particularly numerous. The reason for the importance of vlekken is rooted in the physical and associated sociological setting of the province's farms. The tiny farm villages of Westergo and Oostergo, nestled on terpen, did not lend themselves, structurally, to nonagricultural pursuits. Gradually the resident farmers found it to their advantage to discourage nonfarmers from residing on the terpen. As a result, agricultural and rural nonagricultural pursuits became physically separated; new rural settlements, vlekken, accommodated the latter.[30] As these vlekken grew during the sixteenth and early seventeenth centuries they attracted, because of their freedom from guild and municipal controls, traders and industrial operators who otherwise might have located in cities. This unique situation permits us to present a true picture of urban and rural growth in Friesland by separating the vlekken from the rest of the rural population.

In Friesland, as elsewhere, population growth occurred mainly in the sixteenth and early seventeenth centuries. What remains of a list of men capable of bearing arms compiled in 1552, the Monstercedellen, suggests that the population had already grown a good deal since 1511. A 1554 reference in the *Charter-boek van Vriesland* to the construction of houses where none had previously stood rein-

TABLE 3.6. Population of Friesland, 900–1795

POPULATION PER DISTRICT

Year	Westergo	Oostergo	Zevenwouden	het Bildt
c. 900	14,500	10,000	5,500	
c. 1300	15–16,000	15–16,000	15–16,000	
1511	21,000	20,000	17,500	a
1689	28,689	32,832	21,034	3,222
1714	27,619	31,977	22,661	3,342
1744	27,066	38,375	25,524	3,362
1795	29,960	45,041	33,475	4,196

POPULATION OF VLEKKEN[b]

	Westergo		Oostergo		Zevenwouden	
Year	Rural	Vlekken	Rural	Vlekken	Rural	Vlekken
1511	21,000		20,000		17,500	
1744	22,366	4,700	30,375	8,000	18,924	6,600
1795	25,960	4,000	37,341	7,700	25,175	8,300

POPULATION PER TYPE OF JURISDICTION

Year	Rural	%	Vlekken	%	Cities	%	Total
c. 900	30,000	100	—	—	—	—	30,000
c. 1300	45–48,000	?	—	—	?	?	?
1511	58,000	77	—	—	17,000	23	75,000
1689	66,777	52	19,000	15	42,957	33	128,734
1714	66,599	52	19,000	15	43,644	34	129,243
1744	75,327	56	19,000	14	40,806	30	135,133
1795	92,672	59	20,000	13	44,824	28	157,496

SOURCES: *900:* B. H. Slicher van Bath, "The Economic and Social Conditions in the Friesian Districts from 900 to 1500," p. 100. *1300:* RA Leeuwarden, Staten van Friesland, no. 9, Cohieren van Stemgerechtigden (1640). *1511: Aanbreng van 1511;* also, for approximations of the urban population, see RA Brussel, Papiers d'Etat et de l'Audience, no. 1429, De Monstercedellen van 1552; Gemeentearchief van Franeker, Priviligeboek van 1536. *1689, 1714, 1744:* P. J. D. van Slooten, "Frieslands volkstellingen der 18ᵉ eeuw met opgave der gealimenteerden," in *Friesche Volksalmanak voor het Schrikkeljaar 1888,* pp. 129–60; RA Leeuwarden, Staten van Friesland, no. 14, Omschryvinge van familien in Friesland (1744). *1795: Volks-Telling.*

ᵃ Het Bildt was drained in 1505 and settled in the decades thereafter. Its population in 1511 is not known, but it cannot have been large.

ᵇ There is no agreed upon, or official list of vlekken. The population figures here refer to the following 15 vlekken: Koudum, Molkwerum, Woudsend, Makkum in Westergo; Kollum, Grouw, Bergum, Surhuisterveen, Drachten in Oostergo; Oldeboorn, Lemmer, Gorredijk, Joure, Heerenveen, Balk in Zevenwouden.

forces the impression given by the Monstercedellen.[31] The record of the expansion of city walls tells a similar tale: a comparison of the maps of Hindeloopen made by Jacob van Deventer in 1558 and by Schotanus in 1667 shows the city area to have doubled in the intervening period. The density of settlement cannot be described from van Deventer's map, but in 1667 the houses were closely packed. No gardens or courts graced this industrious, seafaring city. Harlingen grew to become the province's chief port and industrial center. Between 1570 and 1650, successive expansions and harbor extensions took place, as the maps of the city show.[32]

All in all, Friesland's population trends show a strong similarity to those of Holland, although the rates of change here were less dramatic. The population doubled between 1511 and the mid-seventeenth century, when Faber estimates the total population at the 145,000–155,000 level.[33] Thereafter, population declined by about 10 percent until the mid-eighteenth century when growth resumed, although at a slower pace than in the sixteenth century.

The relative rates of increase between urban and rural population are of particular interest since the unique situation described earlier permits us to distinguish urbanized villages from the overall rural population. The 11 cities managed to increase their share of the total population from 23 percent in 1511 to 33 percent in the late seventeenth century. Most of this increase is accounted for by the brisk growth of the 3 largest cities, Leeuwarden, Harlingen, and Sneek. Even more impressive, however, is the growth of the vlekken. These 15 villages scattered about the province either did not exist or were nothing more than small farm villages in 1511. By the eighteenth century they contained about 19,000 persons, 15 percent of the total population. The remaining rural population, which increased by less than a quarter between 1511 and 1689, fell from 77 percent to just over half of the total population between those two dates.

The great majority of the farm hamlets grew not at all; population growth concentrated in a small number of cities and vlekken. In the grietenij Wymbritseradeel, for instance, the population of 25 hamlets grew from about 2,450 in 1511 to 2,675 in 1749. Two larger villages grew from 500 to 641 in this period, while the vlek Woudsend grew from a farm village of 24 households to a commercial center of 734 inhabitants.[34] Wymbritseradeel also contributed many people to the city of Sneek, which is surrounded by the grietenij and which grew rapidly, from 1,700–1,900 in 1552 to 4,370 in 1689. This con-

centration process tells more of the transformation of the rural
economy in Friesland than does the rate of population growth.

Groningen

Groningen's population before 1795 is largely *terra incognita,* but
the effort to discover the outlines of its development should be amply
repaid because Groningen is a good province in which to observe
yet another feature of the northern Netherlands' economy: large-
scale reclamation and colonization.

No early sixteenth-century population data exist for Groningen,
but a clue to the approximate rural population level can be gained
from the taxation records compiled during the short rule of the
Saxon dukes. The dukes imposed a *Jaartax,* a tax levied on the rental
value of the land, in both Friesland and Groningen. The tax yielded
about 6,000 gold gulden per year in Groningen, some 40 percent of
the Friesian yield.[35] After taking into account the probably lower
per hectare value of the land in Groningen, it still appears that
Groningen's rural population must have totalled something like half
that of Friesland. As a round figure, we suggest 30,000 as the rural
population of early sixteenth-century Groningen.

In 1795, when the first Groningen census was taken, the population
stood at 115,000. The rural population, at 87,000, was nearly three
times larger than our estimate for the early sixteenth century. The
urban population, on the other hand, grew very little in the course
of these centuries. The only city of importance—Groningen, with
23,770 inhabitants in 1795—already had 19,400 in 1564.[36] This city's
great size should not surprise us when we recall its dominant role in
the provincial economy. This dominance, symbolized by the city's
staple rights, imposed the suppression of all other cities and placed
in the hands of Groningers all the commercial activities of the province. There is much evidence of rapid growth in fifteenth-century
Groningen city. The city's burghers erected a new city hall, wine
storehouses, and church tower between 1443 and 1470 and undertook the expansion of the city in 1469.[37]

The dramatic growth of Groningen's rural population is the chief
phenomenon requiring our attention: when and how did it occur?
A careful examination of the 1795 census reveals that the bulk of the
increase lived in areas reclaimed and colonized since the sixteenth
century. The long-settled farm villages on the clay soils, just as their
counterparts in Friesland, experienced no rapid growth.

A general impression of population change in rural Groningen can be gained from an investigation of the Schatregister voor de Verponding, land-use records of 1630 and 1721, and the Kohier van het Taxatiegeld, a tax register of 1730.[38] A sample of 26 villages of the long-settled district of Fivelingo had 7,982 inhabitants—about 1,600 households—in 1795. Here, the 1630 tax records mention 1,126 households. The timing of population growth here is indicated in a smaller sample of 12 villages where the registers list 546 households in 1630, 542 in 1721, and about 800 in 1795.

But now consider a sample of 13 villages in het Oldampt. Here, where 7,025 persons resided in 1795, we could find only 622 households in 1630. In 1730 the "Taxatiegeld Kohier" listed only 494 taxed households. We are left to conclude that no population growth took place in Fivelingo until after 1721. Then, after taking into account the probability that the fiscal records exclude some poor households enumerated in the 1795 census, the region's population grew by a maximum of 40 percent. In het Oldampt, the center of considerable land reclamation, numbers may have grown, mainly after 1730, by as much as 125 percent.

The "Veenkoloniën" accounted for much of the increased rural population. Uninhabited in 1600, these peat moors of southeastern Groningen were transformed into populous, semi-industrial villages by the activities of capitalist consortia that organized large-scale peat digging for the urban markets of Holland. Beginning in 1612, and continuing throughout the seventeenth century, these entrepreneurs hired hundreds of laborers who dug canals and laid out farm plots on which settlers dug peat and, on the remaining soil, began farming. Shipbuilding, transportation, and related industries quickly sprang up, and by 1795 the Veenkoloniën had a population of over 20,000.[39]

Groningen's fiscal records cannot form the basis for well-founded population statistics. Still, the crude estimates entered in table 3.7 are sufficient to show that the province's rural population growth took place mainly in the Veenkoloniën and het Oldampt—regions of large-scale reclamation. The Westerkwartier, Hunzingo, and Fivelingo, which paid 90 percent of the provincial land tax in 1520, held but 60 percent of the rural population in 1795.[40] In Groningen, as in the other provinces, migration greatly altered the distribution of population as the economy expanded.

TABLE 3.7. Population of Groningen, 900–1795

	Urban			Rural			
Year	Groningen	Other	W-H-F-t[a]	Westerwolde	Oldampt	Veenkoloniën	Total
900	0	.....	11,100	.....	1,400	0	12,500
1520	......	.....	[..........30,000[b]..........]			0	....
1564	19,400	.....	......	.....	....	0	....
1630	......	.....	36,000[c]	.....	c. 7,000	......	....
1721–40	20,680	.....	36,000[c]	.....	c. 7,000	......	....
1795	23,770	4,358	48,177	5,008	13,883	20,028	115,224

SOURCES: 900: Slicher van Bath, "Economic and Social Conditions in the Friesian Districts," p. 100; 1740: Tegenwoordige Staat van Groningen, 21:10. All other dates are described in the text; see notes 35, 36, 38, 40 for this chapter.

[a] Westerkwartier, Hunzingo, Fivelingo, and t' Gorecht.

[b] Includes W-H-F-t, Westerwolde, and Oldampt.

[c] At least 36,000.

GENERAL DEMOGRAPHIC CHARACTERISTICS

Many of the population estimates made in the foregoing sections are, to say the least, tentative. Consequently, we must be cautious in aggregating these estimates into total population statistics for the entire region. Each of the privincial series shows broadly similar tendencies, however, which permit us to describe with some confidence the major demographic periods. Beginning in the early sixteenth century, the region's population, which stood at about 450,-000, increased rapidly in every province. The rate of increase gradually fell, although the timing of this deceleration varied regionally. The growth process ended by the mid-seventeenth century, when the population stood at some 1,100,000, to be replaced by a century-long period of stagnation and in some areas decline. After 1740–50 a low growth rate reestablished itself; the 1795 census recorded a population of 1,154,000. This outline is broadly consistent with the population histories of nearby countries (with the exception of Germany during the Thirty Years' War) but is distinguished from them by more rapid growth rates before 1650 and much slower growth rates after 1750.

The demographic trends of the northern Netherlands pose two questions: why and how did the population grow so rapidly, and why did the population cease to grow?

Immigration

The average annual rate of growth of 0.84 percent that Holland sustained for over 100 years, while not unusual today, had few precedents in the preindustrial era. Large-scale immigration, particularly from the southern Netherlands during and immediately following the revolution against Spain, is often thought to account for this rapid rate of growth. For instance, Antwerp, the commercial center of the entire Burgundian Netherlands, attained a population of 90,-000 in 1566. Immediately after the city's fall to the duke of Alva in 1585, so many citizens fled (and died) that the population fell by nearly 30,000.[41] Presumably, most of that number migrated to Holland. Later, during the Thirty Years' War, thousands of Germans migrated to the Netherlands. The Poorterboeken, municipal registers that enroll new inhabitants who purchase "citizenship" rights, make it possible to gauge accurately the numbers and origins of well-to-do migrants. We can presume that this information broadly reflects trends of lower class migration as well, although a larger percentage of the poor probably always came from nearby areas than did the well-off.

The origins of new poorters in Leiden, as calculated by Posthumus, are indicated in table 3.8. It should be noted that Leiden,

TABLE 3.8.   Origins of New Poorters in Leiden, 1365–1799
(In percentages)

Period	Holland	Rest of Republic	Belgium	France	Germany	Other
1365–99	80.1	10.8	6.9	. . .	1.2	1.0
1400–49	83.1	12.0	3.8	. . .	1.1	0.0
1450–99	79.1	12.5	3.6	. . .	4.0	0.8
1500–74	67.8	17.1	7.2	. . .	6.4	1.5
1575–1619	15.9	9.1	38.4	24.5	7.6	4.5
1620–99	32.5	16.9	14.6	13.7	18.8	3.5
1700–99	42.2	24.6	3.1	4.5	21.8	3.8

SOURCE: Posthumus, *Lakenindustrie*, 1:377–88, 2:44, 62, 886, 1042.

a seat of the textile industry, attracted more than its share of foreigners since spinners and weavers from the moribund textile centers of Flanders moved there en masse.

During the peak period of foreign immigration, 1575–1606, 7,217

new poorters entered Amsterdam. Their origins as compiled by van Dillen, are displayed in table 3.9.

TABLE 3.9.   Origins of New Poorters in Amsterdam, 1575–1606
(In percentages)

Within the Republic		Foreign Origins	
Holland	26.3	Belgium	20.6
Utrecht and Gelderland	9.3	France	1.5
Overijssel	10.6	Germany	14.4
Friesland, Groningen, and Drenthe	10.8	England	0.9
Zeeland, Brabant, and Limburg	5.4		
Total	62.4	Total	37.4

SOURCE: J. G. van Dillen, *Bronnen tot de geschiedenis van het bedrijfsleven en het gildewezen van Amsterdam, 1512–1601.*

Natural Increase

Immigration from the southern Netherlands and Germany, while sizable and occasionally of strategic importance, cannot account for the extraordinary growth of the Dutch population. Only a high rate of natural increase could produce the population trends outlined above; a simple arithmetic exercise will make this clear. We make the following assumptions: the five largest cities of Holland experienced birth rates no greater than their death rates; they could grow only by migration from elsewhere. (This, as will be shown later, is a very optimistic assumption.) One-half of the migrants to the cities came from outside Holland. The migrants from Holland came from the countryside. What then, would be the rate of natural increase necessary for the rural population of 1514 to produce by 1660 the rural population of that date plus half the increase observed in the five largest cities between 1570 and 1660? The 140,000 rural dwellers of 1514 grew to 300,000; if they also yielded half the 311,000 migrants who crowded into the cities, their yearly growth rate would have been 0.9 percent. Thus if the crude death rate were, say, 32, the birth rate necessary to generate the population this model requires would be 41; whatever the death rate, the birth rate would have to be 9 per thousand greater. The assumptions of our model were designed to produce a lower limit estimate of the required rate of natural increase. Mortality in the largest cities greatly exceeded natality, and the many smaller cities also required a steady influx from the countryside to permit the growth of their populations. This exercise

makes clear, however, that despite immigration the rate of natural increase must have been large. How did it arise?

Two explanations compete for our attention; one asserts that the death rate fell and another that the birth rate rose. The first does not appear very persuasive. During the era of rapid population growth the Dutch fought a long war of liberation. The armies that moved over the area could hardly have bettered health conditions. Until the late sixteenth century the problems of securing a regular grain supply provoked periodic famine conditions, most notably in 1536, 1557, and 1566.[42] Inundation sometimes proved to be a killer, and the major floods of 1570, if the reports of them are to be trusted, killed over half the inhabitants of two Friesian grietenijen alone.[43]

The region did not enjoy a reputation as a healthy place in which to live. Until health measures—introduced in the nineteenth century —reduced the danger of malarial and typhoid fevers, the inhabitants of the lowlands suffered a higher death rate than did those in higher-lying provinces.[44] The English ambassador, Sir William Temple observed that, "They are generally not so long lived as in better airs; and begin to decay early, both men and women, especially at Amsterdam. . . . The diseases of the climate seem to be chiefly the gout and the scurvy; but all hot and dry summers bring some that are infectious among them, especially in Amsterdam and Leyden." [45] The writer of an account of Overijssel, a sandy-soil province, wrote disparagingly of the province's climate, but noted that when compared to Holland, Overijssel was a healthy place indeed, and that Hollanders moving to Overijssel found their health much improved.[46]

Health conditions in the northern Netherlands deteriorated after 1598, when the frequency of plague epidemics increased markedly. Amsterdam, an especially hard hit city, recorded burials (see table 3.10) that implied crude death rates periodically exceeding 100 (i.e., a decimation of the population). In Rotterdam, van der Woude and Mentink found crude death rates of 120 to 135 per thousand occurring repeatedly in the decade 1625–35.[47]

The plague epidemics ceased after the 1660s and so did population growth. Ironically, the population moved forward during an era of numerous hazards to life. When their impact lessened, population growth ceased.

We are left with a rising birth rate to account for the upsurge of population. The chief indicator of fertility rates in this period is the

TABLE 3.10. Burials in Amsterdam
during Plague Years, 1617–64

Year	Burials	Approximate Crude Death Rate
1617	8,449	90
1623	5,929	56
1624	11,795	112
1625	6,781	60
1635	8,177	60
1636	17,193	140
1655	16,727	125
1663	9,756	50
1664	24,148	120

SOURCE: J. H. F. Kohlbrugge, "Over den invloed der steden," pp. 372–74.

average age at which brides marry. Small changes in the marriage age, a statistic highly sensitive to economic conditions,[48] could result in sizable changes in the birth rate.[49] Unfortunately, the available evidence is not voluminous. Van Nierop calculated the ages of *bridegrooms* in Amsterdam between 1578 and 1601; she found that 53 percent married before their twenty-fifth birthdays.[50] A study of Amsterdam brides, whose average age at marriage was lower than that of bridegrooms, found that 60.9 percent married before their twenty-fifth birthdays in 1626–27; their average age at marriage was 24 years, 6 months. By 1676–77 the average age had risen sharply to 26 years, 6 months. This trend continued in the eighteenth century: in 1726–27 the age of brides averaged 27 years, 2 months, and in 1776–77, 27 years, 10 months.[51]

In the early seventeenth century, when we observe a rapid rate of population growth, the average age at marriage stood at a low level. The gradual diminution and cessation of growth that occurred in the course of the seventeenth century was matched by a gradual increase in the marriage age and, hence, a reduction of fertility. The demographic model introduced earlier associated high fertility with an increasing marginal productivity of labor—a phenomenon likely to occur in an economy where men are rapidly adopting new techniques, pioneering new branches of commerce and industry, and transforming agricultural practices.

Another demographic characteristic associated with a developing economy is migration. Since migration also reflects changes in socioeconomic structure, a picture of the size and pervasiveness of population movements is of great interest.

Although the subregional population statistics introduced earlier repeatedly display trends that can be accounted for only by widespread mobility, we have no information that permits a direct measurement. But the few pieces of evidence we could gather from the Tiende Penning Cohieren uphold this interpretation. In Twisk I traced the names of the heads of households through three registers —for 1553, 1558, and 1562. In 9 years over 55 percent of the inhabitants either died or moved away. In the 4-year interval 1558–62, 40 percent disappeared, a rate of disappearance confirmed by a similar exercise performed on the registers of the village of Beets. Here, of 88 heads of households in 1558, only 50 remained in 1561, a 43-percent decrease.

The disappearance rate can be traced over a longer time span in the Tiende Penning Cohieren of Diemen, an agricultural village near Amsterdam. Of the 89 heads of households recorded in 1543, 47 remained in 1553. Ten had been replaced, apparently, by relatives (i.e., widows, sons, or brothers). The rest of the vacated holdings were worked by new, unrelated persons, if we can safely judge this from their names. The 89 peasants of 1543 were further reduced to 21 in 1557, and 3 in 1569. A comparison of the disappearance rates of Twisk, Beets, and Diemen with those corresponding to the mortality levels of preindustrial European populations can support two interpretations: either many households depart and enter the villages each year or the heads of households were all of very advanced age.[52] The former would appear to be the more plausible interpretation.

A special survey taken in 1540 of the population living within 2.5 kilometers of the city walls of Leiden asked each resident how long he had lived there and whence he came. Of 52 respondents, only 8 had lived there all their lives. Despite the fact that over half the respondents exceeded 40 years of age, half had moved to their 1540 residence within the previous ten years, and many mentioned having lived in more than one other village before moving to the vicinity of Leiden. Of those specifying their former residences, only one came from outside the province.[53]

Finally, in mid-seventeenth-century Friesland a pervasive mobility can be noted among the farm population. The probate records of the grietenij Hennaarderadeel indicate not only the names of each deceased farmer's children, they also note the place of residence of the older children. The whereabouts of the children over the age of 20 in 34 households with such children in the period 1651–55 was as follows: 25 remained in their parents' villages; 19 lived elsewhere in Hennaarderadeel (the grietenij embraced 12 villages and hamlets); 40 lived elsewhere in rural Friesland (many in the vlek of Makkum); 23 lived in Friesian cities; 4 lived in cities in Holland; the whereabouts of 16 are unknown.[54] Even when we assume that the "unknowns" lived in their parents' villages, this source shows that of the children of landed farmers, 70 percent left the village and 53 percent left the grietenij in which they had been brought up.[55]

This information is not consistent with the frequently evoked image of the stable rural society of the ancien régime, where sons succeed their fathers on ancestral homesteads. Such a stable succession hardly characterized the landed farmers; surely we cannot suppose it characterized the growing rural proletariat of the northern Netherlands.

On the contary, the restructuring of the economy engendered an enormous movement of people into the centers of new activity. Thus we witness the particularly rapid growth of population in the Zaanstreek, the peat district of central Holland, the riverbank villages of the Alblasserwaard and the Krimpenerwaard, the vlekken of Friesland, and the Veenkoloniën of Groningen—all centers of nonagricultural activity. The growth of these regions in the sixteenth century (excepting the Veenkoloniën) accounts in part for the stagnation of urban population before the Revolution, when the cities' hold on industrial activity was very weak. After the Revolution the cities, infused with new men and invigorated by new commercial opportunities, regained their leading role, and the rate of rural population growth gradually declined as migration to the cities became more and more frequent.

Stagnation

Shortly after the mid-seventeenth century, population growth ceased, to be replaced in many areas by a substantial decline. Why did this occur?

This question takes on added importance because of the historical controversy surrounding a "general crisis" in the mid-seventeenth century. Since the appearance of Eric Hobsbawm's articles describing the "crisis of the seventeenth century," numerous studies, particularly in France, have supported the contention that by 1660 at the latest the western European economy encountered frustrations to growth that engendered economic dislocation, increased political despotism, and exposed the economy to crises of subsistence.

A number of Dutch economic indicators uphold this theory of crisis: admiralty excise tax records show that the shipping volume of Dutch ports entered a long period of highly unstable secular stagnation after 1650; passenger volume on intercity ferry services peaked in 1661–62 and fell gradually thereafter; Leiden textile output reached its high point between 1654 and 1667.[56]

The sources of economic expansion in the Dutch economy showed signs of exhaustion. Our demographic model does not make an unambiguous prediction of how the population responds to such an economic situation; a variety of options exist. There is evidence that suggests that fertility fell. We noted earlier that the average age at which women married increased during the seventeenth century. A reduction in the average size of families should be expected as a consequence. A special census of the village of Twisk, taken in 1715, recorded a population with a disproportionately large number of bachelors and spinsters and a very small average household size of 3.32.[57] (A sample of 100 English communities between 1574 and 1821, analyzed by the Cambridge Group for the History of Population and Social Structure, exhibited an overall average household size of 4.8.) Van der Woude's investigation of the size of 4,089 households, 72 percent of which fall in the period 1672–1748, found the average household to consist of 3.7 members.[58] Widespread celibacy, late marriage, and, perhaps, birth control must stand behind these data, but we cannot be certain that they reflect conditions common to the entire region. Both Twisk and the villages investigated by van der Woude lie in the Noorderkwartier, which experienced a particularly severe fall in population after 1650.

More general evidence of a reduced average family size comes from an unlikely quarter: the notarial records of the estates of deceased farmers. They show a distinct reduction in the number of beds per household in the third quarter of the seventeenth century (see chapter 6, p. 218). This downward trend holds good even when the households are controlled for wealth. That is, families of comparable economic status owned fewer beds in the late seventeenth century than they had fifty years earlier. Can we conclude from this information that families with fewer beds also had fewer members?

The sectoral analysis introduced earlier in this chapter attracts our attention to another possible cause of population stagnation: the high degree of urbanization. In Holland urban population grew from 50 percent to 63 percent between 1514 and the eighteenth century, but of even greater importance is the growth of the larger cities. In the same interval Holland's population living in cities of at least 10,000 inhabitants increased from one-fifth to over half of the total. Since the desperately high death rates of preindustrial cities are notorious, and since mortality appears to have been correlated to the size of cities, the urban growth of the northern Netherlands must have exercised a powerful influence on the region's overall demographic trends.[59]

The baptism and burial registers of Amsterdam, although not an unimpeachable source, show an enormous gap between the crude death rate at an average level of 43.5, and the birth rate, which usually stood well under 40.[60] The maintenance of the city's population at the 200,000 level, where it apparently stood from the 1660s until the late eighteenth century, required under these conditions an annual net immigration that we estimate, conservatively, at 1,700 persons. This estimate is not inconsistent with the civil marriage records of Amsterdam, which show that each year from 1660 to 1800 about half of all persons married in the city were born elsewhere.[61]

The much quoted study of Rotterdam provides us with a trustworthy measurement of average net yearly immigration. In the first half of the eighteenth century the city received about 100 immigrants per year. This influx could only slow the decline of the city's population. In the second half of the century a yearly average of 350 (or 7 per thousand inhabitants) settled in Rotterdam to permit a modest recovery.[62]

Raw baptism and burial figures of the early eighteenth century, compiled for the other major cities by the contemporary demographers Kersseboom and Struyck, all produce crude death rates substantially above the birth rates.[63] Even after discounting these figures for the likelihood that they overestimate the gap between the two rates, we must still conclude that the cities of at least 10,000 suffered a negative rate of natural increase of at least 5 per thousand inhabitants.

So, even though the cities of Holland ceased growing, their demand for rural migrants did not cease. The consequences of this high urban mortality can perhaps best be seen if we once again resort to a model.

This model, similar to one employed by the English historical de-mographer E. A. Wrigley, will employ the 1795 census figure for the northern Netherlands. Then, the region's urban population con-sisted of 490,000 in cities of at least 10,000 inhabitants and 142,000 in smaller cities. The rural population stood at 522,000. These fig-ures broadly reflect the demographic characteristics of the late seven-teenth and eighteenth centuries. If we set the rate of natural increase of the smaller cities at 0 and that of the larger cities at −5 per thou-sand, we can determine that the cities needed 2,450 new settlers per year to maintain their indicated strength. If we further assume that the average age of migration is twenty, we can reckon that the mi-grants represent the survivors of a cohort which at birth was half again as large. Finally, if we assume that all the migrants came from the northern Netherlands, we can determine that the rural sec-tor, if its population was not to decline, needed to produce a yearly excess of births over deaths representing a rate of natural increase of 7 per thousand inhabitants. That is, whatever the crude death rate, the birth rate had to be 7 per thousand higher. If we generously estimate net immigration from outside the region at 30 percent of the total, then the rate of natural increase is reduced to 5 per thou-sand. Even this rate of natural increase frequently proved difficult to surpass, as is shown by the first overall vital rates available for the Netherlands, which date from 1811.

We need hardly wonder that the Dutch population ceased its growth in the late seventeenth century and did not again experience

TABLE 3.11.   Crude Birth and Death Rates in the Northern Netherlands, 1811

Province	Birth Rate	Death Rate	Rate of Natural Increase	Percentage of Population in Urban Areas
Bouches de la Meuse (South Holland)	34.1	34.2	−0.1	
Zuider Zee (North Holland and Utrecht)	33.7	35.8	−2.1	63%
La Frise (Friesland)	30.1	24.7	+5.4	
Ems Occidental (Groningen and Drenthe)	31.8	26.5	+5.3	27%
Kingdom of Holland	32.9	30.9	+2.0	

SOURCE: Rates derived from data in d'Alphonse, p. 553.

a pronounced demographic upswing until well into the nineteenth century, when health improvements finally began to force down urban death rates. A turn-of-the-century Dutch demographer who was sensitive to this problem described it in a way that proves that historical model building, if controversial, is nonetheless not novel. "We see," he observed, "that the cities of earlier times can be likened to the Minotaur, which gobbled up the children of the Greeks, and that hygiene was the Theseus which disarmed the monster. Athens, to stay with this image, was the countryside, which sent each year its hecatombs to the cities." [64]

Until the nineteenth century a highly urbanized region imposed an enormous demographic burden on the rural population, a burden with important ramifications. The economic consequences of this demographic phenomenon can perhaps best be characterized as an "urban safety valve" (to set on its head a much abused theory of American history). An agrarian structure that expelled its surplus members supplied the needed manpower to maintain urban populations. This migration mechanism preserved a balance between the various economic sectors. Such a balance preserved, in turn, the dominant position of the cities with their high-cost industries, conservative economic policies, and jealous regard for their vested interests.[65]

The eighteenth-century Republic has often been described as economically and politically "petrified." In searching for causes historians have pointed to the designs of foreign powers and, domestically, to moral decay.[66] Surely this migration mechanism, which so directly affected both the urban and rural economies, must be included in the analysis.

It should be noted that regions with large urban populations did not invariably follow this demographic course. Between 1675 and 1795 the population of Overijssel, a landward province, increased by 89 percent yet it experienced deurbanization; the population of its cities fell from 28 percent to 20 percent of the total. The absence of urban migration caused a buildup of population in the countryside with the consequent proliferation of a cottar class (which found its salvation in the rise of a rural textile industry).[67] Overijssel's demographic characteristics were shared in the southern Netherlands by Flanders and, apparently, Brabant.[68] These contrasting migration patterns make clear that accounts of migration that consider only the "pull" factor (in this case the attractive power of the cities) are often insufficient. I would emphasize that a "push" factor—the structure of the agrarian economy and whether it absorbs or expels surplus population—played a major role in determining the course of urbanization and, hence, the character of rural economic life.[69]

The investigation of demographic change in the northern Netherlands has provided us with several suggestive generalizations about both the region's rapid growth and its later stagnation. They must be offered tentatively; our models and indirect evidence cannot substitute for demographic analysis based on a knowledge of vital rates. The special weaknesses of Dutch parish registers prevent our offering more firmly established details. We can place some confidence in the long-term trends, however, and they support our view that agricultural specialization, industrial growth, and urbanization were not isolated processes. They occurred together, fed upon each other, and partially depended upon a mechanism of population growth shaped by the agrarian structure of the region.

4. The Transformation of the Rural Economy

THE SPECIALIZATION MODEL APPLIED
TO THE NORTHERN NETHERLANDS

The economies of Europe expanded vigorously during the sixteenth century. Increased demand stimulated by the price inflation and population growth pressed upon the productive resources and forced organizational and technical changes designed to accommodate the new circumstances. The signs of expansion could be seen everywhere: domestically in land reclamation, new city walls, harbor extensions, enlarged fleets, and abroad in the European penetration of other continents. Expansion there was in abundance; a more elusive phenomenon was growth.

Improvements in the qualities as well as the quantities of the productive factors—land, labor, and capital—occurred only sporadically. As a consequence, economic expansion invariably encountered frustrations which, in time, brought the process to a fitful halt. Real wages fell as grain became increasingly scarce, labor productivity fell as peasants divided holdings, and unemployment condemned ever growing numbers of workers to take up the beggar's staff. These seemingly inevitable processes enriched the owners of the scarce grain and land and promoted ossification of social, political, and, inevitably, economic relations.

When the expansion phase flagged in the early seventeenth century, it left a rich legacy of problems and only a few souvenirs of economic growth. Le Roy Ladurie's massive study of Languedoc in the sixteenth and seventeenth centuries describes this process at work, as does, in abstract terms, the peasant model of rural development introduced in chapter 1 above.

The economy of the northern Netherlands expanded probably more rapidly than any other in Europe. In the process, new institutions and new techniques were developed which distinguished this economy from others and stimulated its further expansion. Here new financial institutions, shipbuilding techniques, textile methods, and many lesser improvements drove up the productivity of labor and capital. Fully as remarkable as the commercial and industrial achievements of the northern Netherlands, and closely connected to it, was a thoroughgoing transformation of the rural economy.

In the course of the sixteenth and seventeenth centuries a rural economy emerged which differed qualitatively as well as quantitatively from that of the preceding era. The specialization model, introduced in chapter 1, describes its principal characteristics and explains the distinctions between it and the more common course of events portrayed in the peasant model. It is worth noting that the restructured rural economy, although overshadowed by the urban economy during the sixteenth and seventeenth centuries, endured long after the urban economy fell into decay. The enhanced productivity of agriculture and related rural activities provided the material basis for the development of the Dutch economy in the nineteenth century, when the commercial and industrial glories of the "Golden Age" were but memories.

The sources of rural growth must be sought in the peasant household. In the early sixteenth century the essential features of regional and international specialization existed. To expand its scope, to generate large scale commodity flows, and to stimulate organizational and technological improvements, a third level of specialization had to come into play. Reorganization of peasant households rather than their simple proliferation held the key to a productive rural economy responsive to urban and international markets and capable of stimulating, by its own demand, output in other sectors.

The essentially unspecialized peasant households that characterized Dutch rural society in the early sixteenth century developed in the course of the economic expansion of the sixteenth and early seventeenth centuries into commercial, highly capitalized farm enterprises. Surrounding these new households, nonagricultural specialists in crafts, transportation, marketing, fuel supply, and education arose to provide goods and services that the unspecialized households of earlier times had endeavored to provide for themselves. In short, the peasantry, *the* rural class, became the farmers, *a* rural class.

The new occupational structure that evolved reflected the changed economic nature of the rural household. The peasant household of the early sixteenth century was relatively self-contained; the farm household of the seventeenth century, on the other hand, displayed strong linkages with other economic functions. Backward linkages stimulated investment in drainage improvements, established a commerce in fertilizer and fodder, called forth craftsmen of all sorts, and supported education. Forward linkages maintained a closely knit structure of transportation and marketing services and permitted the development of an international trade in agricultural commodities, which formed an essential lubricant of the vast Dutch trading empire.

This chapter is devoted to the description of the important elements of this transformation. To strengthen the plausibility of this economic process and to render it comprehensible, I shall begin by examining a small area, one Friesian grietenij. After displaying the main trends in the transformation of this fairly typical district's economic life, I shall return to a discussion of the entire northern Netherlands.

IDAARDERADEEL: 1511–1749

Idaarderadeel, a grietenij about 69 square kilometers in area, comprises 8 villages situated on the margins of the marine clay soil, where it merges with the extensive peatlands of central Friesland.

In 1511 the 184 households of the grietenij cultivated no more than 3,800 hectares of the ill-drained land.[1] Endemic winter flooding plagued the inhabitants in the operation of their farms and condemned about 40 percent of the grietenij to the status of wasteland.

The Idaarderadeelians (!) lived in an egalitarian community. The hoofdelingen (petty nobility) owned most of the land, it is true, and they found their way into the office of grietman as well, but the vast majority of the inhabitants owned or rented sufficient land to be considered secure by the standards of the time. The 179 schotschietende huizen of the grietenij, which represented the substantial, enfranchised farmsteads of earlier centuries, had attached to them pasture, meadow, and sometimes arable plots totalling at least 30, but rarely over 80 pondematen (between 11 and 30 hectares). Although the *Aanbreng van 1511* may have excluded a few poor landless households, it listed only 5 households that had to content themselves with "loose pieces" of land. No one used fewer than 4 hectares (see table 4.1).

The population in 1511, numbering no more than 1,000 to 1,100 souls, existed in a state probably not unlike that of earlier centuries when the schotschietende huizen system had been devised. Canals, roads, and drainage works were so scarce and the economic value of the area consequently so meager, that the new rulers, the Saxon dukes, exhorted the *Landdag* to bring about improvements in order to increase tax revenues.

TABLE 4.1.   Distribution of Farm Size in Idaarderadeel, 1511–1769

Size of Farm in Pondematen	1511	1700	1713	1741	1769
0.1– 9.9	0	9	0	0	0
10 –19.9	2	8	1	1	1
20 –29.9	17	12	6	4	5
30 –39.9	23	13	6	6	6
40 –49.9	48	28	26	21	21
50 –59.9	37	29	26	27	27
60 –69.9	23	34	46	45	43
70 –79.9	10	35	33	38	39
80 –89.9	11	12	22	22	22
90 –99.9	6	14	7	7	8
100 and over	7	27	25	23	25
Unknown			3	3	1
Total	184	221	201	197	198

SOURCES: *Aanbreng van 1511;* RA Leeuwarden, Rekenkamer Archief, Belasting Co-hieren, Floreen-Cohier van de Reële 100ste Penning van alle vaste Goederen gelegen in de grietenie van Ijdaarderadeel, 1713, 1741, 1769; J. Kooistra, "Agrarisch Idaarderadeel in de achtiende eeuw."

NOTE: A sizable increase in the cultivated land area between 1511 and 1700 shifted the size distribution upward but did not appreciably change the nature of the distribution. Also note that the distributions for 1511 and 1700 include all land users, while those for 1713 and later include only the lands of schotschietende huizen. "Loose pieces" of land are excluded in these years.

In the century and a half that followed, the face of Idaarderadeel and even more the economic and social relations under which the people lived changed fundamentally. In 1552 much had already changed. The Monstercedellen of that year found among the 179 schotschietende huizen 230 men capable of bearing arms. It also listed 91 other men, nearly 50 of whom were in poverty, from house-holds using little or no land.[2] Many of these latter probably lived in houses that the pastor and vicar of Grouw had built in the village center. In 1542 the *Charter-boek* records the names of the inhab-itants of the vicar's 10 houses; they include a cooper, weaver, basket-maker, and tailor.[3] Most of the new landless class, which already made up 28 percent of the grietenij's population, lived in Grouw, the largest of the villages. None lived in the 4 small hamlets. Their pres-ence increased Idaarderadeel's population to approximately 1,300 in the mid-sixteenth century.

Among the farmers, land improvement efforts got underway. The *Charter-boek* gives us an indication of this when it tells of a certain

Dodo Edezoon, who in the years following 1528 "dug and ditched" and brought under cultivation sufficient wasteland owned by the church of Grouw to be charged 12 gulden in rent by 1541. Dodo found the rent too high and declared he would rather abandon the land than pay the rent. This he did in the following year.[4] His brashness caused the compilers of the *Charter-boek* to include his story; there must have been many other Dodos clearing new land who are unknown to us because they did not give up their hard won fields. This is clear enough in 1700 when the Floreen-Cohier lists almost 5,500 hectares under cultivation, which is about 1,700 hectares more than was listed in the *Aanberg van 1511*.[5] (In 1833 the first cadastral survey found 6,534 hectares developed and taxable among the 6,900 hectares of the grietenij.)

The provincial government and local people initiated projects to improve navigation on the meandering waterways in and around Idaarderadeel and to better drainage through the installation of windmills and sluices. As a consequence, the chronicler Winsemius described the grietenij in 1622 as low-lying and unfruitful were it not for the "watermills," dikes, and sluices that prevented yearly flooding and permitted the development of good cow pastures.[6] Already in 1580 the improvements in soil quality must have been considerable because the rental value of the land had increased over 8 times since 1511, while prices and wages increased by much less.[7]

After 1552 no population data stand at our disposal until 1689, but we can confidently assert that the population grew rapidly, particularly in the chief town, Grouw. The growing agricultural surpluses required merchants less distant than those in Leeuwarden and Sneek, the nearest cities. Grouw acquired regular weekly markets and a weighhouse, and it became a considerable shipping center.[8] Grouw, along with a dozen other villages all over Friesland, became a vlek.

A record of the boats passing through the little city of Sloten on their way to Holland between 24 May and 30 August 1582 reveals that of the 240 boats that passed, 10 were from Grouw. The boats from Grouw transported mainly butter and cattle, and they appeared in the list with increased frequency toward the end of the period covered, a fact that reflects the concentration of dairy marketing in the late summer and fall. Grouw's commercial activity would have appeared greater still had the extant list not ended in August.[9]

By 1644 the growing commercial needs of Idaarderadeel's farmers required the establishment of a regular shipping service, "following the example and the good use made by large villages of the country-side as well as by the cities." Scheduled boat services travelling over newly improved canals connected Grouw and Warga to Leeuwarden, the provincial capital, and Grouw and Roordahuysen to Sneek, the principal butter market.[10]

The prosperous agriculture and well-developed commercial facilities of the area attracted investors from not only Leeuwarden but Amsterdam as well. In 1632, eight men from these cities invested 64,000 gulden in a project to drain a 185-hectare lake, the Wargaastermeer. Documents describing agricultural methods employed on the new land, which fell dry in 1644, tell of heavy manuring and instructions to the windmill operator to keep the new polder dry throughout the winter—the season when earlier generations had, as a matter of course, given their fields over to the ubiquitous waters of central Friesland.[11]

All these developments suggest the growth of agricultural output in Idaarderadeel. When we examine the farms themselves, this suggestion is confirmed. The size of dairy herds in early sixteenth-century Holland rarely exceeded 10, although the typical herd numbered 5 or 6 head. Unfortunately we know nothing of herd size in early sixteenth-century Idaarderadeel. In the 1560s, however, the average herd size in the immediately adjacent Zuidertrimdeel of Leeuwarderadeel was 14.1; in the 1620s herd size in Idaarderadeel had grown to 23.0; and in the 1690s 26.5 head of cattle made up the average herd. Calves and heifers made up over one-third of the herds, which indicates that Idaarderadeel's farmers were breeders as well as dairymen. The rising importance of breeding is reflected in the increased percentage of farmers owning bulls in the course of the seventeenth century.[12]

The growth of dairy herds required larger barns. In the late sixteenth century, farm inventories describe the *oud Friese langhuis*, a farmhouse style of great antiquity and cramped dimensions. By the early seventeenth century new farmhouse types appeared. The *Friese boerenhuis* and the *stelp*, capable of stalling larger herds and storing large quantities of hay and fodder, quickly became the typical farmhouse in Idaarderadeel.

The population of the grietenij continued to grow until about the mid-seventeenth century: the census of 1689 counted 2,522 inhabitants. In just over 150 years the population increased 250 percent, but the number of farmers increased by only 12 percent. Despite the vigorous land reclamation movement, few new farms came into being, and as the average size of farms grew, only a few were split in two. The "stemcohier" of 1640 listed 215 schotschietende huizen.[13] Table 4.1 makes evident the characteristic stability of the farm structure.

The population of the grietenij changed very little between 1689 and 1749. The number of households using more than a few hectares of land held steady at about 200 throughout this period as it had, indeed, throughout the preceding 4 or 5 centuries. The much larger number of landless households also remained quite stable: the Quotisatie Cohier of 1749 enumerated 734 households in the grietenij, 550 of which were headed by nonfarmers. What place was there in the economy of Idaarderadeel for the landless two-thirds of the population?

The stability of population and economic relations in the area from the mid-seventeenth until the mid-eighteenth century suggests that the Quotisatie Cohier of 1749, a village-by-village enumeration of heads of households, their occupations, and their tax statuses, can probably tell us much about the culmination of the process of economic development at work in Idaarderadeel throughout the 150 years after 1500.

The large nonagricultural population was not distributed evenly over the countryside. In the 4 small terp hamlets of Idaard, Aegum, Warstiens, and Friens, the 32 farmsteads recorded in 1511 continued to dominate the scene; in the eighteenth century, only 8 nonfarm houses stood there.[14] The population growth of the grietenij concentrated in the larger villages and particularly in Grouw. Already in the mid-sixteenth century this village attracted the poor and landless. A prosperous religious institution built and rented houses, and the location of the village on or near a number of waterways encouraged the development of marketing institutions as the farms developed to produce increasingly large agricultural surpluses. In 1552 nonfarmers made up one-third of the men capable of bearing arms in Grouw; in 1749 the village numbered 60 farm families, 31 farm laborers, and 307 workers in other branches of the economy. Table 4.2 shows the occupational distribution of the Grouw and the rest of Idaarderadeel.

The nonfarm population that grew between 1500 and about 1650 found its employment not in rural industry financed and organized from an urban center but in activities directly related to the agricultural sector. There grew in the midst of the farm populations a ship-

TABLE 4.2.   Occupational Distribution of Idaarderadeel, 1749

Occupational Category	Grouw	Roordahuysen, Warga, Wartena	Friens, Idaard, Aegem, Warstiens	Total
Agriculture	60	87	33	180
Fishing	8	2	0	10
Farm labor[a]	31	35	9	75
Glass, brick, pottery	1	1	1	3
Construction, boat and wagon making	33	27	0	60
Wood and straw crafts	5	6	0	11
Leather crafts	12	16	0	28
Smiths and metal crafts	3	1	0	4
Clockmaking	3	0	0	3
Textile trades	10	9	0	19
Food preparation	6	8	0	14
Merchants	11	7	1	19
Storekeepers and peddlers	5	4	2	11
Transportation services	38	49	2	89
Inn- and tavernkeepers	1	1	0	2
Professional and "well-to-do"	6	14	0	20
Schoolmasters	1	1	3	5
Government officials	1	0	0	1
Day laborers	55	36	0	91
Unknown	17	35	0	52
Widows	29	19	0	48
Total	336	358	51	745

SOURCE: RA Leeuwarden, Rekenkamer Archief, Quotisatie Cohieren van 1749, no. 14e.

[a] Only farm laborers heading independent households are enumerated. All servants living in the households of their employers are subsumed in such households. The higher average household size of the farm hamlets suggests that many farmers employed live-in servants. In 1795 there were 298 live-in servants in Idaarderadeel.

ping and shipbuilding industry, a colony of merchants who acted as intermediaries between the farmers, the agricultural markets at Grouw and the urban markets, and a service and petty trade sector that provided clothing, leather goods, ironware, foodstuffs, and consumer articles such as furniture, clocks, glass, and candles. In the course of the seventeenth century the inventories of deceased farmers show a gradual increase in the variety and luxury of their possessions.

The egalitarian image Idaarderadeel's society projects in 1511 is quite untenable in the later seventeenth century, when the social structure reflected in the Quotisatie Cohier of 1749 had developed. A relatively homogeneous group of peasants dominated society in 1511. It is unlikely that they kept many servants or hired labor on a permanent basis. In 1749 the farmers form a relatively prosperous sector of a much more complex society. They hire labor but own no more than 7 percent of the land they work (they owned 18 percent in 1511). The hoofdelingen are now clearly the dominant political force. They and city dwellers are the beneficiaries of the dismantling of the monasteries and the gradual sale of church lands. In 1749 at least one-third of the population depends on wage labor; over 100 households could be described only as "poor workers."

Farm specialization formed the basis of the grietenij's economic reorganization. Farmers and merchants invested in land improvement schemes and in construction to enlarge the scale of dairy farming. Subsidiary tasks disappeared from the peasant household to be taken up by craftsmen and merchants in the larger villages. The new demands of large-scale commercial farming maintained a force of day laborers prepared to work in dike and canal maintenance and seasonal tasks of all sorts.

OCCUPATIONAL SPECIALIZATION WITHIN THE PEASANTRY

As the rural population of the northern Netherlands grew, a farmer class, which increased very little in number, gradually became distinguishable. When the rural population ceased growing in the later seventeenth century, this farmer class consolidated its position. A combination of factors, among them polder drainage and a resurgence of aristocratic landownership, stimulated the assembly of landholdings sometimes larger even than the farms of the early sixteenth century, when the unimproved quality of the fields rendered them much less productive. This social and economic transformation is confirmed by several sorts of evidence.

Villages that developed no nonagricultural activities did not share in the upsurge of population common to the countryside as a whole. This suggests that the population increment swelled the ranks of callings other than farming. In chapter 3 attention was drawn to the separate courses of population growth in the river bank and interior villages of the Krimpenerwaard, Alblasserwaard, and Ijsselmonde, and in the hamlets and vlekken of Wymbritseradeel in Friesland.

The Friesian grietenij Wonseradeel provides another particularly clear example of this phenomenon. There, the coastal hamlet of Makkum, where 46 households lived in 1546, developed into a vlek of considerable importance as the center of a brick and ceramics industry. Its rise to a town of 775 households in 1714 occurred in sharp contrast to the nearby agricultural villages of Kornwerd, Engwier, Zurich, and Wons. Their aggregate population of 140 households in 1546 actually fell to 107 in 1714. Population trends such as this are prima facie evidence that the farm population did not grow.

Where farmers and nonfarmers did not live in separate villages, village population data are of no use to us; we must turn to other sources to follow the course of events outlined above.

Consider Alphen aan den Rijn, a village bordering the Oude Rijn River in the center of Rijnland. In the course of the sixteenth century its population more than tripled. How can we determine if its agricultural population increased in like measure?

The Morgenboeken, records of landowners and land users upon which the drainage board taxes were levied, date from 1541, when the directors of the Hoogheemraadschap van Rijnland ordered a new survey of the land. Together with the Tiende Penning Cohieren and the Verponding Cohieren, they permit us to trace the general course of both the total and agricultural population of Alphen, but an enormous collating task stands between the old folios and the statistical tables we desire. As a consequence I have selected a few years for careful examination of the number of houses and the distribution of land among owners and users.

In 1514 the *Informacie* recorded 83 houses containing 400 communicants (i.e., about 600 inhabitants). The most reliable of the Tiende Penning Cohieren, complied in 1562, listed 179 houses. The list of land parcels yielded 154 separate land users. Many of these, however, lived elsewhere and used a parcel in Alphen to supplement holdings in their own villages. This accounts for the fact that only 87 households resident in Alphen could be identified as land users. What of the remaining households? The "Cohier" identified 68 as living in the village center (*dorp*); only 5 of these ranked among the land-using households.[15] In this new, rapidly growing village center clustered the nonagricultural households—the merchants, craftsmen, bargemen, and brickworks laborers.

In 1572, 142 households, including outsiders, used land in Alphen and in 1575, directly after war-related inundations laid waste the vast majority of Alphen's fields, 209 houses stood here, while the land was distributed among 148 persons, nonvillagers included. From these data we can discern a gradual increase of total population together with a stable number of land users.[16]

Ninety-three years later the constancy of the farm population is again observed in the Morgenboeken. Since the polder administration continued to work with a field survey of 1541, these records are extremely difficult to use; because of the likelihood of error, no attempt was made to compute the small holdings. In 1716, when the village fields were freshly surveyed for an updating of the Morgenboeken, a reliable and complete picture is once again available. Then the population stood somewhere between the 1,477 reached in 1622 and the 1,636–1,849 range indicated by the weerbare mannen list of 1749. The number of land users, including outsiders, stood at 159, a figure comparable with those of the mid-sixteenth century. The Verponding of 1732 permits us to single out those land users resident in Alphen. Unfortunately, it excluded the users of small parcels. The 87 farmers listed in 1732 were but little fewer than the 98 farmers and 6 horticulturalists listed in the occupational census of 1807, when the village numbered 2,136 inhabitants.[17]

The data, brought together in table 4.3, are less than we could desire. We can only occasionally segregate nonresident land users and the garden plots of nonfarmers. But the conclusion is clear enough: the number of farmers in Alphen remained constant while the total population rose dramatically. The surplus population congregated in the newly invigorated village center, a concentration process common to many other villages as well. Around an ancient church site or crossroads new houses sprang up and sometimes markets and other urban functions took root.

Bodegraven, which claimed 100 houses in 1514, could count 236 within its jurisdiction in 1732. Only 134 were farmhouses; of the remaining number, 150 were clustered together in the village center. In Zoetermeer the 56 houses of 1514 grew to 132 inhabited houses in 1732. Only 36 were farmhouses; of the rest 44 were situated in the village center.[18]

This phenomenon extended to the villages of predominantly arable soil as well. Het Bildt, a Friesian grietenij reclaimed from the sea in 1505 and colonized by Hollanders, numbered 183 land users according to the rent roll of 1527. The large tracts in the hands of a few individuals at that time indicate that the colonization was not

TABLE 4.3.   Land Distribution in Alphen, 1562–1732

Landholdings in Morgen	1562		1572	1575	1668	1716	1732
	excl.	incl.	incl.	incl.	excl.	incl.	excl.
0.1– 4.9	3	11	16	25	?	44	0[a]
5 – 9.9	9	25	33	35	?	25	5
10 –14.9	9	18	19	24	29	21	14
15 –19.9	12	13	18	15	22	17	16
20 –24.9	11	12	17	21	15	10	13
25 –29.9	11	12	11		7	14	12
30 –34.9	8	9	4		5	11	10
35 –39.9	6	6	8	27	4	7	7
40 –44.9	8	8	11			5	5
45 –49.9	2	2	3		2	2	0
50 –59.9	3	4	2	1		3	1
60 –75	5	5	0	0		0	0
Unknown	—	—	—	—	—	—	4
Total	87	125	142	148	?	159	?
Total over 10 morgen	75	89	93	88	85	90	82
Total households	179	179	?	209	?	?	386

SOURCE: See notes 15, 16, and 17.

NOTE: Excl. indicates the exclusion of nonresident land users; incl. indicates the inclusion of such land users.

[a] The 1732 Verponding records do not enumerate the smallest farms or the ownership of fragments of land, consequently, the number of holders of small parcels is not known.

yet completed. In the rent roll of 1536 these large parcels were divided and 240 land users now lived in het Bildt, 184 of whom used at least 10 morgen.[19] The process of colonization was now nearing completion, for the Monstercedellen of 1552 listed 254 men from ploeggangen (farms) and 76 "working men and others who have neither ploeggangen nor land." [20] In 1749, when the population of het Bildt approached 3,400—at least triple the 1527–36 population—the number of farmers totalled 163,[21] and the census of 1807, likewise, counted 155 farm households among the 841 households and 5,000 inhabitants of the grietenij.[22]

The pattern described in Idaarderadeel and in Alphen recurred in het Bildt and, in fact, all over the northern Netherlands. The Quotisatie Cohieren consistently indicate that there had been little increase in the farm population between 1511 and 1749 in Friesland. In Holland the same situation prevailed. In 22 Rijnland villages, which numbered 1,151 houses in 1514, the Verponding of 1732 listed

4,024 inhabited houses, 1,012 of which were "farmhouses." By the same token, in 15 Rijnland villages, where the 1807 census counted 737 farm households, the 1732 Verponding listed 723 farmhouses.[23] In 66 villages scattered throughout Holland the Verponding of 1732 listed 9,471 inhabited houses, including only 3,217 farmhouses.[24]

Clearly, in the course of the sixteenth and seventeenth centuries, the growth of the rural population of the northern Netherlands went hand in hand with an occupational differentiation that produced a distinct class of farmers. Despite the growing rural population this class operated farms of a considerable size. In fact, as the seventeenth century progressed, many areas witnessed movement toward consolidation. By the end of our period large, improved farms covered the landscape of the northern Netherlands. Horticultural districts and actively exploited peat bogs formed the chief exceptions to this generalization.

The growth of demand for peat sent swarms of laborers to villages where the authorities permitted peat digging. In the second half of the sixteenth century Ter Aar was such a village. Immediately adjacent lay Oudshoorn, which forbade peat digging to protect its soil for agriculture. In Ter Aar the 60 percent of the residents who in 1543 used at least 10 morgen commanded three-quarters of the village land; in 1600, users of at least 10 morgen made up only 16.4 percent of the inhabitants and controlled half the village land. Users of under 5 morgen, mainly peat diggers, increased over twelvefold and the land subject to their shovels and dredging equipment increased from 4 to 25 percent of the total. Because of the peat diggers the 2,100 morgen of Ter Aar became divided into ever more numerous (and ever smaller) parcels: 166 in 1543, 931 in 1600.[25]

Land distribution trends in neighboring Oudshoorn stand in sharp contrast to those of Ter Aar. Not until 1680 did Oudshoorn permit peat digging. Then, moving from exhausted bogs elsewhere, peat diggers quickly overran the village. The movement to consolidate lands into larger farms also operated at this time. By 1732 Oudshoorn's landholding distribution showed none of the characteristics of earlier days. A handful of large farmers and over 150 peat diggers now dominated a village where a rather cohesive peasant society had earlier reigned.[26]

The peat industry's effect on landholding size did not end here. When the last peat had been dug from a bog and the laborers moved on, leaving behind them a desolate landscape of inundated fields and

TABLE 4.4.   Distribution of Landholdings in Oudshoorn and Ter Aar, 1543–1732

| | Ter Aar | | | | Oudshoorn | | | | |
| Size of Holdings in Morgen | 1543 | | 1600 | | 1544 | | 1576 | | 1732 | |
	no.	%	no.	%	no.	%	no.	%	no.	%
0.1– 4.9	21	17.0	264	66.6	30	30.0	32	23.7	157	66.8
5 – 9.9	28	22.6	68	17.2	19	19.0	46	34.1	35	14.9
10 –24.9	50	40.3	57	14.4	38	38.0	48	35.6	24	10.2
25 –49.9	22	17.7	6	1.5	12	12.0	8	5.9	19	8.1
50 and over	3	2.4	1	0.3	1	1.0	1	0.7	0	0
Total	124	100.0	396	100.0	100	100.0	135	100.0	235	100.0

SOURCE: See notes 25 and 26.

abandoned buildings, capitalists often initiated land reclamation projects. These will be discussed in detail later; here our only concern is the effect of these schemes on landholding size distribution. In Zoetermeer, a depleted peat bog was drained in 1668 and parcelled to make 26 farms of 33 morgen each. This, plus an earlier drainage project of 7 farms, accounted for almost all of the 36 farms listed in the 1732 Verponding Cohier.[27]

In the Noorderkwartier urban investors financed the drainage of dozens of lakes, ranging in size from a few hectares to over 6,000 hectares. Between 1600 and the 1640s land reclamation completely

TABLE 4.5.   Size of Agricultural Holdings on Noorderkwartier Polders

Size of Holding in Morgen	Beemster	Purmer	Schermer	Wormer	Zijpe	Heer Hugo	Total
30	100	0	0	0	230	0	330
20	150	100	0	0	0	0	250
15	30	0	400	120	0	220	770
10	52	0	0	0	0	0	52
Total	332	100	400	120	230	220	1402

SOURCES: *Extract Uyt het Octroy van de Beemster met de Cavel-Conditien; Octroy van de Purmer;* Belonje, *De Schermeer,* p. 29; Blink, *Boerenstand,* 2:25; A. Zijp, "Hoofdstukken uit de economische en sociale geschiedenis van de polder Zijpe in de 17e en 18e eeuw," p. 33; Belonje, *De Heer-Hugowaard,* p. 6.

altered the structure of farm size in many areas. In chapter 2 we noted the paucity of large holdings in this area, where seafarers and fishermen made up a large portion of the rural population. During the first half of the seventeenth century the 6 largest drainage schemes added over 1,400 new farms to the Noorderkwartier.

The tendency of seafaring activities to concentrate in larger centers during the seventeenth century also stimulated the rural inhabitants of the Noorderkwartier to improve their land and assemble larger farms. Thus, Broek in Waterland, a village noted in the sixteenth century for its active merchant and seafaring economy,[28] turned increasingly to agriculture as nearby Amsterdam attracted successful merchants away. In 1624 and 1632, local investors financed the drainage of the Belling, Broeker, and Buikerslooter lakes, which, together, created about 750 morgen of new land. A cow or two kept by seafarers' wives had earlier characterized Broek's agriculture; now in the seventeenth century the village land, augmented by a large part of the newly drained lakes, supported about 40 dairy farmers who specialized in supplying fresh milk to the Amsterdam market. In 1769 Broek's 38 dairy farmers owned 663 cattle.[29]

In the seafaring communities clustered in the southwestern corner of Friesland, among them Staveren, Hindeloopen, Molkwerum, and Workum, a similar metamorphosis occurred. To accommodate the family cows of the seafarers' wives these places maintained common pastures. For instance, in 1640, 158 men owned the commons of Hindeloopen. On this 1,225-pondematen common they held 286 cows. By 1719 the commons had been enclosed, and the number of landowners much reduced. In 1753 only 30 farmers operated the land; they converted some of the land to arable and considerably increased the size of their herds. A similar development took place in all these maritime villages.[30]

Areas of land reclamation and old seafarers' towns held no monopoly on the process of consolidation; it occurred in all districts. In Tekkop, a village near the Holland-Utrecht border, the population grew not at all between 1562 and 1732, but it does not follow that the village's 460 morgen remained distributed as before. Table 4.6 clearly shows the consolidation of the land into fewer, larger farms.

A similar concentration process can be ascertained in Papekop, a village of 800 morgen in Utrecht. It occurred, we should note, together with a gradual reconstruction of the landowning role of the nobility. This process was abetted in the late seventeenth century when the purchase of seigneuries and the construction of country seats became widespread among the urban regents. They did not operate estates or shed their commercial interests, but it would be

TABLE 4.6. Distribution of Landholdings in Tekkop, 1561–1732

Size of Holdings in Morgen	1561 no.	1561 %	1732 no.	1732 %
(No land)	0	0	10	35.7
0.1– 9.9	8	28.6	2	7.1
10 –19.9	10	35.7	0	0
20 –29.9	6	21.4	9	32.1
30 –39.9	2	7.1	4	14.3
40 –49.9	2	7.1	3	10.7
Total	28	99.9	28	99.9

SOURCES: ARA, Staten van Holland voor 1572, Tiende Penning Cohieren, no. 1448; Leggers der Verponding Cohieren, no. 505.

TABLE 4.7. Distribution of Landholding and Landownership in Papekop, 1540–1680

LANDHOLDING

Size of Holdings in Morgen	1540 no.	1540 %	1600 no.	1600 %	1680 no.	1680 %
0.1– 9.9	13	27.1	14	28.6	8	20.0
10 –19.9	20	41.6	25	51.0	11	27.5
20 –29.9	12	25.0	8	16.4	14	35.0
30 and over	3	6.3	2	4.0	7	17.5
Total	48	100.0	49	100.0	40	100.0

LANDOWNERSHIP

Class	Number of Morgen 1540	1600	1680
Owned by user	283	427	299.5
Church, charity	285.5	136.5	222
Nobility	17	33.5	162.5
Others	179.5	132	119.5
Total	765	729	803.5

SOURCES: RA Utrecht, Staten van Utrecht, no. 143-1–143-4, Mannuaal van het Oudschildgeld van het Sticht; no. 971, Blaffard van het Oudschildgeld over het Nederquartier, Overkwartier en de steden Wijk, Amersfoort, en Rhenen; no. 972, Blaffard van het Oudschildgeld . . . , 1680.

wrong to think that the Dutch bourgeoisie remained immune to the blandishments of the aristocratic life style.

Friesland provides the clearest example of land accumulating in the hands of a nobility. Here, where landownership led directly to political power (see p. 57), the resurgence of the hoofdelingen after 1650 led inexorably to the concentration of landownership in their hands.[31]

Finally, an overview of tax registers in Groningen shows that the pattern of land distribution remained constant between 1630 and 1721. After the confiscation of monastic property in 1595 a large part of the land was controlled by the provincial government. Their administration, as recorded in the Statenboeken, opposed the division of farms. Even before 1595, stability was the rule, if the evidence of the village of Stedum is any indication.

TABLE 4.8. Distribution of Landholdings in the District of Fivelingo and the Village of Stedum, 1553–1721

Size of Holdings in Grazen	1553		1630		1721	
	no.	%	no.	%	no.	%
Fivelingo						
0.1– 9.9			230	33.5	255	36.7
10 –19.9			100	14.6	102	14.7
20 –59.9			249	36.2	221	31.8
60 –99.9			92	13.4	97	14.0
100 and up			16	2.3	19	2.7
Total			687	100.0	694	99.9
Stedum						
0.1– 9.9	15	18.2	18	19.6	30	30.6
10 –19.9	14	16.9	20	21.7	14	14.3
20 –59.9	41	49.3	40	43.5	37	37.8
60 –99.9	13	15.7	14	15.2	17	17.3
100 and up	0		0		0	
Total	83	100.0	92	100.0	98	100.0

SOURCES: RA Groningen, Staten van Stad en Lande, 1594–1798, Schatregister voor de Verponding, 1630, nos. 2133–36; Schatregister . . . 1721, no. 2143; Postma, *Kleihoeve*, pp. 67–68.

Only in het Oldampt, where reclamation efforts on the Dollart added thousands of hectares to the cultivated land area in the late seventeenth and eighteenth centuries, do we find evidence of en-

TABLE 4.9. Distribution of Landholdings
in Midwolder Hemrick, 1630–1721

Size of Holdings in Diemten	1630		1721	
	no.	%	no.	%
0.1– 9.9	52	51.0	45	37.8
10 –19.9	28	27.4	17	14.3
20 –59.9	21	20.6	40	33.6
60 –99.9	1	1.0	15	12.6
100 and over	0	0	2	1.7
Total	102	100.0	119	100.0

SOURCES: Same as table 4.8.

larged holdings. Midwolder Hemrick more than doubled its cultivated area between 1630 and 1721, but land-using households increased by only 17 percent since established farmers added newly
reclaimed land to their existing holdings to build large commercial
enterprises.

Data concerning population trends, occupational distribution, and
land distribution from every part of the northern Netherlands confirm the generality of the course of events examined in Idaarderadeel
in the preceding section. Between the early sixteenth and mid-seventeenth centuries, when the rural population grew rapidly, a class of
farmers developed from among the mass of the peasantry. In the
century after about 1650 we ascertained in many areas a tendency
toward the augmentation of the size of the larger farms. In this
physical and social setting were agricultural techniques introduced
and specialized production undertaken.

TECHNICAL CHANGE THROUGH SPECIALIZATION AND TRADE

An agricultural transformation requires more than a change in
social structure; implicit in the notion is change in agricultural techniques and increased yields and output. What evidence have we of
such changes in the northern Netherlands?

A sense of change is difficult to acquire in this matter because
descriptions of agricultural practices in the sixteenth century are rare.
But one aspect of the transformation stands out clearly: the growth
of scale. Rural households reorganized their activities; they shed from
their work schedules a wide variety of tasks necessary to sustain the
household in a regime of relative self-sufficiency and concentrated

their efforts on the remaining tasks, the more strictly agricultural tasks. In a word, they specialized. An indicator of specialization is the growth of the scale of production, and in areas predominantly engaged in livestock husbandry, the growth of herd size shows this development most clearly.

Livestock Husbandry

Happily, we know something about the size of herds in the early sixteenth century. In chapter 2 I presented the information on this subject recorded in the *Informacie* of 1514. Data from all over Holland confirmed that only the largest farmers held as many as 12 head of cattle and that the average peasant typically possessed a herd of 4 to 6 head. Many households, particularly in the Noorderkwartier, had to content themselves with a cow or two. The wretched quality of the pastures, upon which a single cow often required over 4 morgen for its summer grazing, insured that few households would maintain large herds—and insured, too, that the household's members would take up many subsidiary employments to support themselves. In this context a large increase in herd size on farms of approximately constant size implies two major changes. In the first place, herd size could not increase without improvements in pasture quality. This required investment of capital and labor and the adoption of new techniques designed to maintain pasture quality at a high level. In the second place, an enlarged herd required an increase of labor time devoted to its care. In the late eighteenth century milking cows and preparing butter and cheese absorbed the full energies of one milkmaid for approximately 9 cows.[32] Should a household's herd double in size from 9 to 18 while the labor strength of the household itself remained unaltered, the need of the household to redirect its labor time would be clear. Milking, churning, curdling, etc., would now absorb the energies of two persons. Maintaining the drainage installations, spreading manure and sowing grass seed on the pastures, cutting and storing hay, breeding and tending to calves —all these activities would, likewise, demand a much increased labor commitment. Enlarged barns, additional equipment, and more frequent trips to market necessarily follow from such a change, not to mention a contraction of the labor time devoted to activities not associated with the dairying enterprise.

So, the trends of herd size are of considerable importance to our investigation. Notarial records provide us with the only comprehensive and trustworthy information on this subject. Very poor persons rarely left any record in these sources, but most farmers had the financial standing to require a formal testament and an inventory of their belongings after their death. Our study covers 471 farm households: 406 in Friesland, where the earliest inventories date from the 1550s, and 65 from Holland and western Utrecht, where they date from the 1650s.

Rather than aggregating all the data, I have arranged them chronologically and by agricultural districts. They are presented in table 4.10. The first district, made up of the Friesian grietenijen of Barradeel and the Noordertrimdeel of Leeuwarderadeel, possesses marine clay soils well suited to arable agriculture. In the course of the sixteenth and seventeenth centuries farmers in this area increased their arable at the expense of pasture and meadow. The second district—the Zuidertrimdeel of Leeuwarderadeel, Idaarderadeel, and Hennaarderadeel—consists of *knipklei,* a soil badly suited to arable use. In 1511 this district had nearly as much land under arable crops as the first district, but the farmers gradually abandoned arable agriculture in favor of specialization in dairying and cattle breeding.[33] The growing importance of breeding is indicated by the increased percentage of young cattle in the composition of herds and the increased frequency of bull ownership. (A farm on which young cattle make up over a third of the herd can generally be assumed to engage in breeding and selling mature cattle. Farms where the percentage is significantly under this figure probably buy cattle from others.) The final district consists of 3 noncontiguous areas of central Holland and western Utrecht, all predominantly livestock-raising areas.

The growth of herd size can be estimated for 4 villages in central Holland—Aarlanderveen, Oudshoorn, Alkemade, and Noordwijkerhout—by comparing the *Informacie*'s description of herd size in 1514 (see chap. 2) with a census for 1807. Reckoning from the statements made by the village elders we can ascertain that 314 households, about 1800 inhabitants, owned just under 1,300 head of cattle in these villages. In 1807, although the population of the 4 villages had grown to 7,600, cattle-owning households numbered but 326. They owned 5,462 head of cattle,[34] 4 times more than in 1514. Presumably most of this increase took place in the sixteenth and seventeenth centuries.

The accuracy of the Friesian data depends on the representative-

TABLE 4.10. Average Size of Cattle Herds in the Northern Netherlands, 1550–1723

	#	(1)	(2)	(3)	(4)	(5)	(6)	(7)	(8)
DISTRICT ONE[a]									
Leeuwarderadeel, Noordertrimdeel									
1566–74	42	14.5	10.4	1.7	2.4	28.3%	2.4	2.2	19.0%
1583–99	55	17.3	11.8	2.8	2.7	30.6	2.9	2.9	32.7
1616–41	34	16.0	10.4	2.6	3.0	35.0	3.0	2.7	23.5
1677–86	30	16.1	9.7	2.3	4.1	39.8	4.2	2.3	26.7
1711–23	10	15.5	8.2	2.5	4.8	47.1	4.4	3.7	30.0
Barradeel									
1651–66	21	12.4	9.4	0.3	2.7	24.2	5.1	0.7	23.8
1679–92	16	10.7	6.6	0.9	3.2	38.3	5.2	1.3	12.5
DISTRICT TWO[b]									
Leeuwarderadeel, Zuidertrimdeel									
1566–74	17	14.1	10.4	1.2	2.5	26.2	1.4	1.4	11.8
1583–99	18	20.0	13.3	3.1	3.6	33.5	1.7	1.6	11.1
1616–41	14	21.1	14.1	3.1	3.9	33.3	2.5	5.0	21.4
1677–86	16	23.7	14.6	3.9	5.2	38.4	1.0	1.4	31.2
1711–23	10	24.8	13.0	5.2	6.6	47.6	2.7	3.6	40.0
Hennaarderadeel									
1550–65	41	15.5	9.7	2.0	3.8	37.4	1.2	2.7	7.3
1595–1600	19	16.9	12.5	1.7	2.7	26.0	1.3	3.7	31.6
1646–54	33	18.0	12.1	2.7	3.2	32.8	0.8	2.7	30.3
Idaarderadeel									
1605–23	20	23.0	15.3	3.8	3.9	33.5	0.1	1.3	20.0
1676–1702	29	26.5	16.2	4.4	5.9	38.9	0.5	1.5	55.0
DISTRICT THREE[c]									
Woerden area									
1651–61	21	25.2	17.4	2.7	5.1	31.0	1.2	2.0	
Ronde Venen									
1670–85	30	14.6	10.1	1.0	3.5	30.8	0.2	0.5	

(Continued)

TABLE 4.10—*Continued*

	#	(1)	(2)	(3)	(4)	(5)	(6)	(7)	(8)
Alphen area									
1680–92	14	18.2	?	?	?	?	2.5	?	
Beemster polder									
1640	332	18.1	12.1	3.0	3.0	33.1	1.2	6.0	

SOURCES: RA Leeuwarden, Nedergerechten Archieven, weesboeken (see chap. 6, n. 1 for detailed references); RA Utrecht, Rechterlijke Archieven, nos. 1089–1810; ARA, Notariëele Archieven, nos. 166–76, 8514–18; Bouman, p. 251. (The Beemster figures are not based on an inventory analysis, but are averages of data covering the entire polder.)

NOTE: # Number of inventories upon which the data are based.

    (1) Total cattle.
    (2) Milk cows.
    (3) Calves.
    (4) Heifers (all cattle that have not yet calved and are under 3 years old).
    (5) Percentage of herd consisting of young cattle (calves and heifers).
    (6) Horses and colts.
    (7) Hogs.
    (8) Percentage of inventories listing at least 1 bull.

  [a] An area in which farmers specialized increasingly in arable agriculture.
  [b] An area in which farmers specialized increasingly in livestock husbandry.
  [c] Noncontiguous areas engaged primarily in livestock husbandry.

ness of the inventory sample, and the analysis of herd size in Holland depends on the truthfulness of the village elders. The precision of these calculations can certainly be questioned, but the trend seems unmistakable: except in regions that specialized in arable farming, the size of herds grew significantly in the sixteenth and seventeenth centuries.

All cows are not created equal. I would mislead the reader if I considered only the size of herds in this examination of the growing scale of activity in the agricultural household. Larger, more productive beasts provided another source of such growth, and there are signs of the improved feeding and breeding practices necessary to attain this result in the record of Dutch agriculture. Everywhere, cattle relied during the summer months on pasture grasses for their feed. The crucial problem arose in providing winter feed. From the end of September until March or April, cattle were stalled and fed hay. Shortages of hay in the case of a late spring or because of other climatic adversity could greatly harm the herds. The development of a regular, long-distance trade in hay could alleviate local shortages, and there is evidence in the seventeenth century that hay exports from the more remote parts of Friesland to Holland had become of great importance.[35] More important than hay trade was the rise of alternative and supplemental fodders.

Oilcakes, the pressed pulp of rape and coleseed, became an important concentrated cattle feed. Rape and coleseed, the oil of which was used in soap making, as a lighting fluid, and as a cooking oil, became a common crop in the course of the sixteenth century. In the early seventeenth century the strong demand for these oils encouraged a great expansion of coleseed production. This will be considered at a later point; here our interest focuses on the by-product of the oil-pressing process, the oilcakes. For every kilogram of oil pressed, well over one kilogram of cattle feed became available. The proliferation of oil-pressing windmills in the Zaanstreek, the principal production center—from 2 in 1610 to 45 in 1630 and to 140 in 1731 —therefore added a whole new dimension to the livestock-feeding practices of the region. In the two months following 16 July 1672 the freight carried by boat from the Zaanstreek village of Wormer to Friesland and Groningen included 10,000 oilcakes.[36] At its peak— which was apparently attained many decades before 1731—the Zaanstreek's output of oil reached at least 12 million kilograms while the oilcake by-product totalled at least 20 million kilograms.[37]

In the last third of the sixteenth century Abel Eppens, a Groningen farmer, wrote in his chronicle of using these cakes as a fodder in times of hay shortages. Their expense prohibited a more widespread use.[38] In the seventeenth century their frequent presence in farmers' inventories indicate that their use had become general.

The introduction of clover leys in the rotation pattern effected another improvement in both the standards of cattle feeding and arable agriculture. In 1644 Sir Richard Weston found clover leys common in the Land van Waas, in central Flanders; Weston's *Discours of Husbandrie used in Brabant and Flanders* recommended its adoption in England as part of a system of convertible husbandry that later became known as the "Norfolk Rotation."[39] Clover played a central role in the eighteenth-century agricultural revolution in England as it had in the seventeenth century in Flanders.[40] Both the port books of a number of English ports and Charles Wilson, in his study of Anglo-Dutch trade, record an active import trade in Dutch clover after 1620.[41]

Despite this trade in clover we would be in error to assume that clover played as important a role in the improvement of agriculture in the northern Netherlands as it did in Flanders and later would in East Anglia. Rotation systems used in arable districts along the great rivers (in West Brabant, the Betuwe, and in Utrecht near Wijk bij Duurstede) included clover,[42] and it appears that ley husbandry became common in the early seventeenth century along the dune coast of Holland. In most other parts of the northern Netherlands, however, farmers continued to rely on permanent pastures. References to the use of clover on permanent pastures are not common, but a considerable improvement in pasture quality occurred nonetheless.

The pastures benefitted from both improved drainage and regular manuring. From the inventories of Friesian farmers, it appears that the sixteenth-century practice of using manure exclusively as a fuel and a fertilizer for arable gave way in the seventeenth century to its use as fertilizer on pastures as well.[43] In the late seventeenth century the chronicler of Rotterdam, Gerard van Spaan, described the nearby livestock raising village of Kralingen as follows: "One hundred and fifty years ago Kralingen was a miserable little place with but a few houses; the land was of so little value that a large field was sold for a piece of butter. The reason for this was that in those olden times the farmers had no knowledge of fertilization. But since the farmers have become human [!] and fertilize the fields, . . . much improvement has been made." [44]

Early eighteenth-century rental contracts in the village of Ouderkerk not only insist that all the manure be kept on the farm but go on to stipulate that both the owner and the tenant shall purchase a certain number of boat loads of muck (stygeraerde) that the tenant, at his expense, must spread over the pastures.[45] At the same time a Warmond farmer claimed that he could graze 3 cows per morgen by spreading peat ash and liquid manure on his pastures, which he then sowed with clover.[46]

We can conclude that the predominantly natural pastures of the early sixteenth century, reliant on the droppings of grazing beasts for fertilizer, were transformed in the seventeenth century by the deliberate sowing of grasses and by systematic fertilization.

Breeding improvements before the eighteenth century occurred rather fortuitously.[47] The absence of accurate scientific knowledge about this matter did not prevent farmers from experimenting, however, and in the seventeenth century the provincial governments attempted to protect livestock quality by legislation. The Staten of Friesland insisted in 1610 that no bulls under 2 years of age be used and that all towns and large villages hire a *stierhouder* or *bolleman* to chaperone the bulls. The Staten insisted that stud horses be four years old, of Friesian origin, and selected by the grietman. In 1663 the minimum height of the stud horses was defined by law. The existence of a *bulman* to control breeding is confirmed also in the Noorderkwartier village of Wormer by a local ordinance of 1680.[48]

These efforts to improve the breed and increase the weight of livestock appear to have produced the desired result. Holland and Friesland exported cattle in the seventeenth century and the recipients inevitably noted their large size among their desirable characteristics. Trow-Smith, in his study of British livestock, cited cattle imported from North Holland as the main reason why the cattle of eastern England were superior to those of the rest of the island.[49] Abel, in his study of German agriculture, referred to numerous instances of Friesian and Holland cattle on the estates of seventeenth- and early eighteenth-century Prussia and Saxony. In 1725 Czar Peter the Great bought Dutch cattle for breeding purposes.[50]

If improved breeding and feeding methods increased the weight of Dutch milk cows, it also increased their milk yield, but the evidence on this matter is anything but plentiful. In the absence of yearly milk output figures, we must attempt to calculate such figures from data on butter and cheese production and average or maximum daily milk yields. Such calculations can rarely be made with an acceptable degree of accuracy. The butterfat content of the milk, the lactation period of the beasts, the amount of milk used in the feeding of calves, and the prevalence of whey cheese production—data almost always unknown to us—crucially affect any attempt to draw the information we seek from the above data.

Slicher van Bath compiled milk output statistics from all over Europe. He could find only isolated examples from before 1800, at which time a pattern of different average yields could be discerned. According to the Dutch Agricultural Inquiry of 1800, yields per cow ranged from 1,100 to 1,800 liters per year, the lower yields being most common in the eastern provinces. German data indicate yields in the Rhineland comparable to those of Holland, while in the eastern areas, yields were considerably lower. In Schleswig-Holstein yields averaged no more than 700 liters per year, while in Denmark 600 liters was most common. In the sixteenth and seventeenth centuries yields around 700 liters are consistent with the yearly butter and cheese output attributed to cows in various parts of Germany and

Denmark. The unusually well kept records of Robert Loder, a farmer in Oxfordshire, England, indicate that his milk cows gave forth 790 to 860 liters per year in 1618.[51]

In the northern Netherlands the relatively high yields observed in 1800 had been attained by at least the early seventeenth century. Rienck Hemmema, a Friesian farmer, kept records between 1570 and 1573 that show his dairy cows each yielding an average of at least 1,350 liters per year.[52] Abel Eppens, the Groningen farmer, recorded East Friesian milk yields for the 1580s in his chronicle. They suggest that Hemmema's cattle were not unusual at that time.[53] The historian of the Beemster polder recites a yearly cheese output per cow in 1640 that corresponds to Noorderkwartier cheese output in 1800, when it was very high indeed—the equivalent of over 2,000 liters per year.[54]

Growing herds and increased milk yields per cow combined to increase the total milk output per farm. This is reflected in the dairy equipment found on Friesian farms. During the century beginning in 1550 the farmers of Hennaarderadeel increased their stock of pails, cheese presses, and vats—many of which contained costly copper and iron parts. The most costly utensil in the dairy of a farmer specializing in butter production was, oddly enough, the cheese kettle in which the whey was heated. In Hennaarderadeel in 1554–62 only two-thirds of the farmers with at least 10 milk cows owned a cheese kettle. The average capacity of those in use was just over 0.50 *ton* (see Glossary). In 1595–1600 all large farmers possessed cheese kettles and their average size was now 0.75 *ton;* by 1646–54 the average had risen considerably to 1.25 *ton*.[55]

Arable Crops

When we examined the situation around 1500, we determined that the distribution of arable land in the northern Netherlands was undergoing rapid change (see chapter 2, pp. 71–72). The dominance of livestock husbandry notwithstanding, arable land played an important role in many parts of the region. But it was a rapidly changing role. The development of a strongly linked, international economy caused local needs and relative prices to be superseded by supply and demand forces determined on a much larger—an international—scale. When this occurred many arable fields could yield larger profits in the new, larger economy if turned to pasture. On the other hand, land in other areas, well suited to crops for which there had hitherto been an insufficient local market, could now be devoted to the production of those more profitable commodities.

Such a process of resource reallocation in adjustment to markets and relative prices determined in a more extensive area was occurring in the northern Netherlands throughout the sixteenth century. As a consequence the region experienced notable changes in its land use practices.

Waddinxveen, which paid a large barley tithe in the fifteenth century, possessed no arable land in the seventeenth century.[56] In Haastrecht, where a 4-field rotation system played an important role in the sixteenth century, the villagers cultivated only 58 morgen of arable in 1668, and that was mainly planted to hemp.[57] In Twisk, the 16 percent of the land listed as arable by the Tiende Penning Cohier of 1562 represented a noteworthy reduction from the previous century;[58] Assendelft reported in 1514 that it no longer raised arable crops; Oostzaan still mentioned it, but by mid-century no longer did so in its land-use documents.[59] The extensive arable fields of fifteenth-century Ter Aar disappeared in the sixteenth century.[60] In Friesland the 2 to 10 percent of the land that lay under crops in Baarderadeel, Rauwerderhem, and the Zuidertrimdeel of Leeuwarderadeel in 1511 all but disappeared a century later.

The reallocation process encouraged arable contraction in many areas.[61] But, at the same time, a few districts responded by increasing their commitment to arable farming. Thus, in the Friesian grietenijen of Barradeel, Achtkarspelen, and the Noordertrimdeel of Leeuwarderadeel, the 13 to 22 percent of the land under crops in 1511 was much augmented in the following century (see note 33 above). In Holland, the island of Voorne became a veritable granary in the sixteenth century. The island's chief city, Brielle, shipped large quantities of grain to other parts of Holland.[62]

The prospect of profit from certain arable crops stimulated urban capitalists to drain a series of large lakes in the Noorderkwartier. These newly created arable lands added a new dimension to agriculture in this watery peninsula. The drainage projects that reclaimed the peat bogs of central Holland also added much arable land to a hitherto pasture region. The clay soils exposed after the peat had been stripped away proved good for arable agriculture. Thus, Zegwaard, wholly pasture in 1562, was almost wholly arable after the reclamation of its exhausted peat bogs.[63] In yet other areas farmers converted

pastures to orchards and horticultural land. In Oegstgeest, Leyderdorp, and Zoeterwoude, all villages surrounding the city of Leiden,
the *Verponding* of 1632 recorded 278 morgen under horticultural
crops where only a few morgen had been put to that use 100 years
earlier.[64] Akkersloot, where the *Enqueste* of 1494 tells us that only a
little arable existed, was described in the *Tegenwoordige Staat van
Holland* in 1750 as a considerable horticultural center.[65]

New demand patterns, new trade opportunities, and new resource
endowments, produced by investors who responded to the first two
factors, brought about a vast, complex change in the distribution and
character of arable land in the northern Netherlands. In the midst of
these changes farmers introduced new rotation systems and heavier
fertilization practices that increased average crop yields.

A discussion of rotation systems in the northern Netherlands is
hampered by the frequent absence of any system at all. Virtually nowhere did the traditional 2- or 3-field rotation system obtain. In many
predominantly pastoral areas the arable consisted of a few small
parcels of soil built up above the general level of the land. A continuous cropping of whatever commodities the farmer chose could be
carried out on these small, carefully tended, and abundantly ferti-
lized parcels.

Elsewhere, there predominated single- or multiple- (4 or more)
field systems, which lent themselves to a variety of rotation systems
and to a degree of flexibility that defies description. On the lands of
Rienck Hemmema, the sixteenth-century Friesian farmer, the successive crops between 1571 and 1573 betrayed no systematic alternation. On 4 of his 5 fields Hemmema sowed pulses at least once during
the 3 years, while on the fifth field he planted successive winter and
summer grains. The importance of pulses and absence of fallow here
is noteworthy. Over a century later, between 1688 and 1692, the
rotation on 4 fields supervised by the churchwardens of Engelum,
Friesland, also displayed no obvious system, but here, too, pulses or
coleseed appeared every second or third year between winter and
summer grains and no land was left fallow.[66]

A compilation of tenancy contracts drawn in the seventeenth century reveals that fallow was a common requirement. A 33-pondematen
farm in Barradeel leased for 5 years in 1619 restricted the arable to 5
pondematen, which had to lie fallow 1 of the 5 years. A 5-year lease
drawn in 1691 required that 10 of the farm's 64 pondematen be
fallow stubble at the end of the lease.[67] In nearby het Bildt, a 7-year

lease of a 51-morgen farm in 1686 stipulated that each year at least 3.5 morgen be left fallow.[68] Perhaps the farmers contravened these requirements, because an examination of the 685 pondematen of arable of 24 farms in Barradeel between 1651 and 1695 discovered only 12 pondematen, or 1.75 percent, fallow.[69]

In Holland we can observe more systematic crop rotation patterns. On the South Holland islands a 7-year rotation called *heventijd* was common. It typically included 1 year of fallow and an alternation of grain with a wide variety of pulses and industrial crops. Such a permissive system lent itself to frequent adaptation to changing market conditions.

Rotation systems featuring convertible husbandry are strongly associated with improved agricultural techniques. Although convertible husbandry was long known and used in Flanders, we note its introduction in Holland not before the first half of the seventeenth century. A study of the lease contracts of the Sint Elizabeths Gasthuis (hospital) in Haarlem shows that the 6- or 7-year leases common in the 1580s and 1590s included no stipulations about fallow. After 1645, leases, typically for 5 years, made for the same lands (mainly in dune coast villages) stipulated 3 years of cropping followed by 2 years of *dres*—arable land laid to artificial grass.[70] According to F. Sjoerds in his chronicle of 1765, a similar system of convertible husbandry was introduced into Friesland around 1734.[71]

To the extent that northern Netherlands farmers followed rotation systems those systems consisted of at least 5 courses, often without fallow, and included frequent crops of pulses and cole and rapeseed. This flexibility suited the changeable urban demand characteristics of the region but could hardly have been attained so rapidly had the farm population not been freed of manorial restraints and common field restrictions. These agricultural practices further required an adaptable farm population and tenurial arrangements that encouraged farmers to invest and take risks on new crops. Finally, all the crop rotation patterns outlined above, with their infrequent or nonexistent fallows, required heavy manuring and frequent, deep plowing.

The changeability of the crop mix extended beyond the introduction of exotic crops to satisfy an increased urban demand. The basic grain crops also underwent a change in their relative importance, as shown by table 4.11, which indicates the land put under different crops on the marine clay soils of Friesland.

TABLE 4.11.   Percentage Distribution of Crops in Northern Friesland, 1566–1695

Period

Crop	1570[a]	1566–76[b]	1583–98[c]	1603–05[d]	1627–33[e]	1643[f]	1662–64[g]	1651–95[h]	1677–86[i]
Wheat	29.8	4.9	20.9	11.0	38.0	31.1	33.5	45.9	15.9
Winter and summer barley	43.3	51.0	51.1	81.2	18.5	31.1	10.3	19.1	20.1
Oats	17.0	16.0	4.4	2.0	9.4	0	6.2	6.2	30.5
Rye	0	0	6.7	0	8.5	3.5	7.2	10.8	.4.5
Beans	3.5	8.1 ⎱ 12.9		1.8	7.9	17.3	10.3	9.8	16.6
Peas	6.4	5.7 ⎰		1.4	12.2	7.0	5.7	3.3	1.0
Cole and rapeseed	0	0	1.3	2.3	0	0	5.2	3.1	5.8
Others— unknown	0	14.5	2.7	0	4.3	0	21.6	0	5.5
Fallow	0	0	0	0	1.2	0	0	1.8	0

SOURCES: *1570:* Rienck Hemmema, "Rekenboek off Memoriael van Rienck Hemmema," *Estrikken,* no. 14 (1956); compiled in Slicher van Bath, "Landbouwbedrijf," passim. *1566–76, 1583–98, 1627–33, 1662–64, 1651–95, 1677–86:* RA Leeuwarden, Nedergerechten Archieven, weesboeken. *1603–05:* P. Gerbenzon, "Het Aantekeningenboek van Dirck Jansz."; compiled in Spahr van der Hoek and Postma, *Friese landbouw,* 1:124. *1643:* Sannes, p. 423.

[a] Farm of Rienck Hemmema in Franekeradeel.
[b] 10 farms and 50 pondematen of arable in Leeuwarderadeel.
[c] 13 farms and 112.5 pondematen arable in Leeuwarderadeel.
[d] Farm of Dirck Jansz. in het Bildt.
[e] 10 farms and 127 pondematen of arable in Wonseradeel.
[f] Farm of Jacob Harmens in het Bildt.
[g] 4 farms and 98 pondematen of arable in Franekeradeel and Wonseradeel.
[h] 24 farms and 683.5 pondematen of arable in Barradeel.
[i] 6 farms and 154.5 pondematen of arable in Leeuwarderadeel.

Between the late sixteenth and late seventeenth centuries barley fell from its position of preeminence; wheat, a crop of more exacting production requirements, assumed the first place. Other gainers were rye, beans, and coleseed. Nongrains in general took up a larger amount of the arable land in the latter period. The increased importance of wheat suggests that farmers reorganized their crop mix to increase the proportion of their output sold on the market. Wheat was preeminently merchantable; farm folk rarely ate it themselves. In the 1570s Rienck Hemmema sold 92 percent of his wheat crop while he sold only 63 percent of his barley crop. To feed his household and servants, Hemmema purchased rye.[72]

The judicious rotation of crops, the frequent cropping of legumes, and the adoption of convertible husbandry improved soil fertility. But a far more important source of fertility in the agricultural system of the northern Netherlands was manure. Arable agriculture benefitted from a large, and growing, supply of manure, which can claim primary responsibility for the region's capacity to suppress bare fallows and increase arable yields.

Normally, manure supplies tend to diminish during a period of rapid population growth. The growing demand for grain causes arable to expand at the expense of pasture. This, in turn, forces a reduction of herd size and a reduction in manure supplies.[73] An escape from this famous "vicious circle" requires the reorganization of the rotation system to make the arable fields contribute to the fodder supply. This permits herd size to be maintained or increased despite the reduction of pasture and prevents the supply of manure from falling. New sources of fertilizer supply from outside the farm enterprise occasionally are discovered to break the "vicious circle." Flemish agricultural techniques pioneered in both these avenues of escape; the extraordinary amounts of all sorts of fertilizer that the Flemings applied to their fields never failed to amaze foreign observers.[74] The Flemings could pride themselves in their possession of a vocabulary rich in specialized terms for every sort of fertilizer and fertilization practice.

The overwhelmingly arable character of the Flemish farm made manure provision the chief function of farm livestock. The Flemish farmers stalled their cattle year round so that they might most efficiently fulfill this function. Constant stalling, of course, obviated the need for pasture but required the cultivation of large quantities of fodder crops.[75]

In the northern Netherlands, where livestock husbandry provided the mainstay of agriculture, an adoption of Flemish practices could not be entertained. The Flemings' great concern for manure was unnecessary in an economy where the number of cattle per hectare of arable land was much greater. Without going to the great pains of the Flemish farmer, the northern Netherlander could adequately fertilize his fields.

Of course, certain wasteful practices had to cease. In Friesland, and probably elsewhere, dried cow dung served as a fuel in the sixteenth century. Repeated edicts prohibiting this practice were of little avail until increased peat supplies became available.[76]

The cultivation of industrial crops and the systematic fertilization of pastures as well as arable, practices begun in earnest in the late sixteenth century, placed new demands on the manure supplies. Tobacco cultivation, which flourished in the environs of Amersfoort after 1625, required undreamed of quantities of sheep dung.[77] The Veenkoloniën of Groningen required heavy fertilization to permit their agricultural use after the peat had been dug away.[78] The intensification and extension of agriculture could not go forth without an increased supply of fertilizer and a rationalization of its use.

Urbanization and industrialization, stimuli to agricultural intensification, also provided the source for new fertilizers. By the mid-seventeenth century most cities had franchised men to collect refuse and sell and deliver it to farmers. The brickworks sold *verval*, the residual clay earth of their production process, soap boilers sold the ash that they produced as a residue, and numerous industries sold peat ash.[79]

The most remarkable manure distribution system focused on the city of Groningen. The city supervised the exploitation of the Veenkoloniën and strongly desired that agriculture be established in the area once the peat was stripped away. The unfertile sandy soil that lay under the peat required heavy manuring to be made productive, so to encourage settlement the city offered night soil to colonists at no charge.[80] The city established a special organization to husband all manner of night soil and send two-thirds of it to the Veenkoloniën and one-third to the Oldampt district, the prosperity of which also directly benefitted the city.[81]

All the night soil of Groningen could not satisfy the needs of the Veenkoloniën, where thousands of colonists were taking up the plow in the seventeenth century. To secure larger quantities of manure the city offered an import bounty of 10 gulden per *voer*.[82] With this incentive added to the need for a return freight, shippers who transported the peat of the Veenkoloniën to Holland returned with boatloads of night soil.[83] The outbound ships also carried sheep and pigeon dung to satisfy the extraordinary demand for those commodities emanating from the tobacco growing district around Amersfoort.[84]

The manure trade also developed, on a less dramatic scale, in other areas. Le Francq van Berkhey noted that in 1758 eleven specialized *vuilnisvaarders* (night soil shippers) operated in Leiden alone.[85] Both the tenure contracts and the notary records of land operated by trustees for minors provide abundant evidence that the purchase of manure to supplement farm supply was a commonplace. The owner of a farm in Alphen in 1680 permitted his tenant to purchase, at the owner's expense, 25 to 30 gulden worth of night soil to supplement the farm manure; another landowner in Zegveld directed his tenant to buy 4 potter's prams worth of verval each year. The owner was to pay for the verval, but the tenant had to shoulder the costs of its distribution on the fields. In the same village the obligatory purchase of night soil was written into many tenancy contracts.[86]

In the Ronde Venen, small hemp fields absorbed enormous quantities of cattle dung. To fertilize the pastures the farmers resorted to dealers in night soil from both Amsterdam and Utrecht. The amounts purchased are recorded in the records of trustees administering the lands of minors. A single farmer purchased as much as 12 boatloads, costing 136 gulden, in a single year. Three boatloads, costing 42 gulden, were purchased in one year for distribution over no more than 4 morgen of pasture.[87]

The unique records of the Friesian farmer Rienck Hemmema permit us to view the entire manure economy of a farm. The manure provided by his 14 to 16 cows and 4 horses did not suffice to meet the high fertilization requirements he set for his 8.5 hectares of arable land. In 1571 he supplemented the 196 wagonloads of manure produced over a 2-year period by his livestock with 50 wagonloads purchased in the nearby city of Franeker. In 1573 he purchased 113 wagonloads in Franeker. With this outside source of supply he manured about 1.5 hectares per year, or about 70,000 kilograms per hectare once every 6 years.[88]

Later information shows a similar level of manuring in other parts of the region: 62,000 kilograms once every 8 years near Wijk bij Duurstede, Utrecht, in 1809; at least 50,000 kilograms per hectare once every 7 years in Zeeland in 1700; and 14,000 kilograms, apparently yearly, around Enkhuizen in 1800.[89] The manuring practices in other parts of Europe, as compiled by Slicher van Bath, rarely attain this level; only Flemish farmers manured as heavily as the Dutch farmers in these examples.[90]

New rotation patterns and heavy manuring increased crop yields in the northern Netherlands. Before the sixteenth century the average grain yields throughout Europe rarely exceeded 4 or 5 times the quantity of seed sown. At the beginning of the nineteenth century eastern European farmers still had to content themselves with a yield ratio of 4:1, but in Italy, France, and northern Germany farmers could expect yield ratios of 6:1 or 7:1, while in England and the Low Countries 10:1 or 11:1 was the rule.[91]

If we ask when these high yield ratios were first attained, the data leave us in the dark. Most yield ratios are derived from estate accounts; where estates do not exist—as in the northern Netherlands—we must rely on occasional references left by extraordinary individuals. We know, for instance, that Rienck Hemmema, the Friesian farmer who compulsively recorded the minutiae of his farm management for three years beginning in 1570, enjoyed yield ratios of over 10:1 for wheat and 8:1 for barley. Were his yields common for that period? We have only a few scraps of evidence from notarial records to aid us in placing Hemmema's yields in perspective.

In 1582 the notary drawing up the inventory of Tjalke Naniesz. of Stiens, Leeuwarderadeel, carefully noted the yield on a freshly harvested field of winter barley: the yield ratio was exactly 10:1. If we compare the quantities of grain stored on the premises of deceased farmers to the arable lands attached to their holdings, we can sometimes get a rough idea of the average yields. In the case of Teeckle Blaessen of Wynaldum, Barradeel, who died in 1680, his oats yield of 179 lopen indicated a yield ratio of at least 10:1. The widow of Welmoedt Redgers of Tzummarum, Barradeel, also got at least 10:1 yields on her 23 pondematen sown to various grains in 1692.[92]

The new rotation systems and heavy manuring practices had another purpose besides increasing grain yields: they were necessary to the introduction of new crops. The growing urban and industrial demand of the region together with the development of international trade encouraged a diversification of northern Netherlands agriculture away from grains and toward industrial and horticultural crops.

Dairy farmers throughout the Krimpenerwaard and western Utrecht maintained hemp gardens near their farmhouses as a source of extra income. The hemp could be prepared during the winter months and then sold to ropeworks located in the villages and cities.

In Zegwaard the tithe records of the capital, van Sint Marie, show the value of the crop to have increased from an average of 1,200 gulden in 1568–90 to 5,000 gulden in 1660–70.[93] In 1726 the entire Krimpenerwaard produced 1.3 million kilograms of hemp.[94]

On the South Holland islands and on the Zeeland islands a specialized madder cultivation developed as demand for textile dyestuffs increased during the seventeenth century. By the early eighteenth century, before growing English demand greatly increased the production of the commodity, yearly madder production averaged over 5 million kilograms valued at 2.5 million gulden.[95]

Hops, flax, rape, and coleseed were special crops of longer standing, but their cultivation, that of the latter two in particular, increased in the seventeenth century. Rape and coleseed were apparently the beneficiaries of the increased real incomes of the region, which generated a strong demand for lighting oil and soap. The growing demand for these crops played an important role in persuading urban capitalists to invest in land reclamation schemes beginning in the 1610s. Coleseed production was the first reason given by the investors in the Beemster polder project in their request for governmental permission to drain the lake.[96]

Horticulture

The relative prosperity and the technical achievements of the northern Netherlands is well expressed in the development of horticulture. Throughout Europe in the sixteenth century, vegetables, fruits, and plants could be found only in the private gardens of wealthy persons or in the immediate outskirts of cities. The diets of the vast majority did not include vegetables in any quantity; primitive transportation facilities dictated their production within or just outside the town walls. Beginning in the late sixteenth century the northern Netherlands combined a widespread demand for horticultural crops with a transport network and new scientific information to make possible their large-scale production in rural areas.

The historian of Dutch horticulture could find only limited horticultural activity, in the outskirts of Leiden and a few other cities, until the end of the sixteenth century.[97] Thereafter it developed to take an important place in the rural economy. In the Noorderkwartier village of Broek op Langedijk, the Tiende Penning Cohier of 1562 gives no indication of horticultural activity; by 1603 the villagers petitioned for a reduction of taxes complaining of the destruction of garden crops by bad weather.[98]

In Beverwijk and Heemskerk horticulture arose after 1610, when the reclamation of many small lakes and marshes in the vicinity made available new arable land that competed with the older arable fields, whose owners turned to horticulture, in an effort to find a profitable use for them. By the mid-seventeenth century the secretary of Beverwijk described vegetable growing as an activity in "daily increase." [99]

The profusion of works on horticultural subjects written here in the second half of the seventeenth century reflects the leadership of Dutch horticulture. By then large-scale market gardening dominated not only the suburbs of large cities, but a number of rural districts as well. The Streek, a densely populated strip of villages between Hoorn and Enkhuizen, transformed its arable fields into garden plots specializing in cabbages and roots. Velius, the chronicler of Hoorn, claimed that many pastures had been transformed into gardens because the soil was extraordinarily well suited to the Hoorn carrot, or yellow root.[100]

The Langedijk, north of Alkmaar, became known for onions, canary seed, mustard, and coriander seed, as well as a variety of roots.[101] The sandy soil of the dune coast was well suited to horticultural crops. The area around Heemskerk and Beverwijk, which enjoyed direct access to Amsterdam via the Ij, kept busy a regular schedule of market boats between the two points by importing night soil and exporting garden produce.[102]

Two villages became known as centers of tree culture. One of them, Aalsmeer, also produced fruit, particularly strawberries. Ferries delivered garden produce to Amsterdam several times a week.[103] Boskoop, the other tree center, had 20 nurseries in 1611 and later in the century exported its products all over Europe.[104]

In Friesland, too, garden crops became important. Berlikum, in Barradeel, grew as a horticultural center and in the inventories of the mid-seventeenth century one frequently encounters cherries, carrots, cabbages, and turnips.[105]

What is worthy of note in this expansion is its spatial distribution. Horticulture was no longer tied to the immediate environs of the cities; benefitting from good transportation, it sought locations offering the greatest relative advantage, where large-scale production could take place for many markets.

MARKETS

Technical changes and improved practices for which technical change would be too august an appellation played an integral role in raising the efficiency with which farmers used their productive resources. The stimulus to employ new techniques must be sought mainly in the symbiotic relationship between growing urban and international markets and an adaptive rural economy. But to make this relationship effective, markets must connect the centers of supply and demand. An especially important feature of the rural transformation in the northern Netherlands, therefore, was the sturdy and extensive infrastructure of local markets and transportation facilities that arose to fasten the farms securely to the urban and international economy.

Since the sort of agricultural specialization described in the preceding section could not have occurred in a closed economy, markets and trade played a particularly important role here. This discussion can claim added interest because the trade flows generated by a specialized Dutch agriculture played a crucial role in the development of the great trading cities. Urban demand stimulated rural change, to be sure, but the rural change was of a kind that stimulated new growth in urban commerce.

There are many levels at which trade is conducted. My aim here will be to describe the structure and development of local and regional markets, give an impression of the volume of agricultural commodities handled, and then pass on to international trade, where discussion will focus on both the volume of agricultural trade and its role in the overall Dutch economy.

In a region of many cities one can expect many marketplaces. The direct distances between cities in the provinces of Holland, Utrecht, and Friesland rarely exceeded 20 kilometers. Only in Groningen, where a single city suppressed all other marketplaces, did a different pattern emerge. Yet the dense network of urban marketplaces with which the region entered the sixteenth century soon proved to be inadequate to the needs of the increasingly commercial farmers—or so they thought, for requests for market privileges from villages became numerous during the sixteenth century. We noted earlier the development of vlekken in Friesland. In Holland, too, rural places established regular markets and sought to provide services to the agricultural population that had hitherto been the prerogative of the cities. Naturally, the established cities strenuously protested this movement. They petitioned the emperor for legislation to preserve their monopolies and to prevent the use of scales in the country-side.

The emperor obliged them with appropriate legislation and the cities remained by far the most important marketplaces, but they never suppressed the village markets, and for our purposes the important point is that during the sixteenth century rural society felt a need for more closely spaced markets. Why, for instance, should the West Friesian village of Niedorp request in 1557 the right to establish a weekly market and two yearly markets? In their request they complained that "the farmers now must go three mijl (about 15 kilometers) to either Alkmaar or Hoorn." [106] Why was the trip to these major market towns, which Niedorpers had been making for generations, now such a burden? Conceivably the Niedorpers felt aggrieved by the merchants in the cities; perhaps they were getting lazier. But similar requests from villages all over the northern Netherlands indicate that a more general motivation lies at the root of the Niedorpers' request. We suggest that the rising output of dairy products—which are marketed more frequently through the year than are grains—made the distance to market a greater burden than it had been. The farmers had more business to transact at the marketplace and therefore wanted a more convenient one.

In 1602 the cities of Friesland obtained a resolution from the provincial assembly forbidding all nonurban scales except where they had existed for at least 40 years. Presumably, there had been a proliferation of markets in the period after 1562. The markets in the older vlekken had to be tolerated since many of the 9 village markets established before 1562 had become the equal of their urban counterparts and paid substantial rents and fees to the provincial government. In the seventeenth century the scales of Kollum and Joure each returned, according to contemporaries, more than 4 or 5 times the rent of those of the smaller cities.[107]

The increased frequency of commercial dealings on the part of the rural population encouraged butter dealers to locate in the countryside as well as in the market cities. The incomplete register of the marks of Friesian butter dealers, drawn up in 1627–28, records 16 dealers in Sneek, the seat of the butter trade, and 13 in Dokkum, another important urban dairy market. In the grietenij of Rauwerderhem, 5 of the 6 villages had a resident butter dealer, in Ferwerderadeel 8 dealers resided in 4 villages, and in Oostdongeradeel, within a few miles of Dokkum, 5 dealers resided in 3 villages. The more complete register of 1727 shows butter dealers residing in the vlekken in numbers which approached that of the middle-sized cities, while dozens of small villages all over the province had 1 and sometimes 2.[108]

The growth of rural marketplaces did not thwart the growth of the older, urban centers. These latter continued to dominate all commodity markets and their growth broadly reflected (although they perhaps understated) the growth of output. How much did agricultural output increase? The entire preceding analysis of technical and organizational change in the farm household stressed the effect of those changes on the volume of production. We should be able to find some reflection of those changes in the records of the marketplaces.

Unfortunately, municipal archives and city chronicles leave us little information on this subject. Each city levied a fee on each pound or measure of produce brought to its scales for weighing. If we knew the proceeds of the market fees and knew the rates charged, we could trace the course of agricultural production. But such information has rarely been preserved because the cities often farmed out the right to collect the market fees. The yearly rental of the "farm" could be useful to our purpose, but even this information is hardly ever left to us. After the mid-seventeenth century a few major markets leave some data on the yearly volume of butter and cheese, but by then the great upsurge is over.

For evidence concerning the earlier period we must rely, for the most part, on evidence of the physical expansion of the weigh-houses and market squares. Because Alkmaar, the major cheese market of the Noorderkwartier, possesses a most beautiful weigh-house tower that contains a remarkable mechanical clock, a number of antiquarians have been inspired to delve into its history. Their labors permit us to sketch the expansion of Alkmaar's cheese market in considerable detail.

The first mention of the weighhouse (Waag) in Alkmaar occurs in 1408. Then it was described as a very important market to which the inhabitants of Texel, Wieringen, and Huisduin travel to market their produce.[109] No other reference of use to us can be found until 1557. In that year the weighhouse receipts were farmed for 760 gulden per year, and the city fathers expanded the weighhouse and the market area in front of it to accommodate a growing commerce.[110]

Further expansion of the market square, at the expense of adjacent buildings, occurred in 1566 and 1572, when the weighhouse receipts were farmed for 1,000 gulden.[111] In 1577, Alkmaar petitioned the count of Holland for financial concessions so that the waterways leading to the weighhouse might be deepened.[112]

A major improvement occurred in 1582 after the liberation of Alkmaar and Holland from Spanish rule. Adjacent to the weighhouse stood a large structure (with the remarkable clock) that had served a religious function for which the triumphant Protestants had no use. The city took it over and reconstructed it as part of the weighhouse. At the same time the city fathers expanded the market square once again.[113]

In 1605 the market square again required more space and in 1612 a fourth scale was added to the three scales with which the weighhouse had operated for some time. The market square gained in area again in 1678 and 1680, whereupon no further evidence of weighhouse expansion presents itself until 1876.[114]

Yearly statistics of the amount of cheese brought to market in Alkmaar are available for 1706–09 and 1758–1816. They show that during the entire eighteenth century, when no further expansion of the weighhouse took place, the volume of marketed cheese exhibited no upward trend: volume fluctuated between 6 and 7 million pounds.[115] A great increase in the quantity of marketed cheese must have occurred during the sixteenth and early seventeenth centuries, particularly between 1557 and 1612, when the weighhouse, its market square, and approaches were all transformed to accommodate an expanded commerce.

Two factors affected the amount of cheese marketed at Alkmaar: the degree of specialization of the farmers and the productivity of their cattle, and the extent of Alkmaar's market area. The reference of 1408 shows the market area stretching to distant islands. We know that in the seventeenth century the city's market area was much more compact. Wieringen and Texel islands now possessed their own markets, and the village of Schagen, north of Alkmaar, held a market that cut into Alkmaar's hinterland.

These examples of market area contradiction must be matched against the large tracts of productive land that early seventeenth-century land reclamation projects brought into being at the doorstep of the city. The city's capitalists were themselves active in these projects, and the city administration never failed to insist that the roads and canals of the larger drainage projects be constructed to lead directly to Alkmaar. Agreements to that effect gained the city's markets 620 new farmers on the Schermer and Heer Hugowaard polders in the 1630s.[116]

But the major expansion phase of the Alkmaar market predates the period of impolderization, and, indeed, the Florentine traveler Guicciardini described the city in 1566 as "a very rich city since its surrounding lands are very fertile and filled with an uncountable number of cattle; more cheese and butter is produced here than in any other district in all of Holland." [117]

In Holland south of the Ij, Gouda's weighhouse received more cheese than any other. Its grain market, important in the fourteenth century, all but disappeared in the late sixteenth century, but the large wheel-shaped cheeses came in such profusion that in 1664 the city fathers ordered built a new, larger weighhouse.[118] An impression of the magnitude and trend of the cheese trade in this city can be gained from the record of weighhouse receipts, which are preserved in 10-year averages for the period 1641–1730. The weighhouse fee was 1 stuiver per 100 pounds. Records for 1748–52, which give the exact amount of marketed cheese plus the weighhouse receipts, indicate that the latter includes receipts for other commodities besides cheese and must be deflated by 10 to 15 percent to give the true amount of cheese brought to market (table 4.12).

The low figures for the 1650s might be accounted for by an epidemic of hoof and mouth disease that occurred in the early years of the decade.[119] The low figures that begin with the decade 1711–20 obviously reflect the epizootics that struck first in 1714 and recurred periodically until the 1760s. In many areas farmers lost over half their livestock to this plague in a single year. Still, this catastrophe by itself cannot account for Gouda's persistently lower cheese market activity in the eighteenth century. Conceivably, other market towns gained a competitive advantage in attracting the farmers of central Holland; a more probable explanation is that peat digging reduced the importance of dairying in this region. Moreover, once the land was reclaimed it was found to be suitable for arable agri-

TABLE 4.12.   Record of Weighhouse Receipts
and Cheese Marketed in Gouda, 1641–1752

Decade	Average Yearly Market Receipts in Gulden	Volume of Cheese Marketed Yearly in Pounds
1641–50	2,718	4,892,000
1651–60	2,230	4,014,000
1661–70	3,012	5,422,000
1671–80	3,545	6,380,000
1681–90	3,496	6,292,000
1691–1700	2,322	4,180,000
1701–10	2,379	4,282,000
1711–20	1,525	2,746,000
1721–30	1,520	2,736,000
1748–9		3,120,175
1750		2,886,845
1751		2,486,450
1752		2,691,735

SOURCE: GA Gouda, nos. 624, 625.
NOTE: For the decades 1641–50 to 1721–30, the
volume of cheese marketed yearly in pounds was
estimated at 90% of yearly receipts. From 1748
on, the recorded volume is used.

culture. The resulting readjustment of the area's rural economy
caused a further diminution of Gouda's cheese market: in 1804 it
received only 1,944,000 pounds.[120]

Rotterdam, whose market enjoyed only local significance in the
sixteenth century, developed an important trade in agricultural
commodities in the seventeenth century. The madder crops of the
South Holland islands all found their way to Rotterdam, making
it the center of the European madder trade. Rotterdam's cheese
market dates from 1611 and its butter house from 1619; in the
following decades its dairy trade increased sufficiently to warrant a
transfer of the butter market to larger quarters in 1654.[121]

The cheese market of Oudewater warranted a new weighhouse in
1595,[122] and Purmerend, which had contented itself in the sixteenth
century with a trade in eel, became, after 1612, the third largest
cheese market of the Noorderkwartier when the Beemster polder
added hundreds of farms to the city's market area. Around 1640
the polder produced yearly 800,000 pounds of cheese, making it a
considerable contributor to Purmerend's cheese market, which in

the eighteenth century received between 2.5 and 3 million pounds of cheese per year.[123]

In Hoorn a chronicler relates that in 1612 the market received about 150,000 pounds of cheese each week. Assuming this figure refers only to the weeks of active trade (and not to an average of all weeks, which would include the winter weeks when the dairy markets were dormant), Hoorn received about 3.6 million pounds per year in the early seventeenth century.[124] After 1763, when yearly statistics become available, Hoorn received between 4.2 and 5.5 million pounds.[125] The seventeenth-century chronicler of the city, Velius, pridefully described Hoorn's busy market days with the following story: "Out of curiosity some foreigners stood outside the Noorderpoort of Hoorn on a market day to count the wagons which rode in and out. They found that just under one thousand passed. If one were to add to that the wagons coming through other gates and then add the husbandmen who come by barge to the city then one can understand the busyness of the city's market. Many merchants come daily from the Maas and Rhine rivers to attend the markets here. Many Hoorn citizens occupy themselves in the dairy produce trade, and cheese is sent as far as Spain, Italy and elsewhere." [126]

In Friesland the markets displayed no less vigor than those in Holland. Leeuwarden, so its historian tells us, experienced such an increase in its trade after 1580 that a new butter weighhouse was constructed in 1595.[127] As the primary cattle market of the province, 7,500 head were said to pass through its markets yearly in the mid-seventeenth century.[128]

Heerenveen, a vlek that did not exist before the early seventeenth century, was by the end of that century the seat of a flourishing agricultural trade based upon farms many of which also did not exist a century earlier. In 1727 a Heerenveen resident in Amsterdam felt moved to write an account of his home town in which he described the weekly market as a cornucopia of grain and meat. In the fall 300 to 400 wagons each week hauled produce to Heerenveen and boats sailed to Amsterdam, Groningen, and all the Friesian cities delivering the produce of this recently settled district.[129]

Sneek received rights to hold a butter market only in 1456 but, despite its late start, it rose to become the principal butter market of the province—a province whose farmers specialized in butter production to such an extent that most of its cheese was made from decreamed milk. The records of this important market are complete from 1711 on, when the city fathers decided to administer the weigh-house directly. Until then the market had been leased to franchisers who paid a yearly fee for the privilege of its exploitation. Their yearly payments are known for most years beginning with 1610. The franchise payments up to 1703 and the revenue from direct exploitation from 1711 on are presented in graph 4.1.

These data confirm our expectation of a sharp increase in volume during the early decades of the seventeenth century followed by long-term stability. The much reduced franchise payments beginning in 1687 reflect a reduction in weighhouse fees. The fee for marketing a *ton* of butter was reduced by a third. When the figures are inflated to correct for this market volume, stability is restored until the sharp drop in 1702–03. In 1711, when direct evidence is first available, the apparent volume of marketed butter stood at an extraordinarily low level. The complex tariff structure of the Sneek market prevents our making exact calculations of the market volume in that year, but it stood at less than half the level of the 1730s and 1740s, when yearly butter volume stood at roughly 2 million pounds.[130] During these two decades the butter market yielded the city a yearly revenue of about 2,100 gulden. In this light the yearly fees of 1,600 to 1,700 gulden paid by the butter market franchisers between the 1630s and 1670s can reasonably be expected to represent a comparable volume of butter.

A comprehensive view of dairy production in eighteenth century Friesland is provided by the *Tegenwoordige Staat van Friesland*, a systematic survey of the history, political system, and economy of the province published in 1785–89. There the claim is found that in 1762 all the scales of the province weighed 6.7 million pounds of butter, 1.5 million pounds of cheese, and 4 million pounds of decreamed cheese.[131] The markets of Sneek and Dokkum together accounted for about half this volume.[132] At current prices, as quoted by Posthumus, Friesland's marketed dairy output exceeded 3.5 million gulden.

In the Noorderkwartier of Holland, the total weight of cheese brought yearly to all the district's markets fluctuated between 16 and 20 million pounds after 1767, when complete figures are first available.[133] No overall market statistics exist for other parts of the northern Netherlands, nor have we any such figures for the sixteenth

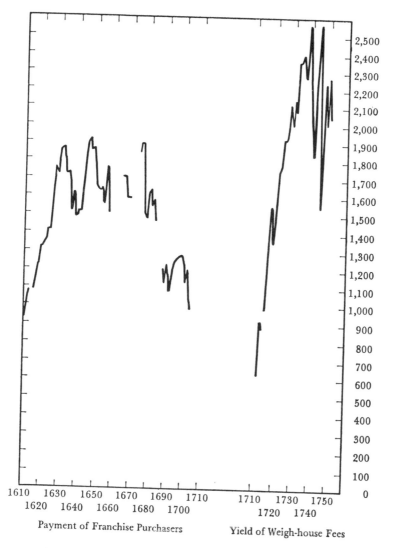

Payment of Franchise Purchasers	Yield of Weigh-house Fees

Graph 4.1. Sneek Butter Market Receipts, 1610–1750.

SOURCES: GA Sneek, Verpachtingsboeken, nos. 396–98; Collectieboeken van de Stads-waag, nos. 417–56. The calculation of physical quantities is complicated by the fee structure of the Sneek market. The fee per unit varied with the size of the shipment and with the status of the marketer; that is, there existed rates for merchants and for "outsiders." These various fees did not change in the period 1711–50.

century. The data we can muster tell us only that by the mid-seventeenth century at the latest the farms of the region were organized to produce large quantities of dairy products; the description of market development suggests the rest—that the farms had not been so organized in the early sixteenth century and that the transition required an expansion, in both number and size, of the market network.

INTERNATIONAL TRADE

Reorganization of agriculture along lines described above could never have taken place in an economy closed to trade. One cannot live on butter, cheese, and cabbages alone; and one cannot live on hemp, madder, flax, and coleseed at all. The specialization process must be understood in the context of the growth of international, or, perhaps more properly, interregional, trade.[134]

A change in the relative proportions with which the northern Netherlands was endowed with the factors of production—land, labor, and capital—provided an opportunity for reorientation of agricultural production. If each commodity is produced with a characteristic combination of the factors of production, an unequal increase of the factors will require a disproportionate increase in the production of the commodities that use most the factor increasing in quantity most rapidly. This readjustment necessarily forces a reduction of the output of the other commodities.[135] This consequence of an unequal increase of the various factors of production will be observed only if the economy can, in fact, allow an alteration in the proportions in which it produces the various commodities. If one or more of the commodities that would suffer a reduction in output were a necessity for which no sufficient alternative supply could be found, the efficient employment of the factors of production would be thwarted. Instead, the economy would be induced to find new production techniques for the commodities in question which would fully utilize the relatively more abundant factor of production. The law of diminishing returns asserts that this alternative would yield lower returns in rents, wages, and interest to the abundant factors of production than those received before the increase in factor endowments occurred. In short, in a closed economy the relative increase of a factor of production used in an extensive manner in the production of a necessary commodity will condemn that economy to a less efficient use of all its factor endowments.

Returning to the northern Netherlands, we can describe the economy in the course of the sixteenth century as one where the supply of labor and capital increased relative to land. Had they been devoted to grain production, both would have suffered a sharp fall in marginal productivity. Capital invested in livestock husbandry and related drainage improvements promised to be profitable, but livestock husbandry is labor-extensive in comparison to grain production. Both labor and capital could combine profitably in the production of industrial and horticultural commodities. But if output were altered in the direction of these more profitable commodities, how would surplus labor be absorbed, how would the population be fed, and how could the increased output of specialized crops find vent? Trade is the obvious answer to these questions, but in an era when regular, long-distance trade in grains hardly existed, the ability of foreign trade to expand in scope sufficiently to permit these changes in the northern Netherlands could justly be doubted. The creation of a large-scale trade in bulky commodities was one of the great accomplishments of the sixteenth-century international economy.

We have discussed the development of trade in agricultural commodities in the northern Netherlands in highly stylized terms. Contemporaries did not consider the alternatives as we have described them, and abrupt reversals in the economy's output mix did not occur. Throughout the fifteenth century grain production had probably been declining. In the early sixteenth century the region was certainly a net importer of grains and an exporter of dairy and industrial commodities. But in the course of the sixteenth and early seventeenth centuries, and in the face of international price movements, the tendencies of the earlier period were pushed forward at an accelerated pace. The rural economy moved more rapidly away from autarky. Developments in the rural economy imposed a "pro-trade bias"; imports of grain and exports of home-produced goods increased at a faster rate than did total output. In short, the rural economy vigorously responded to a partially self-created opportunity to specialize and produce for international markets.

By the early seventeenth century Europe's largest fleet of sailing vessels delivered enormous quantities of grain to Amsterdam and took from all Dutch ports cheese, butter, madder, tobacco, oils, and the exotic fruits of garden and nursery, not to mention the manufactured goods that utilized domestic hemp, flax, coleseed, dyestuffs, peat, and clay. Amsterdam's role as Europe's entrepôt and purveyor of bread grains was based on the dominance of its merchants in the Baltic trade, a trade that could grow to its enormous importance in part because of the Dutch rural sector's ability to respond positively to the opportunities international trade made available.

Exports

When we turn from models and theories and confront the stern matron who guards historical fact, what do we find? The few sources that refer to fifteenth- and early sixteenth-century foreign trade indicate that dairy products were exported, but on a small scale. Rhineland Germany and the North Sea and Baltic coastlands provided the major markets for Dutch products, which consisted primarily of cloth, herring, soap, and various manufactured goods. Besides these, agricultural products did not cut an imposing figure. In 1439–41 the *pondtol* of Kampen, a port of the Ijssel river and a gateway to Germany, registered the passing of some 200,000 pounds of cheese and 138,000 pounds of butter in a 22-month period.[136] A century later, in 1542, a record of shipments from Amsterdam records only a trickle of dairy products besides large quantities of herring, soap, cloth, and oil. The record of shipments up the Rhine from Utrecht in 1542 mentioned dairy products more frequently: 24 of 88 boats that left Utrecht between 3 July and 2 August 1542 carried at least a partial load of either butter or cheese.[137]

Edicts and resolutions forbidding the export of foodstuffs during times of dearth in the fifteenth and sixteenth centuries usually included dairy products.[138] Only one instance is recorded of complaints from the citizens forcing the amendment of an edict to exempt dairy products from the ban.[139] These fragments suggest that by the 1540s dairy exports had not yet assumed the economic importance that characterized them in the seventeenth century.

After the revolution against Spain, the new Republic established admiralties, each of which held the right to levy and collect tolls and fees on international shipping at the ports under their jurisdiction. The admiralties rarely kept proper import and export statistics since they levied their charges on the tonnage of ships rather than on their contents. The Republic's unusual import and export regulations deny us the trade statistics that provide the standard fare of

the economic historians of other countries. We must content ourselves with a few morsels which, unfortunately, whet the appetite
without satisfying it.

TABLE 4.13. Cheese Exports from the Admiralties
of Amsterdam and the Maas (Rotterdam), 1649–
1792, and Imports from the Netherlands at the
French Port of Rouen, 1669–1776
(In pounds)

Year	Amsterdam	The Maas	Rouen
1649	2,626,503	....	....
1667–68	1,662,904	....	....
1669	....	....	1,914,000
1680	1,221,600	1,899,000	....
1683	....	....	1,917,000
1728–33	....	....	1,598,000[a]
1753	1,750,000	2,500,000	....
1767–76	....	....	985,000[a]
1774	3,533,000	....	....
1784	....	2,400,000	....
1792	7,500,000	4,856,000	....

SOURCES: H. Brugmans, "Statistiek van den in- en
uitvoer van Amsterdam, 10 October 1667–20 September
1668," *BMHG* 19 (1898): 125; N. W. Posthumus,
"Statistiek van den in- en uitvoer van Rotterdam en
Dordrecht in het jaar 1680"; L. van Nierop, "Uit de
bakermat der Amsterdamsche handelstatistiek," p. 145;
N. W. Posthumus, Statistiek "van den in- en uitvoer van
Amsterdam in het jaar 1774"; Johan de Vries, "Admirali-
teit op de Maaze"; ARA, Admiraliteitscolleges, no. 693.
Statistics of French imports of Dutch cheese in Pierre
Dardel, *Navires et marchandises dans les ports de Rouen et du
Havre au XVIIIᵉ siècle*, pp. 171, 552.
[a] Figure represents an average for the period.

The data brought together in table 4.13 show that cheese exports
from the largest Dutch ports barely sufficed to supply the demand
of a single French port. This puzzling situation warns us to use
these data with care. Amsterdam, the great entrepôt, was not the
main dairy market; hence table 4.13 presents no more than the tip
of the cheese iceberg. The main export center was Hoorn, a port
for which no statistics are available but which was described as the
"cheese provisioner of all of Europe." [140]

The trade figures of the Amsterdam and Rotterdam admiralties indicate a volatile export of between 3 and 5 million pounds per year. Hoorn and the other Noorderkwartier ports must have added substantially to the export figures. How much is hinted at by the import figures of the French port of Rouen. When one considers that the most important cheese importers were now Italy and the Iberian peninsula,[141] that the London market absorbed ever increasing quantities,[142] and that Dutch cheese so dominated the Belgian market that domestic dairies retreated to a concentration on butter production,[143] it becomes clear that the outflow of cheese greatly exceeded the amounts recorded in Amsterdam and Rotterdam.

The earliest overall cheese export figures date from the period of French occupation. In 1803 exports totalled 18.7 million pounds. The stable record of eighteenth-century cheese production indicates that late seventeenth-century production and exports probably approached the 1803 figure. The fragmentary cheese export statistics are consistent with the course of development indicated by the market volume statistics: from a low level in the early sixteenth century, specialized agricultural output increased rapidly until some point in the mid-seventeenth century, after which overall stability reigned for well over a century.

Other commodities have left even less satisfactory export statistics. Tobacco and madder, unknown or insignificant crops in the sixteenth century, enjoyed a vigorous export trade during the seventeenth century, and a trade in horses, dairy cattle, and fattened oxen with England and the southern Netherlands attained a considerable importance.[144] This trade in livestock was, in fact, part of a larger network of trade in which the northern Netherlands played an important importing role as well. Danish farmers on the Jutland peninsula bred oxen that they drove to the Netherlands in ever increasing numbers during the sixteenth century. By the early seventeenth century the toll of Rendsburg, in Schleswig, registered the passage of an average of 40,000 head per year.[145] Many oxen also found their way to Holland by sea, and in 1624 the Zuider Zee port of Enkhuizen became the main Danish oxen market. In that year almost 12,000 oxen arrived in Enkhuizen via the sea route.[146] Some of these beasts were transported farther, to the southern Netherlands and France, but most stayed to be fattened on the lush pastures of Holland and slaughtered for urban consumption and for the provisionment of ships.[147]

Imports

Far overshadowing oxen imports in importance to both the urban and rural economies of the northern Netherlands were grain imports. This trade played such a central role in the Dutch economy that Amsterdam's merchants dubbed it the *Moedernegotie* (the mother commerce). The ability of the region to secure regular grain supplies in large quantities from distant places at once formed the basis of the shipping and commercial economy of Amsterdam, which became the main European market for grain, and permitted the efficient specialization of agriculture. This specialization, in turn, further stimulated foreign trade.

In the fifteenth and early sixteenth centuries, the evidence, meager as it is, indicates that foreign sources of grain supplied but little of the region's total grain demand. People in grain deficit areas had to rely, primarily, on nearby areas of surplus. The *Informacie* of 1514 informs us that Ijsselmonde supplied Dordrecht and Rotterdam and the *Enqueste* of 1494 cites the chief commerce of the city of Woerden as the relaying of grain from rural Utrecht to Leiden.[148] The Groningers relied on grain produced just over their province's borders in East Friesland. In his chronicle, Abel Eppens tells of farmers and merchants sailing to Lier, Wener, and Reen to buy grain to supplement their own production.[149]

In 1554 the toll of Geervliet, located near Dordrecht, recorded that some 2,400 last of wheat and rye passed by for regional distribution.[150] This volume of grain, sent from a small agricultural district, serves to put in proper perspective the role that grains from the Baltic played in the fifteenth and early sixteenth centuries. Polish exports (to all destinations) amounted to no more than 3,000 last in 1460 and 10,000 last by 1500.[151] (One last is approximately equal to two modern tons, or about 2,000 kilograms).

After the first years of the sixteenth century this limited, mainly local trade in grains was supplemented by a long-distance trade of much greater volume. The increased population of the northern Netherlands looked to these new sources for the necessary increase of their grain supply. The Baltic, Poland in particular, became the major, but not only, source of this additional grain. By the second half of the sixteenth century, durable trade links connected the Polish and Dutch economies.

Under the conditions of low agricultural productivity prevailing in eastern Europe, the western markets could be supplied only by the diffusion of demesne economy led by noblemen with both the desire to capture the profits that grain exports could yield and the power to enserf the peasant population. Under the direction of the nobility, Poland's economy was transformed to become the grain supplier of the Netherlands.[152]

Producing the grain needed by the large urban population of the northern Netherlands required, under the low productivity of grain production current in Poland and much of Europe, the exertions of an entire nation. The following exercise presents a hypothetical situation that reflects the conditions under which Poland produced the grain surplus that the Dutch market regularly purchased.

Polish yield ratios hovered around 4:1 during the sixteenth century. Let us assume that farmers sowed an average of 200 liters of seed per hectare, cultivated 2 hectares per capita, followed a 3-field rotation, and supported a domestic nonfarm population one-fifth the size of the total population. These assumptions reflect Polish conditions as nearly as we can tell. In order to produce under these conditions an exportable surplus of 40,000 last, which was the average Polish grain export of the period 1600–50, a farm population of 1,556,000 had to cultivate 2,315,000 hectares of arable land. After feeding the farm population and 390,000 nonfarm Poles an average of 200 kilograms each, the economy portrayed in this model had sufficient exportable grain to feed, at the same level of consumption, no more than 400,000 persons; that is, 17 percent of total output could be exported.[153]

In fact, Maçzak's study of the Polish grain trade found that the economy, despite its organization specifically to produce the largest possible grain surplus, exported no more than 12 percent of its rye output and 5 percent of wheat output in the late sixteenth century —and even less in the eighteenth century.[154] This gives an impression of the vast resources of land and labor needed to produce exportable grain surpluses in most of Europe during the sixteenth century. The urban growth and rural specialization of the northern Netherlands depended upon an ability to command the surplus of literally hundreds of thousands of serfs and millions of hectares of land.

The small Polish grain exports of the late fifteenth century grew rapidly in the early sixteenth century. In the period 1562–99 a yearly average of 50,000 last of rye and wheat passed through the Danish Sound, 77 percent of it in Dutch bottoms. During the first half of the seventeenth century the volume of Baltic grain exports averaged 68,500 last per year; again, Dutch bottoms carried 77 percent of this total.[155]

In 1630 a Dutch observer wrote that "from 1560 until now we have taken an average of 40,000 last of grain from the Baltic, although there have been years when it has reached 70,000; add to this that we take yearly from the Bight of Denmark and France 6,000 last of barley." [156]

After the middle of the seventeenth century Baltic ports supplied the northern Netherlands with less grain than in earlier decades. From 1650 to 1699 Dutch bottoms carried 70 percent of an average yearly export of 55,800 last, and in the first half of the eighteenth century the average yearly volume fell to 32,000 last. But now other regions began to play a larger role in the provisionment of grain to the northern Netherlands. The southern Netherlands, France, and, in the early eighteenth century, England began producing considerable surpluses. This not only reduced the demand for Baltic grains, which the merchants of Amsterdam reexported in times of famine, but also made the Dutch themselves less dependent upon Baltic suppliers.[157]

In the last decades of the seventeenth century we can discern a revival of domestic grain production. Zeeland in the southwest and Groningen in the northeast began sending regular shipments to the traditional grain-deficit areas and to the cities. The reorientation of internal trade routes that this revival brought about is made evident in the complaints, made in the 1690s, of the barge men of Gouda: "each ten to twelve days a shipper from Goes (in Zeeland) [comes] with wheat, barley, oats, peas, beans, and such, so that the hauling of grain from Amsterdam [the import point for Baltic grains] to Gouda is by-and-large finished, and diminished daily." [158]

In Groningen, which imported grain in the sixteenth century, grain production increased, particularly in the Oldampt area, to permit exports to Friesland, Utrecht, and Holland at the end of the seventeenth century, and agitation began for the construction of a grain exchange, which was finally established in the late eighteenth century.[159]

The relative importance of the various sources of Dutch grain supply changed in the course of the sixteenth and seventeenth centuries. In the absence of overall grain consumption and net import statistics, we cannot precisely calculate the extent of the region's grain deficiency. But the record of grain imports to Amsterdam suggests that, in the mid-seventeenth century, foreign grain fed well over half the million inhabitants of Holland, Utrecht, Friesland, and Groningen (see table 4.14).

TABLE 4.14. Total and Net Grain Imported
at Amsterdam, 1649–80
(In lasts)

Year	Total	Reexported	Net Import
1649	112,901	46,049	66,852
1667–68	63,829	1,864	61,965
1680	64,535	8,394	56,141

SOURCES: A. E. Christensen, *Dutch Trade to the Baltic about 1600; Studies in the Sound Toll Register and Dutch Shipping Records*, p. 407; H. Brugmans, "Statistiek van den in- en uitvoer," p. 125; J. G. van Dillen, "Stukken betreffende den Amsterdamschen graanhandel omstreeks het jaar 1681." During the grain crisis of 1698–99 Amsterdam officials reported that the city's yearly grain imports totaled 76,000 last. Of this, the city required 10,000 for consumption and 7,500 for brewers and distillers. Altogether, they reported, 43,000 last was destined for domestic consumption while the rest was reexported (cited in H. Brugmans, *Opkomst*, p. 114).

Per capita grain consumption estimates for this period vary widely, from over 200 kilograms to under 100 kilograms per year. If each person consumed 200 kilograms, one last (about two tons) would feed 10 persons for one year; 60,000 last would feed 600,000 persons. During the eighteenth century net grain imports from the Baltic declined. Amsterdam received 34,500 last in 1740 and an average of 24,000 last in 1803–09.[160] This reflected both a shift in the source of supply (which now made Rotterdam and other ports import points of some consequence) and a shift in consumption habits. Rice and, after 1740, potatoes probably acted as substitutes for bread consumption. Van der Woude found that in 1798 the entire province of Holland consumed 49,000 last of grain (per capita urban consumption 127 kilograms, rural consumption 108 kilograms).[161] This amount was less than the net import of Amsterdam a century earlier.

These diverse statistics are sufficient to show that the region was much more than marginally dependent on foreign grain. The dense population and specialized economy could not have arisen had the region not been able to draw upon all of Europe, and Poland in particular, for its grain.

Relieved of the need to devote resources to grain production, the Dutch could utilize them in forms of production that gave a greater return. Labor could be released from agriculture in greater quantities for employment in both rural and urban industry and trade. Abundant capital could be invested in land improvements and in new equipment to produce specialized crops for which an urbanizing economy provided a buoyant demand. The new activities of the rural sector could avoid the need for large numbers of horses and other draft animals that provided the power needs of arable agriculture. Feeding such beasts absorbed labor and land in much larger quantities than did the water- and wind-based techniques developed by the Dutch. All together, the rural sector greatly improved its allocation of resources during the period we have examined. This improvement both permitted and was a result of urban economic development.

5. Prices, Wages, Rents, and Investments

This analysis of the rural economy has stressed real factors and avoided discussing money phenomena except in theoretical terms. But if, as I maintain, the upsurge of economic activity and the many structural changes brought in its train were indicative of an economy enjoying an enhanced productivity of its productive factors, we should be able to see this fact reflected in the trends of prices, wages, and rents. For instance, if land became more productive, we should expect its rental value to increase relative to other goods; if labor productivity rose significantly more than elsewhere, real wages should increase relative to those elsewhere. Of course, there are many other price relationships that must also be taken into account, and short-term price fluctuations generate what scientists cleverly call "surface noises," which obscure secular trends.

To examine these questions, we need extensive and reliable price series. Price data are certainly plentiful at an earlier date than any other kind of numerical economic information, but wage and rent statistics, where they exist at all, are much less satisfactory. The enormous labor of N. W. Posthumus, who published two volumes of Dutch price data as part of the international price history project, forms the basis of our analysis.[1] My own price and wage statistics supplement his in a few instances; I have brought together rent data from both published and archival sources to shed light on that subject.

To interpret this sort of information we must first bring order to it. The efforts of Wilhelm Abel and B. H. Slicher van Bath to construct an analytical framework of secular price changes in pre-industrial Europe provide us with the necessary broad view.[2] (See chap. 1, app. B.) Both authors divide agrarian history into periods of expansion and contraction that are determined by changing supply and demand conditions for grain. From about 1500 until the mid-seventeenth century Europe experienced a period of agrarian expansion. The growth of population made grain relatively scarce, drove up its price, and, as a consequence, depressed real wages. Falling real wages forced people to curtail consumption of luxuries and nonnecessities in order to maintain a minimum grain consumption. This substitution diminished demand for pastoral and manufactured goods. The course of relative prices encouraged farmers to reduce pastoral activities in order to increase grain production. In a period of contraction the relative abundance of grain and its consequent low price produce just the opposite effect. The contraction phase is more properly called a grain depression since nongrain producers are not necessarily affected adversely.

Implicit in this schema is the assumption that during a period of population increase agricultural output will tend to fall behind and that overall labor productivity will not increase sufficiently to compensate for an increased dearness of grain. Relative inelasticity in the response of these two factors is basic to the schema and typical of European experience, since the schema is based on the observed performance of European economies from Carolingian times to the nineteenth century. It corresponds, for instance, to the course of events described by E. Le Roy Ladurie in sixteenth- and seventeenth-century Languedoc which he termed the *grand cycle agraire*.[3] Our earlier descriptions of the agrarian economy of the northern Netherlands should prepare us to expect price phenomena that diverge from this general schema.

The main price movements are presented in a series of graphs. The first shows real prices in 5-year averages; the others show indexes in 5- and 25-year averages. To guard against erroneous conclusions based on the peculiarities of any single base period I have constructed indexes based on 4 separate periods: 1450–74, 1530–44, 1575–99, and 1725–49.

The following are the most significant trends: dairy prices, especially butter, increased at a more rapid rate than did grains, especially the main bread grain, rye. The 1530–44 and 1575–99 base period indexes both show dairy prices outstripping grains except for brief crisis periods in the 1590s and 1630s. With its forceful population expansion during the period 1500–1650 we would expect the northern Netherlands to experience the price trend typical of most of Europe, namely grain prices outdistancing dairy prices. After 1650, when population growth ceases, grain demand weakens, and real incomes creep upward all over Europe, we expect dairy prices to rise relative to grains—an expectation confirmed by the 1725–49 base index.

Between the early sixteenth and the seventeenth centuries meat

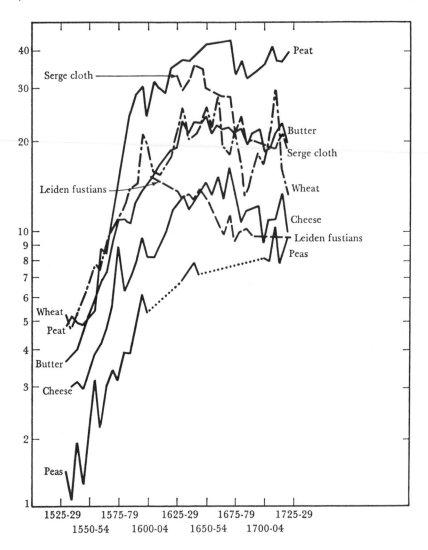

Graph 5.1. Relative Prices of Seven Commodities in Five-Year Averages, 1530–34 to 1720–24.

SOURCE: N. W. Posthumus, *Inquiry into the History of Prices in Holland.*

prices rose more rapidly than grain prices. This too contravenes expectations. Oxen prices show no strong rising trend during the first half of the seventeenth century. Thereafter, in conformity with general European trends, oxen prices increase relative to grains.

Textiles, the major manufactured good, suffered constantly fall-

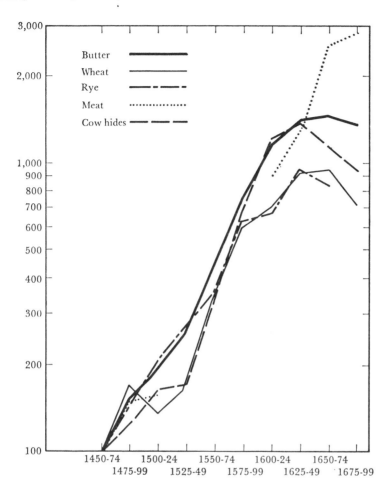

Graph 5.2. Relative Prices of Five Commodities in 25-Year Averages, 1450–1699. (1450–74 = 100)

SOURCE: Posthumus, *Inquiry.*

ing prices from the early seventeenth century, when the first data are available, to the second quarter of the eighteenth century. As a consequence, throughout the seventeenth century agricultural producers found textile products becoming steadily cheaper.

Finally we should note that peat, the principal fuel of home and industry, experienced a price increase between 1550 and 1594 which exceeded that of all other major commodities. Thereafter peat prices continued to gain relative to many commodities.

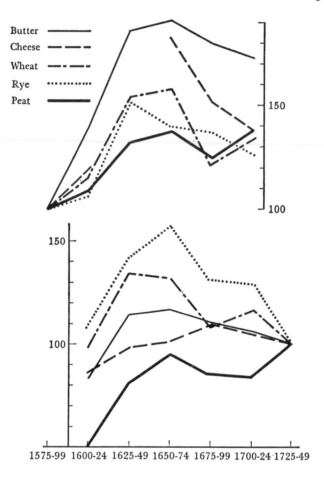

Graph 5.3 Relative Prices of Five Commodities in 25-Year Averages, 1575–1749.
(*Upper graph:* 1575–99 = 100; *lower graph:* 1725–49 = 100)

SOURCE: Posthumus, *Inquiry.*

Price series for many important commodities are fragmentary and
therefore cannot be used in this survey of long-term trends. We can
state, however, that during the period of the most vigorous population and price increase, during the second half of the sixteenth
century, many commodities experienced price increases at least as
great as grain prices; among them are bricks, lime, cowhides, hay,
and peas. Commodities with conspicuously weak prices during the
inflationary period included herring, salt, paper, soap, and rape oil.

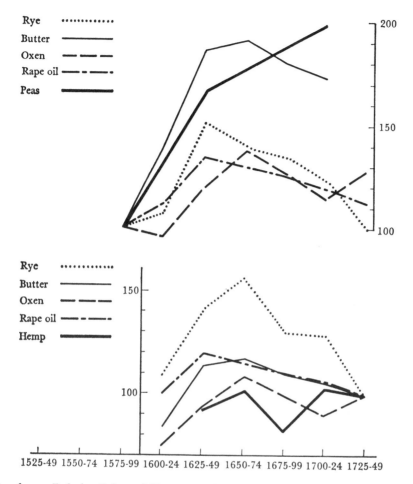

Graph 5.4. Relative Prices of Six Commodities in 25-Year Averages, 1575–1749. (*Upper graph:* 1575–99 = 100; *lower graph:* 1725–49 = 100)

SOURCE: Posthumus, *Inquiry*.

The incomplete price information at our disposal raises more questions than it answers. Our discussion here must concentrate on two issues of particular importance to our primary subject. First, we must try to account for the failure of grain prices to outstrip others during the sixteenth and early seventeenth centuries, or rather, the ability of livestock-related products in particular to out-strip grain prices during a period of Europe-wide grain scarcity.

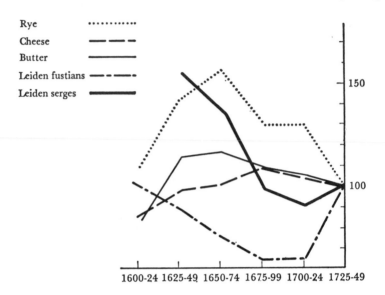

Graph 5.5. Relative Prices of Five Commodities in 25-Year Averages, 1600–1749. (1725–49 = 100)

SOURCE: Posthumus, *Inquiry*.

Second, we must confront the problem of real wages. This second issue obviously will relate to the first, since a trend of real wages inconsistent with the predictions of the general schema has the effect of invalidating much of the schema's predictions of relative price movements.

The farmer who sold butter and purchased rye received 30 percent more rye for every pound of butter he sold in the fourth quarter of the sixteenth century than in the first or second quarters. In the first quarter of the seventeenth century he received over 80 percent more rye and after a brief period in the second quarter of the century, when rye prices rose steeply, that margin of advantage returned and, by the final quarter of the seventeenth century, increased even more. A comparison of rye with beef and cowhide prices produces a similar conclusion. In most other parts of Europe this was not the case. Rye and grains in general were among the commodities whose prices were increasing most rapidly.

The exceptional quality of Dutch price trends in these basic commodities surely contributed to the specialization process described above, but what can explain the trends themselves? It is conceivable that the growing importance of the Baltic-Amsterdam grain trade can account for the price trends. Grain prices in northwestern Europe were generally among the highest in all of Europe while grain prices in eastern Europe were always the lowest, usually less than half those of northwestern Europe when measured in silver or gold. The development of a strong trade link between these two zones, even without a reduction of transport costs, must tend to produce a convergence of factor prices and commodity prices. The growing importance of the trade link on the course of prices can be measured by correlation analysis. The German historian Achilles has calculated the coefficients of correlation for rye prices in Danzig and Amsterdam and in Danzig and Utrecht, and between Lübeck and the two Dutch cities. The results appear in table 5.1.

TABLE 5.1.   Coefficients of Correlation between
Rye Prices of Pairs of Cities, 1500–1700

Cities	Period	r	$\pm$	σ_r
Lübeck-Utrecht	1501–1550	0.519		0.143
Lübeck-Utrecht	1551–1600	0.440		0.132
Danzig-Utrecht	1551–1600	0.686		0.080
Danzig-Amsterdam	1601–1650	0.881		0.033
Danzig-Amsterdam	1651–1700	0.917		0.023
Lübeck-Amsterdam	1601–1650	0.879		0.035
Lübeck-Amsterdam	1651–1700	0.909		0.026

SOURCE: W. Achilles, "Getreidepreise und Getreidehandelsbeziehungen," pp. 54–55.

NOTE: r can vary between $+1$ and -1. $+1$ indicates a complete positive correlation, -1 a complete negative correlation, and 0 complete random correlation between the two variables. The precise meaning of intermediate values is open to question, but values of above 0.8 are usually considered indicative of a high degree of correlation, while values below 0.6 are often held to indicate the absence of meaningful correlation.

As time passed, the price series of the Dutch and Baltic cities became more sensitive to each other and by the mid-seventeenth century followed a very similar course indeed. Achilles' study presented the coefficients of correlation between a number of other cities. Nowhere else, not even between cities within a single state, did similarly high values arise.

The increasingly strong correlations do not mean that the absolute gap between the price series fell and that the prices in the two areas converged, but that result is certainly a possibility implicit in the growing volume of trade between these two points.[4] Braudel's and Spooner's price data indicate that such a convergence indeed took place. Their graphs show that the range of wheat prices, reckoned in grams of silver, tended to narrow in the course of the sixteenth and seventeenth centuries, and that Dutch prices (series are given for Utrecht, Arnhem, and Amsterdam) were clustered toward the upper limit of the price range in the fifteenth and early sixteenth centuries and more often than not found themselves near the arithmetic average of all prices after the first third of the seventeenth century.[5]

A tentative conclusion can be offered that the growth of trade cheapened the price of grain, which in the northern Netherlands could be produced only at high cost. If this is so, the region's economy enjoyed large savings in the form of relatively lower grain prices which, given grain's importance in any economy of that time, liberated funds for other purposes.

This leads to the second question: what was the trend of real wages? During the course of the sixteenth century the purchasing power of wage incomes all over Europe fell precipitously. In southern England farm laborers' purchasing power fell by 60 percent between 1500 and 1610–19; the rye-value of farm wages in Germany fell by 33 to 50 percent between 1491–1500 and 1591–1600.[6] All over Europe the high wages attained in the labor-scarce fifteenth century were eaten away by sharply rising prices that far outstripped the increase in wage rates. Most explanations of this phenomenon point, in one way or another, to the rapid growth of population as the underlying cause of falling real wages. A pre-industrial economy with static technology is characterized by a stable labor demand curve; an outward shift of the labor supply curve would invariably provoke a sharp decline in marginal productivity and, hence, in real wages.

But the northwestern corner of Europe, where, as we have seen, the labor supply curve shifted outward with a vengeance, appears to have escaped most of this real-wage erosion. Scholliers's study of the standard of living in Antwerp, the metropolis of the Burgundian Netherlands and a city closely linked to the pre–1585 economy of our region, shows that construction laborers' purchasing power, measured in terms of rye, fell only 16 percent between 1501–05 and 1596–1600, while purchasing power in terms of a "basket of goods" actually increased.[7] In 1596 the wage structure in Antwerp became petrified. Exactly the same wage rates stood from then until well into the eighteenth century. As a result, purchasing power fell considerably until the mid-seventeenth century, whereafter it gradually recovered.[8]

Although Posthumus's wage data for Holland are fragmentary, a comparison between these data and Scholliers's for Antwerp reveals some useful information. The wage structure and level in Holland was similar to that of Antwerp in 1595–1600. Thereafter, while Antwerp's wages stand unaltered, Holland's wage rates rise until the 1640s when rigidity sets in here, too, for a full century. Measured against Posthumus's cost of living index, the purchasing power of unskilled labor fell, between 1501–20 and 1615–19, by only 8 percent, while real wages for outdoor work and hay mowing rose by from 5 to 12 percent. Table 5.2, using 1580–84 as a base, displays some wage-price relationships in the seventeenth century.

TABLE 5.2. Index of Wages and Cost of Living in Holland, 1580–1699
(100 = 1580–84)

Period	Unskilled Laborer	Hay Mower	Bricklayer's Helper	Shipbuilder-carpenter	Cost of Living Index
1580–84	100	100	100	100	100
1625–49	361	204	209	182	211
1650–74	—	—	225	310	282
1675–99	—	—	229	327	202

SOURCES: Posthumus, Lakenindustrie, 2:217, 1014–17; H. Brugmans, Opkomst, p. 154.

The evidence of Scholliers and Posthumus, taken together, suggests that wages in the northern Netherlands were unique in resisting the massive erosion of purchasing power experienced elsewhere. The peak price levels attained in the mid-seventeenth century undoubtedly exceeded wage increases, but by the 1670s prices had fallen back, and from then on the characteristic tendency of a grain contraction phase of the agrarian cycle asserted itself: prices, led by grain prices, fell while the "sticky" wage rates remained fixed, causing purchasing power to increase.

Farm labor received a wage which in the mid-seventeenth century varied between 15 stuivers and 1 gulden per day.[9] Resident farm servants received room and board plus a money wage that varied enormously. The yearly wages owed farm servants as recorded in Friesian farm inventories in the period 1562–76 ranged from fl. 3.2

to fl. 15.12, with half the observations between 5 and 10 gulden. In the period 1634–66 the range spread from 11 to 116 gulden, with half the observations between 30 and 50 gulden. By 1718–30 the range was 28 to 129 gulden; half the observations stood between 70 and 90 gulden.[10] Frequently, a shirt or a pair of shoes supplemented these monetary payments. If a solitary farm-wage reference for 1500 is of any value—it tells of a Friesian convent paying about 4 gulden plus a shirt and a pair of shoes[11]—then we can conclude that real wages held up very well indeed during the era of price inflation. What is perhaps more worthy of attention is the continued rapid increase of farm laborers' wages after the mid-seventeenth century. All the admittedly fragmentary evidence of urban wages tells of stable or falling money wages after 1650. Still, the great variance of the 76 observations upon which the above figures are based dictates extreme caution in drawing conclusions.

For what it is worth, we can observe that those who paid wages complained frequently that they were too high. Pieter de la Court, the astute observer of the Dutch economy, wrote in 1662, "the farmers must pay such high salaries and day wages to their servants that they live with great difficulty while their servants are very comfortable. And the same discomfort is felt by men in the cities, where the craftsmen and servants are more unbearable than in any other land."[12] In 1667 a publicist for the textile industry complained that the "day wages in combing, carding, spinning, and weaving are about half as much [in England] as must be paid here."[13] Posthumus found that in 1741 the wage rates for weavers in Leiden, Tilburg (a seat of rural textile production in Brabant), and Vervier (in Belgium) were related to each other in the proportions 3:1.5:1.[14]

Some of the caution induced by our limited statistical evidence can be dispelled by another sort of historical evidence, that which tells of a great interest in labor-saving farm equipment beginning in the second half of the seventeenth century. The fields of grain were few, but productive, and as labor costs rose, the labor-intensive winnowing and threshing processes became increasingly costly bottlenecks. Efforts to reduce the labor requirement of these activities took the form of introducing the Chinese winnowing mill to Europe in the late seventeenth century and, in the early eighteenth century, of employing the horse-drawn threshing block.[15]

The most significant labor-saving innovation of the period was the *karnemolen,* a large, horse-powered butter churn. On a large dairy farm the labor-intensive process of butter churning could absorb the labor of several milkmaids. The steady increase of farm laborers' wages apparently triggered a spate of invention to reduce this expense. Several mechanical churns gained patents in the 1660s. Their installation required a considerable space in a reconstructed dairy. These costly, indivisible, labor-saving devices were rapidly adopted by the larger farms. Peasant inventories of Leeuwarderadeel in 1677–86 list them on 35 percent of farms with at least 10 milk cows; in 1711–50, 72 percent of such farms possessed karnemolens. Apparently, the threshold herd size for the profitable use of the karnemolen stood near 10, for few smaller farms acquired them.[16]

Much of the complaining about high wages can undoubtedly be attributed to the uniquely high taxation of the seventeenth-century Dutch Republic and its reliance on excise taxes.[17] But a more fundamental explanation must be provided to account for the observation that real wages fell very little, if at all, while in the rest of Europe they fell precipitously. An argument introduced earlier, that the economy in its expansion underwent qualitative as well as quantitative changes, suggests the needed explanation: specialization and the introduction of new techniques increased productivity. As a result, employment expanded fast enough to absorb the enormous increase in population without suffering it to accept reduced wages. If this interpretation can be upheld, we can account for the unique character of many price trends in the region. Since real wages did not fall and growing grain imports dampened the upward trends of grain prices, demand for other goods—dairy and horticultural products and manufactured goods—held up better than in other parts of Europe.

The introduction of new, more productive, practices in dairy farming contributed to these price and wage phenomena. Price movements between 1550 and 1650 seem to reflect a change in cattle-feeding practices and an increased productivity of milk cows. Posthumus compiled the price data of all the commodities in table 5.3 except those for milk cows. His milk cow series begins in 1620; before that date he found only scattered observations for the period 1565–68. I have supplemented those observations with the sale prices of 132 milk cows in 1565–71 recorded in the Weesboeken of Friesland. All these data permit us to build an index of milk cow prices using 1565–71 as a base period.

Between 1550–74 and 1600–24 the price of hay and oilcakes—

TABLE 5.3.   Index of Milk Cow, Cheese, and
Butter Prices, 1565–1654
(100 = 1565–71)

Period	Milk Cows	Cheese	Butter
1565–71	100	100	100
1620–24	363	248	252
1645–49	467	—	301
1650–54	—	308	333

SOURCES: Posthumus, *History of Prices*, vol. 2; RA Leeuwarden,
Nedergerechten Archieven, weesboeken.

livestock fodder—increased by 360 and 375 percent, respectively,
while milk cow prices apparently increased somewhat less and butter and cheese prices increased much less—260 and 215 percent,
respectively. Rape oil, of which oilcakes are a by-product, increased
in price by only 100 percent. We can conclude from these price
trends that the demand for fodder rose enormously as farmers strove
to improve the quality of their herds. The more rapid increase of
milk cow prices than those of their principal products is, in all
probability, a reflection of the success of farmers' efforts to improve
the productivity of their beasts.

The discussion of price and wage trends tells us much about the
economy in general. There remains yet the question of the profitability of agriculture. The course of prices and wages suggests partial answers, but before we can attempt a fuller answer to the
question, the course of rents must be charted.

RENTS

In chapter 2 I presented a survey of rental values in the early
sixteenth century. At that time soil quality differences caused rents
to vary greatly, from as little as 4 stuivers per morgen to over 20
times that amount. In the following century and a half, rents increased considerably; the rate of increase varied with the qualities
of the soil, the location, the amount of drainage improvement, and
the level of the drainage tax levied on the land. These many variables prevent us from citing the rental history of small parcels as
representative of general trends. Numerous tendencies exist, and
they should be accounted for separately.

Graph 5.6 displays the data at our disposal. Between 1511–14 and
1580 all indicators show a rapid increase; on average, rents rose

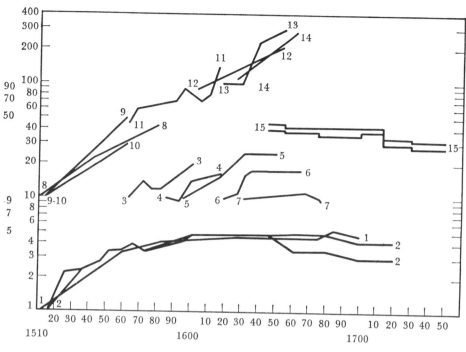

Graph 5.6. Rental Values in the Northern Netherlands, 1510–1740.

KEY AND SOURCES:

1. Rent on a farm in Goutum, Friesland, owned by the Sint Antoni Gasthuis in Leeu-warden. Spahr van der Hoek and Postma, *Friese landbouw*, 1:131. Entry fines of 1,000 gold gulden were levied in 1626 and 1669. These are not included in the graph.

2. Rents paid in het Bildt, Friesland. Sannes, vol. 1, passim. Excluded from the graph are entry fines levied regularly from 1635 until 1700. After the last two entry fines, those of 1686 and 1693, fell in arrears, this practice was ended.

3. Rent on a farm near Haarlem owned by the Sint Elizabeths Gasthuis of Haarlem. GA Haarlem, Archieven van het Sint Elizabeths Gasthuis, no. 53/1.

4. Rental income of confiscated monastic lands in Friesland. Van Apeldoorn, *Kerkelijk goederen*, p. 396.

5. Rental income of confiscated monastic lands in Groningen (22,655 hectares until 1608, when a portion was sold). Roelfsema, *De klooster- en proosdijgoederen*, pp. 81–82.

6. Rent on a farm in Bozum, Friesland. Spahr van der Hoek and Postma, *Friese land-bouw* 1:171. At each renewal an entry fine was levied: 1619 and 1628, 1,000 gulden; 1632, 1,400 gulden; 1635–65, 1,500 gulden. After 1665 the rent was reduced, but the new amount is unknown.

7. Rent on a farm in Marsum, Friesland. Spahr van der Hoek and Postma, *Friese land-bouw*, 1:172.

8. Average rent of 10 farms in 1511, 1543, and 1580. *Aanbreng van 1511; Beneficiaal-boeken van Friesland; Register van geestelijk opkomsten.*

(continued on p. 188)

fourfold. In the 1570s and 1580s this advance was cut short when the war of liberation, with its disruption of rural life in many areas, rendered the land unprofitable.

After 1590 the upward tendency is resumed by some indicators, but not all. The reformation and the attendant confiscation of church property threw contractual obligations into confusion. Some farmers took the opportunity to press for recognition of their rights to hereditary tenure and fixed rents and sometimes managed to avoid paying rent to anyone for many years.[18] The rents paid by the farmers of het Bildt, for instance, increased little after 1590 despite the constant efforts of the new landlord, the provincial government of Friesland. Litigation and overt resistance on the part of the farmers, who considered themselves hereditary tenants on the basis of prerevolutionary lease agreements, succeeded in frustrating the efforts of the province to increase rents.[19] But most farmers were not so lucky. The rental receipts of the confiscated monastic lands of Friesland and Groningen, which represent tens of thousands of hectares, show the pre-1580 trend reestablished after 1590. The level of Groningen rents rose nearly 50 percent between 1596 and 1632. Thereafter, they were stable until the 1650s. In Leeuwarderadeel, rents listed among the debts of deceased farmers in 1718–20 stood at nearly 3 times the level of 1580, when, in turn, they were 3 times the level of 1511.[20]

The average rent levied on 1,039 hectares in the Noorderkwartier owned by the Burgerweeshuis (orphanage) of Amsterdam increased by 154 percent between 1627 and 1662 from fl. 10.14 to fl. 27.4 per morgen. The average rent on the lands of the Sint Elizabeths

9. Average rent levied in Ouderkerk aan de Amstel. *Informacie;* ARA Staten van Holland voor 1572, Tiende Penning Cohieren, 1562. The average rental value of 3 farms in 1730–34 was 6 times the average of 1562. RA Haarlem, Notarieële Archieven, Huurcontracten.

10. Average rent levied in Tekkop. *Informacie;* ARA Staten van Holland voor 1572, Tiende Penning Cohieren, 1562.

11. Rent on a 3.5-morgen parcel in Lisse owned by the Sint Elizabeths Gasthuis of Haarlem. GA Haarlem, Archieven van het Sint Elizabeths Gasthuis, no. 53/1.

12. Rent on a farm near Haarlem. GA Haarlem, Archieven van het Sint Elizabeths Gasthuis, no. 52/2.

13. Rent on a 4-morgen parcel near Haarlem. GA Haarlem, Archieven van't het Sint Elizabeths Gasthuis, no. 53/2.

14. Average rent on 1,039 morgen owned by the Burgerweeshuis of Amsterdam. GA Amsterdam, Burgerweeshuis Archieven, no. 127.

15. Maximum and minimum rental prices on the Beemster polder, Holland. Bouman, p. 267.

Gasthuis (hospital) of Haarlem in the 1650s confirms the validity of the Amsterdam figures.[21] In the same villages where rents of over 20 gulden per morgen were typical, the *Informacie* of 1514 had cited average rents of between 1 and 2 gulden. The overall rent increase in the century and a half following 1514 appears to have been at least tenfold, and often very much more.

In the 1650s the first indications of lower rents appear. The increasingly common practice of imposing entry fines as a supplement to yearly rents obscures the precise extent of the decline, however, and only in the 1680s, when rent reductions become general and complaints of mounting arrears are widespread, can we be certain of a marked decline in the profitability of agriculture.

The lack of precision with which we must content ourselves in describing the trend of rent in the northern Netherlands makes comparison with price trends difficult. In table 5.4, however, it is

TABLE 5.4. Index of Rye and Butter Prices and the
Approximate Course of Rents, 1500–1674
(100 = 1500–24)

Period	Rye	Butter	Rent
1500–24	100	100	100
1525–49	132	133	—
1550–74	177	233	—
1575–99	309	397	400[a]
1600–24	333	608	—
1625–49	467	741	800[b]
1650–74	421	758	1400[c]

SOURCES: Rye and butter prices from Posthumus, *History of Prices*, vol. 2; rent index from my estimates based on data in graph 5.6.
[a] Period = 1580.
[b] Period = 1632; 800 represents minimum.
[c] Period = 1662.

clear that beginning with a 1500–24 base, rents rise far above rye prices and remain above them and that after 1580, rents tend to outstrip butter prices. Textiles, building materials, and most other goods rise more slowly than dairy prices or grains during the entire period under discussion. Thus, we are left with the impression that the leading character of rents reflects strongly increasing profitability, particularly between 1580 and 1650, when dairy prices decisively break away from the general course of agricultural prices.

Another factor that cannot be overlooked is the impact of improved drainage on rents. In 1543 some haylands in Ypekolsga, Friesland, were described as follows: "In the past, the above mentioned lands were so crummy that a pondemaat did not rent for more than six stuivers in the time of Heer Sicko [1511]. Thereafter they were improved, and rented for ten stuivers, and after that, in the time of his Imperial Majesty [Charles V] a pondemaat rented for fifteen stuivers (because of the good regulation of dikes and dams), and now rent for eighteen stuivers, more or less." [22] A contemporary attributed the tripling of rents in 32 years to physical improvements, which allowed output to increase.

But land improvement in the Netherlands was a double-edged sword. The most important improvements occurred through cooperative action, and that required taxation. In the *Informacie* of 1514 villagers occasionally remarked that high drainage taxes depressed rents, despite the productivity of the soil. The rise of rents is the more remarkable because of the steep increase in taxes, both drainage and general revenue taxes, assessed upon the land.

Drainage authorities were, and are, small and numerous. This hinders assembling their tax data; but the *morgengeld* assessed by one of the largest of these authorities, the Hoogheemraadschap van Rijnland, will give an impression of the course of these levies (see graph 5.7).

In most provinces a general assessment on landed property formed the base of the taxation system. In Holland this was known as the Verponding and in Friesland as the *Floreentaux*. The Friesian levy underwent no alteration from its inception in 1511 until the beginning of the nineteenth century. In 1511 the Floreentaux levied an assessment of 3 stuivers on each floreen's worth of land (a floreen was a gulden of 28 stuivers). The amount assessed rose steadily, particularly after the Revolution, finally attaining the rate of 6 gulden, 6 stuivers (126 stuivers) per floreen in 1688. The tax rate had increased forty-twofold. [23]

The fact that rents attained very high levels relative to those of prices of various goods despite the high, and increasing, tax burden must attest to the profitability of agriculture in the region. A considerable increase in the productivity of the land must stand behind this phenomenon.

When agricultural prices began to fall after 1660, rents fell also. Although the evidence provides no dramatic demonstration of a sudden general collapse of land values, there is plentiful evidence

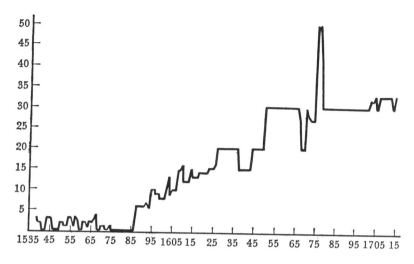

Graph 5.7. Tax per Morgen of Taxable Land Levied by the Hoogheemraadschap van Rijnland, 1537–1715. (In stuivers per morgen)

Source: Jhr. D. T. Gevers van Endgeest, *Hoogheemraadschap van Rijnland,* vol. 2, appendix 27.

of large-scale sale and abandonment of land in the late seventeenth and early eighteenth centuries. In 1686 the administrators of the Burgerweeshuis of Amsterdam decided to review during the following decade the receipts and expenditures for each parcel of land. If the rental income did not provide at least a 3 percent return over all costs, including administration costs, the parcel was to be sold. In 1700 much of the Weeshuis lands were, indeed, sold. The lands of the Sint Elizabeths Gasthuis of Haarlem, with the exception of parcels nearby the city, were also sold in 1723 and 1739–40.[24] The proceeds of these land sales were reinvested in negotiable paper.

Small landowners also felt the decline of the profitability of land as the Register van de Transporten makes clear. This document, drawn up in 1755, records all lands in the Noorderkwartier, the ownership of which was transferred to the provincial government because of the inability of the previous owners to pay the taxes and other charges attached to them. Beginning around 1700, hundreds of morgen, occasionally over 100 morgen in a single village, lay abandoned for this reason.[25]

A fall in the profitability of landownership, and presumably of farming itself, is clear to see in these events. The cattle plagues that began in 1714 and the menace of rotting dike timbers, which first presented itself at about the same time, also lead us to the conclusion that farm profits could not be maintained at their earlier levels in the last quarter of the seventeenth and the first quarter of the eighteenth centuries. Weak agricultural prices encountered stubbornly irreducible costs, led by taxes, and thereby eliminated profits.

INVESTMENTS

During the century and a half after 1500 the course of rents is consistent with the statement made elsewhere that agricultural land became increasingly more valuable. The price trends certainly contributed to this: the "terms of trade" of dairy farmers improved during much of this period. Physical improvements of the land and additions to equipment also enhanced its profitability. But these last mentioned factors should be seen as a reflection of the new profitable opportunities in the rural sector. Investment in the rural sector deserves a careful investigation. It is frequently assumed that capital investment in peasant economies is negligible. In the northern Netherlands the enormous sums sunk into the land, transport routes, buildings, and the people of the rural society were crucial to the thoroughgoing specialized economy that arose there. The prospect of profit induced the flow of capital, but it would not have come had appropriate institutional and legal forms not existed. We shall discuss in turn investments made in the rural sector by urban capitalists, the rural dwellers themselves, and the government.

Urban Capitalists

The most impressive and enduring achievements of the Dutch during our period may well have been the land reclamation projects. In their age-old struggle against the sea the Dutch could claim only a partial success, and even that stood threatened in the sixteenth century, when it appeared that rising seas, natural subsidence, and inland lakes created by peat digging might decisively gain the upper hand. Beginning in the late sixteenth century and attaining its full glory in the first half of the seventeenth century, a land reclamation effort arose, led and financed by urban capitalists, which changed the face and shape of the region and secured it from the very real dangers of extensive, permanent inundation. The largest of these projects required the organized efforts of thousands of laborers and taxed the ingenuity of surveyors and hydraulic engineers to overcome technical problems of considerable complexity. These projects also required determination on the part of provincial, municipal, and village governments, since tax abatements, condemnation rights, the alteration of trade routes, and the destruction of fishing grounds necessary to the prosecution of the schemes generated bitter conflicts.

The heroic character of the Dutch battle against the sea continues —even in the space age—to appeal to men's imagination, and Goethe's *Faust,* it may be recalled, found some resolution to a life of searching and striving by directing a vast land-reclamation project. Yet we must not be deceived about the motives behind land reclamation. The merchants and traders of Amsterdam and other cities who directed the numerous drainage projects of the early seventeenth century did not see their activities in the light of Faust's heroic grandeur. They were speculators. By 1600 the value of land had increased considerably; the prospect of uncovering soils well suited to the production of industrial crops enhanced the likely value of reclaimed land; techniques of arranging windmills in a multiple-pumping system made the projects feasible, as did the recent availability of a sizable proletarian labor supply. Finally, merchants, their coffers overflowing with profits from an expanding trade, actively sought new investment opportunities. The stage was set for investment in land reclamation projects.

The numerous lakes, large and small, that dotted the Noorderkwartier made that peninsula an enormous sponge and provided the setting for the major projects. The first of them, and the first to indicate that the government would pursue a policy encouraging such schemes, occurred in 1561 when Klaas Hendrikszoon of Alkmaar drained the Vroonmeer near his city. The first large project, the drainage of the Zijpe, an inundated coastal area, began in 1596. Over 3,000 workers and 1,000 horses labored on this project, which the Staten van Holland encouraged by granting exemptions from various taxes for periods of 5 to 20 years.[26]

The largest single project, the drainage of the Beemster lake, began in 1608. Some of the wealthiest merchants of Amsterdam joined Johan van Oldenbarnevelt, the ill-starred Grand Pensionary of Holland, to invest altogether 1,492,500 gulden in this project to create over 7,100 hectares of new land. In 1612, after having erected 43 windmills and having overcome unforeseen difficulties, the polder could be occupied. The speculative investment paid off handsomely:

almost immediately the 123 investors began receiving yearly rental payments totalling over a quarter million gulden, or an apparent annual rate of return of nearly 17 percent.[27]

In the 20 years after the successful drainage of the Beemster, wealthy capitalists in cities large and small eagerly invested in a succession of polders that transformed the waterlogged Noorder-kwartier into a well-drained agricultural district. In 1635 over 1.1 million gulden, mostly from Alkmaar, went into the Schermer polder,[28] and by 1647 the small Noordeindermeer's drainage marked the completion of the projects in this district.

The specialized construction teams that had gone from lake to lake now sought projects farther afield. The same group of men who drained the Noordeindermeer drummed up support for a drainage project in central Holland, where peat digging had created vast, shallow lakes. Under their direction the Wildevenen, an inundated area of 585 hectares, fell dry in 1655, and a few other exhausted peat bogs were similarly rehabilitated.[29] But the profitability of agricultural land fell after the middle of the century, slowing the pace of reclamation to a virtual standstill.

Before the reclamation boom ended, however, enormous sums of capital had added tens of thousands of hectares to the region, but most dramatically to the Noorderkwartier (see table 5.5).

TABLE 5.5.   Average Amount of Land Reclaimed
Yearly in the Netherlands, 1565–1714

Period	Hectares Per Year	Period	Hectares Per Year
1565–1589	317	1640–1664	1150
1590–1614	1431	1665–1689	487
1615–1639	1762	1690–1714	495

SOURCE: Blink, *Boerenstand*, 2:112–13.

A project often advocated but never attempted involved the drainage of the huge Haarlemmermeer, a lake covering 18,000 hectares in the triangle between Amsterdam, Haarlem, and Leiden. The arguments advanced in publications intended to gain support for the scheme give an illuminating glimpse into the nature of the rural society and the way that contemporaries viewed its functioning.

Anthonie de Hooch led a consortium that wished to drain the lake in 1617. His request stressed as benefits of the scheme the halt-

ing of further land erosion (for the lake increased its size contin-
ually), employment, and a larger tax base: "[the area will be
benefitted] in the first place by the demand, and repercussions from
it, for myriad amounts of laborers, i.e., husbandmen, dike workers,
engineers, surveyors, carpenters, masons, smiths, and other sorts of
people, who otherwise, for lack of work, leave in large numbers each
year for Flanders, Emderland [East Friesland], France, and elsewhere to seek work, to the detriment of the tax revenue and the
population of the land, besides the fact that the scarcity of land
causes many to go to other kingdoms to seek it, so that, as time
goes on, whole families leave to live elsewhere." [30]

The stress laid on emigration abroad was undoubtedly exag-
gerated, but movement to the cities, and the slackening of population growth in the countryside by this date, are confirmed by our
examination of population trends in chapter 3. In 1630 another
effort to stimulate interest in the scheme, which involved the noted
hydraulics engineer Jan Adriaenszoon Leeghwater, presented a more
detailed argument: at a cost of 3.6 million gulden Leeghwater
estimated the 18,000-hectare polder could be drained. It would set
thousands of dike laborers to work; 1,000 new farms would provide
farmers with the land they sorely needed; people from afar would
be attracted to the area; the drained land would provide large
amounts of butter, cheese, and livestock that could be exported
abroad; the sand needed for the project would come from the dune
lands and create fruitful land for farming there as well; consumption and production would expand.[31]

Finally, a proclamation encouraging drainage projects, printed
in the *Groot Placaatboek* at an unknown date in the seventeenth
century, urged further reclamation, "because the land and the cities
are notably more peopled and inhabited than thirty or forty years
ago, and also because some years ago people began cultivating the
land with notably larger amounts of cole, linseed, and other crops
than had been customary. Besides, year by year notably more oxen
are pastured such that one finds daily that the land in Holland, and
particularly in the Noorderkwartier, is much too scarce, which forces
various persons to seek in all quarters, in high and low, dry, wet and
uncultivated places, in order to transform wasteland at great cost
into good pasture and arable, which despite everything, because of
the great multitude of residents and husbandmen, is not enough to
set the people here in Holland to work and keep them in the coun-

try; thus we see from year to year that various husbandmen depart to France, England, Eastland, Groningen, and other areas to seek work and land." [32]

The drainage of the Haarlemmermeer waited until 1852, but the other projects, hundreds of them all together, added tens of thousands of hectares to the cultivable land of the region. The uniqueness of reclamation from the sea should not keep us from calling attention to the more traditional forms of land reclamation. Wasteland in all sections of the region was brought under cultivation, often in well-capitalized, large-scale projects. The sand-covered lands along the dune coast and in the interior district of het Gooi yielded up much new cultivable land as merchants stripped off the sand and transported it to the low-lying pasture lands where this commodity enjoyed a steady demand for embankment repair and construction projects. In 1625 a group of urban capitalists received permission to remove the sand and improve a waste area in het Gooi which became the new village of 's-Graveland. [33]

The reclamation along the dune coast between 1632 and 1654 is recorded in a special register. Nearly a thousand morgen of arable land were cleared of sand in this period in the string of villages between Haarlem and The Hague. [34]

All these efforts together, the largest of them financed by urban capitalists, greatly increased the cultivable area of the region. In Holland alone, the approximately 255,000 hectares that appear to have been improved and taxed in 1514, grew to 440,000 hectares at the time of the first cadastral survey in 1833. Of this increase, seas and lakes yielded almost half; the rest consisted of the improvement of wastelands and exhausted peat bogs. [35]

The Rural Population

Urban capitalists financed the most dramatic examples of investment in Dutch agriculture, but the more important work of improving the quality of existing land, protecting it from the constant threats of inundation, and endowing it with the buildings and equipment needed for increased productivity fell to the rural dwellers themselves.

A perennial problem of agriculture has been, and is yet, how capital investment can be made when possession and entrepreneurial decision making is divided between owner and renter and how projects requiring cooperation and compromise can be carried out in an economy of small, individual enterprises. Many an agrarian reform has floundered on the rocks of peasant individualism and tenant-owner conflict.

Rural society in the northern Netherlands enjoyed tenurial customs that permitted tenants to invest in the equipage of their farms (see chap. 1, p. 16); it also benefited enormously from the drainage boards, or waterschappen (see chap. 2, p. 28). These ancient institutions adapted successfully to the needs of a specializing agriculture and provided the framework in which the farmer—be he owner or tenant—could invest capital in land betterment without fear that the bulk of the benefits would accrue to others.

Traditionally, dike maintenance was an obligation divided among the villages that benefitted from it; they, in turn, divided their stretch of dike among the land users who were each made responsible for a specific segment. The waterschappen supervised this system and fined the negligent. Perhaps the most significant change in the operation of the drainage authorities at the local level was the replacement of this system with one of professional dike maintenance. The danger of neglect and the increased complexity of the dikes played a role in fostering this change, but its principal cause was the same as that which stimulated the farmers to engage in specialized agricultural production: by ceasing to work on the dikes themselves and paying a tax for the hired labor that took over the tasks, the farmers increased the amount of time they could devote to their farm operations. This substitution was part of a general economic change that commercialized agriculture and called into being a rural proletariat to labor at special tasks formerly performed by an undifferentiated peasantry. The shift did not occur all at once: in the early sixteenth century few examples of professional dike maintenance could be found; not until the beginning of the eighteenth century had it spread to all areas.

In 1493 the residents of Houtwoudingerambacht, in the Noorderkwartier, transformed their dike maintenance obligations into a purely financial obligation when they installed *dijkmeesters* to supervise the work.[36] Then this practice was still rare, but by the early seventeenth century its desirability became manifest to many through the example of the professional dike management employed on the newly drained polders. The experience of the new polders encouraged the regents of Westzaan to switch to communal dike maintenance in 1637,[37] and by 1649 the unified maintenance of the great encircling dike of West Friesland ensured the triumph of the new system.[38]

In mid-sixteenth-century Friesland the need to strengthen greatly the Vijfdeelen dike, which extended along the coast from Wonseradeel to het Bildt, provided the opportunity for initiating professional dike maintenance. Those who lived near the dike maintained it until 1574 when the provincial government assumed this responsibility. The government increased the basic land tax to finance its new obligation and immediately set 300 men to work under the Spanish soldier Caspar de Robles to strengthen this crucial bulwark.[39]

Not until 100 years later, in 1673, do we read of the professionalization movement gaining momentum in Friesland; in that year maintenance of Zuider Zee dikes was reorganized. By 1718 most of the Friesian dike system was communally maintained.[40] This gradual transformation of the dike maintenance burden into a financial one redirected enormous amounts of labor. The large, and growing, financial burden, on the other hand, placed a great pressure on the farmers to produce for the market. The scope of these dike maintenance activities was considerable and so impressed Sir William Temple, the British ambassador to the Dutch Republic, that he wrote in 1673: "The flatness of the land exposes it to the danger of the sea, and forces them to infinite charge in the continual fences and repairs of their banks to oppose it; which employ yearly more men, then all the corn of the province of Holland could maintain (as one of their chief Ministers had told me)." [41]

The communalization of dike maintenance was not the only change benefitting commercial agriculture. As noted above, the waterschappen provided a framework in which capital investment in land betterment could proceed. On the local level improving soil quality required the creation of a local improvement district—a polder. This entailed encircling a small area with a dike and building one or more windmills to pump water from the enclosed area. The cost of such schemes was considerable: a common 8-sided windmill cost 3,500 gulden to construct in 1574 and over 5,500 gulden by 1670;[42] the windmill operator, who resided in the structure, commanded a salary of about 100 gulden per year plus a supply of candles (since his responsibilities required frequent night work).

The villagers of Ter Aar impoldered their lands into three separate polders between 1570 and 1609. In the first of them, the

Noordeinde polder, land users paid a polder tax (above and beyond the morgengeld of the Hoogheemraadschap van Rijnland, of which they were a part) of 15 stuivers. The result of this large investment was evident in the village's Morgenboeken: that of 1568 described many fields as *leege weer*—empty lands; the term disappeared by 1600.[43]

The drainage conditions of the 6 villages of Waterland, north of Amsterdam, suffered from chronic storm floods in the late sixteenth century. After taking various unsatisfactory half-measures, the 6 villages agreed to a common drainage policy in 1649. Strengthened embankments and the construction of a number of windmills followed from this decision and thus enabled the area to specialize in commercial milk production for the Amsterdam market.[44]

These accounts of Ter Aar and Waterland are typical of village after village throughout the northern Netherlands. Thus, while polders were few in 1500, and many areas were protected only by the sea and river dikes of the larger drainage authorities, local polders and windmills to regulate drainage abounded by 1670. In fact, in Rijnland the "saturation point" had been reached.[45]

The nineteenth-century historian of Rijnland went to the trouble of describing each of the area's hundreds of polders, telling when they were created and how many windmills they had. His review shows that the resident farmers undertook an enormous investment program between 1590 and 1630.[46] Rather than labor at these tasks themselves, the farmers chose increasingly to hire others so that they might devote their labor to commercial agriculture. They paid increased local taxes to finance the raising of interior dikes, the construction of sluices and windmills, and the support of windmill operators, and they paid increased taxes to the hoogheemraadschappen to improve major sluices and sea and river dikes. We noted earlier that the tax imposed by the Hoogheemraadschap van Rijnland rose from 2 or 3 stuivers per morgen in the first half of the sixteenth century to at least 30 stuivers by 1650. This tenfold increase, far in excess of overall price increases, gives an indication of the raised standards of drainage maintenance that the rural population insisted upon—and paid for. Since rents also rose enormously in this period, we might be justified in observing that the returns to capital thus invested were high.

But, to end this story of improvement on a sour note, drainage expenditures could be a double-edged sword. After the mid-seventeenth century, when very few drainage improvements took place and the general price level declined, the expenditures of the drainage boards continued to increase. The expenditures of the Hoogheemraadschap van Rijnland, which stood at 87,000 guldens in 1675, rose to 104,000 in 1700 and 154,000 in 1725, before falling back to 110,000 in 1750.[47] In this period we cannot avoid the conclusion that rising expenditures reflected rising costs, which struck directly at the profitability of agriculture in the decades after 1680.

The investment in land was a necessary part of the effort to increase the intensity of land use. This, in turn, required further investments in buildings and equipment. The farm structures used in early sixteenth-century Friesland were the linear descendants of the oud Friese huis. These structures, as described in Friesian laws of the eleventh through fourteenth centuries, consisted of a one-room space for man and livestock, surrounded by wattle walls and decked with a reed roof resting on beams. Originally the fireplace was an open place on the floor, and smoke escaped through an open space in the roof. By the sixteenth century a living room-kitchen had been separated from the stalls, and during the century a milk room was often added as well.[48]

The average size of the medieval oud Friese huis appears to have been 9 vakken, or sections of about 2 meters each, which marked the crossbeam intervals and conveniently marked off each cow stall. A 9-vak house, thus, was about 18 meters long, by 8 meters wide, the standard width of this method of construction. Such a structure could neither offer much storage space for farm products nor house a large herd. By the mid-sixteenth century the need for more space had forced the farmers to elongate their houses somewhat. Farm inventories of Leeuwarderadel between 1566 and 1576 show the oud Friese huis to be universal. The average length was now 14 vakken. Almost half of the 27 buildings described in the inventories had separate milk rooms of 2 or 3 vakken, and many of the larger farms possessed a separate small building of 3 or 4 vakken.[49]

The process of elongation allowed the farmer to adapt the oud Friese huis to new requirements, but these structures continued to suffer from an intrinsic lack of storage space for bulky commodities. Beginning in the late sixteenth century Dutch farmers began experimenting with other architectural types. They needed a farm building capable of providing a larger amount of space so hay could be protected from the elements, larger herds could be stalled, and the household could live more comfortably. A number of different types evolved and spread, the most important being the North Holland stelp, the Friesian boerenhuis, and the Groninger *schuur*. Each of these types possessed lofty barns that brought hay storage into the structure and featured a large milk room and much more elaborate living quarters. From the one living room-kitchen of the oud Friese huis the farmer now moved into a suite of rooms, sometimes adorned with a parlor for special occasions and a "summer kitchen" on the cool side of the building to which the family retreated during the summer months. Besides spaciousness, which improved the standards of farm operations and reflected a growing scale of production, the new structures incorporated new construction materials that reflected an increased prosperity. Wattle and daub and thatching yielded to brick construction and tile roofs, at least over the living quarters.[50]

The new farm types can be traced back to the last decades of the sixteenth century. In Leeuwarderadeel, farm inventories from the period 1566–74 describe only the old style of structures. In 82 inventories preserved from the period 1583–92, however, we find 2 farms described in a novel way; they record the presence of a schuur, or barn.[51] Widespread construction of the new farm types began only in the early seventeenth century. In Holland, the reclamation projects of the period popularized the stelp (this style spread to Friesland in the wake of land reclamation projects financed by Hollanders);[52] in Groningen, the secularization of monastic lands in 1595 set the stage for adoption, in the decades thereafter, of farm types developed in Friesland.[53] The process of adoption can be observed in Leeuwarderadeel: in 1616–19, 9 of 33 farm inventories record the presence of a schuur; by 1634–41 the frequency had increased to 11 of 17.[54]

The new, larger farm buildings did not spread beyond the northern Netherlands. The eastern provinces of the Republic, which distinguished themselves in so many ways from the maritime region, continued to possess small, simple buildings in which man and beast shared the same space. These structures could accommodate much less produce, livestock, and equipment and afforded their inhabitants a minimum of comfort. They persisted in these districts throughout the seventeenth, eighteenth, and into the nineteenth centuries.[55]

The farmers financed the construction of the new, large farm-houses even when they leased the land. Tenurial customs typically reserved this expense to the lessee but stipulated that the owner, should he wish to end the tenure of the lessee, must first buy out the lessee's interest in the attached buildings. This arrangement, described in chapter 1, provided the tenant farmer with the security necessary to allow him to improve his farm, yet it gave the owner recourse should he be dissatisfied with his tenant.

The rebuilding of Dutch rural society took place on many levels and reflected both the profitability of agriculture and the fortunate institutional endowment of the region, which elicited large amounts of capital from the rural people themselves.

Fuel and Transportation

The rural economy benefitted from investments in fuel production and in transport facilities. Investment funds in these two fields, often linked together in single projects, came from virtually every segment of society.

The premier fuel of the region, for all purposes, was peat. Until the sixteenth century farmers dug most of the peat, and only an occasional heavy user, such as a brewer, attempted to organize peat digging on a permanent basis using hired labor. The principal areas of exploitation lay in the villages of Holland between the Ij and the Maas River.

The growth of Antwerp during the sixteenth century stimulated many rural dwellers in Holland to specialize in peat digging and transporting to supply the growing Brabant market. By the mid-sixteenth century concern about land destruction had prompted the Staten van Holland to levy a prohibitive duty on peat exports in an attempt, apparently unsuccessful, to stem its outward flow, which then totalled perhaps 4 million *tonnen* (of 350 pounds per *ton*) per year.[56]

The rapid growth of Holland's cities and of peat-using industries beginning in the 1570s reoriented the peat industry to domestic markets. But the demand had now attained a higher level of magnitude; systematic, large-scale production was needed to meet it. This required investment to bring under exploitation remote, virgin peat bogs.

Noblemen were the first to invest in massive peat-digging enterprises. In Groningen the Ewsum family, richest in the province,

began hiring laborers and digging canals in 1565. They had to sink
a considerable amount of capital into the project before returns
could be expected, so in 1572 they joined with a consortium of
Cologne capitalists in forming a company to continue the effort.
The company's periodic needs for increased capitalization gradually
reduced the size of the Ewsum's interest until 1584, when creditors
demanded the sale of Ewsum property and the company fell completely into the hands of the urban capitalists.[57]

A similar fate befell the Friesian hoofdelingen who initiated peat-
digging efforts in southeastern Friesland and the Utrecht noblemen
who, in the early seventeenth century, acquired Groningen monastic
lands and began exploitation of the vast peat bog later to be known
as the Veenkoloniën.[58] By the 1620s urban capitalists, mainly from
Holland, had full control of the peat-digging operations in Groningen and Friesland. The companies under their control dug
canals, established villages to house thousands of temporary laborers,
and shipped enormous quantities of peat to the cities of Holland.

Peat digging in Holland, while not under the control of companies, had become the province of specialists. In the 1530s peat
diggers developed new techniques that permitted the dredging of
peat from below the water table. From then on peat digging became both more carefully controlled and a more specialized under-
taking.

We have no overall peat output statistics, but fragmentary evidence suffices to impress us of its importance. In the Rijnland
village of Zegwaard, yearly production rose from 35–40,000 tonnen
in 1520–21 to 140–150,000 tonnen during the 1560s. Some 200 peat
diggers, 130 residents of the village, occupied themselves in the
Zegwaard peat bogs. Output continued to increase until 1632, when
371 peat diggers dug 250,000 tonnen. Thereafter, peat output in
Zegwaard declined; in the period 1680–1700 yearly production
hovered between 60,000 and 75,000 tonnen.[59]

But when the peat bogs of one village declined, others took their
place. In Stompwijk and Wilsveen, 195 peat diggers were active in
1650. Their output exceeded 150,000 tonnen. Oudshoorn, which
earlier forbade peat digging, lifted the ban in 1680, and by the end
of the century output approached 100,000 tonnen per year. By the
1740s, production stood at 3 times the 1700 level.[60] To gain a
sense of the importance of this industry to the rural economy, the
output of these villages must be multiplied by the dozens of villages

in central Holland which, at any given time, were active seats of the peat industry.

Everyone consumed peat, but the greatest demand was in the cities, where heavy fuel-using industries were located. The excise records of Leiden show the yearly consumption of peat to have risen from 450,000 tonnen in 1605–09 to 680,000 tonnen in 1660–64.[61] The *turfaccijn* of Haarlem for 1679 indicates a consumption of at least 300,000 tonnen, while the bleaching works located in the dunes outside Haarlem needed 120 to 150,000 tonnen per year in the mid-seventeenth century.[62]

Friesland's chief port, Harlingen, used more peat than all the other cities of the province combined, according to the chronicler Winsemius. Another chronicler, Schotanus, is more informative in explaining the city's appetite for peat. Brick and tile works, salt refineries, lime kilns, breweries, distilleries, and paper mills—all important fuel users—located here because peat shippers could readily find return cargoes at this distribution point for imported goods. As a result, freight rates to and from this port were lower, and the skippers' profits higher than to any other city in Friesland.[63]

Much more could be said about the peat industry of the region, but the foregoing should suffice to uphold the contention that peat had an impact on the economy that can be compared to the impact of coal in nineteenth-century Europe. An important benefit conferred by the coal industry upon the European economy was the heavy-duty transportation network constructed to move the bulky fuel. This network also served in the transportation of other commodities which, by themselves, could not have supported the new transport facilities. Similarly, the peat industry called into being a network of waterways with deep draft and capacious locks to move the fuel from often remote peat bogs to urban markets.

At strategic points on this network fuel-intensive industries flourished and at many other points, villages of skippers, barge workers, shipbuilders, sail makers, and saw millers formed. In effect, the transportation industry in many areas grew as a backward linkage of the peat industry. The result was an increasingly efficient transport network at the service of rural economic activities which, by themselves, could not have generated the transportation demand to stipulate the improvements in scale and technique that occurred at the behest of the peat industry.

Mile after mile of canal, particularly in Friesland and Groningen, was dug or improved to serve the peat industry; many more owed their construction to governmental and urban interests anxious to improve interurban and rural-urban communications.

When the Saxon dukes won control of Friesland in 1498, one of their first actions was to exhort the local grietmannen and urban patriciates to invest in canal improvements. The decades of anarchy that ended upon the accession of Duke George had witnessed the deterioration of what transport arteries there were, so the task in this province was doubly difficult. The *Charter-boek van Vriesland* records a spate of canal projects begun in the early sixteenth century. Monasteries, the provincial government, the cities, and the grietmannen all played a role in financing them.[64]

The extension of dikes and the drainage of bodies of water increased the need for artificial waterways and locks. For instance, the drainage of het Bildt in 1505 closed the sea route from Leeuwarden to Harlingen; the inland route, consisting of a collection of small, circuitous canals, needed to be replaced by a substantial, direct canal. This was done in 1507.[65]

Similar developments can be cited all over the region, but the construction of new arteries was often frustrated by the conflicting interests of rival cities. Particularly in Holland, where Haarlem, Gouda, and Dordrecht claimed special privileges over the internal canal routes, many projects could not be brought to fruition, and trade was often forced to follow traditional routes and use outmoded facilities.[66]

Virtually all traffic on the canal system consisted of private haulage. Before the 1580s, regular commercial services connected only a few important cities. Regular service between Amsterdam and Utrecht dated from the fourteenth century, and in 1529 Amsterdam-Hoorn service was begun.[67] Beginning in the 1580s a period of some 80 years ensued in which city after city established regular services, operated by guilds, while villages empowered boatmen with franchises to establish regularly scheduled services to market cities. By the mid-seventeenth century virtually every city was connected to every other city by at least a weekly sailing. Major routes enjoyed daily, and sometimes twice or thrice daily, schedules.

A traveler's handbook of 1689, the *Reisboek door de Vereenigde Nederlandsche Provinciën,* listed all regular services. As an example, Dordrecht offered the traveler or shipper weekly or twice weekly sailings to Gouda, Leiden, Geertruidenburg, Utrecht, Haarlem,

The Hague, Schoonhoven, Heusden, Breda, 's-Hertogenbosch, and Middelburg, plus a long list of villages. Daily service was offered to Rotterdam, Bergen op Zoom, Antwerp, and Gorinchem.[68]

Services that connected the villages with the cities were variously called *beurtvaarten, marktschepen,* or *damschuiten.* The growth of local boat (and wagon) service can be illustrated in the vicinity of Alkmaar. In 1607 the city paid two-thirds of the cost of a new road built to the nearby village of Oudorp. Later in the century new canals with towpaths were built from Alkmaar north to Schagen and the Zijpe polder, eastward to Hoorn, and south to Purmerend and Amsterdam.[69] In 1658 daily *snipschuit* (covered canal boat) service began operating between Alkmaar and Niedorp; the following year Opmeer acquired a similar service, and later Oudkarspel and Schagen were taken up in the growing net of daily services from Alkmaar.[70] In 1708 the chronicler Burger van Scoorl described the damschuiten routes serving the village of Schagen, north of Alkmaar: "There are three damschuiten which regularly make two trips per week to Amsterdam, Wednesday and Saturday, to deliver there and to bring back the goods at the service of the citizens. There are also two damschuiten which go to Haarlem every Wednesday. They bring back, especially, beer. There are also three damschuiten which travel every Friday to Alkmaar to bring cheese, cole, and other things and to bring back all manner of goods." Finally, the chronicler relates that 2 teamsters maintained a weekly service north to den Helder.[71]

In the sixteenth century the efforts to replace or improve the old canal system were motivated in large part by the inadequate size of existing canals and locks. For the seventeenth century there exists abundant evidence of a continued increase in the size of inland vessels. Beginning in 1637 the resolutions of the Groningen municipal government refer repeatedly to conflicts over locks in various parts of the region that were inadequate to accept Groningen's peat boats. The efforts to increase the size of the boats delivering peat from the Veenkoloniën to the city met the determined resistance of the peat transporters guild, but improvements were made nonetheless, and locks in the Veenkoloniën themselves required enlargement by the end of the century.[72] In most of Holland's cities, inland transportation workers belonged either to a *Grootbinnenlandvaarders-gilde* or a *Kleinbinnenlandvaardersgilde* (large or small inland transporters guild), depending on the size of their vessels. In Amsterdam in 1669 the former guild raised the minimum size of vessels whose owners were eligible for membership from 15 to 24 last.[73]

The culmination of the internal transportation "revolution" occurred in the 3 decades following 1630 when urban capitalists financed the construction of an extensive network of *trekvaarts*. A trekvaart was a canal, usually newly constructed and as straight as possible, equipped with a towpath. Access to these canals was limited, their main function being to provide a speedy through route for passengers. The first trekvaart, built in 1632, connected Amsterdam and Haarlem. Thereafter new canals, almost always financed by the cities connected, reached out from all the principal cities of the region.

These new arteries represented a sizable investment of capital. The Leiden-Woerden-Utrecht trekvaart, which consisted of a canalization of the Oude Rijn River, was typical of the numerous projects. This venture, financed by the 3 cities connected, required the construction of over 100 bridges for the towpath and cost 295,000 gulden, or 6,000 gulden per kilometer. The Haarlem-Leiden trekvaart cost twice as much per kilometer since it required the digging of an entirely new canal. Its total construction cost amounted to 354,000 gulden. In Friesland, the Leeuwarden-Harlingen route, finished in 1647, cost each city 52,000 gulden.[74] The magnitude of investment becomes apparent when one considers that at least 600 kilometers of trekvaart were constructed in the period 1632–65.

Map 5.1 shows the trekvaart routes and other major waterways of the seventeenth century. They formed a closely knit network in which virtually every town was enmeshed. The city of Groningen built trekvaarts to every corner of the province that it so completely dominated; they provided such a high standard of transportation service that even in the late nineteenth century a historian could write, "if there is one thing which the province, and above all the city, can boast of it is her canals. The rise and prosperity of the city and province must be ascribed even into our day to the digging of the waterways through which both agriculture (by the promotion of improvements and drainage) and trade and shipping (through the opening of new routes) were remarkably encouraged." [75] When we read in the travel manual of 1687 that the city of Groningen

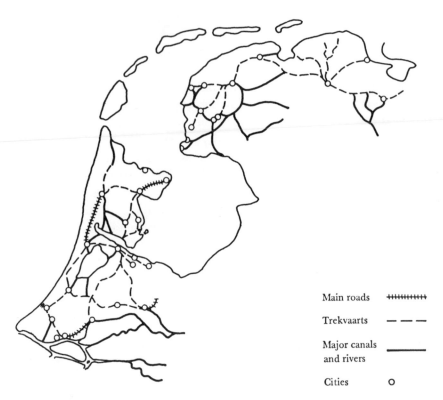

Map 5.1. Internal Waterways in the Netherlands, c. 1660.

Main roads	++++++++++
Trekvaarts	— — —
Major canals and rivers	———
Cities	o

was daily connected with the Friesian border by 4 departures, with Delfzijl by 4, and with 4 other rural districts by 1 boat each, we can understand this enthusiasm.

In the more densely populated provinces of the region, the frequency of service greatly exceeded that provided in Groningen. In neighboring Friesland 4 *trekschuiten* per day left Leeuwarden on each of 4 routes, destined for Franeker-Harlingen, Bolsward-Workum, Dokkum (and on to Groningen), and Sneek. Five daily sailings connected a variety of Friesian cities with Enkhuizen and Amsterdam in Holland.

Within Holland, the frequency of canal boat service on the trekvaarts was probably unique in all of Europe. Amsterdam was connected with Haarlem, Hoorn, and Zaandam with hourly service from sunup to sundown. Between Haarlem and Leiden 10 boats and between Leiden and The Hague 9 boats operated each way daily. Between The Hague and Delft service was twice hourly, and between Delft and Rotterdam hourly.[76]

On most routes the peak passenger volume was attained in the 1660s. Then, the Haarlem-Amsterdam route handled 300,000 passengers per year, the Haarlem-Leiden route 130,000, and the Leiden-Delft route 170,000. Leiden and Amsterdam were also connected by overnight "sleeping barges" that carried 12,000 passengers per year.[77] The volume of shipping connecting the cities with the countryside can be judged from a reckoning, made in the mid-eighteenth century, that from Amsterdam alone 800 boats departed each week plying regular beurtvaart routes that connected that city with over 180 cities and villages.[78]

This system of intercity and urban-rural canal services arose between the end of the sixteenth and the mid-seventeenth centuries. It so increased the efficiency of internal transportation that the rates charged apparently increased much less than the general price level. Few sixteenth-century data are available to chart the precise course of transportation rates; we do know, however, that the Haarlem-Amsterdam and Haarlem-Leiden freight tariffs were stable between 1598 and 1632 and rose very little thereafter. Passenger tariffs between Haarlem and Amsterdam increased only 20 percent between 1520 and 1713, while the general price level more than quadrupled.[79]

The advantages conferred on the Dutch economy by this extensive, efficient transportation system were not lost on contemporaries. Sir William Temple, the astute English ambassador to the Republic, noted in 1673 that "one horse shall draw in a boat more than [what] fifty can do by cart, whereas carriage makes a great part of the price in all heavy commodities." Temple also cited another advantage of efficient transportation that strikes a very modern chord: "By this easy way of travelling [the Dutch canals] an industrious man loses no time from his business, for he writes, or eats, or sleeps while he goes; whereas the time of labouring or industrious men is the greatest native commodity of any country." [80]

The State

In most of Europe during our period the impact of the State on the rural society can be simply said: the State taxed the rural people. The revenues raised in the rural areas flowed to the seat of power, where it maintained the functions of government and supported the court. Ecclesiastical organization reinforced this pattern; church revenues, before the Reformation, tended to flow from the country-side to the seats of bishops, and to Rome. Neither the State nor the Church was a conspicuous investor in the rural sector.

In the northern Netherlands the situation was little different. Here, in the seventeenth century, the tax burden was probably heavier than anywhere else in Europe, and despite the presence of large prosperous cities, much of the burden fell on the users of land.[81] In the most urbanized province, Holland, the principal tax was the Verponding. It was levied as a percentage of the rental value of all real property. This tax was reassessed in 1632 when, according to graph 5.6, rents were approaching a historic high. In the century after 1650 the Verponding pressed ever more heavily on the agricultural sector (as prices fell while the tax remained fixed at its 1632 level). Demands for reassessment were assented to only in 1732—and then only houses were reassessed; the land tax remained as of old.[82]

In 1695 Gregory King, the English national income accountant, calculated the per capita total tax burden to be 61 shillings 6 pence in the United Provinces and only 24 or 25 shillings in France and England.[83] The high level of taxation in the northern Netherlands, together with the previously discussed drainage taxes, undoubtedly encouraged the commercialization of agriculture. The option of engaging in self-sufficient husbandry was closed in a society where tax collectors yearly demanded enormous sums of cash. But the fact remains that, except for the drainage taxes, the rural sector got little in return for these extraordinary tax payments.

A more positive encouragement to the rural sector emanated from the State when, during the Revolution, the provincial governments confiscated monastic lands and dedicated their revenues *ad pios usus.* The parish lands were dedicated to the maintenance of the new Reformed clergy. The Catholic clergy had been unable to live from their landed income. To fill the gap they demanded payment for the performance of such official functions as baptism, marriage, and burial, and over the years they elaborated a complex set of customs that required payments to the clergy.[84] The aim of the Reformed Church was to support the new clergy on the land dedicated to that purpose, and to accomplish that aim they consolidated parishes and radically reduced the size of the religious staff.[85]

The most important change came in the dedication of church revenue to education and charity. Before the Reformation, the

Catholic clergy had conducted schools and, of course, charity was no Protestant invention. But the new administration of lands distinguished itself by both energy and efficiency. In the decades after the Reformation, village schools arose everywhere, 5 universities were founded, and the care of orphans, the aged, and the sick was greatly expanded.

In 1574 the synod of Dort proclaimed that all classes of the Reformed Church should urge the establishment of schools in every place in Holland. In Friesland the provincial Staten resolved in 1584 that "the incomes of the former monasteries are designated for the establishment of a university, seminary, or college, and further, to the increased construction of hospitals, poorhouses, orphanages, and others, in both the cities and the countryside." [86] Local histories almost invariably record the installation of the first schoolmaster with or shortly after the entry of the first Reformed minister.

We need entertain no illusions about the preparation of these newly installed schoolmasters. In 1591 Valcoogh, the schoolmaster of Barsinghoorn, wrote a handbook for teachers in which he complained of the clumsiness and stupidity of teachers who can "barely write a name, and [who] sing a psalm offensively." [87] Nevertheless, in the mid-seventeenth century the Church had constructed an impressive educational establishment in both city and country. At that date the 5 universities of the Republic, 4 in the region under discussion, employed 77 professors and enrolled about 600 entering students per year.[88] Ten *gymnasiën* and 62 Latin schools provided advanced instruction in virtually all cities. In Friesland, the state provided scholarships for orphans to both the university and the "triviale" schools that were located in each city and grietenij.

At the base of the school system lay the common schools, what Schotanus, a professor at the University of Franeker, called "the foundation of the Republic and the Church." He went on to boast, in 1667, that all the villages of Friesland, "are adorned with small schools for educating the children in reading, writing and reckoning and the catechism." [89] The truth of his statement is confirmed a century later when the occupational census showed teachers residing in the vast majority of villages; over all, there was 1 for every 401 rural inhabitants.[90]

This investment in basic education should be reflected in literacy statistics. Unfortunately, little is known about literacy in the countryside until the agricultural survey of 1800. Then the response to the question "are there many among the country folk who cannot read or write?" was overwhelmingly negative.[91] But as early as 1566, before the Reformation in the Netherlands, the Italian observer Guicciardini remarked of the Low Countries that "the common people have mostly a beginning knowledge of grammar and just about all of them, yes, even the farmers and country folk, know at least reading and writing." [92] The only statistics available are based on signatures of brides and grooms in the marriage registers of Amsterdam. Those who could sign their own names were defined as literate. In 1660 the literacy rate of grooms with the occupation of seafarer born abroad was 41 percent, of those born in Amsterdam it was 55 percent, and of those born in smaller cities and on the countryside, 59 percent were literate.[93]

TABLE 5.6.   Literacy of Brides and Grooms
in Amsterdam, 1630–1780
(In percentages)

Year	Grooms Literate	Brides Literate
1630	57	32
1660	64	37
1680	70	44
1730	76	51
1780	85	64

SOURCE: S. Hart, "Enige statistische gegevens inzake analfabetisme," p. 4.

As for welfare and charity, here too the energetic administration of former church lands provided a level of services in both the city and the country that has often been remarked upon by foreigners. One of the most impressed observers was the Englishman William Carr, who in 1693 insisted that there was "not a soul born in the States dominions that want warm clothing and dyet and good lodgings if they make their case known to the magestrates." The wretched people Carr saw daily on the streets did not dissuade him of this opinion. "And for the Vagabonds that rove up and down the streets," he said, "they are either Walloons or other strangers as pretend to have been ruined by the late Wars." [94]

The record of expenditure of the administration of the Friesian monastic lands, recorded for 1618 by Winsemius, give a more accurate impression of the impact of such expenditures on the welfare of society. Of the amounts whose purposes can be ascertained, fl. 10,691 went to pay pensions to the deposed Catholic clergy (that is, to such as "acknowledged their concubines and married them");[95] fl. 15,410 went to the support of the University and Latin schools and to the provision of 124 student scholarships; fl. 8,780 supplemented local support of schoolmasters and ministers; fl. 1,981 went for interest payments and expenses; fl. 6,795 went to poorhouse administration.[96]

Urban capitalists and the State, through landownership and taxation, drained large sums of money from the rural sector to the cities, there to be dispersed in support of various activities of no concern to the country folk. But from the time of the Revolution on, urban capitalists began investing in the rural sector on a large scale, and the reform of the Church liberated vast resources for social purposes in both city and country. The mid-seventeenth-century investment in trekvaarts easily surpassed 3 million gulden; the capital invested between 1590 and 1650 in the drainage projects of the Noorderkwartier alone totalled at least 10 million gulden. These sums compare favorably with the capitalization of the East and West India Companies combined.[97] By the early seventeenth century the monastic lands yearly yielded several hundred thousand gulden for the support of education, health, and welfare. At the same time, farmers through the unique drainage authorities of the region were taxing themselves hundreds of thousands of gulden yearly to improve the quality of their soil and were everywhere rebuilding their dwellings and farm structures on new, more spacious, and sturdier lines.

The great period of investment ended by the mid-seventeenth century. Thereafter the monastic lands were gradually sold off to raise funds for general revenues; the falling profitability of land reclamation schemes discouraged urban investors, and the rising seas and increased incidence of timber rot in the early eighteenth century sent dike taxes skyrocketing simply to defend earlier gains. But the 60 or 70 years of vigorous investment endowed the rural society with productive capital resources of lasting value.

6. Characteristics of the New Rural Sector

The rural sector of the northern Netherlands developed in a setting of vigorous urban expansion. The upsurge of population, the explosive growth of foreign trade and shipping, and the spirited development of domestic industry all imposed unprecedented demands on the rural economy. Manpower, foodstuffs, fuel, and export crops all had to be sent forth in much increased quantities if the rural sector was not to impede urban economic expansion. To the modern student of economic development this situation is none other than the typical problem that faces currently developing countries: how can the traditional agrarian sector be made (permitted, induced, forced) to contribute to the growth of the modern industrial sector, and, in particular, how can its elasticity of supply be increased?

Judgments on the importance of agriculture in economic development and nostrums for an "unresponsive" traditional rural sector are as many as there are economists. Without the quantitative data to test our deductions, we can, nevertheless, conclude from our study that the rural sector in the northern Netherlands responded very satisfactorily to its new opportunities. A historical legacy of institutions and customs endowed the region with an adaptive capacity that insured an elastic supply response for a wide variety of productive factors and products needed by the growing cities. Trade provided the remaining needs of the economy. Here, too, the rural sector showed itself capable of adapting to exploit these new opportunities.

The overall transformation of the rural sector substantially follows the course of events outlined in the "specialization model" introduced in chapter 1. The high supply-elasticity common to both the theoretical model and the example of the northern Netherlands could occur primarily because of the development of household specialization. Household specialization produced another result of equal importance to economic growth which we have yet to discuss in full detail: the elasticity of *demand* for many products increased as the household became less self-sufficient.

Each economic unit consumes as well as produces. The impact of demand on the development of manufacturing and commerce depends upon the degree of household specialization, the distribution of income, and the tastes of consumers. Obviously, it makes a difference whether the purchasing power of a commercial agricultural society is concentrated in the hands of a small noble class possessed of a strong urge toward conspicuous consumption or is distributed evenly over a large number of independent farmers inclined to buy such commodities as textiles, ironware, and building materials. Both these examples contrast with a rural population that buys virtually nothing because nothing it might want is available on the market.

How did the farm population in the seventeenth century dispose of its income? What impact did their expenditures have on the rest of the economy? We can hope to answer these questions with the aid of notarized inventories drawn at the death of farmers. These leave us an intriguing and detailed account of their possessions, assets, and debts, as well as information about farm operations. (Farm inventory data on this last subject were introduced in chapter 4.)

The attraction of inventory analysis lies in its promise to divulge detailed, factual information about common people in an era when other sources remain silent, but we must be mindful of its limitations. We possess notarized inventories only of households of some substance; most farmers enjoyed the stature that required such inventories, but the poorest classes do not appear in the records. In most rural places notary records date back to the late seventeenth century; records of the early seventeenth century are few, and for the late sixteenth century they are rare indeed. The exhaustiveness of the inventories—they list every spoon and thimble—together with the eccentricities of local notarial customs pose the problem of presenting hundreds of separate categories of goods in statistical form. This problem is virtually insurmountable for the most crucial consumer goods, textiles and clothing.

Our analysis rests on a collection of 640 inventories drawn between 1550 and 1750.[1] The inventories of farm households were divided into wealth classes based upon the size of a farmer's cattle herd: under 10 or 10 and over. For each district and each wealth class I noted the presence or number of certain possessions. The most plentiful notarial records, and the only records dating from before the mid-seventeenth century, were found in the Weesboeken (orphan books) of the Friesian grietenijen. Those of Hennaarderadeel go back to 1550 and those of Leeuwarderadeel to 1566. Here we can make comparisons between the inventories of an early period and those of the later seventeenth century; elsewhere we must content ourselves with observations of a single period. Even these, however, should impart to the reader a "feeling" for the physical conditions in which the rural population lived.

In the kitchens the notaries found a wide variety of copper, iron, and tinware. Dishes, in the sixteenth century, were made of wood, for the most part. During the seventeenth century tin plates appear in the inventories with increasing frequency in well-to-do households until the end of the century, when porcelain, especially delftware, suddenly appears and rapidly attains an enormous popularity. Glassware is occasionally observed in the 1590s but households rarely have more than a few glasses and bottles until late in the following century. Tin spoons were the main eating utensil. The average Friesian household in the 1570s possessed no more than 12; by the mid-seventeenth century the average rose to 20.

In the milk house the utensils necessary to the dairy enterprise— pails, troughs, churns, cheese presses, and kettles—exhibited a rather high metal content. Copper and tin were particularly widespread. In the mid-seventeenth century the farmers around Woerden possessed an average of 6.5 milk pails, those in Hennaarderadeel possessed 6.8, each of which contained at least metal bindings. As the century progressed, pails made entirely of metal became common.

The most costly pieces of farm equipment, wagons and boats, became more numerous in the course of the seventeenth century. It is tempting to suppose that this reflects more frequent marketing and a growing scale of farm operations. Increased wagon and boat ownership is the more impressive when one recalls that at the same time there grew to importance a professional transport industry, which surely took over many of the functions formerly performed by the farmers themselves.

The furnishings of the farmhouse rarely consisted of more than 2 tables or fewer than 10 chairs and benches. In the course of the seventeenth century a marked increase in the variety and luxury of furniture can be observed. The large oak chests, characteristic of Dutch interior scenes, became common after the mid-seventeenth century. Eight-sided tables, curtains, and carpets are more frequently encountered at the same time, although the last mentioned were observed only in farmhouses near the large cities of Holland. Less re-

TABLE 6.1. Wagon Ownership per Farm Household, 1550–1702

	Period							
Region	1550–62	1566–74	1583–99	1602–19	1616–41	1646–55	1677–86	1676–1702
Hennaarderadeel	0.6	—	—	—	—	1.4	—	—
Leeuwarderadeel NT[a]	—	1.4	1.3	—	1.0	—	2.2	—
Leeuwarderadeel ST[b]	—	0.6	0.8	—	1.4	—	1.8	—
Idaarderadeel	—	—	—	0.6	—	—	—	1.3
Barradeel	—	—	—	—	—	3.1	—	3.1
Woerden	—	—	—	—	—	2.2	—	—
Ronde Venen	—	—	—	—	—	—	—[c]	—

SOURCES: See note 1 for this chapter.
[a] NT refers to Noordertrimdeel, the northern half of Leeuwarderadeel.
[b] ST refers to Zuidertrimdeel, the southern half of Leeuwarderadeel.
[c] Negligible.

TABLE 6.2. Boat Ownership per Farm Household, 1550–1702

	Period							
Region	1550–62	1566–74	1583–99	1602–19	1616–41	1646–55	1677–86	1676–1702
Hennaarderadeel	0.81	—	—	—	—	0.80	—	—
Leeuwarderadeel NT[a]	—	0.33	0.36	—	0.34	—	0.36	—
Leeuwarderadeel ST[b]	—	0.50	0.63	—	0.50	—	0.94	—
Idaarderadeel	—	—	—	0.33	—	—	—	1.31
Barradeel	—	—	—	—	—	0.15	—	0.25
Woerden	—	—	—	—	—	—[c]	—	—
Ronde Venen	—	—	—	—	—	—	2.10	—

SOURCES: See note 1 for this chapter.
[a] NT refers to Noordertrimdeel, the northern half of Leeuwarderadeel.
[b] ST refers to Zuidertrimdeel, the southern half of Leewarderadeel.
[c] Negligible.

fined tastes continued to characterize the farmers of more remote Friesland.

Beds were the most expensive items of furniture; indeed, their costliness caused contemporaries to regard them as one of the most important indicators of a man's status. To us their interest is enhanced by the relation they bear to the size of the rural household. Table 6.3 shows clearly that the number of beds in a household was strongly associated with wealth—poorer households were smaller— and that in all wealth classes, the number of beds per house fell after

TABLE 6.3.   Number of Beds per Household, According
to Wealth Class, 1550–1750

| | | Wealth Class Measured in Size of Cattle Herd | | | |
| | | 10 and over | Under 10 | None | Total |
Region	Period				
Hennaarderadeel	1550–62	6.1	4.6	—	5.3
Leeuwarderadeel	1566–74	5.9	4.9	—	5.5
Leeuwarderadeel	1583–99	5.2	4.0	2.5	4.4
Hennaarderadeel	1595–1600	5.4	4.3	3.0	5.0
Leeuwarderadeel and Wonseradeel	1616–41	6.0	3.8	2.7	4.7
Hennaarderadeel	1646–54	6.2	3.8	3.7	5.1
Leeuwarderadeel	1677–86	4.5	3.4	—	3.9
Idaarderadeel	1676–1702	4.3	2.3	1.3	3.3
Leeuwarderadeel	1711–50	4.6	3.4	2.8	3.8

SOURCES: See note 1 for this chapter.

1650. It would seem difficult to avoid the conclusion that household size declined in the course of the century.

Clocks, porcelain, mirrors, paintings, and books, all of which were scarce or unknown in the sixteenth-century farmhouse, became increasingly common during the seventeenth century. The new acquisitions of the greatest importance, however, were items of silver and gold—buckles, beakers, buttons, spoons, and head ornaments. Possession of luxury articles was the hallmark of the prosperous farmer. In the early seventeenth century the typical Dutch peasant costume—that is, a somber suit festooned with silver buttons and buckles and, for the women, silver or gold head decoration—is first recorded in the inventories. By the end of the century large farmers inevitably possessed these items. Instead of a few silver spoons or a few silver buttons, a prosperous farmer such as Cornelis Pieterse de Lange of Alphen, who died in 1692, owned rings, trinkets, 3 earrings, 4 spoons, several hair brooches, 2 knives, and 69 buttons, all of silver. Claes Spr;onge of Hogeveen died in the same year leaving behind 2 gold and 7 silver buttons, a medallion and chain, 3 keys, 2 knives, 3 spoons and several boxes, all of silver, plus 3 rings, earrings, and other ornaments of gold. Such men were not typical, but neither were they rare. The significance of their possessions becomes apparent when we note that a gold *oorijzer,* a women's head ornament, was valued at fl. 60, and that 8 silver spoons alone were worth fl. 28.10, or the cost of a year's supply of rye for 2 persons in the mid-seventeenth century. Such an assortment of silver and gold would have been highly unusual in a farm population 70 years previous (see table 6.4).

TABLE 6.4. Percentage of Rural Households Possessing
Certain Consumer Goods, 1550–1750

Region	Period	Number of Inventories[a]	Books	Clocks	Mirrors	Silver
Hennaarderadeel	1550–62	42	9.5	0	9.5	23.7
Leeuwarderadeel	1566–74	40	2.5	0	7.5	2.5
Leeuwarderadeel	1583–99	64	3.1	0	18.7	14.6
Idaarderadeel	1611–23	20	5.0	0	15.0	—
Leeuwarderadeel and Wonseradeel	1616–41	83	29.0	0	53.0	36.0
Hennaarderadeel	1646–54	40	22.5	0	95.0	67.5
Barradeel	1651–61	21	38.0	0	—	38.0
Woerden area	1651–61	21	10.0	0	38.0	33.0
Leeuwarderadeel	1677–86	50	32.0	2.0	86.0	46.0
Idaarderadeel	1676–1702	26	19.0	—	46.0	31.0
Barradeel	1679–92	15	53.0	—	—	53.0
Leeuwarderadeel	1711–50	49	55.7	70.5	94.0	63.2

SOURCES: See note 1 for this chapter.
[a] Occasionally, omissions in the sources require that certain inventories be excluded in the calculation of the above averages.

Even in Friesland, remote from the cultural centers of Holland, the urban culture's tastes spread to the farm population. The presence of obviously urban cultural artifacts such as curtains, clocks, books, and, occasionally, paintings testified to the (at least partial) dismantling of the age-old barriers preventing the transmission of values and ideas from city to country. The inventories show that the legendary Dutch farmer, his walls covered with valuable paintings, was, in fact, no legend.

Cornelis Jacobs Maals, who died in Alphen in 1692, left 16 paintings, a mirror, a cloth fireplace-covering, curtains, a variety of decorative tiles, and an eight-sided table. Most farmers had only a few paintings, if they had any, but painted planks, wall hangings, and decorative porcelain were ubiquitous in the late-seventeenth-century farmhouse. By way of comparison, we can point to the 243 inventories of both farmers and townsfolk in Essex, England, drawn between 1633 and 1749. Of that number only 32 had silver of any sort (usually confined to spoons), and only 5 had books, pictures, or maps in their homes. Of the 166 Bedfordshire inventories compiled in 1617–19, 6 households, 3 of which were gentry, owned silver spoons (the only type of silver object) and only 7 percent, half of which were either clergy or gentlemen, possessed books of any kind.[2]

In the course of the seventeenth century, farmers, as their incomes increased, purchased more farm equipment, more elaborate home furnishings, and greater stocks of gold and silver objects. We have yet to consider demand for the most important industrial products of all: textiles. The textile industry was easily the largest in any preindustrial economy. Its importance in the early phases of the Industrial Revolution makes the nature of demand for textile products of great interest to us.

The inventories of the period 1583–99 show textiles of all sorts— bedding, linens, and clothing—valued at over half the total value of movable property excluding livestock. Textiles made up a large portion of total consumption, but the inventories for later periods do not display any overall increase in the quantity of textile consumption. The number of shirts found in inventories of substantial peasants rose dramatically in the early seventeenth century, and the increased frequency of formal costumes decorated with silver buttons tended to enlarge the size of wardrobes, but against these upward trends we must set the reduced demand for bedding. The decline in bed ownership stands behind this trend, as table 6.5 makes clear. In sum, the value of textiles of all sorts made up a steadily falling percentage of the total value of movable property during the period 1583–1750.[3]

The inventories display a noteworthy distinction between the ownership of linens and of woolens. Households possessed the former to the point of superfluity while the latter, even in the homes of the well-to-do, were present only in sober quantities. The average farmer of seventeenth-century Friesland could choose each morning from over a dozen shirts while, in the mid-seventeenth century, his linen chests were laden with nearly 40 bedsheets, 4 handcloths, 6 table- cloths, and a dozen table napkins. Woolens, on the other hand, were scarce. Substantial farmers rarely owned as many as 2 blankets per bed, while lesser folk often owned no more than 1 blanket per bed. Trousers, skirts, and overcoats came in such a bewildering variety of forms that I could devise no satisfactory aggregation, but many households owned only 1 set of woolen clothing (and 1 pair of shoes)

TABLE 6.5.   Textile Holdings of Farm Households Owning
Ten or More Milk Cows, 1550–1750

		Woolens			Linens				
		Blankets		Men's	Bedsheets			Shirts	
Region	Period	To-tal	Per bed	waist-coats	To-tal	Per bed	Table-cloths	Male	Fe-male
Hennaarderadeel	1550–62	11.6	1.9	(1.9)	43.1	7.1	6.5	(5.3)	(4.5)
Leeuwarderadeel	1566–74	11.6	2.0	—	34.3	5.9	6.5	(6.8)	(4.0)
Leeuwarderadeel	1583–99	9.9	1.9	(1.3)	24.2	4.7	5.7	7.0	(3.1)
Hennaarderadeel	1595–1600	12.7	2.3	(1.4)	28.3	5.2	—	7.0	8.0
Leeuwarderadeel and Wonseradeel	1616–41	11.5	1.9	(1.6)	37.4	6.2	6.2	11.9	(10.1)
Hennaarderadeel	1646–54	12.0	1.9	(1.3)	45.6	7.4	6.6	16.6	11.6
Leeuwarderadeel	1677–86	8.1	1.8	1.6	31.6	7.0	3.9	18.3	(18.2)
Leeuwarderadeel	1711–50	8.8	1.9	2.6	30.6	6.7	3.1	14.3	12.3

SOURCES: See note 1 for this chapter.
NOTE: Statistics in parentheses are based on less than half the total number of available inventories.

per person. Wealthy farmers often owned no more than 1 everyday outfit and 1 fancy outfit (with the silver buttons).

The compulsion to accumulate linens that characterizes the farmers—or rather their wives—is shown in the inventory of a widow, Anna Nannige Beverwijk, who died in 1698 in the village of Lisse. Her prosperity is indicated by the possession not only of silver but of a considerable quantity of gold objects. In a house with 3 beds, she saw fit to amass 48 bedsheets and 53 pillowcases; she adorned her tables with 20 tablecloths and 61 table napkins. Lest one dismiss Anna's possessions as eccentric, we cite the inventory of Michael Corneliszoon, an Oudshoorn farmer who died in 1669. His 12-morgen farm, on which he kept 7 milk cows, rank him with the less affluent. His wife, nonetheless, equipped the 3 beds with 66 linen sheets and 55 pillowcases—but only 7 blankets. Or consider Jan Cornelis Schenckerck, an Oudshoorn farmer who died in 1700. He owned 14 morgen and rented some more, on which he raised 17 milk cows. This prosperous farmer, with 3 books and 8 paintings in his house, owned 29 bedsheets, 7 tablecloths, 18 table napkins, and 11 shirts; his wife owned 14 shirts. The household's woolens consisted of 10 blankets, 4 skirts, 3 trousers, 3 pair of socks, and 1 good suit with silver buttons.

Linens were not cheap. In the 1630s notaries valued bedsheets at fl. 1.10 apiece and woolen blankets at no more than twice that amount, fl. 3., apiece. Why then do we observe this persistent dichotomy between the consumption of linens and woolens? Moreover, woolens were becoming cheaper. Throughout the seventeenth century the prices of woolen cloth fell relative to most agricultural products (see graphs 5.1 and 5.5). Why then did consumption not increase? We can only conclude that the demand for woolen textiles was highly inelastic. Rather, the farmers displayed a preference for articles of "conspicuous consumption."

Eric Hobsbawm, in his stimulating essay on the crisis of the seventeenth century, insists that a failure of demand accounted for a large part of the economic frustration of the period. The enrichment of the peasant sector could not support industrial growth, according to Hobsbawm, because peasant wants were traditional: increased income was plowed into land, cattle, hoards, weddings, and funerals. The demand patterns of the Dutch peasants were anything but traditional and unchanging. On the contrary, a wide assortment of new goods, many of them goods that reflect the influence of urban culture, came into vogue. Yet, ironically, hardly any of the new goods could form the basis for modern industries. It appears to be true that rural demand patterns failed to provide markets for important industrial products (porcelain is a notable exception). But this failure cannot be accounted for by a stubborn peasant traditionalism. On the contrary, peasant consumption habits underwent profound changes, but not in the "right" direction.

The inventories often recorded, besides the movable goods, the investments, debts, and cash holdings of the deceased. In the late seventeenth century 47 farmers in Utrecht and Holland left cash holdings averaging 310 gulden each. The cash holdings of Friesian farm households in 1711–23 averaged 289 gulden, or 21 percent of the value of their movable property. Sixteenth-century inventories, on the other hand, record cash holdings that fluctuated between 3 and 8.5 percent of the value of movable property.[4] When one adds to these holdings the value of silver and gold objects, which also rose during the seventeenth century, the increased propensity to hoard wealth becomes clear. This characteristic could hardly fail to affect aggregate demand.

Some farmers invested outside the agricultural sector. A 1638 tax document of the Noorderkwartier village of Opmeer shows that 12 of the 37 farmers owned shares, usually one thirty-second or one-sixteenth, of ships and fishing boats.[5] The inventories record such investments only for farmers in Holland. The Friesians appear to have been innocent of such shares but did occasionally purchase securities.

The inventories more commonly record a tangle of debt and credit between farmers, cattle buyers, village tradesmen, craftsmen, and urban merchants. The ownership of scattered houses and parcels of land, an extension of credit to another villager, a dowry settlement, a debt to a boatwright—these are the financial transactions that bound together virtually all the subjects of our inventories. In Leeuwarderadeel, 22 inventories that gave a complete account of outstanding debts and credits in 1583–99 showed an average debt of 504 gulden and an average credit of 375 gulden (10 of the 22 were in net debt). Eleven Woerden-vicinity inventories for the period 1651–1662 showed an average debt of 1,950 gulden and average credit of 1,280 (only 3 of the 11 were in net debt).

The large sums lent by villagers to each other indicate the substantial financial resources of the rural communities. Cornelis Adriansz. of Niedorp, who died in 1664, left debts that included a loan of 2,000 gulden from a skipper residing in Winkel at 3.15 percent, 300 gulden from a shoemaker in Niedorp at 3.5 percent, 200 gulden from a smith in Oud Niedorp at 4 percent, and 101 gulden from a village farmer at 4 percent. The financial interests of Cornelis Jacobs Maals, who died in Alphen in 1692, included a 270 gulden investment in a lumbership, two *rentebrieven* representing loans of 800 gulden at 3.5 percent and 150 gulden at 4 percent interest, and a provincial government bond valued at 1,000 gulden.

The inventories also record the farmers' numerous petty debts. These are of interest because of the modern image they evoke. Twentieth-century man can empathize with a farmer leaving dozens of small debts to every manner of creditor. Such a situation, moreover, reflects the presence of a thoroughly commercialized rural economy. Consider Claas Spronge of Hogeveen. When he died in 1692, he left fl. 274 in cash, credits totaling fl. 116.17 with people who had bought butter from him, and the following debts: for a year's rental of his land, fl. 293; school costs, fl. 15.13; brewer, fl. 16.4; manure and salt, fl. 7.10; boat repair, fl. 1.12 and fl. 0.12; butcher, fl. 2.13;

baker, fl. 25.14; cabinetmaker, fl. 7.0; doctor, fl. 5.14; and, of course, the grave digger, fl. 8.2. In all, he owed fl. 383.14.

An Utrecht farmer in 1685 left unpaid debts with a lumber merchant, an Amsterdam carpenter who had made him a new chair, the baker, wine merchant, smith, weaver, brewer, shoemaker, carpenter, and a variety of day laborers. Surveying all these petty debts we can conclude that they were most frequently for provisions, including bread, which was rarely baked at home; the next most frequently encountered debt was for carpentry work and boat repair. Also common were debts for textile purchases. Most inventories record a spinning wheel but never a loom. Farmers almost always purchased the cloth and then sent it out to a tailor to be fashioned into garments.

This attempt to describe the changing rural demand patterns in the course of the sixteenth and seventeenth centuries only begins to explore an important aspect of economic life that has received little attention. But the errors of interpretation undoubtedly present in this analysis cannot negate the obvious fact that the new specialized farm households entered the market for a remarkably wide variety of goods and services for both consumption and the operation of the farms.

OCCUPATIONAL DISTRIBUTION

The Groningen farmer Abel Eppens was alive to the revolutionary impact of the economic changes occurring during his own lifetime. He observed in 1566 that during the 30 years since the establishment of Burgundian rule in his province, "the prosperous, populous villages could no longer be satisfied to live off their own produce buying only the utter necessities from the cities with the surplus output which they brought to market. The growing surplus caused new needs to arise and the growing population pressed for new means of livelihood to be developed." [6]

The demand patterns of the farm population stimulated the growth of a rural, nonfarm sector composed of craftsmen, merchants, transport workers, and day laborers. Thus, the relatively undifferentiated peasantry of the early sixteenth century broke up in the century thereafter, and a new social structure arose, reflecting the needs of a commercialized economy. A distinct class of farmers, whose rise we charted earlier, was joined, not by a mass of marginally employed cottars, nor by a wretched body of spinners and weavers exploited in an urban-based putting-out system, but by a wide variety of provisioners of goods and services, by day laborers, and, during the period of peak farm labor demand, by Westphalian migrant laborers.

Occupational information is scarce for the seventeenth century. Fragmentary evidence from a few villages is all that is available to illuminate the occupational structure of that growing body of rural, nonfarm households that our analysis of landholding records uncovered. We must rely, therefore, on a unique Friesian fiscal document compiled in 1749. Tax riots in the previous year provoked the provincial government to consider reform of the tax system. The replacement for the old system was to consist of a quota assigned to each household on the basis of its size, wealth, and the occupation of the breadwinner. Later, the government had second thoughts about the wisdom of reform and the new system was never implemented, but the occupational census that was to lay the basis for the new tax, the Quotisatie Cohieren, remains for the benefit of historians.

An absence of population growth and major economic developments in the century preceding 1749 permits us to use this source to illuminate seventeenth-century developments. To that end the occupational data of 20 grietenijen, 7 vlekken, and the cities of Franeker and Leeuwarden are summarized in table 6.6.

Interpretation of these data is less than straightforward because of two shortcomings of the Quotisatie Cohieren. First, only heads of independent households were enumerated. Other working family members and live-in servants, a numerous group, were simply subsumed into the independent households. As a result, participation in the labor force, which generally exceeds 30 percent in preindustrial economies, stood at only a quarter of the population according to the Friesian records.[7] Live-in servants were recorded in the 1795 census. Then they numbered 14,756, or 9 percent of the total population; they were more numerous in rural areas than in the cities. This large work force did not form a distinct class; the bulk of them were apparently passing through a phase between adolescence and marriage, whereupon they would assume farms or crafts of their own. When this group is added to the heads of households enumerated in table 6.6 they increase the size of the labor force by 30 to 40 percent.

The second shortcoming consists in the frequency with which per-

Table 6.6. Occupations of Heads of Households in Friesland, 1749

Occupational Categories	18 Grietenijen no.	%	7 Vlekken no.	%	Ooststellingwerf & Weststellingwerf no.	%	Leeuwarden no.	%	Franeker no.	%
Agriculture (primary)										
Agriculture	3,742	36.8	217	10.8	730	52.5	126	3.9	65	8.6
Fishing and hunting	126	1.2	19	0.9	7	0.5	7	0.2	0	0
Subtotal	3,868	38.0	236	11.7	737	53.0	133	4.1	65	8.6
Industry (secondary)										
Pottery, brick, glass	26	0.3	9	0.4	1	0.1	31	1.0	28	3.7
Construction	303	3.0	82	4.1	33	2.4	207	6.4	26	3.5
Wood and straw crafts	95	0.9	54	2.7	11	0.8	107	3.3	14	1.9
Leather crafts	270	2.7	56	2.8	41	3.0	115	3.5	28	3.7
Peat, mining[a]	57	0.6	15	0.8	0	0	0	0	0	0
Metal industries	109	1.1	31	1.5	14	1.0	64	2.0	20	2.7
Wagon and boatmaking	105	1.0	82	4.1	6	0.4	25	0.8	15	2.0
Instrument making	15	0.1	10	0.5	0	0	27	0.8	8	1.1
Textile trades	248	2.4	95	4.7	77	5.5	405	12.5	105	14.0
Food preparation	212	2.1	76	3.8	27	1.9	203	6.3	33	4.4
Subtotal	1,440	14.2	510	25.4	210	15.1	1,184	36.6	277	37.0
Trade and Transportation (tertiary)										
Merchant activities	319	3.1	93	4.6	39	2.8 }	199 } 6.2		127	16.9
Retail activities	67	0.7	13	0.7	1	0.1 }			28	3.7
Transportation	621	6.1	350	17.4	45	3.2	251	7.7	86	11.4
Innkeeping	66	0.6	6	0.3	9	0.6	33	1.0	7	1.0
Subtotal	1,073	10.5	462	23.0	94	6.7	483	14.9	248	33.0

Social Services (tertiary)										
Liberal professions	35	0.4	16	0.8	9	0.6	207	6.4	9	1.2
Education	114	1.1	7	0.3	4	0.3	32	1.0	30	3.9
Government service	154	1.5	45	2.3	12	0.9	85	2.6	40	5.3
Military	9	0.1	4	0.2	1	0.1	968	29.9	3	0.4
Religious service	96	0.9	15	0.7	12	0.9	24	0.7	10	1.3
"Well-to-do" persons	36	0.4	42	2.1	6	0.4	0	0	0	0
Subtotal	444	4.4	129	6.4	44	3.2	1,316	40.6	92	12.1
Common laborers	2,639	25.9	539	26.8	287	20.7	108	3.3	70	9.3
Charity	417	4.1	40	2.0	1	0.1	—	—	?	—
Unknown	296	2.9	95	4.7	16	1.2	16	0.5	0	0
Total "occupied"	10,177	100.0	2,011	100.0	1,389	100.0	3,240	100.0	752	100.0
Retired, "old and poor"	88		18		3					
Widows	550		185		26		416		173	
Total households	10,815		2,214		1,418		3,656		925	
Total population	40,746		7,322		6,121		14,270		3,196	

SOURCE: RA Leeuwarden, Rekenkamer Archief, Quotisatie Cohieren van 1749, no. 14e.

[a] The labor force engaged in peat digging is not identified in this occupational census.

NOTE: The 18 grietenijen included in this table are: Achtkarspelen, Baarderadeel, Barradeel, Dantumadeel, Doniawerstal, Engwirden, Franckeradeel, Hennaarderadeel, het Bildt, Idaarderadeel, Haskerland, Kollumerland, Leeuwarderadeel, Lemsterland, Rauwerderhem, Tietjerksteradeel, Wymbritseradeel, Wonseradeel. The vlekken located in these grietenijen—Surhuisterveen, Grouw, Joure, Kollum, Lemmer, Bergum, Woudsend, and Makkum—are not included in these figures. They are, with the exception of Makkum, listed separately under the heading "7 Vlekken."

The occupational categories used in this analysis are those of the Netherlands' census of 1889. More modern categorization schemes are difficult to apply to preindustrial economies and this system has the virtue of having been used by other researchers in occupational analyses of Overijssel in 1795 and the Veluwe in 1749. In the following list of categories, the occupations subsumed thereunder are listed in order of their importance.

(Continued)

Table 6.6—*Continued*

Agriculture: farmer, cottar, cow milker, horticulturalist.

Fishing and hunting: fisherman, hunter, beekeeper.

Pottery, brick, glass: glassmaker, tilemaker, potter.

Construction: carpenter, roofer, painter, mason.

Wood and straw crafts: cooper, cabinetmaker, broommaker, lumbermiller, chairmaker.

Leather crafts: shoemaker, leather tanner.

Peat, mining: *veenbaas*.

Metal industries: smith, silversmith, coppersmith, tinker.

Wagon and boatmaking: boatmaker, wagonmaker, ship carpenter, mastmaker, wheelwright.

Instrument making: clockmaker, windmill maker, gunsmith.

Textile trades: weaver, knitter, tailor, dyer, *spinbaas*.

Food preparation: baker, miller, brewer, butcher.

Merchant activities: The bulk of this category is simply identified as "merchant," but many are further identified as cheese merchant, cattle merchant, etc. Also included in this category are rentiers, brokers, and financiers. (The distinction between this and the previous category is often difficult to maintain.)

Retail activities: shopkeeper, peddler.

Transportation: skipper, bargeman, sailor, ferryman, teamster, peat carrier.

Innkeeping: innkeeper, tavernkeeper.

Liberal professions: surgeon, lawyer, notary, apothecary, chimneysweep, veterinarian, barber, midwife, "rich historian."

Education: schoolmaster, professor.

Government services: Here, a variety of names are applied to local judges, tax collectors, tax investigators, secretaries, policemen, and other officials. Also included in this category are dike and drainage administrators and toll keepers.

Military: At this time the garrison at Leeuwarden was the only one in the province.

Religious service: minister, organist, gravedigger. (No clergy of other than the Reformed Church appear to have been listed.)

Common laborers: laborer, *vrijgezel* (unmarried workers).

Widow: Widows who performed an economic function are listed under that function. Only widows without further identification are listed in this category.

sons were identified as "laborer" (*arbeider*) without any further information that might permit us to determine their actual occupation. In 2 grietenijen, Idaarderadeel and Doniawerstel, farm laborers were distinguished from the others. There they made up 45 and 27 percent, respectively, of the total number of laborers. Many laborers were peat diggers; this is clear from their numerous presence in the vicinity of the peat bogs. Many others were engaged in transport, haulage, and shipbuilding; this is clear from their concentration in centers of such activities. Finally, the inverse correlation between the percentage of a grietenij's labor force engaged in agriculture and the percentage called "laborer" suggests that agriculture was not their primary source of employment.[8]

The data in table 6.6 have been grouped in categories of relatively homogeneous occupational structure; the vlekken have been listed separately from the countryside of which they were jurisdictionally a part in order to demonstrate the degree to which they performed urban functions. The grietenijen of Ooststellingwerf and Weststellingwerf, located in southeasternmost Friesland, have also been listed separately, in this case to illustrate the occupational structure of a more backward, less commercialized district. As we shall see, these 2 grietenijen had more in common with neighboring provinces than with Friesland. Finally, the occupational distributions of 2 cities have been included to stand as a comparison to the rural evidence. They are Leeuwarden, the capital and largest city of the province, and Franeker, a university city, which can probably be held as representative of the other small cities whose occupational structures remain unstudied.

The most striking characteristic of Friesland's occupational structure is the small percentage directly dependent upon agriculture. Even in the purely rural districts, farm households made up but 38 percent of the total. There is virtually no evidence of a cottar class. (Only 2.4 percent of the agricultural households were actually described as cottars.) Besides the agricultural population rural Friesland was inhabited by a large and varied group of craftsmen and provisioners of economic services. These occupational categories are noteworthy because of their dependence on local demand. Export industries, in which the textile trades are usually predominant, played no important role here. The peat industry, of course, served distant markets in Holland, but since peat diggers were identified only as laborers they are not included in the industrial category in table 6.6.

Despite the shortcomings of the Quotisatie Cohieren and its unusability for several grietenijen, we can present an approximation of the division of the province's population into primary, secondary, and tertiary employments by weighting the available data for each geographic-economic sector listed in table 6.6 by that sector's share of the total population and by assuming the laborers are distributed proportionally among the occupational categories. This procedure gives the results indicated in table 6.7.

TABLE 6.7.   Approximation of the Occupational
Distribution of Friesland, 1749

Categories	Rural	Vlekken	Ooststellingwerf & Weststellingwerf	Small Cities	Leeuwarden	Total
Primary						
Agriculture	56.6	17.7	68.0	9.4	4.2	36.7
Secondary						
Industry and crafts	21.1	38.1	19.3	41.0	37.8	29.2
Tertiary						
Trade and						
transportation	15.7	34.5	8.7	36.0	15.2	22.2
Social services	6.5	9.6	4.0	13.5	42.7	11.9
Percentage of total						
population	51.1	14.0	4.5	19.8	10.6	100.0
Percentage of population in category upon						
which data are based	60.0	36.5	100.0	12.0	100.0	53.3

SOURCE: See table 6.6.
NOTE: This approximation is based on the assumption that the laborers are *proportionally* distributed among the occupational categories.

A preindustrial rural population in which the bulk of the labor force is not engaged in either farming or a cottage industry might seem sufficiently unusual to give rise to misgivings about the evidence. Were the numerous craftsmen not, after all, simply small farmers who occasionally practiced a craft and felt warranted, therefore, in styling themselves carpenter or wheelwright? [9] And was the large tertiary sector not swollen, after the manner of present-day underdeveloped countries, with personal servants, petty traders, hawkers, and peddlers who form an economically marginal, underemployed mass? [10] Both these objections are unfounded in the Friesian case. The notarial inventories of rural craftsmen and traders show them to be divorced from agriculture: hardly any owned either farm equipment or livestock beyond a cow or a pig. Furthermore, the agricultural population as recorded in the Quotisatie Cohieren corresponds closely with the situation described in landholding records. For example, Idaarderadeel's occupational register for 1749 records 180 farm households. The land records of 1741 identify 195 farms of all sizes. Of the remaining 537 households of 1749 most lived in the 386 landless houses recorded in the 1741 documents. The remaining 151 households could have used only the "loose" parcels of land, which were not sufficiently extensive to afford many households with more than a garden plot or a tiny pasture. With regard to service employments, merchants and retailers (who were overwhelmingly storekeepers rather than peddlers) were not a disproportionately large part of the total tertiary sector. Their average tax quotas, moreover, make clear that most were not part of an economically marginal group calling themselves merchant or trader for want of a real occupation.

The occupational distribution presented in table 6.7 probably overestimates the percentage of the population engaged in the primary sector since we have reason to believe that the laborers were disproportionately engaged in peat digging, inland transport, seafaring, dike maintenance, and menial work in the various crafts.

These Friesian data can be placed in perspective by comparing them with the occupational census of the Veluwe for 1749, analyzed by H. K. Roessingh, and that of Overijssel for 1795, analyzed by B. H. Slicher van Bath. The Veluwe is a large sandy-soil district of Gelderland with much unproductive land. Overijssel divides into 3 districts: Vollenhove, adjacent to Friesland and bordering on the Zuider Zee, shared in the economic life of the northern Netherlands; Twente and Salland, forming much the larger part of the province, made up part of the sandy-soil eastern Netherlands, which did not share directly in the economic life of the maritime provinces and exhibited rather different social class characteristics. The Overijssel and Veluwe records are comparable to those of Friesland since they, too, enumerate only heads of households. They have the advantage of specifying the occupations of most laborers.

Vollenhove, just as Friesland, consisted of dairy farmers and a large number of peat diggers, transport workers, craftsmen, mer-

TABLE 6.8. Occupational Distribution of
Rural Veluwe and Overijssel

Categories	Vollenhove 1795	Salland 1795	Twente 1795	Veluwe 1749
Agriculture	33.6	70.8	44.1	66.4
Industry and Crafts	37.7	17.5	42.7	22.4
Export Industries:				
Peat and mining	15.6	0.4	0.1	0.4
Textile trades	2.7	2.6	28.7	6.3
Domestic Industries	19.4	14.5	13.9	15.7
Trade and Transport	17.0	8.0	8.0	5.7
Social Services	5.4	3.3	2.8	2.4
Casual Labor	6.3	0.4	2.4	0.0
Unknown	—	—	—	3.1

SOURCES: Slicher van Bath, *Samenleving onder spanning*, pp. 126, 158; H. K. Roessingh "Beroep en bedrijf op de Veluwe in het midden van de achttiende eeuw."

NOTE: The figures for Overijssel include the populations of the small cities. Only the major cities of Kampen, Deventer, and Zwolle are excluded.

chants, and day laborers. The occupational distribution of Friesland and Vollenhove are rather similar. Salland and the Veluwe, on the other hand, were overwhelmingly dependent upon agriculture; their occupational distribution corresponds closely to that of Ooststellingwerf and Weststellingwerf in southeastern Friesland. Twente differed from Salland in that its large cottar class had been organized into a putting-out textile industry.

Clearly, we have before us 2 distinct rural economies. The regions varied in their social structure, while their agricultural sectors possessed different linkages with the nonagricultural economy. We can appreciate this difference by comparing the number of practitioners of various occupations in relation to the rural populations of the two regions. This procedure shows the average "number of customers" that support each producer. It can serve as a rough index of the degree of rural specialization.

The occupational structure in rural Holland appears to have undergone an even more profound transformation than in Friesland. Unfortunately, the available data are especially weak. The first occupational censuses were taken in the early nineteenth century, when the economy was in utter shambles. A hint at the variety in Holland's rural occupational structure is given by the earliest data we have found, in a census document of 1807. It provides an account of the occupational categories into which fell the 47,000 inhabitants

TABLE 6.9.   Population per Worker in Selected Occupations
in Rural Friesland and Overijssel

Population per Worker in:

Occupation	Overijssel	Ooststellingwerf & Weststellingwerf	Friesland
Carpenter	184	183	104
Shoemaker	298	153	153
Wooden shoemaker[a]	852	—	—
Baker	553	556	318
Wagon and boatmaker	2,483	1,020	325
Smith	610	437	388
Teacher	1,073	1,530	401

[a] Wooden shoes, a hallmark of rural Holland, were apparently not widely worn before the eighteenth century. Since they must be considered an inferior substitute for leather shoes, the absence of wooden shoemakers in Friesland probably indicates a higher level of prosperity.

of 40 villages in Rijnland and Delfland. The work force consisted of 8,879 "independent" and 3,824 "dependent" workers. The latter group consisted of servants and laborers resident in the households of the former group. The independent work force was engaged as shown by table 6.10.

The process of rural specialization, in other regions and at other times, has often contributed to making rural societies less "mature" —less well endowed with skills, nonagricultural capital, and opportunities—than before the process took place. In Poland, where the drive to produce a large, exportable grain surplus entailed the enserfment of the peasantry and the construction of gigantic estates, crafts and merchant activities withered. The estate owners, as the volume of their trade grew, arrogated marketing functions from the urban middle class. The concentration of income in their hands produced a demand pattern that could be satisfied only by specialized producers in the largest cities of western Europe. Modern Asian countries have experienced a similar transformation of their domestic economies.[11]

The northern Netherlands escaped this fate. Tenurial customs, the nature of the crops produced, and the balance of economic power among the region's social classes produced specialized farm households with income and demand patterns that supported a dense population of craftsmen and merchants. The rural sector had certainly

TABLE 6.10. Occupational Distribution of Rural Holland
(parts of Rijnland and Delfland), 1807

Occupation	Number	Percentage of "Independent" Work Force
Farmers	1,604	18.1
Horticulturalists	283	3.2
Craftsmen	2,100	23.7
Day laborers	2,605	29.4
Seafarers	467	5.3
Windmill operators	75	0.8
Storekeepers	416	4.7
Merchants	235	2.7
Inn- and tavernkeepers	197	2.2
Contractors	78	0.9
Officials, doctors, jurists, rentiers	330	3.7
Other	463	5.2
Total	8,853	99.9

SOURCE: "Tableau van den Staat en Betrekingen der In- en
Opgezetenen in het kwartier Leyden, departement Maasland
. . . ," in A. G. van der Steur, "Demografische statistiek."

shown its capacity to respond vigorously to new commercial opportunities. It had destroyed the old peasant society and reorganized
itself to expand greatly agricultural production. In the process, a
peasantry adjusted to the limitations of the land had been transformed into an occupationally differentiated population attuned
to the opportunities of international markets. From the vantage
point of contemporary Europeans, the economic development of this
society must have seemed unique. It certainly provoked much jeal-
ousy. From our vantage point the question immediately arises, why
did this course of development cease? Why did a society with these
endowments not continue to develop and produce economic break-
throughs that could lead to industrialization?

This study, primarily concerned with the growth and development of the Dutch economy, cannot hope to provide firm answers
to this question. Yet, our description of the new rural sector suggests
a few observations that could be a useful guide to further research.
First, the economy's demographic and landholding characteristics
prevented the proliferation of a cottar class. The absence of such
an immiserized population both gave the region its appearance of

rural prosperity and closed the path to industrialization via cottage industry which was followed by so many other parts of Europe. Related to this characteristic is a second: the continued urbanization of the northern Netherlands, fed by a continuing flow of migrants from the rural sector. This preserved the power of a conservative, urban industrial structure while, elsewhere in Europe, rural industry was rendering it uncompetitive. Finally, we have shown that the seventeenth-century rural population of the region was economically specialized, mobile, educated, and receptive to urban cultural values. Could it be that these characteristics of "modernization," far from being preconditions for industrialization, actually acted as obstacles to the kind of social and economic changes associated with eighteenth- and nineteenth-century industrial development?

The stagnation of the Dutch economy was obviously affected by exogenous factors, such as foreign mercantilist policies and the "seventeenth-century crisis." Yet, accounts that do not proceed beyond these convenient explanations seem unconvincing. Unfortunately, we can at present only speculate about the importance of the domestic factors indicated by this study.

7. The Rural Sector's Place in the Dutch Economy and in Dutch History

The aim of this study has been to chart the transformation of Dutch rural society, account for its occurrence, and describe its consequences. This necessarily involves us in two distinct fields of study, that of the development economist and that of the Dutch historian. To be of use to the former, the findings must in some measure transcend time and place, while to the latter the unique character of the historical events and conditions justifiably claims priority.

The uniqueness of our region's historical circumstances is indeed striking. The battles against the sea and against Spain in a society with a profoundly pacifist domestic culture produced an environment without a parallel in Europe. I hope I have done these and other features of Dutch society justice in my efforts to fathom economic relationships and patterns of response as well as modes of economic behavior—knowledge of all these being a prerequisite for indulging in comparative discussion, model building, and the application of economic theory.

In order to describe the overall role of the rural sector in sixteenth- and seventeenth-century Dutch economic growth and at the same time assess the validity of some contemporary thinking about this subject, I shall cite a series of general statements by Bruce Johnston and John Mellor describing "agriculture's contribution to economic development" and discuss them in the light of the Dutch case.[1]

> 1. Economic development is characterized by a substantial increase in the demand for agricultural products, and failure to expand food supplies in pace with growth of demand can impede economic growth.

The most striking increase in demand affected horticultural and industrial crops. The urbanization of the region would undoubtedly have been hindered in the absence of the elastic supply response of these crops. The output of traditional food crops may have increased, to judge from the increase in yield ratios, but the region's dependence on imported grains obviously grew enormously. Rural transformation involved specialization in a narrow range of products in accordance with the efficient use of available productive factors. This resulted in growth of both agricultural exports and imports, which brings us to the second statement.

2. Expansion of agricultural exports is likely to be one of the most promising means of increasing income and augmenting foreign exchange earnings.

The Dutch economy benefitted from its ability to import cheap bread grains; this liberated domestic resources for more productive purposes, among which was the production of exported dairy products. Another important benefit of this international specialization was the stimulus it provided to large-scale foreign trade, upon which the Dutch built much of their imposing trading empire. In short, agricultural specialization here brought benefits to the economy that extended beyond the garnering of foreign exchange earnings.

We should note here that statements 1 and 2 are often mutually exclusive. Many economies must choose either agricultural self-sufficiency or specialization and international interdependence. In the Dutch case the unequivocal choice of the second course brought benefits, direct and indirect, far exceeding those which a deliberate pursuit of agricultural self-sufficiency could have brought.

3. The bulk of the labor force of manufacturing and other expanding sectors must be drawn mainly from agriculture.

A society in which a growing rural population resists movement into nonagricultural occupations is subject to a twofold problem. Industry and trade, for want of low-priced labor, are unable to attain their full potential; and agriculture, forced to accommodate an enlarged work force without increased quantities of land or capital, must adopt techniques and customs that perpetuate, and perhaps exacerbate, rural poverty. One of the crucial factors distinguishing the peasant from the specialization models described earlier was the degree to which the farms absorbed increases of the population. The rural transformation of the northern Netherlands, which in many respects followed the specialization model, entailed a redirection of rural labor from agricultural to nonagricultural activities and displayed a farm sector that resisted absorbing an enlarged work force. A stationary farm population succeeded in increasing agricultural production. This was the result neither of an "agricultural revolution" in the technical sense nor of the "peasant-squeezing" conduct of great landowners. Rather, the specialization of farm households in agricultural production—the shedding of numerous nonagricultural pursuits typical of peasant economies—created an elastic agricultural supply function at the same time that larger supplies of labor became available for migration to urban or rural nonfarm occupations. I have shown that this migration phenomenon was crucial to both the development of rural specialization and the growth of the urban sector.

> 4. As the dominant sector of the underdeveloped economy, agriculture should make a net contribution to the capital required for overhead investment and expansion of secondary industry.

We do not have the information about the diverse and obscure flows of capital between sectors of the sixteenth-century Dutch economy that is needed in order to make anything but vague statements on this subject. Despite the absence of large landowners in a position to effect a transfer of resources from agriculture to industry in the manner of the postrestoration Japanese nobleman, profits accumulated by landowners and by farmers themselves did find their way to other sectors of the economy—via taxation in particular and to a lesser extent via the purchase of shares in fishing, shipping, and milling enterprises. But capital flowed in the reverse direction as well, most notably in the development of land reclamation and transportation projects. The major accomplishments of rural capital lay in the development of agriculture's productive capacity itself: the increased output of these farms, the labor released from them, and the demands they placed upon other sectors of the economy played a much larger role in stimulating nonagricultural activities than did the capital extracted from agriculture.

> 5. Rising net cash incomes of the farm population may be important as a stimulus to industrial expansion.

The record of rural change in the northern Netherlands indicates that this last point is of much greater importance than one could gather from the attention usually focused upon it. The "two-sector model" of economic development as formulated by W. Arthur Lewis and by Gustav Ranis and John Fei[2] embodies a crucial simplification that nonagricultural development requires only capital. Lack of markets is no problem, and as a consequence rural demand patterns are of no particular importance to the model. In fact, in this model increased disposable rural income obstructs industrial growth since it hinders the transfer of labor and capital from the rural sector.

In the Dutch case farm demand for manufactured goods and for services grew. The rise of specialized agriculture transformed the farm from a self-contained production unit to one that purchased inputs and specialized services and redirected farm labor from non-agricultural production (handicrafts, clothing, fuel gathering, etc.) to activities directly in support of producing merchantable commodities. This transformation, besides an increased income level, greatly increased the scope and level of farm demand.

The analysis of farm inventories suggested another way in which farm demand probably affected the course of economic development. Farmers' consumption habits changed considerably in the course of the sixteenth and seventeenth centuries but failed to provide sufficient support to commodities which, a century later, acted as leading sectors of the Industrial Revolution. Whether this failure must be primarily ascribed to perverse demand characteristics of the rural people or to a failure on the part of industry to supply such goods cannot now be determined. But, for whatever reason, this situation could partly account for both the stagnation of agricultural output and the decline of Dutch urban industries beginning in the last third of the seventeenth century.

This checklist of agriculture's contributions to economic growth makes clear the importance of agriculture in the growth of the northern Netherlands, not so much in its provision of foodstuffs, as in the total impact it had, directly and indirectly, in fostering the expansion of the urban sector. If this is so, a reexamination of Dutch economic history during these 2 centuries of its greatest international importance is in order.

Z. W. Sneller, in his introduction to a history of Dutch agriculture after 1795, expressed a common view of the Dutch economy. He wrote that "the Republic was focused entirely upon merchant trade" and that "all the other business life of the nation was made serviceable to this merchant trading," with the consequence that "agriculture remained in the twilight." [3] Nearly 2 centuries earlier, Luzac's account of the Dutch economy expressed similar opinions. His 4-volume work scarcely mentioned agriculture. [4] Luzac, in turn, only followed the antiagricultural bias of Pieter de la Court, who in his influential study of the Dutch economy and its trade policy, *Interest van Holland,* written in 1662, thought the encouragement of agriculture of no importance to the fostering of prosperity in the Dutch Republic.[5]

We do not wish to deny the supreme importance of shipping and commerce in the Dutch economy but do wish to place it in the context of the entire economy. Instead of accounting for Dutch trade by invoking the influence of fortuitous circumstances, the singular feats of a single city, or the inherent advantages of geographical location, we must integrate the roles of industry and agriculture with those of shipping and commerce. The interrelationships among these major sectors provided the basis for a flourishing foreign trade. Once this was well established, Dutch traders and seafarers could take advantage of events—discoveries and wars, among them—to extend and perfect their trading system. But behind this seaborne façade stood industrial and agricultural sectors able to respond to new opportunities and to supply the growing needs of the entire economy.[6]

Industries, and not only those attached to the trade of the entrepôt market, grew in importance during the sixteenth and seventeenth centuries. It is desirable that we review some of the foremost industrial achievements to emphasize what is not generally known, that with windmills for motive power, peat for fuel, numerous canals for transport, and an abundance of labor and resources from the rural sector, the Dutch Republic became a major industrial nation.

The woolen textiles industry of Leiden and other cities made the Republic one of Europe's largest textile producers; in the 1650s Leiden's yearly woolens production attained a value of some 9 million gulden and employed an estimated 37,650 workers.[7] The bleaching and dyeing of linens from all over Europe was centered in the vicinity of Haarlem. In the second half of the seventeenth century 80,000 to 100,000 pieces were bleached yearly by firms employing 40 to 50 workers each.[8] In the port cities, sugar refining became an important industry. In 1661 Amsterdam, the foremost refining center, housed 60 refineries that drew upon the peat resources of the Republic to supply sugar to much of Europe.[9]

The Republic's brickworks, by the early seventeenth century, had a total capacity of some 200 million bricks per year. Even when working at only one-half of capacity, the Dutch brick industry during the seventeenth century produced as many bricks per year, on a per capita basis, as did England during the Industrial Revolution of the late eighteenth century.[10] Tile, pottery, and clay-pipe works also flourished in the Republic. Together with the brickworks, they produced important export commodities.

The Dutch shipbuilding industry not only supplied the enormous domestic demand for ships but undercut foreign shipyards to build a goodly portion of many foreign fleets. In the industry's principal location, the Zaanstreek, dozens of wharves produced hundreds of oceangoing vessels each year.[11] The Zaanstreek produced much more than ships. At its peak, in the late seventeenth and early eighteenth centuries, over 600 industrial windmills provided the power for lumber sawing, oil pressing, lead milling for paint, tobacco pressing, starch making, paper making, and a wide variety of lesser industries. Soap boiling and sailcloth weaving also flourished there, in one of the greatest industrial concentrations of Europe.[12]

As we have seen in the course of this study, the growth of many industries and a numerous class of rural craftsmen depended in many ways upon agriculture. Agriculture's ability to supply raw materials and labor and to provide a market for industrial products crucially affected the prospects for industrial growth. Similarly, agricultural specialization, by supplying export crops and migrating labor as well as many resources needed for industrial expansion, greatly stimulated shipping and commerce.

Our study has shown that the rural sector's ability to respond to new opportunities for economic growth and to alter its methods of production depended in large part upon physical, legal, and sociological characteristics inherited from earlier times. The region delimited in this study, the northern Netherlands, possessed a uniformity in these endowments that permitted it to develop a single rural economy, despite its division into 4 separate provinces. The population growth, occupational differentiation, agricultural specialization, and productivity growth experienced by the northern Netherlands stood in striking contrast to the economic history of immediately adjacent regions.

In the province of Drenthe, which abuts Groningen and Friesland, a sparse peasant population cultivated common fields scattered in a sea of wasteland. Throughout the seventeenth century these peasants burned virgin fields before sowing crops of buckwheat and rye for 7 to 8 consecutive years, whereupon they abandoned the fields and moved on to new soil. Despite their abundant land and the nearness of markets they rarely produced an exportable surplus.[13] Primitive techniques, low productivity, and a resistance to commercialization also characterized the rural sector of Overijssel. Slicher van Bath, in his detailed study of the province, showed that far from exporting agricultural commodities to the urban centers of the maritime region, Overijssel often needed to import foodstuffs.

The regional economy of the northern Netherlands, when set in the context of the larger European economy and when compared to adjacent regions, clearly experienced real growth between the early sixteenth and late seventeenth centuries. Its economic history did not display the familiar cyclical pattern—population growth, reduced per capita income, crisis, and recovery. Instead, population growth, which for 2 generations was centered in the rural sector, reacted with the particular endowments of the region to provoke a restructuring of the rural economy. Later, after 1570, an explosive urbanization added a new dimension to the process of economic development. By the 1660s the sources of growth, both urban and rural, had been spent, although it would be wrong to speak of absolute economic decline in many sectors until several decades later.[14] Even then, agriculture must be excepted. This sector had permanently assumed new characteristics which in the nineteenth century would provide the basis of a new economic structure.

The impact of this economic transformation on income levels can only be sketched. No statistical information on this subject exists for the beginning of our period. We know, however, that the northern Netherlands was then no shining center of wealth. The Burgundian government received the vast majority of its tax revenues from Brabant and Flanders. Compared to them, Holland and the other northern provinces were still what they had long been, an economic backwater. Northern cities could claim no important independent commerce; they provided shipping services to the traders of the southern cities and otherwise lived from herring fishing and a minor textile industry.

By the late seventeenth century there was little doubt that the Dutch Republic, and its maritime provinces in particular, possessed the wealthiest populace in Christendom. The English national income accountant Gregory King calculated, in 1688 and 1695, the national income and government revenues of the principal northern European states. He held the Dutch Republic to be the wealthiest of all, with a per capita income in 1695 of £8.2 shillings (about 97 gulden). The per capita income of England he calculated at £7.16 and that of France at £5.18.[15] Eighty years later no less an economist than Adam Smith still had no doubt that the Republic was the wealthiest state in Europe.[16]

Notes, Glossary, Bibliography

Abbreviations Used in References

AAGB   *A. A. G. Bijdragen*

AER   *American Economic Review*

Annales   *Annales (Economies, Sociétés, Civilisations)*

BMHG   *Bijdragen en Mededelingen van het Historisch Genootschap*

BVGO   *Bijdragen voor Vaderlandsche Geschiedenis en Oudheidkunde*

EHR   *Economic History Review*

EHJ   *Economisch-Historisch Jaarboek*

JEH   *Journal of Economic History*

RPG   *Rijksgeschiedkundige Publicatiën*

SEHR   *Scandinavian Economic History Review*

TEG   *Tijdschrift voor Economische Geographie, later, Tijdschrift voor Economisch en Sociale Geografie*

TKNAG   *Tijdschrift van het Koninklijk Nederlandse Aardrijkskundig Genootschap*

TRHS   *Transactions of the Royal Historical Society*

TvG   *Tijdschrift voor Geschiedenis*

VSWG   *Vierteljahrschrift für Sozial- und Wirtschaftsgeschichte*

ZAA   *Zeitschrift für Agrargeschichte und Agrarsoziologie*

For the archives listed on pages 285–86 of the Bibliography, the following designations are used in the Notes:

ARA	GA Amsterdam
RA Brussel	GA Gouda
RA Groningen	GA Groningen
RA Haarlem	GA Haarlem
RA Leeuwarden	GA Hoorn
RA Utrecht	GA Leiden
AH Rijnland	GA Leeuwarden
GA Alkmaar	GA Sneek

Notes

CHAPTER 1

1. Karl Bücher, *Die Entstehung der Volkswirtschaft* [*Industrial evolution*], p. 119; Alan Everitt, "The Marketing of Agricultural Produce," in *Agrarian History of England and Wales, 1500–1640*, vol. 4, ed. Joan Thirsk, p. 496. Bücher found market areas in Germany to be 40 to 50 square miles in the southwest and 60 to 85 square miles in the center. East-Elbian cities, however, served hinterlands of well over 100 square miles. English market towns served hinterlands averaging 70 square miles.

2. See Rogier Mols, *Introduction à la démographie historique des villes d'Europe du 14ᵉ au 18ᵉ siècle.*

3. For a more detailed description of this phenomenon, see Wilhelm Abel, *Agrarkrisen und Agrarkonjunktur*, pt. 2; for a discussion of von Thünen's theory, see Michael Chisholm, *Rural Settlement and Land Use*, chap. 2, and J. H. von Thünen, *Der Isolierte Staat in Beziehung auf Landwirtschaft und Nationalökonomie*. For individual commodities in this process, see R. Dion, *Histoire de la vigne et du vin en France des origines au 19ᵉ siècle* (Paris, 1959); Jan Craeybeckx, *Un grand commerce d'importation: Les vins de France aux anciens Pays-Bas (XIIIᵉ–XVIᵉ siècle)* Paris, 1958); Robert Trow-Smith, *A History of British Livestock Husbandry*, 2 vols. (London, 1957); H. Wiese and J. Bölts, *Rinderhandel und Rinderhaltung im nordwesteuropäischen Küstengebiet vom 15. bis zum 19. Jahrhundert;* W. Achilles, Getreidepreise und Getreidehandelsbeziehungen europäischer Raume im 16. und 17. Jahrhundert."

4. C. T. Smith, *An Historical Geography of Western Europe before 1800*, (London, 1967), pp. 493–94.

5. The rationale behind our repeated assertions that international trade in agricultural commodities stimulates specialization and thereby increases productivity and income is to be found in the Heckscher-Ohlin theory of international trade. Its central proposition is that the introduction of trade will encourage specialization in goods that use intensively the region's abundant factor of production, in exchange for goods using factors scarce in the region. See Bertil Ohlin, *Interregional and International Trade*, chap. 1.

6. Henri Pirenne, *Early Democracies in the Low Countries* (New York, 1963), p. 79.

7. The concentration process is described in detail in Emmanuel Le Roy Ladurie, *Les Paysans de Languedoc*, 1:633–38. Efforts to alter leases to the advantage of the landowners are described in Marc Bloch, *French Rural Society* (Berkeley and Los Angeles, 1966), pp. 130–35; also see R. H. Tawney, *The Agrarian Problem in the Sixteenth Century* (London, 1912), pp. 170–310.

8. This picture of unmitigated disaster for the peasantry must be tempered by a more favorable tendency. The intensification process will give some farmers the opportunity to specialize in the production of an agricultural commodity

that enjoys strong demand in the urban market, such as flax, hemp, madder, vegetables, silk, or olives. The crisis of food supply does not leave such farmers unaffected, but their ability to specialize in production for the market places them in a more promising position.

9. A full discussion of the factors that enter into the transformation needed to allow such trade links to develop is found in appendix C and the article of Hymer and Resnick cited therein. One important prerequisite for the growth of intersectoral trade is that urban-produced manufactured goods be considered superior to their home-produced counterpart by the peasant consumer. A mathematical proof of the necessity of this condition is found in Hymer and Resnick, pp. 496–97. The practical consequence of this observation is that the tastes of the peasant population must be sufficiently "sophisticated" so that most goods are shorn of religious or ritualistic attributes which might require that they be produced within the household and according to a prescribed traditional method. Another consequence is that the urban "manufacturing" sector be sufficiently advanced to enable it to produce goods that are not objectively inferior to similar goods produced within the peasant household.

10. General discussions are available in Richard Koebner, "The Settlement and Colonization of Europe," in *Cambridge Economic History of Europe*, vol. 1, ed. M. M. Postan pp. 1–91, and Slicher van Bath, *Agrarian History*, pp. 54–62. Descriptions of field systems on a national basis include Wilhelm Abel, *Geschichte der deutschen Landwirtschaft vom frühen Mittelalter bis zum 19. Jahrhundert*, pp. 66–76; Bloch, pp. 35–63; Thirsk, *Agrarian History of England and Wales*, 4:5–9 (describing England), 147–52 (describing Wales); A. W. Edelman-Vlam, "De ontwikkeling van de parceelsvormen in Nederland," pp. 141–67; H. L. Gray, *English Field Systems* (Cambridge, Mass., 1915); A. Verhulst, "Les types differents de l'organization domainiale et structures agraires en Belgique au moyen age"; V. Hansen, "The Danish Village: Its Age and Form," *Denmark, Guidebook for the 19th International Geographers Congress* (Stockholm, 1960), pp. 238–53.

11. The view, still often encountered, that rural settlement patterns of today arose in a manner analogous to the "putty-clay" theory of capital investment, and therefore reflect the racial-cultural attributes of the early inhabitants, has been much modified. See Slicher van Bath, *Agrarian History*, pp. 54–55.

12. Friedrich Wilhelm Henning, "Die Betriebsgrössenstruktur der mitteleuropäischen Landwirtschaft im 18. Jahrhundert und ihr Einfluss auf die ländlichen Einkommensverhältnisse"; Joan Thirsk, "Industries in the Countryside"; Thirsk, *Agrarian History of England and Wales*, 4:9–12. On this subject, which requires much further research, see also Rosamond Jane Faith, "Peasant Families and Inheritance Customs in Medieval England," *Agricultural History Review* 14 (1966):77–95; H. J. Habakkuk, "Family Structure and Economic Change in Nineteenth Century Europe," *JEH* 15 (1955):1–12; H. E. Hallam, "Some Thirteenth Century Censuses," *EHR*, 2d ser. 8 (1957):340–61; George C. Homans, "Partible Inheritance of Villagers' Holdings," *EHR* 8 (1937):48–56; Jean Yver, *Egalité entre héritiers et exclusion des enfantes dotés. Essai de géographie coutumière* (Paris, 1966).

13. For a discussion of the economic characteristics of regions consisting over-

whelmingly of free men, see B. H. Slicher van Bath, "Boerenvrijheid," pp. 272–94.

14. For an example of the approach we wish to avoid see Everett M. Rogers, "Motivations, Values, and Attitudes of Subsistence Farmers: Toward a Subculture of Peasantry," in Clifton R. Wharton, ed., *Subsistence Agriculture and Economic Development*, pp. 111–35.

15. G. A. Kooy, *De oude samenleving op het nieuwe platteland: Een studie over de familiehuishouding in de agrarische Achterhoek* (Assen, 1959); William Peterson, "Demographic Transition in the Netherlands."

16. B. H. Slicher van Bath, *Een samenleving onder spanning; geschiedenis van het platteland in Overijssel*, p. 111. See also A. M. van der Woude, "De omvang en samenstelling van de huishouding in Nederland in het verleden." Van der Woude assembles data from the northern peninsula of Holland that reinforce our belief that the maritime and landward regions of the Netherlands differed considerably in family structure.

17. Peter Laslett, "Size and Structure of the Household in England over three Centuries," p. 218; E. A. Wrigley, *Population and History* (New York, 1969), p. 13.

18. In the accounting equation in appendix C, this would have the effect of dividing L_T into two separate supplies of labor, L_T (female) and L_T (male), one of which cannot be transferred from Z to F production.

19. The importance of this phenomenom to our models is discussed in note 9. For a further discussion of the role of sociological factors, see Raymond Firth, "Social Structure and Peasant Economy: The Influence of Social Structure upon Peasant Economies," in Wharton, *Subsistence Agriculture* pp. 23–37.

20. A description of this process in England is found in Tawney, chaps. 1–2. A more general discussion is found in Barrington Moore, Jr., *Social Origins of Dictatorship and Democracy* (Boston, 1966).

21. Bloch, pp. 146–48.

22. H. O. Feith, *Het Groninger Beklemrecht*; G. J. A. Mulder, ed., *Handboek der Geografie van Nederland*, 5:118–19.

23. The three levels of specialization seem perhaps out of order but are in fact in the chronological order in which they appear to begin playing an important role in agrarian development.

CHAPTER 2

1. *Enqueste ende Informatie upt stuck van der Reductie ende Reformatie van den Schiltaelen* . . . , comp. R. J. Fruin (cited hereafter as *Enqueste*).

2. *Informacie up den staet Faculteyt ende Gelegentheyt van de Steden ende Dorpen van Hollant ende Vrieslant* . . . , comp. R. J. Fruin (cited hereafter as *Informacie*).

3. *Informacie*, pp. ix–x, xxiv–xxv.

4. Both terms refer to the "units of tax burden" allocated to each village. Typically, a village burdened with a number of kerven or schotponden divided them among the inhabitants according to their wealth. When the government levied the actual tax burden, it would be divided among the villages according to the number of schotponden they had; the villages would then assess the

inhabitants according to how many schotponden they had. The tax burden represented by one schotpond, thus, could vary from village to village.

5. *Informacie,* pp. 4–5.

6. For an analysis of what lay inside and what lay outside the taxable area, see E. C. G. Brünner, *De order op de buitennering van 1531,* pp. 14–18; also see J. C. Naber, "Een terugblik," p. 13.

7. This 10-percent property tax, opposition to which figures as a catalyst to the Revolt of the Netherlands, has left us numerous registers of land and houses. The interpretation of these registers is not straightforward. The chief problem is that houses of very low value (under 2 gulden yearly rent in the case of 1543) were exempt from the tax. Many village registers record the presence of these exempt houses anyway, but certainty of the completeness of the Tiende Penning Cohieren is not always attainable. The largest number of extant registers are available for 1543 and 1561; the latter is generally considered the most reliable. ARA, Staten van Holland voor 1572, Tiende Penning Cohieren, 1543, nos. 144–440; 1544, nos. 446–532; 1553, nos. 533–871; 1556, nos. 875–1182; 1561, nos. 1191–1518; RA Brussel, Papiers d'Etat et de l'Audience, Cahiers du Xᵉ, XXᵉ, et Cᵉ denier, nos. 618-36, 618-37.

8. *Register van den Aanbreng van 1511 en verdere stukken tot de Floreen-belasting betrekkelijk,* 4 vols., comp. I. Telting (cited hereafter as *Aanbreng van 1511*). *De Aanbreng der Vijf Deelen van 1511 en 1514,* 5 vols., ed. J. C. Tjessinga (cited hereafter as *Aanbreng der Vijf Deelen*).

9. For discussion of the Roman presence in the northern Netherlands see A. W. Byvanck, "De verovering en de bezetting door de Romeinen," and Germaine Faider-Feytmans, "De Romeinse beschaving in de Nederlanden," in *Algemene geschiedenis der Nederlanden,* vol. 1; W. A. van Es, "Friesen en Romeinen," in J. J. Kalma et al., eds., *Geschiedenis van Friesland.*

10. S. J. Fockema Andreae, "Middeleeuwsch Oegstgeest," pp. 260–62.

11. E. W. Hofstee, *Het Oldampt,* 1:187; I. H. Gosses and N. Japikse, *Handboek tot de staatkundige geschiedenis van Nederland,* 3d ed. (The Hague, 1937), p. 119.

12. H. A. Enno van Gelder, "De Hollandse adel in de tijd van de opstand," pp. 130–31; see also H. A. Enno van Gelder, *Nederlandse dorpen in de 16ᵉ eeuw.* This work consists of a number of case studies of villages from Hainault to North Holland, showing the variety of legal and political institutions in the different districts.

13. Johann Samuel Theissen, *Centraal gezag en Friesche vrijheid,* pp. 5–7; C. J. Guibal, *Democratie en oligarchie in Friesland tijdens de Republiek,* pp. 62–85.

14. Enno van Gelder, "Hollandse adel," pp. 130–31; Jan de Vries, "On the Modernity of the Dutch Republic," *JEH* 33 (1973):191–202; A. de Goede, *Swannotsrecht, Westfriesche rechtsgeschiedenis,* 1:405.

15. A general account is found in Koebner, "The Settlement and Colonization of Europe."

16. J. F. Niermeyer, *Delft en Delfland,* p. 60; I. H. Gosses, "De vorming van het Graafschap Holland," *Verspreide Geschriften* (Groningen, 1946), p. 310; H. van der Linden, *De cope,* pp. 70–72. The similarities between colonization in Holland and Germany rest in part, as van der Linden has shown, on the fact

that Hollanders experienced in colonization practices went to Germany, first to the Bremer marshes and later to Prussia, to participate in the colonization movement.

17. Fz. S. Muller and A. C. Bouman, comps., *Oorkondenboek van het Sticht Utrecht,* 4 vols. (Utrecht, 1920–54), vol. 1, document no. 245.

18. Van der Linden, pp. 169, 171, 184.

19. Niermeyer, *Delft en Delfland,* pp. 72–75; S. J. Fockema Andreae, *Het Hoogheemraadschap van Rijnland,* pp. 10, 21, 37, 119; W. J. Diepeveen, *De vervening in Delfland en Schieland tot het einde der 16e eeuw,* pp. 18–24.

20. R.A. Groningen, Inventarissen van de archieven der voormalige zijlvesten en dijkrechten in de provincie Groningen, introduction.

21. Gerhard Werkman, *Kent gij het land der zee ontrukt,* p. 88; Margarethe Adriana Verkade, *De opkomst van de Zaanstreek,* pp. 13–34.

22. P. C. J. A. Boeles, *Friesland tot de elfde eeuw* (The Hague, 1951), pp. 476–78.

23. Hendrik Tjaard Obreen, *Dijkplicht en waterschappen aan Frieslands westkust;* Brand Klaas van den Berg, *Het laagveengebied van Friesland* (Enschede, 1933), p. 14.

24. A. Bicker Caerten et al., *Zuid Hollands molenboek,* p. 75; Fockema Andreae, *Rijnland,* pp. 88–89, 224.

25. Fockema Andreae, *Rijnland,* p. 122.

26. P. van Balen, *Uit de geschiedenis van Waddinxveen,* p. 15.

27. *Informacie,* pp. 293–94, 297.

28. Ibid., p. 298.

29. Ibid., p. 289.

30. M. K. E. Gottschalk, "De ontginning der Stichtse venen ten oosten van de Vecht," *TKNAG* 73 (1956):207–22.

31. Van der Linden, p. 275; a comparison of the land registers of villages in the Ronde Venen shows that between the Mannuaal van het Oudschildgeld of 1540 and the Blaffard van Oudschildgelden of 1600 sizable amounts of new land, *novalia landen,* were brought under cultivation.

32. Archief van het Hoogheemraadschap van Schieland, no. C5, folio 190, "Verzoek van de Heer van Sommelsdijk aan Filips II, 1566," C. de Jong, *De droogmaking van de Wildevenen in Schieland,* p. 14.

33. H. Blink, *Geschiedenis van den boerenstand en den landbouw in Nederland,* 1:290, 310.

34. J. C. Ramaer, "De omvang van het Haarlemmermeer en de meren, waaruit het ontstaan is, op verschillende tijden voor de droogmaking," *Koninklijke Akadamie van Wetenschappen* (1892), p. 296.

35. Werkman, pp. 70–74.

36. "Informacie van het land van Voorne" (1565), in *Enqueste,* p. 312.

37. *Enqueste,* passim.

38. Diepeveen, p. 60.

39. Z. van Doorn, "Enige landbouwhistorische bronnen van Zegveld en Zegvelderbroek," pp. 198–202; see also S. J. Fockema Andreae, "Uit de geschiedenis van een Rijnlandse polder (De Noordeind en Geerpolder onder Ter Aar en Leimuiden)"; van Balen, *Waddinxveen,* pp. 8–15.

40. Ludovico Guicciardini, *Beschrijvinghe van alle de Nederlanden*, p. 9.

41. *Informacie*, passim.

42. Calculated from *Aanbreng van 1511*. The surveying techniques of the early sixteenth century preclude complete accuracy in these calculations.

43. Pierium Winsemius, *Chronique ofte Historische Geschiedenisse van Vrieslant*, p. 522.

44. ARA, Ambtenaren Centraal Bestuur, no. 925, Register van het Centraal Bestuur met Groningen en Drenthe, folio 17. "Staat van de taxen die de Ommelanden van Groningen jaarlijks aan de Hertog van Gelre opbrengen." According to this document of 1520, 155,728 grazen, or about 83,000 hectares, were under cultivation in Groningen excluding the districts of 't Gorecht and Westerwold. At the time of the first cadastral survey, in 1833, cultivated land area was 182,292 hectares.

45. H. J. Keuning, *De Groninger Veenkoloniën*, pp. 52–53.

46. See Slicher van Bath, *Samenleving onder spanning*, for a description of Overijssel; P. Lindemans, *Geschiedenis van de landbouw in België*, for a description of the sandy-soil Kempen of Brabant; and also G. Niermeyer, "Eschprobleme in Nordwestdeutschland und in den ostlichen Niederlanden," 14th International Geographical Congress, *Comptes Rendus* 2 (1938):27–40.

47. Fockema Andreae, "Middeleeuwsch Oegstgeest," p. 262; idem, *Rijnland*, pp. 92–93. From the mid-fifteenth century onward legal developments progressively limited common rights. The right to graze livestock upon the common arable after "St. Petersday" was abolished by 1500 in Oegstgeest, Valkenburg, Katwijk, Hillegom, and Noordwijk—all villages along the dune coast.

48. O. Postma, *De Friesche kleihoeve*, p. 60; J. J. Spahr van der Hoek and O. Postma, *Geschiedenis van de Friese landbouw*, 1:137. One of the last villages to divide its common fields was Eestrum. In 1511 its pastures were still held in common. In 1612 a *schaarbrief* (enclosure patent) was issued dividing the common pasture according to the amount of arable owned by each villager.

49. See O. Postma, "Over de hoevevorming in de Friese zuidwestelijke kuststreek en op Ameland," *TEG* 45 (1954):20–26, 50–55; Johan Hendrik Sebus, *De erfgooiers en hun gemeenschappelijk bezit tot 1568*.

50. *Groot Placaat- en Charter-boek van Vriesland*, 4:416.

51. See H. P. H. Jansen, *Hoekse en Kabeljauwse twisten*, for a general account.

52. J. Kuyper, *De Republiek der Vereenigde Nederlanden in kaart en woord*, p. 28.

53. *Informacie*, pp. 441, 449.

54. Ibid., p. 447; also R.A. Brussel, Papiers d'Etat et de l'Audience, Cahiers du Xe, XXe et Ce denier, no. 618–37.

55. *Informacie*, p. 264.

56. Ibid., pp. 272, 274, 315.

57. ARA, Staten van Holland voor 1572, Tiende Penning Cohieren, no. 915.

58. ARA, Staten van Holland: 1572–1795, 12e Penning Cohier van 1572, no. 1290.

59. G. 't Hart, *Historische beschrijving van het Hoge Heerlijkheid van Heenvliet*. This excellent study makes use of the private archives of the old seigneurial family. The Heren van Heenvliet derive from a branch of the family

of the Heren van Voorne in 1229. The family held the seigneurie until 1612, when the death of the last Heer provided his heirs an opportunity to sell the rights.

60. ARA, Staten van Holland voor 1572, Tiende Penning Cohieren, no. 1194; RA Brussel, Papiers d'Etat et de l'Audience, Cahiers du Xe, XXe et Ce denier, no. 618–36.

61. Informacie, p. 484.

62. Ibid, p. 400.

63. RA Utrecht, Staten van Utrecht, Mannuaal van het Oudschildgeld van het Sticht, nos. 143-1–143-4.

64. H. A. Enno van Gelder, "Friesche en Groningsche edelen in den tijd van den opstand tegen Spanje," p. 39.

65. P. J. Blok, Geschiedenis van het Nederlandsche volk, 2d ed., 4 vols. (Leiden, 1912–15), 2:103.

66. The Chronique of Winsemius, written in 1622, includes rather detailed maps of each of the 31 grietenijen of Friesland. The stinzen are indicated on these maps with a symbol.

67. Theissen, p. 293; Maria Hartgerink-Koomans, Het geslacht Ewsum; geschiedenis van een jonkers-familie uit de Ommelanden in de 15^e en 16^e eeuw, pp. 64–65.

68. Enno van Gelder, "Friesche edelen," p. 41.

69. Aanbreng van 1511; Aanbreng der Buitendijksteren landen van 1546; T. J. de Boer, "De Friesche grond in 1511."

70. 'T Hart, pp. 52–64.

71. Informacie, passim. Beer excises are mentioned in 36 of Holland's villages.

72. S. van Leeuwen, Batavia Illustrata, pp. 854–55; Tegenwoordige Staat van Holland 6:340; 7:427, 438, 516; 8:264, 274, 279; Enno van Gelder, "Hollandse adel," pp. 127–28.

73. Enno van Gelder, "Hollandse adel," p. 134; H. Blink, Boerenstand, 1:244.

74. Blink, Boerenstand, 1:242; Informacie, pp. 620, 623.

75. Enno van Gelder, Nederlandse dorpen, pp. 69–70.

76. Hofstee, 1:145.

77. Enno van Gelder, Nederlandse dorpen, pp. 39–67.

78. H. G. Koeningsberger, "Property and the Price Revolution (Hainault, 1474–1573)." Koeningsberger's study of 2,147 land parcels held in feudal tenure showed that nobles held 62.1 percent in 1474, 69.3 percent in 1502, and 57.1 percent in 1564, measured by value.

79. Postma, Kleihoeve, p. 121; Lambertus Johannes van Apeldoorn, De kerkelijk goederen in Friesland, pp. 69–70; see also the Beneficiaal-boeken van Friesland, 1543, which lists the property of the parish churches.

80. RA Groningen, Rechterlijk Archief, no. 11.

81. E. H. Roelfsema, De klooster- en proostdijgoederen in de provincie Groningen, pp. 37, 46; J. A. Feith, "De rijkdom der kloosters van Stad en Lande," p. 29.

82. J. J. Spahr van der Hoek, Samenleven in Friesland; drie perioden uit de sociale geschiedenis, p. 54; for the distribution of religious houses, see J. H. Brouwer, ed., Encyclopedie van Friesland, p. 413.

83. Van Apeldoorn, *Kerkelijk goederen*, p. 383; J. A. Faber, "Economische op- en neergang," in Kalma et al., *Geschiedenis van Friesland*, pp. 248–49. Their holdings took the form of complete farms (*hoeven*) rather than scattered parcels. The *Aanbreng der Buitendijksteren Landen van 1546* shows that religious institutions owned 16 percent of the land in Barradeel, but only 2 percent of the land in holdings below 10 pondematen (3.7 hectares) in size.

84. ARA, Financie van Holland, "Staat van Ontvangsten en Uitgaven van Cornelis van Coolwijk, Onvanger-Generaal van de Inkomsten der Geestelijk goederen, tot onderhoud van de Predikanten, 1590." Van Apeldoorn sets the income of the confiscated lands of Friesland at 72,159 gulden in 1593 while Roelfsema sets the income of Groningen at 89,000 gulden in 1595.

85. Religious institutions owned over 20 percent in Warmond, Sassenheim, Rijnsburg, Overblokker, and around Alkmaar. In several villages of the Noorderkwartier they owned no land whatsoever; in most others they owned under 10 percent. *Informacie*, pp. 32, 35, 38, 60, 64, 67, 106, 126, 219, 280, 281, 605; ARA, Staten van Holland voor 1572, Tiende Penning Cohieren, nos. 151, 416, 580, 725, 887, 915, 1165, 1202, 1232, 1375, 1448; RA Brussel, Papiers d'Etat et de l'Audience, Cahiers du Xe, XXe et Ce denier, nos. 618-36, 618-37.

86. RA Utrecht, Staten van Utrecht, Mannuaal van het Oudschildgeld van het Sticht, nos. 143-1–143-4.

87. *Aanbreng van 1511*.

88. Diepeveen, p. 63; de Jong, p. 14.

89. Sebus, p. 105; I. H. Gosses, *Stadsbezit in land en water gedurende de middeleeuwen* (Leiden, 1903), p. 6.

90. *Informacie*, pp. 206–14.

91. ARA, Staten van Holland voor 1572, Tiende Penning Cohieren, nos. 901, 1202.

92. *Aanbreng van 1511;* the seafarers of the small coastal cities along the Zuider Zee coast (Staveren, Hindelopen, Workum) left their wives and children to tend a few cattle while they were at sea. As a consequence, common pastures around the cities played an integral role in their economy. On the other hand, such urban residents hardly qualify as a capitalist bourgeoisie, and more distant landownership on their part was uncommon. See Postma, "Hoevevorming."

93. Jan Wagenaar, *Amsterdam in Zyne Opkomst, Aanwas, Geschiedenissen, Voorregten, Koophandel, Gebouwen, Kerken, Straaten, Schoolen, Schutterijen, Gilden en Regeeringe,* 10:176.

94. J. Walvis, *Beschrijving der stad Gouda,* p. 418.

95. Brünner, *Buitennering,* p. 169.

96. *Ibid.* Shortly after its purchase of the seigneurial rights to Zoeterwoude, pressure from Brussels persuaded the municipal government to divest itself of its new acquisition.

97. Blink, *Boerenstand*, 2:197; C. Cau et al., *Groot Placaatboek van Holland en Zeeland,* 9 vols. (The Hague, 1658–1796), 2:2053; E. van Zurck, *Codex Batavus in voce Commerce,* p. 16.

98. Cau, *Groot Placaatboek van Holland en Zeeland,* 1:1268; Brünner, *Buitennering,* p. 126.

99. Christianus Schotanus, *Chroniek van Vriesland,* p. 657. Schotanus relates

that the petition of the Friesian cities argued that their extraordinary expenses for the maintenance of walls and battlements (many of which had been erected in the late fifteenth century) drove tradesmen to the countryside. They asked that all trades and scales be forbidden in the rural areas. See also: Spahr van der Hoek and Postma, *Friese landbouw*, 1:140; Blink, *Boerenstand*, 2:197.

100. In 1540 Leiden requested, and received, an edict restricting yet further than before the nonagricultural activities permitted in the surrounding villages. An inquiry into the economic activities of all persons living within about 2 kilometers of the city's walls showed that 77 households carried out 70 occupations, including secondary occupations. Only a few households cited agriculture as their primary occupation. The inquiry is reprinted in N. W. Posthumus, "Een zestiende-eeuwsche enquete naar de buitenneringen rondom de stad Leiden."

101. They were not, however, the only cities to acquire stapelrechten. In Zeeland, Middelburg held such rights over the island of Walcheren, Zierikzee over Schouwen; in Holland, Brielle exercised them over Voorne, and Naarden over het Gooi. See W. Jappe Alberts and H. P. H. Jansen, *Welvaart in wording: sociaal-economische geschiedenis van Nederland van de vroegste tijden tot het einde van de middeleeuwen*, pp. 112–13; Sebus, p. 122; T. S. Jansma, "Het economisch overwicht van de laat-middeleeuwse stad t.a.v. haar agrarisch ommeland in het bijzonder toegelicht met de verhouding tussen Leiden en Rijnland," p. 94.

102. H. C. H. Moquette, "De strijd op economisch gebied tusschen Dordrecht en Rotterdam," p. 40.

103. Johan van Beverwijk, *'t Begin van Hollant in Dordrecht*, p. 138.

104. H. Blink, "Economische geographie der provincie Groningen historisch beschouwd," *TEG*, 4 (1913):10, 19; P. N. Boekel, *De zuivelexport van Nederland tot 1813*, p. 20.

105. These figures were drawn from the *Informacie* by Naber, "Een terugblik."

106. The Morgenboeken were land registers maintained for all the villages belonging to the Hoogheemraadschap van Rijnland, a drainage authority. They formed the basis for levying polder taxes. The first of the Morgenboeken were drawn up in 1541, following a fresh, and reasonably accurate, survey of the land. Every four years thereafter the information about the users and owners of each parcel was updated. The land was not surveyed again until 1716, however. As a consequence the Morgenboeken became increasingly more cumbersome to use, and apparently less accurate, as the years pass. AH Rijnland, nos. 3258–8414.

107. *Aanbreng der Buitendijksteren landen van 1546.*

108. Diepeveen, p. 63; ARA, Staten van Holland voor 1572, Tiende Penning Cohieren, no. 1281.

109. *Informacie*, p. 117; a special survey of landownership in Opmeer made in 1582 showed that nonresident peasant proprietorship had increased to 36 percent of the total land area. ARA, Staten van Holland: 1572–1795, no. 1290cx; Staten van Holland voor 1572, Tiende Penning Cohieren, no. 901.

110. These figures were calculated from the *Aanbreng der Buitendijksteren landen van 1546*, by O. Postma, "Een Friesch dorp in 1546," *De Vrije Fries*, 27 (1924):8–17.

111. Enno van Gelder, *Nederlandse dorpen*, pp. 40, 41n, 110.

112. See Bloch, pp. 189–96, for a discussion of common misconceptions concerning this problem.

113. Ibid., p. 191; Pierre Goubert, "The French Peasantry of the Seventeenth Century," gives a concise account of French terminology on this matter.

114. The process of formation of hoeven is described for dozens of villages in van der Linden.

115. Postma, *Kleihoeve*. This study investigates the old hoeve system of Friesland and Groningen. Postma's conclusion is that a hoeve of about 50 pondematen (18 hectares) and of 30 grazen (16 hectares) in Groningen were common, pp. 185–86. De Boer, p. 103, comes to a similar conclusion, noting that the *heerd*, a farm of 30 grazen, was the equivalent to a hoeve in Groningen.

116. Quoted in Schotanus, *Chroniek*, pp. 184–85.

117. *Informacie*, pp. 545–47.

118. Van der Linden, pp. 167–70.

119. *Enqueste*, pp. 98–99; *Informacie*, pp. 221–22.

120. It would be wrong to think of the majority of the landless population living in the village to be impoverished. Of the 41 houses in the village, only 13 were valued at less than 7 gulden while 22 were valued at 7 to 11 gulden and 6 were valued at over 11 gulden. ARA, Staten van Holland voor 1572, Tiende Penning Cohieren, no. 1391.

121. *Informacie*, pp. 309–11.

122. Ibid., pp. 302–03.

123. AH Rijnland, no. 8400.

124. D. M. Rodenburg, "De Morgenboeken van Benthuizen."

125. Although only a few respondents described their tax allocation system in sufficient detail to allow a reconstruction of the distribution of wealth in the village, the process used was different in each of these villages. Thus, the value of the schotpond, where it is used, will be observed to be different in each village.

126. *Informacie*, pp. 283–84.

127. Ibid., pp. 274–76.

128. Ibid., pp. 318–19.

129. Ibid., pp. 311–12.

130. Ibid., pp. 569–79.

131. Ibid. pp. 540–68, 415–27.

132. All these figures are drawn from village and city data available in the *Informacie*. A similar inquiry was made into the economic affairs of Brabant in 1526. Calculations of the number of households in poverty made from this *dénombrement* show that about 23 percent of the urban and 30 percent of the rural population was in poverty. J. A. van Houtte, "Maatschappelijke toestanden," in *Algemene geschiedenis der Nederlanden*, 4:240.

133. *Informacie*, pp. 354–55.

134. Ibid., pp. 223–24.

135. Ibid., pp. 286–88.

136. Ibid., pp. 298–99.

137. Ibid., p. 310.

138. *Enqueste*, pp. 107, 108, 117, 135; *Informacie*, pp. 47, 96, 212, 229–34, 312; Brünner, *Buitennering*, p. 149.

139. Diepeveen, pp. 116–19, 151–53.

140. Posthumus, "Een zestiende-eeuwsche enquete," p. 46.

141. Brünner, *Buitennering,* p. 150; *Informacie,* pp. 53–54, 65–66, 217–18, 302, 588, 596; *Enqueste,* pp. 53–54.

142. J. F. Niermeyer, *De wording van onze volkshuishouding,* p. 48; Willem van Ravesteyn, Jr., *Onderzoekingen over de economische-sociale ontwikkeling van Amsterdam gedurende de 16ᵈᵉ en het eerste kwart der 17ᵈᵉ eeuw,* pp. 30–33.

143. A map showing the distribution of these activities is available in M. J. Boerendonk, "Economische aardrijkskunde van Holland omstreeks het jaar 1500."

144. *Informacie,* p. 480.

145. Ibid., p. 479.

146. Ibid., pp. 367–68.

147. Another center of dairy production was Assendelft. Although we know nothing of the size of herds in the early sixteenth century, a quotation, ascribed to both the late fifteenth and late sixteenth century, describes it as follows: "There is a village in this land, called Assendelft, . . . which contains four thousand cows, which give daily, winter and summer reckoned together, at least eight thousand pots of milk. And there are in this district four other villages which, together with the aforementioned Assendelft deliver yearly more milk than Dordrecht has Rhine wine, though it is the wine staple of these lands" (Abraham Ortelius, *Spieghel der Werelt* [Antwerp, 1577]; also cited in H. J. Koenen, *De Nederlandsche boerenstand,* p. 44).

148. *Informacie,* p. 269.

149. Ibid., p. 558.

150. Ibid., p. 283.

151. Ibid., p. 290.

152. *Enqueste,* pp. 112, 255; *Informacie,* pp. 33, 457, 126–27.

153. *Informacie,* pp. 290–91.

154. Ibid., p. 295; *Enqueste,* pp. 152–53.

155. *Enqueste,* p. 5; *Informacie,* p. 213.

156. GA Hoorn, no. 902.

157. *Enqueste,* pp. 7, 9, 11, 18, 19, 29, 64, 69, 73, 82, 90, 92, 131; *Informacie,* pp. 60–61, 110, 167, 565, 568, 577; ARA, Staten van Holland voor 1572, Tiende Penning Cohieren, no. 1210. In Friesland such arable strips can be identified in the *Aanbreng* of 1511 and 1546 by the use of their name in field names. Such strips were called *ware, warren. warkes,* and *saedwallen.* Spahr van der Hoek and Postma, *Friese landbouw,* 2:606–14.

158. *Enqueste,* pp. 110, 112, 115, 116, 131, 136, 145, 174, 183, 185, 187, 191, 199, 207, 218, 224, 226, 229, 231, 235, 250, 252, 254; *Informacie,* pp. 352, 356, 364, 394, 396, 400, 419, 420, 546, 548, 551, 553, 554, 557, 566, 578; Brünner, *Buitennering,* p. 55.

159. Abel, *Deutsche Landwirtschaft,* p. 157.

160. Cited in Blink, *Boerenstand,* 2:17.

161. *Enqueste,* p. 140; *Informacie,* pp. 274–76; J. Honing Jsz Jr., "Een langdurige strijd," *Zaanlandsch Jaarboek, 1932* (Koog aan de Zaan, 1932), p. 108; P. van Balen, *Uit de geschiedenis van Haastrecht,* p. 42; RA Brussel, Pa-

piers d'Etat et de l'Audience, Cahiers du Xe XXe et Ce denier, no. 618–37. Virtually every house in Veen had a small hops field nearby. They were rarely so much as a morgen in size; the entire village of 82 households and 570 morgen included 33.5 morgen of hopland.

162. W. J. Sangers, *De ontwikkeling van de Nederlandse tuinbouw tot het jaar 1930*, p. 58.

163. Blink, *Boerenstand*, 2:244.

164. A good description of the former sort of trade, which shows its inability to lead to a more complex interdependent economy, is found in Sol Tax, *Penny Capitalism*, Smithsonian Institution, Institute of Social Anthropology Publication no. 16.

CHAPTER 3

1. Mols, *Introduction*, 1:100–64.

2. Idem, "Beschouwingen over de bevolkingsgeschiedenis in de Nederlanden (15^e en 16^e eeuw)," p. 214.

3. It is not always possible to distinguish houses from nonoccupied structures; moreover, farmhouses rented as one unit with their land are omitted from the enumeration of buildings.

4. A. M. van der Woude, "De weerbare mannen van 1747 in de dorpen van het Zuiderkwartier van Holland als demografisch gegeven." On the basis of population data for several villages taken a few years earlier by Nicolaas Struyck, van der Woude puts forward upper and lower limit coefficients of 4.35 and 3.85 respectively.

5. Nicolaas Struyck, *Vervolg van de beschrijving der staartsterren, en nader ontdekkingen omtrent den staat van 't menschelyk geslacht*; W. Kersseboom, *Proeven van Politique Rekenkunde*.

6. For an account of demographic sources and the problems which attach to their use, see B. H. Slicher van Bath, "Historical Demography and the Social and Economic Development of the Netherlands," pp. 606–07; idem, "Report on the Study of Historical Demography in the Netherlands," pp. 187–90.

7. Most notably A. M. van der Woude and G. J. Mentink, *De demografische ontwikkeling te Rotterdam en Cool in de XVII en XVIII eeuw*; a summary of this work is to be found in "La Population de Rotterdam au XVIIe et au XVIIIe siècle," *Population* 21 (1966):1165–90. This exemplary work, based on the baptism and burial records of the various congregations of Rotterdam, could produce results only by employing elaborate weighting systems to account for the ever changing proportions that the various religious groups made in the total population of the city.

8. Le Roy Ladurie, 1:633–54.

9. Abel, *Agrarkrisen*, pp. 266–69. Another confirmation that the marginal returns to labor diminished sharply in the preindustrial economy has been produced in Ronald Lee's important study of English population and wage data. See Ronald Lee, "Econometric Studies of Topics in Demographic History," (Ph.D. diss., Harvard University, 1971); idem, "Population in Pre-Industrial England: An Econometric Analysis," *Quarterly Journal of Economics*, forthcoming.

10. T. R. Malthus, *First Essay on Population* (Royal Economic Society reprint), pp. 137–38.

11. Many authorities have compiled evidence in support of this threefold division of the European population. The particularly high death rates of large cities is the best documented feature. See Mols, *Introduction*, 2:305–22; also, below, n. 59, for further citations. The difference in birth rates between agricultural and rural industrial populations is harder to investigate. Evidence in support of this distinction is provided by Peterson, "Demographic Transition in the Netherlands"; J. D. Chambers, "The Vale of Trent, 1670–1800: A Regional Study of Economic Change," *EHR*, supplement no. 3 (1957); P. Deprez, "Demographic Development of Flanders in the Eighteenth Century," in David Glass and D. E. C. Eversley, eds., *Population in History* (Chicago, 1965), pp. 619–20; Rudolph Braun, *Industrialisierung und Volksleben: Die Veränderungen der Lebensformen in einem ländlichen Industriegebiet vor 1800* (Erlenbach-Zürich, 1960).

12. W. Gordon East, *An Historical Geography of Europe* (London, 1935), pp. 129–30.

13. H. van Werveke, *De curve van het Gentse bevolkingscijfer in de 17e en 18e eeum* (Brussels, 1948); R. Boumans, "L'évolution démographique d'Anvers (XVe–XVIIIe siècle)," *Bulletin de Statistique*, vol. 34 (1948).

14. Everitt, "The Marketing of Agricultural Produce," p. 514.

15. The population history of the Netherlands between the time of the Black Death and the beginning of the sixteenth century is not well known. The greatest mystery is the impact of the plague itself. In England, France, and Germany the plague's impact was great, but little evidence of population decimation presents itself in the Low Countries. H. van Werveke's study, "De zwarte dood in de Zuidelijke Nederlanden 1349–1351," and Abel's *Agrarkrisen* both suggest that the intensity of the plague lessened as one neared the northwest corner of Europe. Land reclamation in Holland certainly slackened after 1350, but it did not cease altogether, and *Wüstungen* did not arise. The evidence, sparse though it is, suggests a stationary population. The numerous hearth counts of Brabant in the fifteenth century uphold this view; a hearth count in central Holland (Rijnland) in 1370 indicates that the population fell 23 percent between then and 1494, but 1494 represents a low point of population. The three dates for which the *Enqueste* and *Informacie* provide hearth count data—1477, 1494, and 1514—enclose two periods, the first of which experienced a 20 percent fall, and the second a 15 percent rise of population.

16. Villages 1, 2, 3, and 5 in graph 3.3 distinguish themselves from the others by declining less between 1622 and 1732–47 and falling more rapidly thereafter. All these villages were either part of, or adjacent to, the Zaanstreek, an intensely industrialized region that followed a population course quite independent of the rest of the Noorderkwartier.

17. Struyck, passim. A striking confirmation of the Noorderkwartier's depopulation is found in documents listing all places licensed to sell beer. In 1734 there were only 56 percent as many as in 1669. In the Zuiderkwartier, on the other hand, the number increased by 48 percent in the same period. ARA, Staten van Holland: 1572–1795, no. 4033.

18. From data in A. M. van der Woude, "Weerbare mannen," p. 45.

19. This presumption is based not on demographic evidence, but on indicators of economic activity and tax revenues. These show decline in the first half of the eighteenth century. Yet, from the weerbare mannen lists we know that rural population south of the Ij was *at least* at the level of 1622. The conclusion seems inescapable that population increased further between 1622 and 1660–70. A 10-percent increase, included in graph 3.6, is only a conservative guess.

20. J. A. van Houtte, "Het economisch verval van het Zuiden," in *Algemene geschiedenis der Nederlanden,* 5:222. Van Houtte estimates that in the first decade of the seventeenth century one-third of Amsterdam's population and one-fifth of Rotterdam's was of southern Netherlands origin.

21. J. C. Ramaer, "De middelpunten van bewoning in Nederland voorheen en thans," pp. 36–37.

22. Van der Woude and Mentink, "Population de Rotterdam," p. 1180.

23. S. J. Fockema Andreae et al., *Duizend jaar bouwen in Nederland,* 2:34–35; F. J. Ganshof, "Over stadsontwikkeling tusschen Loire en Rijn gedurende de middeleeuwen," *Verhandelingen van de Koningklijke Vlaamsche Academie van Wetenschappen, Letteren en Schoone Kunsten van België, Klasse der Letteren, enz.,* 3 (1941):47.

24. For examples, see Violet Barbour, *Capitalism in Amsterdam in the 17th Century,* p. 13; Eric Hobsbawm, "The Crisis of the Seventeenth Century," pp. 44–45.

25. A rank-order formula applied to the cities of Holland in 1514, when the 5 largest cities stood at about the same population level, does not fit at all; in 1795, when most cities except Amsterdam were much decayed, it does not fit either. Then, Amsterdam stood far above the rest. But during the seventeenth and early eighteenth centuries the fit is very close indeed and suggests that Amsterdam, large though it was by contemporary standards, did not dominate the region in the manner that London dominated England after 1500. For a historical application of this concept, see J. C. Russell, "The Metropolitan City Region in the Middle Ages."

26. Johan Huizinga, *Dutch Civilization in the Seventeenth Century,* (London: Fontana paperback, 1968), p. 15.

27. See Peter Hall, *The World Cities* (New York, 1966), pp. 95–121.

28. F. J. Fisher, "The Development of London as a Centre of Conspicuous Consumption in the Sixteenth and Seventeenth Centuries," *TRHS,* 4th ser., 30 (1948):37–50; E. A. Wrigley, "A simple model of London's importance in changing English society and economy, 1650–1750."

29. The role of Germany and Belgium as a "hinterland" has not received much attention. See, however, Herbert Kisch, "Mercantilism and the Rise of the Krefeld Silk Industry: variations on an eighteenth century theme"; Jan Craeybeckx, "Les industries d'exportation dans les villes flamandes au XVIIe siècle, particulièrement à Gand et à Bruges," in *Studi in Onore di Amintore Fanfani,* vol. 4 (Milan, 1962), pp. 413–68.

30. Spahr van der Hoek, *Samenleven in Friesland,* pp. 55–68. The nonagricultural character of *vlekken* is demonstrated below in chap. 6.

31. *Charter-boek van Vriesland,* 3:329.

32. Jacob van Deventer, *Nederlandsche steden in de 16e eeuw, plattegronden* (The Hague, 1916–23); Schotanus, *Chroniek van Vriesland*; E. van Hinte, *Sociale en economische geografie van Harlingen* (Harlingen, 1936).

33. J. A. Faber et al., "Population changes and economic developments in the Netherlands," pp. 63–64.

34. RA Leeuwarden, Rekenkamer Archief, Quotisatie Cohieren van 1749, no 14e.

35. O. Postma, "De Saksische jaartax in Friesland," *De Vrije Fries* 44 (1939):71.

36. G. J. A. Mulder, ed., *Handboek der Geografie van Nederland*, 5:149.

37. H. A. Wijnne, *Handel en ontwikkeling van Stad en Provincie Groningen, geschiedkundig beschouwd*, pp. 75–76.

38. RA Groningen, Staten van Stad en Lande, 1594–1798, nos. 2133–36, Schatregister voor de verponding, 1630; no. 2143, Schatregister voor de verponding, 1721; no. 2217, Kohier van het Taxatiegeld, 1730–31.

39. Keuning, *Groninger Veenkoloniën*, p. 68; *Tegenwoordige Staat van Groningen*, 21:214–19.

40. ARA, Ambtenaren Centraal Bestuur, Register van het Centraal Bestuur met Groningen en Drenthe, no. 925, fol. 17, "Staat van de taxen, die de Omme-landen van Groningen jaarlijks aan de Hertog van Gelre opbrengen.

41. Boumans, p. 117.

42. The blockade of the Danish Sound caused grain scarcity in 1536; for an analysis of the later two crises see Astrid Friis, "An Inquiry into the Relations between Economic and Financial Factors in the 16th and 17th centuries; The two crises in the Netherlands in 1557"; Erich Kuttner, *Het hongerjaar 1566*.

43. *Charter-boek van Vriesland*, 3:837. The flood killed, according to reports sent to the provincial government, 957 persons in Westdongeradeel and 1,510 in Oostdongeradeel, plus several hundred in other areas. The severe floods of 1717 are reported to have killed 2,091 persons in Groningen, as well as over 11,000 cattle and 21,000 sheep. (*Naauwkeurige beschrijving der twee voornaamste watervloeden van de XVIII eeuw, in 1717 en 1775* . . . [Amsterdam, 1776; deposited in the Conrad Collection on Dutch Waterways, Stanford University], p. 41.) Even if these figures are trustworthy they would not in themselves prove that mortality was increased by drowning. Rather, the major impact of inunda-tions must be sought in the lasting adverse health conditions that they bring in their wake.

44. F. J. B. d'Alphonse, *Aperçu sur la Hollande*, pp. 553–55. In 1811 infant mortality, which was 218.5 per thousand live births for the kingdom as a whole, stood at 265 and 250 in South and North Holland, respectively, and at only 170 in the rural eastern provinces. Struyck, the eighteenth-century demographer, published figures for 42 Noorderkwartier villages in the 1740s that implied an incredibly high crude death rate of nearly 45 per thousand (Struyck, p. 84).

45. Sir William Temple, *Observations upon the United Provinces of the Netherlands*, p. 186.

46. *Tegenwoordige Staat van Overijssel*, 1:24–29.

47. Van der Woude and Mentink, "Population de Rotterdam," p. 1181.

48. Contemporaries did not fail to appreciate the connection between eco-nomic conditions and family formation. The chronicler of Hoorn, describing

the prosperous conditions of the mid-seventeenth century, wrote that "because the city was stuffed with people, the merchants and tradesmen prospered. Often marriages had to be postponed, not to wait for a suitable occupation, but because of the housing shortage." (Dirk Velius, *Kroniek van Hoorn*, 2:37.)

49. Goren Ohlin devised a preindustrial demographic model based on the fertility and mortality characteristics of eighteenth-century Sweden in order to estimate the sensitivity of the birth rate to the average age at first marriage. He found that for women in their twenties, a one-year delay in marriage reduced the birth rate by approximately 2.5 per thousand. (Goren Ohlin, "The Positive and the Preventive Check.")

50. Leonie van Nierop, "De bruidgoms van Amsterdam van 1578 tot 1601."

51. S. Hart, "Bronnen voor de historische demografie van Amsterdam in de 17e en 18e eeuw."

52. ARA., Staten van Holland voor 1572, Tiende Penning Cohieren, nos. 901, 1217 (Twisk), 803, 1125, 1453 (Beets), 272, 1008, 1327, 1573 (Diemen). For survival rates of preindustrial societies, see Colin Clark, *Population Growth and Land Use* (London, 1967), pp. 34–42, and sources cited therein. There exists, of course, a third interpretation of disappearance rates derived from the Tiende Penning Cohieren: that the records are full of omissions. The village records chosen for analysis here were compiled by listing houses in sequence as the official proceeded along roads in each district of the village. In successive years, the same route was taken. It is probable that each house listed the first year was recorded in succeeding years as well. Whether *all* houses were recorded, or all new houses, we cannot be certain.

53. Posthumus, "Een zestiende-eeuwsche enquete."

54. RA Leeuwarden, Nedergerechten Archieven, weesboeken, no. 8n, vol. 10.

55. On the other hand, only 3 percent ventured beyond the boundaries of Friesland. An examination of the "indemnity registers" in the village of Hillegersberg, near Rotterdam, showed that between 1711 and 1800 the gradually declining population was infused by over 6,100 migrants. In 1804 only one-third of the population had been born in the village. The birthplaces of the immigrants in the period 1711–1800 show that only 12.5 percent came from beyond the modern province of South Holland. Much of this movement was accounted for by the ebb and flow of peat diggers. (R. A. D. Renting, "Onderzoek naar de bevolkingsstructuur binnen het ambacht Hillegersberg.") This, plus the evidence from seventeenth-century Friesland and sixteenth-century Holland, shows that mobility, while taking place at a furious rate, was not far-reaching. Could it be that mobility in the early modern period contrasts with that of the industrial era not so much in frequency as in range?

56. J. C. Westermann, "Statistiche gegevens over den handel van Amsterdam in de 17e eeuw"; GA Haarlem, nos. L 313–23 (1078); N. W. Posthumus, 2:938–39.

57. Gemeentearchief van Twisk, Quohier van alle Familien tot Twisch, 1715, no. 36; Peter Laslett, "Size and Structure of the Household in England," pp. 215–16. Of the 528 persons resident in Twisk in 1715, 136 were husbands and wives, making 68 couples. In addition there were 20 spinsters and 42 bachelors plus 29 widows. Of the 159 households, 94 consisted of 3 or fewer persons.

58. A. M. van der Woude, "Huishouding in Nederland," pp. 223–25. The 4,089 households were drawn from village records dating from between 1622 and 1795.

The 2,943 households that date from the period 1672–1748 possessed an average size rather below the overall average of 3.7. The eighteenth-century demographer Struyck put forward mid-century statistics for 59 Noorderkwartier villages that show an average household size of 3.8 (Struyck, p. 84).

59. Many sources document the inability of urban populations to replenish their numbers without constant immigration. Perhaps the most exhaustive source is still that of the Prussian army chaplain Johann Peter Süssmilch, *Die Göttliche Ordnung in den Veränderungen des Menschlichen Geschlechtes. . . .* See also Eli. F. Hecksher, "Swedish Population Trends before the Industrial Revolution," *EHR*, 2d ser. 2 (1950): 266–77; E. A. Wrigley, "London's importance."

60. J. H. F. Kohlbrugge, "Over den invloed der steden op hare bewoners en op de bewoners van het land," p. 374.

61. Hart, "Bronnen voor de historische demografie van Amsterdam." Between 1660 and 1800 the percentage of all persons who were married in Amsterdam and born elsewhere fluctuated between a minimum of 43 percent and a maximum of 57 percent. In the period 1731–40, to take an example, half of those married, or 2,600 per year, had been born elsewhere. If all migrants to the city were unmarried, and if all married eventually, this figure would approximate the yearly number of immigrants. It would have to be reduced, of course, by an unknown number who left the city in order to become an estimate of net immigration.

62. Van der Woude and Mentink, "Population de Rotterdam," p. 1187.

63. The burial and baptism records for Haarlem (*1*), Delft (*2*), Dordrecht (*3*), Gouda (*4*), Schiedam (*5*), and Amsterdam (*6*) are presented below in the form of a ratio of births per hundred deaths; a dash indicates that data were not available.

Period	(1)	(2)	(3)	(4)	(5)	(6)
1690–99	—	103	—	—	—	—
1700–09	—	97	96	89	—	90
1710–19	80	84	87	96		84
1720–29	60	82	83	87	97[a]	75
1730–39	79	81	92	96		81
1740–49	—	—	—	—	—	78
1750–74	79[b]					84
1775–99						75

SOURCES: Kersseboom, pp. 39–41; *Statistiek der bevolking van Amsterdam tot 1921*, table 179.

[a] An average for the entire period 1710–39. This city of under 10,000 inhabitants was apparently healthier than the larger cities.

[b] For the years 1766–87.

Raw burial and baptism data, upon which the above ratios are based, generally underestimate the rate of natural increase. "Only in the ideal circumstance where all children are baptised before their death and in which stillborn children are not recorded in the burial register are these figures useable without revision" (van der Woude and Mentink, *Rotterdam*, p. 70).

64. Kohlbrugge, p. 383.

65. Our pessimistic conclusions stand in sharp contrast to E. A. Wrigley's own

application of this demographic model to England. He concluded that London's enormous size acted as a stimulant to the economy both by encouraging commercial agriculture and by draining away surplus rural population that otherwise might have inhibited market development. The commercializing impact of London is beyond doubt, yet is it not worthy of note that, as Deane's and Cole's regional analysis in *British Economic Growth, 1688–1959* (Cambridge, 1969) makes clear, the home of dynamic structural change in the English economy of the eighteenth century was found in the north and northwest, where London's demographic impact was weakest?

66. For a review of the arguments see T. J. Kastelein, "Social structure and economic growth in the Netherlands."

67. Slicher van Bath, *Samenleving onder spanning,* chap. 6, passim.

68. A. Cosemans, *De bevolking van Brabant in de XVIIe en XVIIIe eeuw* (Brussels, 1939); Franklin F. Mendels, "Industrialization and Population Pressure in Eighteenth Century Flanders." According to estimates made by Mendels, the rural population of the sandy-soil parts of Flanders grew by 104 percent during the eighteenth century while the Flemish cities grew by only 24 percent. Another sandy-soil region, the Veluwe, a part of Gelderland, also experienced rapid rural population growth and deurbanization during the late seventeenth and eighteenth centuries. See H. K. Roessingh, "Het Veluwse inwonertal, 1526–1947."

69. For further discussion, see chap. 1, where two models of rural development are presented. English researchers have also tried to distinguish agrarian structures according to the degree to which they absorb additions to the population. See Thirsk, "Industries in the Countryside."

CHAPTER 4

1. This figure is drawn from the *Aanbreng van 1511,* which listed all taxable land. We can reasonably assume that all improved land was taxed.

2. RA Brussel, Papiers d'Etat et de l'Audience, no. 1429, De Monstercedellen van 1552.

3. Charter-boek van Vriesland, 3:101. Elsewhere in the *Charter-boek,* the construction of new houses in this grietenij is noted (3:359).

4. *Ibid.,* 3:108.

5. RA Leeuwarden, Rekenkamer Archief, Belasting Cohieren, no. 14b.

6. Winsemius, p. 576.

7. The rental increase figure is based on a comparison of the average of all rents recorded in the *Aanbreng van 1511* and a sample of rents recorded in the *Register van geestelijke opkomsten van Oostergo,* 1580. Price trends are based on N. W. Posthumus, *Inquiry into the History of Prices in Holland.*

8. Gemeentearchief van Idaarderadeel, document no. IV, 289.

9. RA Leeuwarden, Gedeputeerde Staten, Beheer der Finantien, no. 1.

10. M. P. van Buijtenen, *De grietenij Idaarderadeel* (Dokkum, 1947), p. 72.

11. A. L. Heerman van Voss, "De inpoldering van de Wargastermeer en Paulus Jansz. Kley," *De Vrije Fries* 34 (1937):106, 112.

12. The herd size figures are drawn from our study of farm inventories, discussed more fully later in this book. RA Leeuwarden, Nedergerechten Archieven, weesboeken.

13. R. A. Leuwarden, Staten van Friesland, no. 9, Cohieren van Stemgerechtigden, 1640.

14. R. A. Leeuwarden, Rekenkamer Archief, Floreen-Cohier van de Reële
100ste Penning.

15. *Informacie,* p. 310; ARA, Staten van Holland voor 1572, Tiende Penning
Cohieren, nos. 151, 1202. The Cohier of 1544 listed 99 houses. It excluded houses
with a rental value under 2 guldens, but in 1561 there were only 25 houses with
a rental value under 6 guldens. Clearly, population growth was very rapid in the
decades preceding the Revolution.

16. ARA, Staten van Holland: 1572–1795, XIIe Penning Cohier, no. 1290; AH
Rijnland, "Quoyer van . . . den Gebruyckte Landen van den Zomer van
[15]75"; N. W. Posthumus, "Gegevens betreffende landbouw toestanden in Rijnland in het jaar 1575."

17. AH Rijnland, Morgenboeken; ARA, Financie van Holland, Leggers der
Verponding Cohieren, no. 496; A. G. van der Steur, "Een demografische,
agrarische en sociale statistiek van de steden en dorpen in het Kwartier van
Lieden in de jaren 1807–1808."

18. ARA, Financie van Holland, Leggers der Verponding Cohieren, nos. 497,
505.

19. RA Leeuwarden, Bildtrekening van 1527–28, Bildtrekening van 1536–37
(reprinted in H. Sannes, *Geschiedenis van het Bildt,* vol. 3, app. II).

20. RA Brussel, Papiers d'Etat et de l'Audience, no. 1429, De Monstercedellen
van 1552.

21. RA Leeuwarden, Rekenkamer Archief, Quotisatie Cohieren van 1749, no.
14e.

22. RA Leeuwarden, Landdrost Archief, Bevolking statistiek, 1807.

23. ARA, Financie van Holland, Leggers der Verponding Cohieren, nos. 485–
522; van der Steur, "Demografische statistiek," pp. 184–96; *Informacie,* passim.

24. ARA, Financie van Holland, Leggers der Verponding Cohieren, nos. 485–
522.

25. Data from the Morgenboeken of AH Rijnland have been compiled in L.
Jansen, "De morgenboek van het Ambacht Ter Aar in Rijnland, 1543–1680."

26. B. W. van der Kloot-Meyburg, *De economische ontwikkeling van een zuid-
Hollandsch dorp (Oudshoorn) tot in den aanvang der twintigste eeuw,* pp. 5–6.

27. ARA, Financie van Holland, Leggers der Verponding Cohieren, no. 497.

28. *Informacie,* p. 212.

29. W. van Engelenburg, *Geschiedenis van Broek in Waterland,* p. 160.

30. Postma, "Hoevevorming," pp. 23–24.

31. The ownership of schotschietende huizen in the grietenij Opsterland was
divided among the major social classes as follows:

Year	Farmers	Noblemen	Church	Total
1640	288	38	17	343
1698	210	98	25	333
1728	174	145	26.5	354.5

SOURCE: H. G. W. van der Wielen, *Een Friesche
landbouw-veenkolonie,* p. 93.

J. A. Faber, in a lucid study of the emergence of oligarchy in Friesland, has shown that the above trend was present in the province as a whole. In 1640 hoofdelingen held sufficient property to give them 26 percent of the stemmen (votes); in 1698 they controlled 38 percent of the stemmen. Their new stemmen were selectively acquired to maximize the political power gained per gulden invested in land. Thus, in 1640 the hoofdelingen held a majority of stemmen in 4 of the 30 grietenijen while in 1698 they controlled 17—a majority in the provincial assembly. (Faber, "De oligarchisering van Friesland in de tweede helft van de zeventiende eeuw," pp. 44, 48.)

32. R. Trow-Smith, 2:179.

33. This differentiation is shown clearly in the accompanying table, which presents the pondematen of arable land in villages in Leeuwarderadeel in 1511 and 1768.

Village		1511	1768
Stiens	Noordertrimdeel	900	1465
Finkum		330	588.5
Goutum	Zuidertrimdeel	212	10.5
Wirdum		450	0

SOURCE: Spahr van der Hoek and Postma, *Friese landbouw*, 2:627.

The farm inventories also reflect this specialization process and are able to verify that it took place well before the eighteenth century. In Hennaarderadeel, a grietenij that reduced its arable acreage, plows were found on 63 percent of farms with 10 or more milk cows and 35 percent of farms with less than 10 milk cows in 1550–64. Ninety years later the percentages of farms with plows stood at 45 and 18, respectively. In Leeuwarderadeel, 71 to 80 percent of all farm inventories in the Noordertrimdeel record plows throughout the period 1566–1687, while in the Zuidertrimdeel plow ownership falls from 67 percent in 1583–99 to 31 percent in 1677–86.

34. Van der Steur, "Demografische statistiek," p. 189.

35. Spahr van der Hoek and Postma, *Friese landbouw*, 2:206.

36. C. Mol, *Uit de geschiedenis van Wormer*, p. 101.

37. L. A. Ankum, "Een bijdrage tot de geschiedenis van de Zaanse olieslagerij," pp. 49, 53, 232–33. A memorial of 1648 claimed that the entire province of Holland then had 200 oil-pressing mills. Despite the rapid increase in production capacity, oilcakes were regularly imported from the fenlands of England. From an average export of 6,000 to 7,000 cakes per year between 1601 and 1604, the volume increased erratically until 1640, the last year for which information is available, when 55,000 cakes left Boston for the Netherlands. (*The Port Books of Boston, 1601–1640*.)

38. Abel Eppens, *Kroniek van Groningen*, 2:735.

39. Sir Richard Weston, *Discours of Husbandrie used in Brabant and Flanders*.

40. Lindemans, *Landbouw in België*, 1:430.

41. Slicher van Bath, *Agrarian History*, p. 279; Charles Wilson, *Anglo-Dutch Commerce and Finance in the Eighteenth Century*, p. 49.

42. W. J. Dewez, "De landbouw in Brabants westhoek in het midden van de achttiende eeuw," p. 12; Blink, *Boerenstand*, 2:55; G. Wttewaal, "Landbouwkundige beschrijving van een gedeelte der Provincie Utrecht tusschen de Stad Utrecht en Wijk bij Duurstede."

43. Spahr van der Hoek and Postma, *Friese landbouw*, 2:102.

44. Gerard van Spaan, *Beschryvinge der Stad Rotterdam*, p. 167.

45. RA Haarlem, Oud Rechterlijke en Weeskamer Archieven, no. 2595.

46. J. le Francq van Berkhey, *Verhandeling over het Nationaal Gebruik der Turf of Houtassche in Holland*, p. 51.

47. For a full discussion see Trow-Smith, vol. 2.

48. *Charter-boek van Vriesland*, quoted in Spahr van der Hoek and Postma, *Friese landbouw*, 2:236; C. Mol, pp. 127–28.

49. Trow-Smith, 2:15–16.

50. Abel, *Deutschen Landwirtschaft*, pp. 175, 215.

51. Slicher van Bath, *Agrarian History*, pp. 367–68.

52. B. H. Slicher van Bath, "Een landbouwbedrijf in de tweede helft van de zestiende eeuw," pp. 105–08.

53. Eppens, 2:727–28.

54. J. Bouman, *Bedijking, opkomst en bloei van de Beemster*, p. 248.

55. RA Leeuwarden, Nedergerechten Archieven, weesboeken. Another measure of milk output obtained from the farm inventories is the average number of *aden* (decreaming vessels) per cow. In the nineteenth century, when they were made of metal, their capacity averaged 25 to 30 liters. If in earlier centuries, when made of wood, these vessels were of a constant capacity, we might be able to read something into the fact that the average number of aden per milk cow on farms with 10 or more milk cows rose from 1.6 in Hennaarderadeel in 1550–62, to 1.8 in Leeuwarderadeel in 1566–76 and 1583–92, to 2.0 in Leeuwarderadeel in 1616–17 and 1634–41. Inventories in the late seventeenth century show a decline to 1.9 aden per milk cow.

56. Van Balen, *Waddinxveen*, p. 11.

57. Idem, *Haastrecht*, p. 42.

58. ARA, Staten van Holland voor 1572, Tiende Penning Cohieren, no. 1453. The compiler of the 1556 register referred to the arable land as the remnant of the arable land of earlier decades.

59. *Informacie*, p. 61; Aris van Braam, *Bloei en verval het economisch-sociale leven aan de Zaan in de 17ᵉ en 18ᵉ eeuw.*

60. S. J. Fockema Andreae, "Uit de geschiedenis van een Rijnlandse polder, p. 57.

61. Even buckwheat, which was well suited to local soils, apparently suffered a diminution in production. During the grain crisis of 1698 the Pensionaris of Holland suggested that the practice followed in the previous crisis, that of 1630, be followed of setting a maximum price on buckwheat. The reply came that, in contrast to 1630, the Republic was now so dependent on imports that price fixing would simply divert foreign supplies to other lands with higher prices. (See J. G. van Dillen, "Dreigende hongersnood in de Republiek in de laatste jaren der zeventiende eeuw," p. 198.)

62. *Informacie van Brielle en Land van Voorne, 1565, Informacie.*

63. ARA, Staten van Holland voor 1572, Tiende Penning Cohieren, no. 1495; van der Steur, "Demografische statistiek," pp. 184–96.

64. ARA, Financie van Holland, Kohier van het redres-generaal der Verponding, 1632, no. 467; Sangers, *Tuinbouw*, pp. 23–46.

65. *Enqueste*, pp. 49–50; *Tegenwoordige Staat van Holland*, 8:219.

66. Spahr van der Hoek and Postma, *Friese landbouw*, 1:168–69.

67. RA Leeuwarden, Nedergerechten Archieven, huurcontracten.

68. Sannes, 1:413.

69. Compiled from inventories in RA Leeuwarden, Nedergerechten Archieven, weesboeken. The possibility exists that these records may occasionally have omitted fallow from the lists of goods and assets.

70. GA Haarlem, Archieven van het Sint Elizabeths Gasthuis, Landpachtboeken, no. 53 (1479), and Conditien van Huur en verhuur van Landerijen, no. 55 (1493).

71. Foeke Sjoerds, *Algemeene Beschrijvinge van Oud en Nieuw Friesland*, p. 172.

72. Slicher van Bath, "Landbouwbedrijf," p. 97.

73. See Slicher van Bath, *Agrarian History*, p. 16, for a full description of the interrelationship.

74. Von Grouner described the great manure store place near Dendermonde, where, it seemed, the fecal matter of all the cities of the Netherlands was sent, in Slicher van Bath, *Agrarian History*, p. 281.

75. Lindemans, *Landbouw in België*, 2:52.

76. Postma, *Kleihoeve*, p. 170; *Charter-boek van Vriesland*, 5:651, 973.

77. Johannes Jacobus Herks, *De geschiedenis van de Amersfoortse tabak*, p. 150.

78. H. J. Top, *Geschiedenis der Groninger Veenkoloniën*, pp. 160–61.

79. Sangers, *Tuinbouw*, pp. 98–99.

80. Mulder, 5:162–63.

81. H. D. Dorenbos, "De Groningsche landbouw in 1800," *Groningsche Volksalmanak* (1927), p. 21.

82. Ibid.

83. H. Blink, "Economische geographie der provincie Groningen historisch beschouwd," p. 22.

84. Dorenbos, p. 22.

85. Le Francq van Berkhey, *Gebruik der Turf of Houtassche*, p. 81.

86. ARA Notarieële Archieven, no. 171; RA Utrecht, Rechterlijke Archieven, nos. 895, 1791.

87. RA Utrecht, Rechterlijke Archieven, nos. 1782–85, 1808–09.

88. B. H. Slicher van Bath, "Robert Loder en Rienck Hemmema," p. 101.

89. Wttewaal, "Landbouwkundige beschrijving"; M. J. Boerendonk, *Historische studie over den Zeeuwschen landbouw*, p. 184; "De landbouwenquete van 1800" (comp. by J. M. G. van der Poel), *Historia Agriculturae* 2 (1954):83.

90. Slicher van Bath, *Agrarian History*, pp. 279–87.

91. A full discussion is found in B. H. Slicher van Bath, "De oogstopbrengsten van verschillende gewassen, voornamelijk granen, in verhouding tot het zaaizaad, ca. 810–1820." Much of this article is translated in "The Yields of Different Crops

(mainly cereals) in Relation to the Seed, ca. 810–1820"; see, particularly, pp. 34–35.

92. RA Leeuwarden, Nedergerechten Archieven, weesboeken, nos. 1m, 30.

93. Van Doorn, pp. 231–32.

94. Van Balen, *Haastrecht*, p. 43.

95. C. Wiskerke, "De geschiedenis van het meekrapbedrijf in Nederland," p. 30.

96. *Extract Uyt het Octroy van de Beemster met de Cavel-Conditien.* The investors were not mistaken in their expectations. According to the hydraulic engineer Jan Adriaenszoon Leeghwater, "the coleseed crop came up so abundantly [the first year the Beemster was dry] that it was maintained that all the oil-pressing mills in North Holland at that time had enough work to go a whole year long." (Jan Adriaenszoon Leeghwater, *Haarlemmer-meer-boek*, p. 56.)

97. Sangers, *Tuinbouw*, pp. 23–46.

98. ARA, Rekenkamer Archief van der Domeinen in Holland, no. 196; K. M. Dekker, "De landbouw in Broek op Langedijk in het midden van de 16e eeuw."

99. Quoted in P. Hoekstra, *Bloemendaal: proeve ener streekgeschiedenis*, p. 47.

100. Velius, 1:290; Sangers, *Tuinbouw*, p. 79.

101. Blink, *Boerenstand*, 2:23–24.

102. Hoekstra, p. 86.

103. H. Blink, "Opkomst van Aalsmeer, de Europeesche bloemtuin," *TEG* 19 (1928):293–303; *Tegenwoordige Staat van Holland*, 8:249.

104. Aart Vuyk, *Boskoop, vijf eeuwen boomwekerij*, p. 68.

105. *Charter-boek van Vriesland*, 2:858; 3:320, 357.

106. GA Hoorn, no. 2568.

107. Gemeentearchief van Franeker, no. 435; N. E. Algra, *Ein; enkele recht-historische aspecten van de grondeigendom in Westlauwers Friesland*, p. 155 (footnote).

108. RA Leeuwarden, Gedeputeerde Staten, no. 9.1.

109. G. Boomkamp, *Beschrijving van Alkmaar*, p. 4.

110. Boomkamp, p. 110; C. W. Bruinvis, *Geschiedenis van de kaasmarkt, het waaggebouw, en het waagrecht te Alkmaar* (Alkmaar, 1889), p. 5.

111. L. Frankenberg, *In en om de Alkmaarsche waag* (Alkmaar, 1922), p. 44; Bruinvis, p. 5.

112. Bruinvis, p. 13. The count had taken over the administration of the weigh-house finances to punish the city for its part in the *Kaas en Brood* revolt of 1492.

113. C. van der Woude, *Kronyk van Alkmaar*, p. 81; Bruinvis, pp. 15–16; Frankenberg, p. 44.

114. Frankenberg, pp. 33, 43, 44.

115. GA Alkmaar, no. 4636; *Tegenwoordige Staat van Holland*, 2:398; Boekel, p. 210.

116. J. Belonje, *De Heer-Hugowaard, (1629–1929)*, p. 6; idem, *De Schermeer, 1633–1933*, p. 11.

117. Guicciardini, p. 222.

118. C. J. de Lange van Wijngaarden, *Geschiedenis en Beschrijving der Stad van der Goude*, 2:332.

119. C. van der Woude, *Alkmaar*, p. 126.

120. R. Metelerkamp, *De toestand van Nederland in vergelijking gebragt met die van enige andere landen van Europa*, (Amsterdam, 1804), p. 79.

121. Wiskerke, "Meekrapbedrijf in Nederland," p. 74; S. Lois, *Chronycke ofte Korte Waere Beschrijvinge der Stad Rotterdam*, pp. 126, 148.

122. *Teenwoordige Staat van Holland*, 5:40.

123. Bouman, p. 252; Boekel, pp. 210–11.

124. The monthly records of cheese weighed at Alkmaar between 1758 and 1767 show marketing activity to be strongly concentrated in the 6 months between June and November. In this period 88 percent of the cheese was marketed; in the 4 months between January and April only 3 percent of the cheese was marketed. (GA Alkmaar, no. 4636.)

125. Boekel, pp. 210–11.

126. Velius, 1:632–33.

127. W. Eekhoff, *Geschiedkundige beschrijving van Leewarden*, 2:18.

128. Spahr van der Hoek and Postma, *Friese landbouw*, 1:387.

129. J. F. Schouwen, *Korte Beschrijving van 't vlek Heerenveen*, p. 22.

130. *Nederlandsche Jaarboeken*, 1:59; Eelko Napjus, *Historisch Chronyk, of Beschryvinge van Oud en Nieuw Sneek*, pp. 141–42.

131. *Tegenwoordige Staat van Friesland*, 16:579. The butter volume figure quoted in this source is garbled. It reads 38,206 *vierendeel* (of 320 pounds); apparently it should read 83,206 vierendeel.

132. Ibid., 15:253, 265; 14:258, 273.

133. Boekel, pp. 210–11.

134. Before the construction of nation-states as we now know them, distinctions between domestic and international trade were less clear-cut than now. Before the mid-sixteenth century our region had no common ruler, and even after the founding of the Republic, commercial policy varied from province to province.

135. The production effect of factor accumulaton is given by Rybczynski's theorem, which states: "If terms of trade are constant and one factor accumulates there will be an absolute reduction in production of the good which uses this factor less intensively and the good which uses the abundant good more will increase output more than proportionally with output." See Harry G. Johnson, *Money, Trade and Economic Growth*, chap. 4.

136. H. J. Smit, "Het Kamper pondtolregister van 1439–1441," pp. 211–12.

137. RA Brussel, Rekenkamer Archief, "Comte Rendee par Jacques Graumage receveur du centienae derner de la valeur des marchaudises sortant des ports de Hollande du 10 feviere 1542 au 10 feviere suivant," no. 23.365.

138. Winsemius, p. 302; *Charter-boek van Vriesland*, 3:187; Velius, 1:146.

139. *Charter-boek van Vriesland*, 3:22–23.

140. Jacques le Moine de l'Espine and Isaäc le Long, *De Koophandel van Amsterdam*, p. 23.

141. Velius, 1:260, 338.

142. G. E. Fussell, *The English Dairy Farmer 1500–1900*, p. 281.

143. Lindemann, *Landbouw in België*, 1:375. The dairy products sold at the Brabant fairs were overwhelmingly of Flemish origin until the early sixteenth century. In the first half of the sixteenth century "Delftse" butter and "Hollandse" cheese came to dominate the Antwerp markets. (H. van der Wee,

The Growth of the Antwerp Market and the European Economy, 1:210, 217, 221.)

144. Lindemans, *Landbouw in België*, 1:305, 434.

145. Wiese and Bölts, pp. 61–62. Wiese estimate the total export of oxen from Denmark, Schleswig, and Schonen at 20,000 in 1480–1500 and at 55–60,000 in 1600–20, the peak period. Thereafter the trade fell off sharply.

146. Boekel, pp. 39–40; R. M. Molesworth described East Jutland in the following terms in 1692: "This is a plentiful country abounding more especially in cattle; it wants good sea-ports toward the Ocean, notwithstanding which the Hollanders transport yearly great quantities of lean cows and oxen from hence to their more fertile soil, where in a short time they grow so prodigiously fat, through better feeding, in the rich grounds of Holland." (R. M. Molesworth, *An Account of Denmark as it was in the year 1692*, p. 28.) In fact, when Molesworth wrote, the oxen trade had passed its peak. By 1700 the Rendsburg toll registered that no more than 20,000 head passed by in an average year; by 1750 the number had sunk to 10,000 per year. (Wiese and Bölts, pp. 62, 78.)

147. A description of the trade is provided in a law taxing the imported oxen: ARA Staten van Holland: 1572–1795, no. 1365.

148. *Enqueste*, pp. 170–71; *Informacie*, pp. 585–98.

149. Eppens, 2:369.

150. ARA, Grafelijkheid Rakenkamer, Toll van Geervliet, 1554–56, no. 4906. Exemptions in the staple rights of Dordrecht indicate the importance of the grain trade of the upstream grain-producing areas. (van Beverwijk, p. 139.)

151. Abel, *Deutschen Landwirtschaft*, p. 157.

152. See S. Hoszowski, "The Polish Baltic trade in the 15th–18th centuries"; J. Rutkowski, "Le régime agraire en Pologne au XVIIIᵉ siècle," *Revue Historique, Economique et Sociale* 14 (1926):473–505, 15 (1927):66–103; Antoni Mączak, "Export of Grain and the Problem of Distribution of National Income in the years 1550–1650."

153. This exercise uses equations devised by Slicher van Bath in his study of yield ratios in "Oogstopbrengsten," pp. 29–126.

154. Mączak, p. 92.

155. W. S. Unger, "De sonttabellen"; J. A. Faber, "Graanhandel, graanprijzen en tarievenpolitiek in Nederland gedurende de tweede helft der zeventiende eeuw"; idem, "Het probleem van de dalende graanaanvoer uit de Oostzeelanden in de tweede helft van de zeventiende eeuw," pp. 3–28.

156. GA Hoorn, no. 2567, "Klaer-Bericht ofte Aenwysinge hoe ende op wat wijse de tegenwoordige dierte der granen sal konnen geremedieerte werden ende de schipvaert dezer landen vergroot," by Margen Gerbrantsz.

157. An increase of Belgian and French grains supplying the northern Netherlands is indicated in many sources: GA Gouda, no. 2394; Johan de Vries, "De statistiek van in- en uitvoer van de Admiraliteit op de Maaze 1784–1793," 30:236–310, and the French writers on mid- and late seventeenth-century French-Dutch trade, especially Bishop Huet. England exported no more than 1,000 or 2,000 last of grain in the late seventeenth century, but by the first decade of the eighteenth century, the amounts increased rapidly to over 10,000 last. C. Davenant, in his description of Dutch-British trade at this time, claimed that

Holland took three-fifths of all British grain exports. (*Abstract of British Historical Statistics*, comp. B. R. Mitchell with Phyllis Deane [Cambridge, 1962]; Charles Davenant, "An Account of the Trade between Great Britain, France, Holland, Spain, Portugal . . ." 5:424.)

158. GA Gouda, no. 2414.

159. RA Groningen, Pondkamer Archieven, Resolutions of 1669 and 1707; *Tegenwoordige Staat van Groningen*, 21:69.

160. GA Haarlem, no. 1929; d'Alphonse, p. 457.

161. A. M. van der Woude, "De consumptie van graan, vlees en boter in Holland op het einde van de achttiende eeuw." I found per capita consumption in the city of Haarlem to be 105 kilograms (75 kilograms wheat and rye and 30 kilograms buckwheat) in 1733–35. (GA Haarlem, nos. 1142, 1157 [1830].) A review of grain consumption estimates from the sixteenth to the eighteenth century is available in Chr. Vanderbroeke, "Aardappelteelt en aardappelverbruik in de 17e en 18e eeuw."

CHAPTER 5

1. N. W. Posthumus, *Inquiry into the History of Prices.*

2. Abel, *Agrarkrisen*; Slicher van Bath, *Agrarian History*; idem, "Les problèmes fondamentaux de la société préindustrielle en Europe occidentale."

3. Le Roy Ladurie, 1:633–54.

4. It is also likely because of the introduction in the 1590s of the flyboat (*fluitschip*), a utilitarian merchant vessel that gave Dutch shipowners an impressive cost advantage on northern European trade routes for nearly a century. (See Violet Barbour, "Dutch and English Merchant Shipping in the 17th Century.")

5. F. P. Braudel and F. Spooner, "Prices in Europe from 1450 to 1750," pp. 410–11.

6. Abel, *Agrarkrisen*, p. 131.

7. E. Scholliers, *De levenstandaard in de XVe en XVIe eeuw te Antwerpen*, pp. 108–11; see also C. Verlinden, J. Craeybeckx, and E. Scholliers, "Mouvements des prix et des salaires en Belgique aux XVIe siècle."

8. Scholliers, pp. 146–49.

9. AH Rijnland, no. 2825; ARA, Grafelijkheid Rekenkamer, no. 5240.

10. RA Leeuwarden, Nedergerechten Archieven, weesboeken.

11. Spahr van der Hoek and Postma, *Friese landbouw*, 1:462.

12. De la Court, *Interest van Holland ofte gronden van Hollands welvaren*, p. 38.

13. GA Amsterdam, "Vertoog van d' onmooghlijkheidt van 't maken der Engelsche manufacturen hier te landen," no. L.C.8., N.8.

14. N. W. Posthumus, De industrieële concurrentie tusschen Noord- en Zuid-Nederlandsche nijverheidscentra in de XVIIe en XVIIIe eeuw," 2:376.

15. J. M. G. van der Poel, *De landbouw in het verste verleden*, pp. 7–14.

16. Spahr van der Hoek and Postma, *Friese landbouw*, 1:166–67; J. le Francq van Berkhey, *Natuurlijke historie van Holland*, 6:348–412; RA Leeuwarden, Nedergerechten Archieven, weesboeken. Among farms of under 10 milk cows, none possessed karnemolens in 1677–86 while but 23 percent did in 1711–50. For an analysis of the diffusion of laborsaving machinery see the well-known article

of Paul A. David, "The Mechanization of Reaping in the Ante-Bellum Midwest," in Henry Rosovsky, ed., *Industrialization in Two Systems* (New York, 1966), pp. 3–39.

17. Charles Wilson, "Taxation and the Decline of Empires."

18. See 't Hart, p. 146.

19. Sannes, 1:139–238, passim. The province did, however, succeed in imposing entry fines and various extraordinary payments in lieu of rental increases.

20. These figures have been calculated from the *Aanbreng van 1511* (148 pondematen), the *Register van geestelijke opkomsten van Oostergo,* 1580 (274 pondematen), and RA Leeuwarden, Nedergerechten Archieven, weesboeken of Leeuwarderadeel, 1718–20 (157.5 pondematen).

21. The average rent per morgen on 5 farms totalling 119 morgen between 1652 and 1654 was fl. 24.3. (GA Haarlem, Archieven van het Sint Elizabeths Gasthuis, nos. 52/2 and 53/2.)

22. *Beneficiaal-boeken van Friesland,* 1543 (quoted in Spahr van der Hoek and Postma, *Friese landbouw,* 1:632).

23. Van Apeldoorn, *Kerkelijk goederen,* pp. 124–25.

24. GA Amsterdam, Burgerweeshuis Archief, no. 115; GA Haarlem, Archieven van het Sint Elizabeths Gasthuis, no. 40.

25. ARA, Rekenkamer van de Domeinen in Holland, no. 769c.

26. J. Belonje, *De Zijpe en Hazepolder, de ontwikkeling van een waterschap in Holland's Noorderkwartier,* pp. 61–63; Dirk Burger van Scoorl, *Chronyk van Schagen,* p. 254.

27. Bouman, p. 267.

28. Belonje, *Schermeer,* p. 22.

29. De Jong, pp. 34–46.

30. AH Rijnland, no. 1577.

31. AH Rijnland, no. 1578; Leeghwater, *Haarlemmer-meer-boek,* pp. 40–41, 46–52.

32. Carr, *Groot Placaatboek van Holland en Zeeland,* 2:1669.

33. ARA, Archieven der Verschillende Besturen over de Domeinen en Afkomstig van de Voormalige Provincie Holland, no. 755a; *Tegenwoordige Staat van Holland,* 8:119–21.

34. ARA, Financie van Holland, no. 473. A glimpse into the enormous labor involved in reclaiming land inundated by dune sand is given by a document concerning a 20-morgen parcel near Alkmaar. In 1636 it was cleared of 629 bargeloads of sand. The uncovered soil was prepared with at least 20 bargeloads of night soil from Alkmaar. It was then sold to the Burgerweeshuis of Amsterdam for 875 gulden per morgen. (GA Amsterdam, Burgerweeshuis Archief, no. 128.)

35. Naber, p. 16. In Groningen, the land tax register of 1520 records a taxable (improved) area of 83,000 hectares. This figure apparently excludes hayland. In 1833, the cadastral survey records 182,292 hectares under cultivation. ARA, Ambtenaren Centraal Bestuur, Register van het Centraal Bestuur met Groningen en Drenthe, no. 925, fol. 17.

36. De Goede 1:332.

37. G. de Vries, *Het dijks- en molenbestuur in Holland's Noorderkwartier onder de grafelijke regeering en gedurende de Republiek,* p. 477.

38. Velius, 2:39–41; G. de Vries, *Dijksbestuur*, p. 482.

39. Schotanus, *Chroniek van Vriesland*, pp. 201–02.

40. Winsemius, pp. 179–80; Obreen, p. 98.

41. Temple, p. 156.

42. Bicker Caarten, et al., *Zuid Hollands molenboek*, p. 52.

43. Jansen, "Ter Aar," pp. 13–14; Fockema Andreae, "Rijnlandse polder," pp. 61–62.

44. G. de Vries, *Dijksbestuur*, pp. 493–96; *Tegenwoordige Staat van Holland*, 5:521–22.

45. Fockema Andreae, *Rijnland*, p. 224.

46. Jhr. D. T. Gevers van Endgeest, *Hoogheemraadschap van Rijnland*, vol. 2, app. 9.

47. Ibid., vol. 2, app. 26.

48. Fockema Andreae et al., *Duizend jaar bouwen*, 2:210; S. J. van der Molen, *Het Friesche boerenhuis in twintig eeuwen*, p. 40.

49. RA Leeuwarden, Nedergerechten Archieven, weesboeken.

50. Spahr van der Hoek and Postma, *Friese landbouw*, 1:99–100; Fockema Andreae et al., *Duizend jaar bouwen*, 2:230.

51. RA Leeuwarden, Nedergerechten Archieven, weesboeken.

52. Fockema Andrea et al., *Duizend jaar bouwen*, 2:220.

53. H. Dijkema, *Proeve van een geschiedenis der landhuishoudkunde van Groningen*, p. 388.

54. RA Leeuwarden, Nedergerechten Archieven, weesboeken.

55. A commendable display of old farm buildings and practices is to be seen at the Openluchtmuseum in Arnhem, the Netherlands. Although the new styles did not spread inland, they did spread along the coast in the direction of East Friesland and Dithmarschen. See D. Wiaarda, *Die Geschichtliche Entwickelung der Landwirtschaftlichen Verhältnisse Ostfrieslands*, and Abel, *Agrarkrisen*, p. 127.

56. Diepeveen, pp. 116–19, 137. This figure is calculated from a financial report presented to the Staten van Holland. The actual fiscal records of Gouda, the major export center, do not record an export volume above 1.3 million *tonnen.*

57. Hartgerink-Koomans, *Ewsum*, pp. 191–323, passim.

58. *Tegenwoordige Staat van Groningen*, 21:202–03.

59. AH Rijnland, no. 8400.

60. AH Rijnland, no. 2240; Gemeentearchief van Oudshoorn, nos. 106–09; Kloot-Meyburg, *Oudshoorn*, p. 6.

61. Calculated from excise receipts recorded in Posthumus, *Lakenindustrie*, 2:612.

62. GA Haarlem, no. 261 (1828); S. C. Regtdoorzee Greup-Roldanus, *Geschiedenis der Haarlemmer bleekerijen*, p. 185.

63. Schotanus, *Chroniek van Vriesland* p. 259.

64. *Charter-boek van Vriesland*, 2:67, 73, 253, 261.

65. Van Hinte, p. 16.

66. For instance, in 1540 Leiden and Delft, cities that did not share the privileges over control of the canals, petitioned the emperor to permit new

connections between Leiden and Amsterdam that would circumvent the tolls of Haarlem and permit larger vessels to travel between the 2 cities. Nothing came of it. When a new route was built in 1657, Haarlem was able to restrict its use to passengers for a number of years. (AH Rijnland, no. 2796.)

67. *Keurboek van Amsterdam*, D. fol. 136; J. M. Fuchs, *Beurt- en Wagenveren*, p. 55.

68. Jan ten Hoorn, *Reisboek door de Vereenigde Nederlandsche Provinciën, en der selver aangrenzende landschappen en koningrijken.*

69. GA Alkmaar, nos. 1344, 1353–55.

70. GA Alkmaar, nos. 1391, 1393, 1396, 1399.

71. Burger van Schoorl, *Chronyk van Schagen*, pp. 16–17.

72. Resoluties van de Regering der Stad Groningen, deposited in GA Groningen.

73. GA Amsterdam, Archief van der Gilden, no. 40.

74. F. van Mieris, *Beschrijving van Leyden*, 2:471; GA Leiden, no. 136; GA Leeuwarden, no. 127.

75. Wijnne, p. 88.

76. Ten Hoorn; also see William Carr, *Travels through Flanders, Holland, Germany, Sweden, and Denmark.*

77. GA Haarlem, L313–23 (1078); GA Leiden, nos, 59, 132, 136, 137, 239, 279; GA Delft, no. 1093; Fuchs, p. 203.

78. Wagenaar, 2:501.

79. Keuren en Ordonnanten der Stad Haarlem, 2:28, 41, 189, deposited in GA Haarlem; *Keurboek van Amsterdam*, H. fol. 143; J. G. van Dillen, *Bronnen tot de geschiedenis van het bedrijfsleven en het gildewezen van Amsterdam*, 69: 51.

80. Temple, p. 152.

81. Andrew Yarranton, *England's Improvement by Sea and Land to Out-do the Dutch without Fighting, to Pay Debts without Moneys . . .* , pp. 6–7; Temple, pp. 251–52.

82. My attention was drawn to this matter by A. M. van der Woude, who also corrected my information on the operation of the Verponding tax.

83. Gregory King, *Natural and Political Observations and Conclusions upon the State and Condition of England*; Wilson, "Taxation," pp. 10–26. The Republic's tax burden was not only great, it was also divided among the provinces in a highly unequal manner. Each province contributed a fixed percentage to the central government's budget. The maritime provinces, of course, paid the lion's share. The total tax revenue per province at the end of the eighteenth century, recorded on a per capita basis, was between 19.5 and 30 gulden in Holland, Zeeland, Utrecht, and Friesland, while only 7 gulden in Overijssel and Gelderland. (W. M. Keuchenius, *De Inkomsten en Uitgaven der Bataafsche Republiek voorgesteld in eene Nationale Balans . . .* [Amsterdam, 1803], p. 102.)

84. Van Apeldoorn, *Kerkelijk goederen*, pp. 69–70.

85. Ibid., pp. 119–20.

86. Quoted in Blink, *Boerenstand*, 2:95.

87. Schotanus, *Chroniek van Vriesland*, pp. 139–40.

88. This approximate enrollment figure amounts to 2.75 percent of the male cohort that yearly attained the age of 17 in a population of 2 million, subject to a mortality table such as Gregory King describes for the English town of Litchfield. In England at the height of the education boom in the 1630s, students entering Oxford, Cambridge, the Inns of Court, and foreign universities amounted to 2.5 percent of the 17-year-olds. (See Lawrence Stone," "The Educational Revolution in England, 1560–1640," *Past and Present* 28 (1964):57.) Data on enrollments in Dutch universities are available in D. W. Davies, *The World of the Enseviers: 1580–1712* (The Hague, 1954); W. B. S. Boeles, *Frieslands hoogeschool en het Rijksatheneum te Franeker*, 2 vols. (Leeuwarden, 1878–89); *Tegenwoordige Staat van Utrecht*, 11:363–64.

89. Schotanus, *Chroniek van Vriesland*, p. 752.

90. RA Leeuwarden, Rekenkamer Archief, Quotisatie Cohieren van 1749, no. 14e.

91. "Landbouwenquete van 1800," passim.

92. Guicciardini, p. 27. Before him the learned Erasmus, a native of Rotterdam, had remarked of the Low Countries that "nowhere else does one find a greater number of people of average education." Quoted in Carlo M. Cipolla, *Literacy and Development in the West* (London, 1969), p. 45.

93. S. Hart, "Enige statistische gegevens inzake analfabetisme te Amsterdam in de 17e en 18e eeuw."

94. Carr, p. 50.

95. *Charter-boek van Vriesland*, 5:150.

96. Winsemius, p. 752.

97. The Dutch East India Company and the Dutch West India Company, were capitalized, handsomely it was thought at the time, at 6.5 and 7 million gulden, respectively. Van der Woude estimates the capital invested in Noorderkwartier drainage projects at 20 million gulden. See Faber et al., "Population changes and economic developments," p. 54. Our estimate of total investment in these projects is based on an average cost per hectare of 300 gulden times the 35,000 hectares either drained or won from the sea in the period 1590–1650.

CHAPTER 6

1. The following inventories were used in this study. *Friesland*: RA Leeuwarden, Nedergerechten Archieven, weesboeken (Barradeel, no. 30, vols. 1–8; Franekeradeel, no. 2w, vols. 1–7; Hennaarderadeel, no. 5i, vols. 1–10; Idaarderadeel, no. 10j, vols. 1–15; Leeuwarderadeel, no. 1m, vols. 1–43; Wonseradeel, no. 6s, vols. 28–32). *Utrecht*: RA Utrecht, Rechterlijke Archieven, Testamenten (Mijdrecht, nos. 1809–10, 38 vols.; Demmerick, no. 1783, 2 vols.; Wilnis, no. 1836, 2 vols.). *Holland*: RA Haarlem, Oud Rechterlijke en Weeskamer Archieven, weesboeken (Kortenhoef, nos. 3407–11; Niedorp, nos. 5732–34; Beemster, nos. 4081–84; Ouder Amstel, no. 2595); RA Haarlem, Notarieële Archieven, Testamenten (Assendelft, nos. 153–58; Graft, nos. 1609–10, 1614–17); ARA Notarieële Archieven, Testamenten (Alphen aan den Rijn, nos. 166–67, 171–76; Aarlanderveen, nos. 268–71; Oudshoorn, nos. 317–25; Woerden, nos. 8496–98, 8513–18).

2. F. Steer, *Farm and Cottage Inventories in Mid-Essex* (Chelmsford, 1950), pp. 19, 21, 48; F. G. Emmison, "Jacobean Household Inventories," *Bedford Historical Record Society* 20 (1938):1–143. Among the 139 inventories of tradesmen resident in the Sussex country town of Petworth during the period 1610–1760, 18 percent included books, 13 percent included timepieces, 9 percent recorded pictures or maps, while 6.5 percent recorded silver worth at least £10. With the exception of books, nearly all these objects were found only in eighteenth century inventories. (G. H. Kenyon, "Petworth Town and Trades 1610–1760," *Sussex Archeological Collection* 98 (1958):35–44.)

3. For a more complete analysis of peasant demand see my forthcoming article, "Peasant Demand Patterns and Economic Development: A Case Study."

4. The value of these figures is reduced by the great variance in cash holdings. In the case of Holland and Utrecht, for example, the largest hoard totalled 3,673 gulden, while 5 households had no cash at all. A further problem arises in the uncertainty that cannot be dispelled when confronting an inventory which records no cash holdings. Did the notary fail to record the cash or was there none?

5. "Pacht ende Schellingh Boek der Stede ende Heerlijcheyt van Opmeer," in de Goede, vol. 2, app.

6. Eppens, 1:20–21.

7. Simon Kuznets, *Modern Economic Growth: Rate, Structure, and Method* (New Haven, 1966), pp. 72–74.

8. In 5 grietenijen where laborers made up less than 15 percent of the labor force, farmers made up half the labor force. In 6 grietenijen where laborers made up over 30 percent of the labor force, farmers made up but 31 percent. If we assume the demand for farm labor on the farms of the two groups of grietenijen to be similar, we cannot escape the conclusion that the majority of laborers worked in other sectors of the economy. As an extreme example, if *all* laborers in the 5 grietenijen worked on farms, the laborers per farm would have averaged 0.28. At this level of labor demand, only a quarter of the laborers in the 6 grietenijen could have found employment on farms.

9. For regions where such was the case, see Goubert, "The French Peasantry of the Seventeenth Century"; P. de Saint-Jacob, *Les Paysans de la Bourgogne du Nord au dernier siècle de l'ancien Régime* (Paris, 1960).

10. For a discussion of this problem, see P. T. Bauer and B. S. Yamey, "Economic Progress and Occupational Distribution," *The Economic Journal* 61 (1951):741–55.

11. A. Mączak, "Export of Grain." Stephen Resnick, "The Decline of Rural Industry under Export Expansion: A Comparison among Burma, Philippines, and Thailand, 1870–1938," *JEH* 30 (1970):51–73.

CHAPTER 7

1. Bruce Johnston and John Mellor, "The Role of Agriculture in Economic Development."

2. John C. Fei and Gustav Ranis, *Development of the Labor Surplus Economy*; W. Arthur Lewis, "Economic Development with Unlimited Supplies of

Labour," *The Manchester School of Economics and Social Studies* 22 (1954): 139–91.

3. Z. W. Sneller, *Geschiedenis van de Nederlandschen landbouw, 1795–1940*, p. 8. It is not our intention to single out Professor Sneller for criticism. Many others have taken a similar view. See, for instance, the 12-volume *Algemene geschiedenis der Nederlanden*. The writers of this cooperative effort rarely refer to the sixteenth- through eighteenth-century rural economy. The most recent confirmation of this neglect is found in J. G. van Dillen's *Van rijkdom en regenten*, the new standard text for the economic history of the Dutch Republic. Of its twenty-nine chapters only one is wholly and two partially devoted to the rural economy.

4. E. Luzac, *Holland's Rijkdom, Behelzende den oorsprong van den Koophandel en van de magt dezen staat.*

5. De la Court, p. 12.

6. Charles Kindleberger, in *Economic Growth in France and Britain: 1851–1950* (Cambridge, Mass., 1964), emphasized this factor, the importance of which is often overlooked in discussions of the role of foreign trade in economic growth. He wrote, "One cannot really discuss the role of foreign trade in growth without indicating the underlying capacity of the economy to undertake new tasks in depth or to transform. . . . It is not the foreign trade that leads to growth—any stimulus can do it if the capacity to transform is present or can be drawn out of dormancy. Without that capacity a benign stimulus may lull the economy into senescence and a rude one may set it back" (p. 287).

7. Posthumus, *Lakenindustrie*, 3:941; Charles Wilson, "Cloth Production and International Competition in the 17th Century."

8. Regtdoorzee Greup-Roldanus, pp. 102, 324.

9. J. J. Reesse, *De suiker handel van het begin der 17ᵉ eeuw tot 1894*, 1:288.

10. The records of a cartel formed by the brickworks owners of Rijnland, where fully half the nation's brickmaking capacity was located, make us quite well informed about brick production in the mid-seventeenth century. When Rijnland's 35 to 38 brick ovens worked at full capacity, they were each fired 5 times per year, producing 100 million bricks. The other brickmaking centers doubled that figure. H. A. Shannon's index of brick production in England during the Industrial Revolution shows that per capita output varied between 50 and 100 bricks per year. The Dutch industry, in an average year (when the cartel permitted 2 or 3 firings per oven) produced 50 per capita, and had a capacity to nearly double that output. See B. W. van der Kloot-Meyburg, "Een productiekartel in de Hollandsche steen-industrie in de 17ᵈᵉ eeuw," *Bijdragen tot de Economische Geschiedenis van Nederland* 2 (1916):208–38; W. S. A. Arntz, "Export van Nederlandsche baksteen inn vroeger eeuwen"; Johanna Hollestelle, *De steenbakkerij in de Nederlanden tot omstreeks 1560*; H. A. Shannon, "Bricks—A Trade Index, 1785–1849," *Economica*, n.s. 1 (1934):300–18.

11. Barbour, "Dutch and English Merchant Shipping."

12. Van Braam, *Het economisch-sociale leven aan de Zaan*; A. Loosjes, *Beschrijving der Zaanlandsche dorpen*; S. Lootsma, *Historische studiën over de Zaanstreek.*

13. J. Linthorst Homan, *Geschiedenis van Drenthe,* p. 180; Blink, *Boerenstand,* 2:72.

14. The best work on this little studied phase of Dutch economic history is Johan de Vries, *De economische achteruitgang der Republiek in de achtiende eeuw.*

15. Gregory King, *Observations and Conclusions.*

16. Adam Smith, *Wealth of Nations,* 2 vols. (New York: Cannon ed., 1904), 1: 353.

Glossary

For the weights and measures listed below, modern equivalents are given. It should be noted that the system of measuring varied from city to city, or province to province, and in some cases from village to village. By the early seventeenth century, the weights and measures of Amsterdam had become the most important.

Words set in small capitals in the glosses below are defined elsewhere in the Glossary.

DIEMT. In Groningen, usually a measure of hayland; equivalent to the amount of meadow 1 man could mow in 1 day (about 0.5 hectare).

FLOREENTAUX. The basic land tax of Friesland, established 1511.

GEMET. In Holland south of the river Maas, 300 square ROEDEN (0.46 hectare).

GRAS (pl. GRAZEN). In Groningen, a unit of pastureland corresponding to the amount of land needed for the summer grazing of 1 cow. These units necessarily varied from place to place, but typically represented approximately 0.5 hectare.

GRIETENIJ (pl. GRIETENIJEN). The basic rural jurisdictions into which the province of Friesland was divided. Each of the 30 grietenijen consisted of several villages and hamlets.

GRIETMAN (pl. GRIETMANNEN). The chief judicial and executive official of the GRIETENIJEN in Friesland.

GULDEN. The unit of account in the Netherlands' currency system. From the reign of Charles V the gulden of 20 STUIVERS, or carolusgulden, became standard. Until then, and later in certain regions such as Friesland, the gold gulden, or Floreen, of 28 STUIVERS was widely used. The gold gulden remained in use in the Friesian land tax, the FLOREENTAUX.

HOEVE (pl. HOEVEN). Farms of a standard size originally designated as an area sufficient for the maintenance of a family. In areas of systematic land reclamation, the hoeven were the basis of field parcelization; in older areas they served chiefly as an administrative and fiscal concept.

HONDSBOSSE MORGEN. In Holland north of the Ij, a unit of land of 800 square ROEDEN (0.98 hectare).

HONDSBOSSE ROEDA. In Holland north of the Ij, a unit of length (3.108 meters).

HOOFDELING (pl. HOOFDELINGEN). Members of the chief landowning and political families of rural Friesland; a de facto aristocracy.

HOOGHEEMRAADSCHAP. A regional drainage authority embracing several WATERSCHAPPEN responsible for major dikes, sluices, and drainage channels. It is directed by a *dijkgraaf*, originally an appointee of the count of Holland, and a body of elected representatives known as the *hoogheemraad*.

KOEGANG. In Friesland, a unit of pastureland similar to the Groningen GRAS (approximately 1.5 PONDEMATEN, or 0.5 hectare).

KONINGSROEDA. In Friesland, the basic unit of measurement (3.913 meters).

LAST. A volume measurement used in shipping and international trade. The Amsterdam last became the basic unit of measure of the international grain trade (3,003.6 liters, or, when measuring rye, 2000 kilograms). The Amsterdam last was divided into 25 MUD.

LOPEN. A Friesian measure for grain and seed (when measuring ryeseed it equals 83.3 liters).

LOPENSTAL. In Friesland, a unit of arable land of a size sufficient to exhaust 1 LOPEN of seed (approximately 1 PONDEMAAT, or 0.367 hectare).

MIJL. A distance measure, the Hollandse mijl equalled 2,000 RIJNLANDSE ROEDEN (7.4 kilometers).

MORGEN. In Holland and Utrecht (as well as other parts of the Netherlands and Germany), a unit of land that varied in size from region to region, and often from village to village. The most important variants were the RIJNLANDSE MORGEN and the HONDSBOSSE MORGEN.

MORGENGELD. A drainage tax levied on land by HOOGHEEMRAADSCHAPPEN.

MUD. A unit of measurement, especially of grain. (In Amsterdam 1 mud equals 120 liters.) Twenty-five mud equals 1 Amsterdam LAST.

POND. The pond, usually divided into 16 ounces, was used everywhere but varied in weight between 0.46 and 0.50 kilograms.

POORTER. An urban resident possessed of burghal rights. Typically, the acquisition of such status required the payment of a fee; *poorterschap* was a condition of entry into most trades and professions above the most menial.

PONDEMAAT (pl. PONDEMATEN). In Friesland, the basic unit of land measurement; equal to 240 square KONINGSROEDA (0.367 hectare).

RIJNLANDSE MORGEN. In central Holland, a land measurement of 600 square RIJNLANDSE ROEDEN (0.85 hectare).

RIJNLANDSE ROEDA. In central Holland, a unit of length (3.767 meters).

ROEDA (pl. ROEDEN). The basic unit of length in all the provinces of the northern Netherlands; there were many different roeden, of varying lengths. See HONDS-BOSSE ROEDA; KONINGSROEDA; RIJNLANDSE ROEDA; STADSROEDA; STICHTSE ROEDA.

SCHIPPOND. A unit of weight of cheese, usually 320 POND.

SCHOTSCHIETENDE HUIS. A Friesian farmstead and its attendant land (called a *ploeggang*) invested since medieval times with voting rights (STEM) in this "peasant republic." These rights were vested in the owner of the farm; they formed the basis of political authority in Friesland.

STADSROEDA. In Groningen, a unit of length (4.091 meters).

STEM (pl. STEMMEN). The votes of the owners of SCHOTSCHIETENDE HUIZEN that chose GRIETMANNEN and representatives to the provincial assembly (*staten*) of Friesland.

STICHTSE ROEDA. In Utrecht, a unit of length (3.756 meters).

STINZEN. The fortified dwellings of the Friesian HOOFDELINGEN. In the sixteenth century the ownership of stinzen was a distinguishing feature of true HOOFDE-LINGEN.

STUIVER. The basic monetary unit of the coinage. 20 stuivers made up one carolus-gulden. A stuiver, in turn, consisted of 8 duiten, a copper coin. In 1621 the silver content of the stuiver was 0.57 gram.

TERP (pl. TERPEN). Refuge mounds built in Roman and early medieval times in

Friesland and Groningen. They were gradually built up to form the nucleus of hamlets and villages since, until a system of dikes was completed, they formed the only permanently inhabitable places in much of the region.

TON (pl. TONNEN). A unit of weight whose specific value varies with the commodity. A ton of peat weighed 350 POND; a ton of butter, equal to 4 VIERENDEELS, varied between 288 and 320 POND. *Ton* is italicized in the text, to distinguish it from the English ton.

VERPONDING. The basic land tax of Holland, levied on the rental value of real property as assessed in 1632 and 1732.

VIERENDEEL. A quarter of a TON, or vat, of butter; from 72 to 80 POND.

VLEK (pl. VLEKKEN). Villages grown beyond mere agricultural settlements into centers of industry or trade, but without the political autonomy characteristic of chartered cities. The term is most often applied to Friesland, but such places existed throughout the northern Netherlands.

WATERSCHAPPEN. Local drainage boards.

Bibliography

The materials consulted for this study are listed below in five categories: the archival collections, published primary sources, secondary materials published before 1820, unpublished secondary materials, and secondary materials published since 1820. This last category is not complete. For further references the reader is directed to the endnotes and to my dissertation, "The Role of the Rural Sector in the Expansion of the Dutch Economy" (Yale University, 1970).

ARCHIVES

The Netherlands' archive system consists of a central archives in The Hague, provincial archives in each provincial capital, municipal archives, and special collections, of which the most important for our purposes are those of the drainage authorities. The following list gives the names of the archives, the shortened designations used in the notes, and, wherever necessary, the separate collections that were consulted. For more detailed information the reader is referred to the notes.

Algemeen Rijksarchief, 's-Gravenhage (ARA)
  Admiraliteitscolleges
  Ambtenaren Centraal Bestuur
  Financie van Holland
  Grafelijkheid Rekenkamer
  Notarieële Archieven
  Rekening der Admiraliteiten in de Generaliteits Rekenkamer
  Rekenkamer van de Domeinen in Holland
  Staten van Holland voor 1572
  Staten van Holland: 1572–1795
Rijksarchief Brussel—Archives Générales du Royaume, Bruxelles (RA Brussel)
  Papiers d'Etat et de l'Audience
  Rekenkamer Archief
Rijksarchief in Groningen (RA Groningen)
  Pondkamer Archieven
  Rechterlijk Archief
  Staten van Stad en Lande, 1594–1798
  Voormalige Zijlvesten en Dijkrechten
Rijksarchief in Noord-Holland (RA Haarlem)
  Notarieële Archieven

Oud Rechterlijke en Weeskamer Archieven
Rijksarchief in Friesland (RA Leeuwarden)
    Gedeputeerde Staten
    Landdrost Archief
    Nedergerechten Archieven
    Rekenkamer Archief
    Staten van Friesland
Rijksarchief in Utrecht (RA Utrecht)
    Rechterlijke Archieven
    Staten van Utrecht
Archief van het Hoogheemraadschap van Rijnland (AH Rijnland)
Gemeentearchief van Alkmaar (GA Alkmaar)
Gemeentearchief van Amsterdam (GA Amsterdam)
    Archief van de Gasthuizen tot 1875
    Archief van der Gilden
Gemeentearchief van Gouda (GA Gouda)
Gemeentearchief van Groningen (GA Groningen)
Gemeentearchief van Haarlem (GA Haarlem)
    Archieven van het Sint Elizabeths Gasthuis
Gemeentearchief van Hoorn (GA Hoorn)
Gemeentearchief van Leeuwarden (GA Leeuwarden)
Gemeentearchief van Leiden (GA Leiden)
Gemeentearchief van Sneek (GA Sneek)

PUBLISHED PRIMARY SOURCES

De Aanbreng der Vijf Deelen van 1511 en 1514. Edited by J. C. Tjessinga. 5 vols. Assen, 1943–53.

Alphonse, F. J. B. d'. *Aperçu sur la Hollande, 1811.* Reprinted in Centraal Bureau voor de Statistiek, *Bijdragen tot de Statistiek van Nederland,* n.s. no. 1. The Hague, 1900.

Beneficiaal-boeken van Friesland, 1543. Compiled by G. T. N. Suringer. Leeuwarden, 1850.

Dillen, J. G. van. "Summiere staat van de in 1622 in de provincie Holland gehouden volkstelling." *EHJ* 21 (1940):167–89.

Enqueste ende Informatie upt stuck van der Reductie ende Reformatie van den Schiltaelen voertijts getaxeert ende Gestelt Geweest over de landen van Hollant ende Vrieslant, gedaen in den jaere 1494. Compiled and with an introduction by R. J. Fruin. Leiden, 1876.

Extract Uyt het Octroy van de Beemster met de Cavel-Conditien. Purmerend, 1696.

Gerbenzon, P. "Het Aantekeningenboek van Dirck Jansz." *Estrikken,* no. 31 (1960).

Groot Placaat en Charter-boek van Vriesland. Compiled by G. F. Baron thoe Schwartzenberg en Hohenlansberg. 5 vols. Leeuwarden, 1768–93.

Hemmema, Rienck. "Rekenboek off Memoriael van Rienck Hemmema," with introductions by B. H. Slicher van Bath, J. H. Brouwer, and P. Gerbenzon. *Estrikken,* no. 14 (1956).

Informacie up den staet Faculteyt ende Gelegentheyt van de Steden ende Dorpen van Hollant ende Vrieslant om daernae te reguleren de nyeuwe Schildtaele, gedaen in den jaere 1514. Compiled and with an introduction by R. J. Fruin. Leiden, 1866.

"De landbouwenquete van 1800," compiled by J. M. G. van der Poel. *Historia Agriculturae,* vol. 1–3 (1953–56).

Meilink, P. A. "Gegevens aangaande bedrijfskapitalen in den Hollandschen en Zeeuwschen handel in 1543." *EHJ* 8 (1922):254–77.

Octroy van de Purmer. Amsterdam, 1722.

Oldewelt, W. F. H. "De beroepsstructuur van de bevolking der Hollandse stemhebbende steden volgens de kohieren van de familiegelden van 1674, 1715 en 1742." *EHJ* 24 (1950):81–161, 25 (1951):167–248.

———. "De scheepvaartstatistiek van Amsterdam in de 17ᵉ en 18ᵉ eeuw." *Jaarboek Amstelodamum* 45 (1953):114–51.

Oorkondenboek van het Sticht Utrecht. Compiled by S. Muller Fz. and A. C. Bouman. 4 vols. Utrecht, 1920–54.

The Port Books of Boston, 1601–1640. Compiled and with an introduction by R. W. K. Hinton. Hereford (Lincoln Record Society), 1956.

Posthumus, N. W. "Een zestiende-eeuwsche enquete naar de buitenneringen rondom de stad Leiden." *BMHG* 33 (1912):1–95.

———. "Statistiek van den in- en uitvoer van Amsterdam in het jaar 1774." *BMHG* 38 (1917):516–28.

———. "Statistiek van den in- en uitvoer van Rotterdam en Dordrecht in het jaar 1680." *BMHG* 34 (1913):529–37.

De Provinciekaarten van Jacob van Deventer. Compiled by B. van 't Hoff. The Hague, 1941.

Register van den Aanbreng van 1511 en verdere stukken tot de Floreenbelasting betrekkelijk (including *Aanbreng der Buitendijksteren landen van 1546*). Compiled and with an introduction by I. Telting. 4 vols. Leeuwarden, 1879.

Register van geestelijke opkomsten van Oostergo, 1580. Compiled by J. Reitsma. Leeuwarden, 1888.

"Het schultregister van Jacob Koorn, 1734–1748," with an introduction by L. S. Meihuizen and J. A. Kuperus. *Historia Agriculturae* 9 (1968): 179–374.

Slooten, P. J. D. van. "Frieslands volkstellingen der 18ᵉ eeuw met opgave der gealimenteerden." In *Friesche Volksalmanak voor het Schrikkeljaar 1888.* Leeuwarden, 1888.

Smit, H. J. "Het Kamper pondtolregister van 1439–1441." *EHJ* 5 (1919): 109–296.

"Staat van Ontvangsten en Uitgeven van Cornelis van Coolwijk, Ontvanger-generaal van de Incomsten der Geestelijke Goederen, tot onderhoud van de Predikanten, 1590," compiled by H. C. Rogge. *Kroniek van het Historisch Genootschap gevestigd te Utrecht* 30 (1874):17–70.

Steur, A. G. van der. "Een demografische, agrarische en sociale statistiek van de steden en dorpen in het Kwartier van Leiden in de jaren 1807–1808." *Leids Jaarboekje* 57 (1965):184–96.

Vermeulen, P. J. "Bevolking van het platte land der provincie Utrecht in 1632." *Tijdschrift voor Oudheiden, Statistiek, Zeden en Gewoonten, Regt, Genealogie en Andere Deelen der Geschiedenis van het Bisdom, de Provincie en de Stad Utrecht* 1 (1847):198–208.

Volks-Telling in de Nederlandsche Republiek. Compiled by order of the Commissie tot het ontwerpen van een Plan van Constitutie voor het Volk van Nederland. The Hague, 1796.

Vries, Johan de. "De statistiek van in- en uitvoer van de Admiraliteit op de Maaze, 1784–1793." *EHJ* 29 (1961):188–259, 30 (1963):236–310.

Zurck, E. van. *Codex Batavus in voce Commerce.* Amsterdam, 1664.

SECONDARY MATERIALS PUBLISHED BEFORE 1820

Alkemade, K. van. *Beschrijvinge van den stad Brielle.* 2 vols. Brielle, 1729.

Beverwijk, Johan van. *'t Begin van Hollant in Dordrecht.* Dordrecht, 1640.

Boomkamp, G. *Beschrijving van Alkmaar.* Alkmaar, 1747.

Burger van Scoorl, Dirk. *Chronyk van Medenblik.* Hoorn, 1728.

———. *Chronyk van Schagen.* Hoorn, 1722.

Burrish, Onslow. *Batavia Illustrata.* London, 1728.

J. C. [Coleri, Johannes?] *De verloop, en onfeylbaren Almanack, oorsprongh en vastetijdt der heylige dagen, Iten ontdeckengh van de wonderlijke wecking der Natuur, Eygenschappen van Beesten en Kroyden, Plichten der Huyshouding, Visscherije, en Landt-Bouwery.* . . . Amsterdam, 1661.

Carr, William. *Travels through Flanders, Holland, Germany, Sweden, and Denmark.* London, 1693.

Court, Pieter de la. *Interest van Holland ofte gronden van Hollands welvaren.* Amsterdam, 1662.

Davenant, Charles. "An Account of the Trade between Great Britain, France, Holland, Spain, Portugal . . . ," 1715. In *The Political and Commercial Works of Charles Davenant.* 5 vols. London, 1771.

Eppens, Abel. "Kroniek van Groningen." Compiled by J. A. Feith and H. Brugmans. *Werken van het Historisch Genootschap,* 3d ser., no. 27 (1911).

Francq van Berkhey, J. le. *Natuurlijke historie van Holland.* 9 vols. Amsterdam, 1769–1811.

———. *Verhandeling over het Nationaal Gebruik der Turf of Houtassche in Holland.* Amsterdam, 1779.

Googe, Barnabe. *Foure Bookes of Husbandrie.* London, 1577.

Graswinckel, Dirck. *Placcaet-Boeck op 't Stuck van de Lijf-Tocht.* Leiden, 1651.

Guicciardini, Ludovico. *Beschrijvinghe van alle de Nederlanden.* Translated by Cornelis Kiliaan. Amsterdam, 1612. Originally published as *Des Crizione de Tutti i Paesi-Bassi,* 1567.

Hoorn, Jan ten. *Reisboek door de Vereenigde Nederlandsche Provinciën, en der selver aangrenzende landschappen en koningrijken: Behelzende, benevens een naauwkeuringe beschrijving der Steden, een aanwijzing van de Schuit- en Wagen vaarten.* Amsterdam, 1689.

Hortensius, Lambertius. *Opkomst en Ondergang van Naarden.* Naarden, 1573.

Huet, P. D. *Memoirs sur le commerce des Hollandais.* Paris, 1658. Published in English as *Memoirs of the Dutch Trade in all the States, Kingdoms, and Empires of the World.* London, 1703.

Kersseboom, W. *Eerste, Tweede, Derde Verhandeling tot een Prove om te weeten de probable menigte des volks in de Provintie van Holland en West-Vrieslandt.* . . . The Hague, 1742.

———. *Proeven van Politique Rekenkunde.* Amsterdam, 1739.

King, Gregory. *Natural and Political Observations and Conclusions upon the State and Condition of England.* London, 1696.

Lange van Wijngaarden, C. J. de. *Geschiedenis en Beschrijving der Stad van der Goude, 1817.* Reprint edited by J. N. Scheltema. Gouda, 1879.

Leeghwater, Jan Adriaenszoon. *Haarlemmer-meer-boek.* Amsterdam, 1641.

Leeuwen, S. van. *Batavia Illustrata.* The Hague, 1685.

Lois, S. *Chronycke ofte Korte Waere Beschrijvinge der Stad Rotterdam.* Rotterdam, 1746.

Loosjes, A, *Beschrijving der Zaanlandsche dorpen.* Zaandam, 1794.

Luzac, E. *Holland's Rijkdom, Behelzende den oorsprong van den Koophandel en van de magt van dezen Staat.* 4 vols. Leiden, 1780–83.

Malthus, T. R. *First Essay on Population.* London, 1798. Reprint. London (Royal Economic Society), 1926.

Mieris, F. van. *Beschrijving van Leyden.* 3 vols. Leiden, 1765–70.

Moine de l'Espine, Jacques le, and Isaäc le Long. *De Koophandel van Amsterdam.* Amsterdam, 1714.

Molesworth, R. M. *An Account of Denmark as it was in the year 1692.* 3d ed. London, 1694.

Napjus, Eelko. *Historisch Chronyk, of Beschryvinge van Oud en Nieuw Sneek.* Sneek, 1772.

Nederlandsche Jaarboeken. 19 vols. Amsterdam, 1747–65.

Parival, Jean-Nicolas. *Les delices de la Hollande.* Amsterdam, 1678.

Schotanus, Christianus. *Chroniek van Vriesland.* Franeker, 1664.

————. *De Geschiedenissen Kerkelyk ende Wereldtylyck van Friesland Oost ende West; beginnende van d' eerste geheuchtenis ende voltrocken tot op 1583.* Franeker, 1658.

Schouwen, J. F. *Korte Beschrijving van 't vlek Heerenveen.* Amsterdam, 1727.

Sjoerds, Foeke. *Algemeene Beschrijvinge van Oud en Nieuw Friesland.* Leeuwarden, 1765.

Spaan, Gerard van. *Beschryvinge der Stad Rotterdam.* Rotterdam, 1738.

Struyck, Nicolaas. *Vervolg van de beschrijving der staartsterren, en nader ontdekkingen omtrent den staat van 't menschelyk geslacht.* Amsterdam, 1753.

Süssmilch, Johann Peter. *Die Göttliche Ordnung in den Veränderungen des Menschlichen Geschlechtes.* . . . 3d ed. 3 vols. Berlin, 1775.

Tegenwoordige Staat der Vereenigde Nederlanden. 23 vols. Amsterdam, 1739–1803. (Holland, vols. 1–8, 1742–50; Utrecht, vols. 11–12, 1758–72; Friesland, vols. 13–16, 1785–89; Groningen [Stad en Lande], vols. 20–21, 1793–94; Overijssel, vols. 1–4, 1781–1803.)

Temple, Sir William. *Observations upon the United Provinces of the Netherlands.* London, 1673.

Valcooch, D. A. *Chronycke van Leeuwenhorn voortyden ontrent der Sypen.* Alkmaar, 1599.

Velius, Dirk. *Kroniek van Hoorn,* 4th ed. 2 vols. Hoorn, 1740.

"Verzameling van nauwkeurige lijsten opgemaakt uit oorspronkelijke registers betreffende sterfde, geboorte en huwelijken in 's Gravenhage: 1755–1773." The Hague, 1774.

Wagenaar, Jan. *Amsterdam in Zyne Opkomst, Aanwas, Geschiedenissen, Voorregten, Koophandel, Gebouwen, Kerken, Straaten, Schoolen, Schutterijen, Gilden en Regeeringe.* 10 vols. Amsterdam, 1767.

Walvis, J. *Beschrijving der stad Gouda.* Gouda, 1713.

Weston, Sir Richard. *Discours of Husbandrie used in Brabant and Flanders.* London, 1645.

Winsemius, Pierium. *Chronique ofte Historische Geschiedenisse van Vrieslant.* Franeker, 1622.

Woude, C. van der. *Kronyk van Alkmaar.* 2d ed. The Hague, 1746.

Yarranton, Andrew. *England's Improvement by Sea and Land to Out-do the Dutch without Fighting, to pay Debts without Moneys.* . . . London, 1677.

Ypey, N. *Verhandeling over den Uitvoer van 't Hooi, in een drietal gekroonde prijsverhandelingen.* . . . Harlingen, 1781.

UNPUBLISHED SECONDARY MATERIALS

Brummelkamp, J. "Grondgebruik in Aarlanderveen," 1934. Economisch-Historisch Bibliotheek, Universiteit van Amsterdam.

Dekker, K. M. "De landbouw in Broek op Langedijk in het midden van de 16ᵉ eeuw," 1957. Bibliotheek of the Afdeling Agrarische Geschiedenis, Landbouwhogeschool, Wageningen.

Hart, S. "Bronnen voor de historische demografie van Amsterdam in de 17ᵉ en 18ᵉ eeuw," 1965. Paper presented to the Historisch-Demografische Kring, 24 May 1965; deposited in GA Amsterdam.

Jansen, L. "De morgenboek van het ambacht Ter Aar in Rijnland, 1543–1680," 1935. Economisch-Historisch Bibliotheek, Universiteit van Amsterdam.

Keulen, B. van. "Beroepsstructuur van Leeuwarden in 1749," 1967. Deposited in GA Leeuwarden.

Klein, D. "De spreiding van enkele middenstands beroepen op het Groninger platteland in 1730," 1960. Bibliotheek of the Afdeling Agrarische Geschiedenis, Landbouwhogeschool, Wageningen.

Kooistra, J. "Agrarisch Idaarderadeel in de achtiende eeuw," 1963. Bibliotheek of the Afdeling Agrarische Geschiedenis, Landbouwhogeschool, Wageningen.

Kramer, J. H. "De bevolkingsterkte van Gouda tussen 1550 en 1650," 1950. Deposited in GA Gouda.

Mendels, Franklin F. "Industrialization and Population Pressure in Eighteenth Century Flanders," 1969. Ph.D. diss., University of Wisconsin.

Ohlin, Goran. "The Positive and Preventive Check, A Study of the Rate of Growth of Pre-Industrial Population," 1955. Ph.D. diss., Harvard University.

Rodenburg, D. M. "De Morgenboeken van Benthuizen," 1934. Economisch-Historisch Bibliotheek, Universiteit van Amsterdam.

Slicher van Bath, B. H. "Voorlopige systematische bibliografie van de Nederlandse demografische geschiedenis," 1962. Bibliotheek of the Afdeling Agrarische Geschiedenis, Landbouwhogeschool, Wageningen.

Snoep, J. "De Morgenboeken van Aalsmeer," 1934. Economisch-Historisch Bibliotheek, Universiteit van Amsterdam.

SECONDARY MATERIALS PUBLISHED SINCE 1820

Abel, Wilhelm. *Agrarkrisen und Agrarkonjunktur: Ein Geschichte der Land- und Ernährungswirtschaft Mitteleuropas seit dem hohen Mittelalter.* 2d ed. Hamburg-Berlin, 1966.

———. *Geschichte der deutschen Landwirtschaft vom frühen Mittelalter bis zum 19. Jahrhundert.* Stuttgart, 1962.

Achilles, W. "Getreidepreise und Getreidehandelsbeziehungen europäischer Räume im 16. und 17. Jahrhundert." *ZAA* (1959):32–55.

Algemene geschiedenis der Nederlanden. 12 vols. Utrecht, 1949–58.

Algra, N. E. *Ein; enkele rechthistorische aspecten van de grondeigendom in Westlauwers Friesland.* Groningen, n.d.

Ankum, L. A. "Een bijdrage tot de geschiedenis van de Zaanse olieslagerij." *TvG* 73 (1960):39–57, 215–51.

Apeldoorn, Lambertus Johannes van. "De historische ontwikkeling van het grondbezit in Friesland." *De Vrije Fries* 27 (1924):185–228.

———. *De kerkelijk goederen in Friesland.* Leeuwarden, 1915.

Arntz, W. S. A. "Export van Nederlandsche baksteen in vroeger eeuwen." *EHJ* 23 (1947):57–133.

Baasch, Ernst. *Holländische Wirtschaftsgeschichte.* Jena, 1927.

Baerderadiel, In geakunde. Drachten, 1957.

Balen, P. van. *Uit de geschiedenis van Haastrecht.* Stolwijk, 1937.

———. *Uit de geschiedenis van Waddinxveen.* Waddinxveen, 1940.

Barbour, Violet. *Capitalism in Amsterdam in the 17th Century.* Ann Arbor, 1963.

———. "Dutch and English Merchant Shipping in the 17th Century." *EHR* 2 (1929):261–90.

Becht, Harold E. *Statistische gegevens betreffende den handelsomzet van de Republiek der Vereenigde Nederlanden gedurende de 17ᵉ eeuw (1579–1715).* The Hague, 1908.

Beekman, A. A. *De Republiek in 1795. Geschiedkundige atlas van Nederland.* The Hague, 1913.

Belonje, J. *De Heer-Hugowaard (1629–1929), een geschiedenis van den polder.* Alkmaar, 1929.

———. *De Schermeer, 1633–1933.* Wormerveer, 1933.

———. *De Zijpe en Hazepolder, de ontwikkeling van een waterschap in Holland's Noorderkwartier.* Wormerveer, 1933.

Bicker Caarten, A., et al. *Zuid Hollands molenboek.* Alphen aan den Rijn, 1961.

Bijnouwer, J. T. P., and R. Lijsten. *Nederlandsche boerenerven.* Amsterdam 1943.

Blink, H. "Economische geographie der provincie Groningen historisch beschouwd." *TEG* 4 (1913):8–22.

———. *Geschiedenis van den boerenstand en den landbouw in Nederland.* 2 vols. Groningen, 1902.

Boekel, P. N. *De zuivelexport van Nederland tot 1813.* Utrecht, 1929.

Boer, T. J. de. "De Friesche grond in 1511." *Historische Avonden* 2 (1907):95–114.

Boerendonk, M. J. "Economische aardrijkskunde van Holland omstreeks het jaar 1500." *TEG* 30 (1939):127–48.

————. *Historische studie over den Zeeuwschen landbouw.* The Hague, 1935.

Boorsma, P. *Duizend Zaanse molens.* Wormerveer, 1950.

Boserup, Ester. *The Conditions of Agricultural Growth.* London, 1965.

Bouman, J. *Bedijking, opkomst en bloei van de Beemster.* Amsterdam, 1857.

Boxer, C. R. *The Dutch Seaborne Empire: 1600–1800.* New York, 1965.

Braam, Aris van. *Bloei en verval van het economisch-sociale leven aan de Zaan in de 17ᵉ en 18ᵉ eeuw.* Wormerveer, 1944.

Brouwer, J. H., ed. *Encyclopedie van Friesland.* Amsterdam, 1958.

Brugmans, H. *Opkomst en bloei van Amsterdam.* Amsterdam, 1944.

Brugmans, I. J. "De Oost-Indische Compagnie en de welvaart in de Republiek." *TvG* 61 (1948):225–31.

————. *Paardenkracht en mensenmacht: Sociaal-economische geschiedenis van Nederland, 1795–1940.* The Hague, 1961.

Bruijne, F. H. de. *De Ronde Venen.* Rotterdam, 1939.

Brünner, E. C. G. "De ontwikkeling van het handelsverkeer van Holland met oost Europa tot het einde der 16ᵉ eeuw." *TvG* 41 (1926):353–71.

————. *De order op de buitennering van 1531.* Amsterdam, 1921.

Bücher, K. *Die Entstehung der Volkswirtschaft.* Tubingen, 1893.

Bureau voor statistiek en voorlichting der gemeente 's Gravenhage. *Zeven eeuwen 's Gravenhage.* The Hague, 1948.

Burke, G. L. *The Making of the Dutch Towns.* London, 1956.

The Cambridge Economic History of Europe. Vol. 1: *The Agrarian Life of the Middle Ages,* edited by M. M. Postan, 2d ed. Cambridge, 1966. Vol. 4: *The Economy of Expanding Europe in the Sixteenth and Seventeenth Centuries,* edited by E. E. Rich and C. Wilson. Cambridge, 1967.

Chayanov, A. V. *The Theory of Peasant Economy.* Edited and translated by Daniel Thorner, Basile Kerbley, and R. E. F. Smith. Homewood, Ill., 1966.

Chisholm, Michael. *Rural Settlement and Land Use.* New York, 1967.

Christensen, A. E. *Dutch Trade to the Baltic about 1600. Studies in the Sound Toll Register and Dutch Shipping Records.* Copenhagen and The Hague, 1941.

Cistozvonov, A. N. "Agrarnye otnošenije v Južnoj Gollandii, Amsterlante i Choojlante po materialam opisej 1494 i 1514 godov." *Srednie Veka* 17 (1960):164–95.

————. "Agrarnye otnošenija v Severnoj Gollandii po materialam opisej 1494 i 1514 godov." *Srednie Veka* 19 (1962):125–41.

Cools, R. H. A. *De strijd om den grond in het lage Nederland; het proces van bedijking, inpoldering en droogmaking sinds de vroegste tijden.* Rotterdam, 1948.

Dardel, Pierre. *Navires et marchandises dans les ports de Rouen et du Havre au XVIIIe siècle.* Paris, 1963.

Dewez, W. J. "De landbouw in Brabants westhoek in het midden van de achttiende eeuw." *Agronomisch-Historische Bijdragen* 4 (1958):1–65.

Diepeveen, W. J. *De vervening in Delfland en Schieland tot het einde der 16e eeuw.* Leiden, 1950.

Dijkema, H. *Proeve van een geschiedenis der landhuishoudkunde van Groningen.* Groningen, 1851.

Dillen, J. G. van. *Bronnen tot de geschiedenis van het bedrijfsleven en het gildewezen van Amsterdam, 1512–1601.* RPG, vol. 69 (1929), vol. 78 (1933).

————. "Dreigende hongersnood in de Republiek in de laatste jaren der zeventiende eeuw." In idem, *Mensen en Achtergronden.* Groningen, 1964.

————. "Leiden als industriestad tijdens de Republiek." *TvG* 59 (1946): 25–51.

————. "Stukken betreffende den Amsterdamschen graanhandel omstreeks het jaar 1681." *EHJ* 3 (1917):70–106.

————. *Van rijkdom en regenten. Handboek tot de economische en sociale geschiedenis van Nederland tijdens de Republiek.* The Hague, 1970.

Dissel, E. F. van. "Grond ineigendom en in huur in de ambachten van Rijnland omstreeks 1545." In *Catalogus over Leiden en omgeving, nr. 8987.* n.d.

Doorn, Z. van. "Enige landbouwhistorische bronnen van Zegveld en Zegvelderboek." *Historia Agriculturae* 7 (1963):193–277.

Edelman-Vlam, A. W. "De ontwikkeling van de parceelsvormen in Nederland." In Ministerie van Landbouw en Visserij, *Landbouwgeschiedenis,* pp. 141–67. The Hague, 1960.

Eekhoff, W. *Geschiedkundige beschrijving van Leeuwarden.* 2 vols. Leeuwarden, 1846.

Engelenburg, W. van. *Geschiedenis van Broek in Waterland.* Haarlem, 1907.

Enno van Gelder, H. *De Nederlandse munten.* Utrecht, 1968.

Enno van Gelder, H. A. "Friesche en Groningsche edelen in de tijd van den opstand tegen Spanje." In *Historische opstellen, opgedragen aan H. Brugmans.* Amsterdam, 1929.

————. "De Hollandse adel in de tijd van de opstand." *TvG* 45 (1930): 113–50.

————. "Nederlandse dorpen in de 16^e eeuw." *Verhandelingen der Koninklijke Nederlandse Akademie van Wetenschappen, Afdeling Letterkunde,* n.s., vol. 59 (1953).

————. "Een Noord Hollandse stad, 1500–1540," *BVGO,* 4th ser. 8 (1910):428–31.

——. "De tiende penning." *TvG* 48 (1933):1–36.

Faber, J. A. "De buitenlandse scheepvaart en handel van Harlingen in de jaren 1654 en 1655." *AAGB* 14 (1967):34–71.

——. "Economische op- en neergang." In J. J. Kalma *et al.*, eds., *Geschiedenis van Friesland*. Drachten, 1968.

——. "Graanhandel, graanprijzen en tarievenpolitiek in Nederland gedurende de tweede helft der zeventiende eeuw." *TvG* 75 (1962):533–39.

——. "De oligarchisering van Friesland in de tweede helft van de zeventiende eeuw." *AAGB* 15 (1970):39–64.

Faber, J. A., H. K. Roessingh; B. H. Slicher van Bath, A. M. van der Woude, and H. J. van Xanten. "Population changes and economic developments in the Netherlands: a historical survey." *AAGB* 12 (1965): 47–113.

——. "Het probleem van de dalende graanaanvoer uit de Oostzeelanden in de tweede helft van de zeventiende eeuw." *AAGB* 9 (1963):3–28.

Fei, John C., and Gustav Ranis. *Development of the Labor Surplus Economy*. Homewood, Ill., 1964.

Feith, H. O. *Het Groninger Beklemrecht*. 2 vols. Groningen, 1828.

Feith, J. A. "De rijkdom der kloosters van Stad en Lande." In *Groninger Volksalmanak*, pp. 1–21. Groningen, 1902.

Fockema Andreae, S. J., E. H. ter Kuile, and R. C. Hekker. *Duizend jaar bouwen in Nederland*. 2 vols. Amsterdam, 1957

Fockema Andreae, S. J. "Bronnen voor de geschiedenis van de landbouw." In Ministerie van Landbouw en Visserij, *Landbouwgeschiedenis*, pp. 171–83. The Hague, 1960.

——. "Embanking and drainage authorities in the Netherlands during the Middle Ages." *Speculum* 27 (1952):158–67.

——. "Uit de geschiedenis van een Rijnlandse polder (de Noordeind en Geerpolder onder Ter Aar en Leimuiden)." *Leids Jaarboekje* 52 (1960): 57–69.

——. "Grondeigenaars en grondgebruikers in een hoekje van Holland." In *Ceres en Clio, zeven variaties op het thema landbouwgeschiedenis*. Wageningen, 1964.

——. *Het Hoogheemraadschap van Rijnland*. Leiden, 1934.

——. "Middeleeuwsch Oegstgeest. " *TvG* 50 (1935):256–75.

——. "De Nederlandse staat onder de Republiek," *Verhandelingen der Koninklijke Nederlandse Akademie van Wetenschappen, Afdeling Letterkunde*, n.s., vol. 68 (1961).

——. *Studiën over waterschapsgeschiedenis*. 8 vols. Leiden, 1950–52.

Friis, Astrid. "An Inquiry into the Relations between Economic and Financial Factors in the 16th and 17th centuries; The two crises in the Netherlands in 1557." *SEHR* 1 (1953):193–241.

Fuchs, J. N. *Beurt- en Wagenveren*. Amsterdam, 1946.

Fussell, G. E. *The English Dairy Farmer: 1500–1900.* London, 1966.

Gevers van Endgeest, Jhr. D. T. *Hoogheemraadschap van Rijnland.* 2 vols. The Hague, 1871.

Gieysztorowa, Irene. "Research into Demographic History of Poland. A Provisional Summing Up." *Acta Poloniae Historica* 18 (1968):5–17.

Glamann, Christof. *Dutch-Asiatic Trade, 1620–1740.* Copenhagen, 1958.

Goede, A. de. *Swannotsrecht, Westfriesche rechtsgeschiedenis.* 2 vols. Utrecht, n.d.

Gottschalk, M. K. E. "De ontginning der Stichtse venen ten oosten van de Vecht." *TKNAG* 73 (1956):207–22.

Goubert, Pierre. *Beauvais et le Beauvaisis de 1600 à 1730.* 2 vols. Paris, 1960.

——. "The French Peasantry of the Seventeenth Century." *Past and Present,* no. 10, 1956. Reprinted in Trevor Aston, ed., *Crisis in Europe, 1560–1660,* pp. 150–76. New York, 1967.

Guibal, C. J. *Democratie en oligarchie in Friesland tijdens de Republick.* Assen, 1934.

Hart, G. t'. *Historische beschrijving van het Hoge Heerlijkheid van Heenvliet.* Den Helder, 1949.

Hart, S. "Enige statistische gegevens inzake analfabetisme te Amsterdam in de 17e en 18e eeuw." *Maandblad Amstelodamum* 55 (1968):3–6.

——. "Historisch-demografische notities betreffende huwelijken en migratie te Amsterdam in de 17e en 18e eeuw. *Maandblad Amstelodamum* 55 (1968):63–69.

Hartgerink-Koomans, Maria. *Het geslacht Ewsum; geschiedenis van een jonkers-familie uit de Ommelanden in de 15e en 16e eeuw.* Groningen, 1938.

Henning, Friedrich Wilhelm. "Die Betriebsgrössenstruktur der mitteleuropäischen Landwirtschaft im 18. Jahrhundert und ihr Einfluss auf die ländlichen Einkommensverhältnisse." *ZAA* 17 (1969):171–93.

Herks, Johannes Jacobus. *De geschiedenis van de Amersfoortse tabak.* The Hague, 1967.

Hobsbawm, Eric. "The Crisis of the Seventeenth Century." In Trevor Aston, ed., *Crisis in Europe: 1560–1660.* New York, 1967. Originally published as "The General Crisis of the European Economy in the Seventeenth Century." *Past and Present,* no. 5 (1954), pp. 33–53; no. 6 (1954), pp. 44–65.

Hoekstra, P. *Bloemendaal: proeve ener streekgeschiedenis.* Wormerveer, 1947.

Hofstee, E. W. *Het Oldampt.* 2 vols. Groningen, 1937.

Hollestelle, Johanna. *De steenbakkerij in de Nederlanden tot omstreeks 1560.* Assen, 1961.

Hömberg, Albert K. *Wirtschaftsgeschichte Westfalens.* Münster, 1968.

Hoskins, W. G. *The Midland Peasant; the Economic and Social History of a Leicestershire Village.* London, 1957.

――――. "The Rebuilding of Rural England, 1570–1640." *Past and Present*, no. 4 (1953), pp. 44–59.

Hoszowski, S. "The Polish Baltic trade in the 15th–18th centuries." In *Poland at the 11th International Congress of Historical Studies in Stockholm.* Warsaw, 1960.

Hovij, J. *Het vorstel van 1751 tot instelling van een beperkt vrijhavenstelsel in de Republiek.* Groningen, 1966.

Hymer, Stephen, and Stephen Resnick. "A Model of an Agrarian Economy with Nonagricultural Activities." *AER* 59 (1969):493–506.

Jansen, H. P. H. *Hoekse en Kabeljauwse twisten.* Bussem, 1966.

Jansma, T. S. "Bijdrage tot de agrarische geschiedenis van Texel, voornamelijk in de zestiende eeuw." *Landbouwkundig Tijdschrift* 61 (1949):525–47.

――――. "Het economisch overwicht van de laat-middeleeuwse stad t.a.v. haar agrarisch ommeland in het bijzonder toegelicht met de verhouding tussen Leiden en Rijnland." *Leids Jaarboekje* 58 (1966):93–108.

Jappe Alberts, W., and H. P. H. Jansen. *Welvaart in wording: sociaal-economische geschiedenis van Nederland van de vroegste tijden tot het einde van de middeleeuwen.* The Hague, 1964.

Jeannin, P. *L'Europe du nord-ouest et du nord aux XVIIe et XVIIIe siècles.* Paris, 1969.

Jellema, D. "Friesian Trade in the Dark Ages." *Speculum*, 30 (1955):15–36.

Johnson, Harry G. *International Trade and Economic Growth.* Cambridge, Mass., 1967.

――――. *Money, Trade and Economic Growth.* Cambridge, Mass., 1962.

Johnston, Bruce, and John W. Mellor. "The Role of Agriculture in Economic Development." *AER* 51 (1961):566–93.

Jong, C. de. *De droogmaking van de Wildevenen in Schieland.* Voorburg, 1957.

Jonge, J. A. de. *De industrialisatie in Nederland tussen 1850 en 1914.* Amsterdam, 1968.

Kalma, J. J., J. J. Spahr van der Hoek, and K. de Vries, eds. *Geschiedenis van Friesland.* Drachten, 1968.

Kamen, Henry. "The Economic and Social Consequences of the Thirty Years War." *Past and Present*, no. 39 (1968), pp. 44–61.

Kastelein, T. J. "Social structure and economic growth in the Netherlands." In *First International Conference of Economic History*, pp. 489–93. Stockholm, 1960.

Keuning, H. J. *De Groninger Veenkoloniën, een sociaal-geografische studie.* Amsterdam, 1933.

Kindleberger, Charles P. *Foreign Trade and the National Economy*. New Haven, 1962.

Kisch, Herbert. "Prussian Mercantilism and the Rise of the Krefeld Silk Industry: variations upon an eighteenth century theme." *Transactions of the American Philosophical Society*, n.s., vol. 58, pt. 7 (1968).

Klein, P. W. "De heffing van de 100ᵉ en 200ᵉ penning van het vermogen te Gouda." *EHJ* 31 (1965):41–62.

Kloot-Meyburg, B. W. van der. *De economische ontwikkeling van een zuid-Hollandsch dorp (Oudshoorn) tot in den aanvang der twintigste eeuw*. The Hague, 1920.

Kniphorst, C. L. *Geschiedkundig overzicht van de verveening in Drenthe*. Assen, 1872.

Koenen, H. J. *De Nederlandsche boerenstand*. Haarlem, 1858.

Koeningsberger, H. G. "Property and the Price Revolution (Hainault, 1474–1573)." *EHR*, 2d ser. 9 (1956):1–15.

Kohlbrugge, J. H. F. "Over den invloed der steden op hare bewoners en op de bewoners van het land." *De Economist* 56 (1907):372–93.

Koster, P. *Hoorn in de middeleeuwen*. Amsterdam, 1928.

Kranenburg, H. A. H. *De zeevisscherij van Holland in den tijd der Republiek*. Amsterdam, 1946.

Kruizinga, J. H. *Watergraafsmeer*. Amsterdam, 1948.

Kuttner, Erich. *Het hongerjaar 1566*. Amsterdam, 1949.

Kuyper, J. *De Republiek der Vereenigde Nederlanden in kaart en woord*. Leiden, 1898.

Laslett, Peter. "Size and Structure of the Household in England over three centuries." *Population Studies* 23 (1969):199–223.

Le Roy Ladurie, Emmanuel. *Les Paysans de Languedoc*. 2 vols. Paris, 1966.

Lindemans, P. *Geschiedenis van de landbouw in België*. 2 vols. Antwerp, 1952.

——. "De Vlaamse landbouw in de 16ᵉ tot de 18ᵉ eeuw en zijn betekenis voor de landbouw in West Europa." In Ministerie van Landbouw en Visserij, *Landbouwgeschiedenis*, pp. 99–105. The Hague, 1960.

Linden, H. van der. *De cope*. Assen, 1956.

Linthorst Homan, J. *Geschiedenis van Drenthe*. Assen, 1947.

Lootsma, S. *Historische studiën over de Zaanstreek*. 2 vols. Koog aan de Zaan, 1939–50.

Lubimenko, I. "The Struggle of the Dutch with the English for the Russian Market in the Seventeenth Century." *TRHS*, 4th ser. 7 (1924): 27–51.

Maçzak, Antoni. "Export of Grain and the Problem of Distribution of National Income in the years 1550–1650." *Acta Poloniae Historica* 18 (1968):75–98.

Meertens, P. J. *De lof van den boer; de boer in de Noord en Zuid Nederlandsche letterkunde van de middeleeuwen tot 1880.* Amsterdam, 1942.

Mellor, John W. *The Economics of Agricultural Development.* Ithaca, 1966.

Ministerie van Landbouw en Visserij, Directie van Landbouw. *Landbouwgeschiedenis.* The Hague, 1960.

Mol, C. *Uit de geschiedenis van Wormer.* Wormerveer, 1966.

Molen, S. J. van der. *Het Friesche boerenhuis in twintig eeuwen.* Assen, 1942.

————. *Opsterlan, skiednis fan in Waldgritenij.* Drachten, 1958.

Mols, Rogier. "Beschouwingen over de bevolkingsgeschiedenis in de Nederlanden (15ᵉ en 16ᵉ eeuw)." *TvG* 66 (1953):201–19.

————. "De Bevölkerungsgeschichte Belgiens im Lichte des heutigen Forschung." *VSWG* 46 (1959):491–511.

————. *Introduction à la démographie historique des villes d'Europe du 14ᵉ au 18ᵉ siècle.* 3 vols. Louvain, 1955.

Moquette, H. C. H. "De strijd op economisch gebied tusschen Dordrecht en Rotterdam. *TvG* 41 (1926):40–63.

Mulder, G. J. A., ed. *Handboek der Geografie van Nederland.* 5 vols. Zwolle, 1949–53.

Naber, J. C. "Een terugblik." *Bijdrage van het Statistisch Instituut* 4 (1885):1–48.

Niermeyer, J. F. *Delft en Delfland.* Leiden, 1944.

————. "Landbouw en handel in Friesland in de 13ᵉ eeuw." In *Economisch Historische Opstellen.* Amsterdam, 1947.

————. *De Wording van onze volkshuishouding.* The Hague, 1946.

Nierop, Leonie van. "De aanvang der Nederlandsche demographie." *EHJ* 5 (1919):192–208.

————. "De bruidgoms van Amsterdam van 1578 tot 1601." *TvG* 48 (1933):337–59; 49 (1934):136–60, 329–44; 52 (1937):144–63, 251–64.

————. "Uit de bakermat der Amsterdamsche handelstatistiek." *Jaarboek Amstelodamum*, vol. 13 (1915), vol. 15 (1917).

————. "Het zielenaantal van Amsterdam in het midden van de achttiende eeuw." *Maandblad Amstelodamum* 38 (1951):151–54.

Noorden, D. J. "De bevolking van 's Gravenzande en Zand Ambacht, 1680–1795." *Zuidhollandse Studiën* 14 (1968):73–94.

Obreen, Hendrik Tjaard. *Dijkplicht en waterschappen aan Frieslands westkust.* Bolsward, 1956.

Ohlin, Bertil. *Interregional and International Trade.* Cambridge, Mass., 1957.

Oldenhof, Harm. "Biroppen yn Frjentsjeren amkriten foar 200 jier." *It beaken* 20 (1958):54–70.

Peterson, William. "Demographic Transition in the Netherlands." *American Sociological Review* 25 (1960):334–47.

Pirenne, Henri. "The Place of the Netherlands in the Economic History of Medieval Europe." *EHR* 2 (1929):20–40.

Poel, J. M. G. van der. *De landbouw in het verste verleden*. Assen, 1961.

———. "De teelt van meekrap." In *Ceres en Clio,* pp. 129–65. Wageningen, 1964.

Posthumus, N. W. "Gegevens betreffende landbouw toestanden in Rijnland in het jaar 1575." *BMHG* 35 (1914):169–85.

———. *De geschiedenis van de Leidsche lakenindustrie.* 3 vols. The Hague, 1939.

———. *Inquiry into the History of Prices in Holland.* 2 vols. Leiden, 1946–64.

———. "De industrieële concurrentie tusschen Noord- en Zuid-Nederlandsche nijverheidscentra in de XVIIe en XVIIIe eeuw." In *Mélanges d'histoire offerts à Henri Pirenne 1886–1926,* 2:369–78. Brussels, 1926.

———. The Tulip Mania in Holland in the Years 1636 and 1637." *Journal of Economic and Business History* 1 (1929):434–66.

Postma, O. "Fan boer en ambacht." *It beaken* 20 (1958):121–32.

———. *De Friesche kleihoeve.* Leeuwarden, 1934.

———. "Over het Friesche boerenhuis in de 16^e en 17^e eeuw." *De Vrije Fries* 34 (1937):6–28.

———. "Over de positie van het vlek in Friesland in de tijd van de Republiek." *De Vrije Fries* 44 (1960):51–58.

Ramaer, J. C. "De middelpunten van bewoning in Nederland voorheen en thans." *TKNAG* 38 (1921):1–38, 174–215.

Ravensteyn, Willem van, Jr. *Onderzoekingen over de economische-sociale ontwikkeling van Amsterdam gedurende de 16de en het eerste kwart der 17de eeuw.* Amsterdam, 1906.

Reesse, J. J. *De suiker handel van het begin der 17^e eeuw tot 1894.* 2 vols. Haarlem, 1908–11.

Regtdoorzee Greup-Roldanus, S. C. *Geschiedenis der Haarlemmer bleekerijen.* The Hague, 1936.

Renting, R. A. D. "Onderzoek naar de bevolkingsstructuur binnen het ambacht Hillegersberg." *Rotterdams Jaarboekje* 5 (1957):217–43.

Roelfsma, Ena H. *De klooster- en proostdijgoederen in de provincie Groningen.* Groningen, 1928.

Roessingh, H. K. "Beroep en bedrijf op de Veluwe in het midden van de achttiende eeuw." *AAGB* 13 (1965):181–274. Partially translated as "Village and Hamlet in a Sandy Region of the Netherlands in the middle of the 18th century." *Acta Historiae Neerlandica* 4 (1970):105–29.

———. "Het Veluwse inwonertal, 1526–1947." *AAGB* 11 (1964):79–150.

Rogier, J. P. "De betekenis van de terugkeer van de Minderbroeders te Delft in 1709." *Archief voor de geschiedenis van de katholieke kerk in Nederland* 2 (1960):169–204.

Russell, J. C. "The Metropolitan City Region in the Middle Ages." *Journal of Regional Science* 2 (1960):55–70.

Sangers, W. J. "Amsterdam's betekenis voor de groententeelt in de 17de eeuw." *TEG* 38 (1947):52–55.

———. *De ontwikkeling van de Nederlandse tuinbouw tot het jaar 1930.* Zwolle, 1952.

Sannes, H. *Geschiedenis van het Bildt.* 3 vols. Franeker, 1951–56.

Sauvy, Alfred. *Théorie Générale de la Population.* 2 vols. Paris, 1963.

Schaik, P. van. "De economische betekenis van de turfwinning in Nederland." *EHJ* 32 (1969):141–205, 33 (1970):186–235.

Schillemans, C. A. "De houtveilingen van Zaandam in de jaren 1655–1811." *EHJ* 23 (1947):171–315.

Scholliers, E. *De levensstandard in de XVe en XVIe eeuw te Antwerpen.* Antwerp, 1960.

Scholtens, H. J. J. *Uit het verleden van midden-Kennemerland.* The Hague, 1947.

Schoorl, Henk. *Isaäc Le Maire; koopman en bedijker.* Haarlem, 1969.

Schraa, P. "Onderzoekingen naar de bevolkingsomvang van Amsterdam tussen 1550 en 1650." *Jaarboek Amstelodamum* 46 (1954):1–33.

Sebus, Johan Hendrik. *De erfgooiers en hun gemeenschappelijk bezit tot 1568.* Amsterdam, 1933.

See, Henri. "Le commerce des Hollandais à Nantes pendant la minorité de Louis XIV." *TvG* 41 (1926):246–60.

Siemens, B. W. *Historische atlas van de provincie Groningen.* Groningen, 1962.

Slicher van Bath, B. H. "Accounts and diaries of farmers before 1800 as sources for agricultural history." *AAGB* 8 (1962):3–34.

———. *De Agrarische geschiedenis van West Europa, 500–1850.* Utrecht, 1960. Translated as *Agrarian History of Western Europe, 500–1850.* London, 1963.

———. "Agriculture in the Low Countries, ca. 1600–1800." In *Relazioni del X Congresso Internazionale de Scienze Storiche, Storia Moderna,* vol. 4. Firenze, 1955.

———. "Boerenvrijheid," *Economisch-Historische Herdrukken.* The Hague, 1964.

———. "The Economic and Social Conditions in the Friesian districts from 900 to 1500." *AAGB* 13 (1965):97–134.

———. "Historical Demography and the Social and Economic Development of the Netherlands." *Daedalus* 97 (1968):604–21.

———. "De invloed van de economische omstandigheden op de technische ontwikkeling van de landbouw in het verleden." *Landbouwkundig Tijdschrift* 74 (1962):149–79.

————. "Een landbouwbedrijf in de tweede helft van de zestiende eeuw." *Agronomisch-Historisch Bijdragen* 4 (1958):67–188.

————. *Mensch en land in de middeleeuwen: bijdragen tot den geschiedenis der nederzetting in oostelijk Nederland.* Assen, 1944.

————. "De oogstopbrengsten van verschillende gewassen, voornamelijk granen, in verhouding tot het zaaizaad, ca. 810–1820." *AAGB* 9 (1963): 29–126. Substantially translated as "The Yields of Different Crops (mainly cereals) in Relation to the Seed, ca. 810–1820," *Acta Historiae Neerlandica,* 2 (1967):26–106.

————. "Les problèmes fondamentaux de la société préindustrielle en Europe occidentale, une orientation et un programme." *AAGB* 12 (1965):3–46.

————. "Report on the Study of Historical Demography in the Netherlands." *Problèmes de Mortalité, Les congrés et colloques de l'université de Liège* 33 (1965):185–98.

————. "The Rise of Intensive Husbandry in the Low Countries." In J. S. Bromley and E. H. Kossman, eds., *Britain and the Netherlands.* London, 1960.

————. "Robert Loder en Rienck Hemmema." *It beaken* 20 (1958):89–117.

————. *Een samenleving onder spanning; geschiedenis van het platteland in Overijssel.* Assen, 1957.

Sneller, Z. W. *Geschiedenis van de Nederlandschen landbouw, 1795–1940.* Groningen, 1943.

————. "De opkomst van de plattelandsnijverheid in Nederland in de 17e en 18e eeuw." *De Economist* 77 (1928):691–702. Translated as "La naissance de l'industrie rurale dans les Pays-Bas aux 17e et 18e siècle." *Annales de histoire économique et sociale* 1 (1929):193–202.

Spahr van der Hoek, J. J. *Samenleven in Friesland; drie perioden uit de sociale geschiedenis.* Drachten, 1969.

Spahr van der Hoek, J. J., and O. Postma. *Geschiedenis van de Friese landbouw.* 2 vols. Drachten, 1952.

Staring, W. C. H. *De binnen- en buitenlandse maten, gewichten en munten van vroeger en tegenwoordig.* Schoonhoven, 1871.

Statistiek der bevolking van Amsterdam tot 1921. Mededeelingen van het Bureau van Statistiek der gemeente Amsterdam, no. 67 (1923).

Steur, A. G. van der. "Het aantal inwoners van Warmond in de loop der eeuwen." *Holland: Regionaal-Historisch Tijdschrift* 1 (1969):70–82.

Swart, F. *Zur Friesischen Agrargeschichte.* Leipzig, 1910.

Tanguy, Jean. *Le Commerce du port de Nantes au milieu de XVIe siecle.* Paris, 1956.

Theissen, Johann Samuel. *Centraal gezag en Friesche vrijheid.* Groningen, 1907.

Thirsk, Joan., ed. *Agrarian History of England and Wales, 1500–1640,* vol. 4. Cambridge, 1967.

―――. "Industries in the Countryside." In F. J. Fisher, ed., *Essays in the Economic and Social History of Tudor and Stuart England.* Cambridge, 1961.

Thünen, J. H. von. *Der Isolierte Staat in Beziehung auf Landwirtschaft und Nationalökonomie.* Rostock, 1826.

Top, H. J. *Geschiedenis der Groninger Veenkoloniën.* Veendam, 1893.

Topolski, J. "La regression économique en Pologne du XVIe au XVIIIe siècle." *Acta Poloniae Historica,* vol. 7 (1962).

Unger, W. S. *De levensmiddelenvoorziening der Hollandsche steden in de middeleeuwen.* Amsterdam, 1916.

―――. "De sociale en economische structuur van Dordrecht in 1555." *De Economist* 64 (1915):461–507.

―――. "De sonttabellen." *TvG* 41(1926):137–55.

Vanderboeke, Chr. "Aardappelteelt en aardappelverbruik in de 17e en 18e eeuw." *TvG* 82 (1969):49–68.

Verhulst, A. "Bronnen en problemen betreffende de Vlaamse landbouw in de laat-middeleeuwen (XIIe–XVe eeuw)." *Agronomisch-Historisch Bijdragen,* vol. 7 (1964).

―――. "Les types differents de l'organization domainiale et structures agraires en Belgique au moyen age." *Annales* 11 (1956):61–70.

Verkade, Margarethe Adriana. *De opkomst van de Zaanstreek.* Utrecht, 1952.

Verlinden, C., J. Craeybeckx, and E. Scholliers. "Mouvements des prix et des salaires en Belgique au XVIe siècle." *Annales* 10 (1955):173–98.

Voorthuijsen, W. D. *De Republiek der Verenigde Nederlanden en het mercantilisme.* The Hague, 1964.

Vooys, A. C. de. "De Bevolkingsspreiding op het Hollandse platteland in 1622 en 1795." *TKNAG* 70 (1953):316–30.

Vooys, A. C. de, and J. M. G. Kleinpenning. *Bronnen voor het regionale onderzoek in Nederland.* Groningen, 1963.

Vrankrijker, A. C. J. de. *Naerdencklant; Gooische studien over koptiende, enz.* The Hague, 1947.

―――. "De Textielindustrie van Naarden; de nieuwe industrie in de 17de en 18de eeuw." *TvG* 51 (1936):264–83.

Vries, G. de. *Het dijks- en molenbestuur in Holland's Noorderkwartier onder de grafelijke regeering en gedurende de Republiek.* Amsterdam, 1876.

Vries, Johan de. *De economische achteruitgang der Republiek in de achttiende eeuw.* 2d ed. Leiden, 1968.

Vuyk, Aart. *Boskoop, vijf eeuwen boomwekerij.* Boskoop, 1966.

Wee, H. van der. "De economie als factor bij het begin van de opstand in de Zuidelijke Nederlanden." *Bijdragen en Mededelingen betreffende de Geschiedenis der Nederlanden* 83 (1969):15–32.

———. *The Growth of the Antwerp Market and the European Economy.* 3 vols. The Hague, 1963.

———. "Typologie des crises et changements de structures aux Pay-Bas (XVe–XVIe siècle)." *Annales* 18 (1963) 209–25.

Wee, H. van der, and Th. Peeters. "Een dynamisch model voor de seculaire ontwikkeling van de wereld handel en de welvaart (12e–18e eeuw)." *TvG* 82 (1969):233–49. Translated as "Un modèle dynamique de croissance interseculaire du commerce mondial (XIIe–XVIIIe siècle)." *Annales* 25 (1970) :100–26.

Werkman, Gerhard. *Kent gij het land der zee ontrukt.* Bussem, 1948.

Werveke, H. van. *Miscellanea Medaevalia.* Gent, 1968.

———. "De zwarte dood in de Zuidelijke Nederlanden, 1349–1351." In *Mededelingen Koninklijke Vlaamse Akademie voor Wetenschap (Letteren),* 1950.

Westermann, J. C. "Statistische gegevens over den handel van Amsterdam in de 17e eeuw." *TvG* 61 (1948):3–15.

Wharton, Clifton, R., ed. *Subsistence Agriculture and Economic Development.* Chicago, 1969.

Wiaarda, D. *Die Geschichtliche Entwickelung der Landwirtschaftlichen Verhältnisse Ostfrieslands.* Emden, 1880.

Wielen, H. G. W. van der. *Een Friesche landbouw-veenkolonie; bevolkingstudies van de gemeente Opsterland.* Amsterdam, 1930.

Wiese, H., and J. Bölts. *Rinderhandel und Rinderhaltung im nordwesteuropäischen Küstengebiet vom 15. bis zum 19. Jahrhundert.* Stuttgart, 1966.

Wijnne, H. A. *Handel en ontwikkeling van Stad en Provincie Groningen geschiedkundig beschouwd.* Groningen, 1865.

Wilson, Charles. *Anglo-Dutch Commerce and Finance in the Eighteenth Century.* Cambridge, 1941.

———. "Cloth Production and International Competition in the 17th century," *EHR,* 2d ser. 13 (1960):209–21.

———. "The Economic Decline of the Netherlands." *EHR* 9 (1939): 111–27.

———. *Profit and Power: A Study of England and the Dutch Wars.* London, 1957.

———. "Taxation and the Decline of Empires." *BMHG* 77 (1963):10–26.

Winkler, Klaus. *Landwirtschaft und Agrarverfassung im Fürstentum Osnabrück nach dem Dreissigjährigen Kriege.* Stuttgart, 1959.

Wiskerke, C. "De geschiedenis van het meekrapbedrijf in Nederland." *EHJ* 25 (1951):1–144.

Woude, A. M. van der, and G. J. Mentink. *De demografische ontwikkeling te Rotterdam en Cool in de XVII en XVIII eeuw.* Rotterdam, 1965. Partially translated as "La Population de Rotterdam au XVIIᵉ et au XVIIIᵉ siècle." *Population* 21 (1966):1165–90.

Woude, A. M. van der. "De consumptie van graan, vlees en boter in Holland op het einde van de achttiende eeuw." *AAGB* (1963):127–54.

———. "De omvang en samenstelling van de huishouding in Nederland in het verleden." *AAGB* 15 (1970):202–41.

———. "De weerbare mannen van 1747 in de dorpen van het Zuiderkwartier van Holland als demografisch gegeven." *AAGB* 8 (1962):35–76.

Wrigley, E. A. "A simple model of London's importance in changing English society and economy, 1650–1750." *Past and Present,* no. 37 (1967) pp. 44–70.

Wttewaal, G. "Landbouwkundige beschrijving van een gedeelte der Provincie Utrecht tusschen de Stad Utrecht en Wijk bij Duurstede." *Tijdschrift ter bevordering van Nijverheid* 2 (1834):1–42.

Zijp, A. "Hoofdstukken uit de economische en sociale geschiedenis van de polder Zijpe in de 17ᵉ en 18ᵉ eeuw." *TvG* 70 (1957):29–48, 176–88.

Index

Aalsmeer: horticulture in, 154

Aanbreng van 1511: described, 23–24

Aarlanderveen, 30; herd size in, 70, 138; population of, 93

Abbekerk: bourgeois landownership in, 45; population of, 92

Abbenbroek, 36; bourgeois landownership in, 46

Achtkarspelen: cultivated land in, 33; farm size in, 59; arable land in, 145

Aegum, 125–26

Akkersloot: horticulture in, 146

Albert of Saxony, 33

Alblasserwaard, 36, 62, 87, 96, 113, 127; poverty in, 67

Alkemade: herd size in, 70, 138

Alkmaar, 50, 154, 156; rural landownership of, 45; development of cheese market in, 157–58; investors in polders from, 194; local transport services from, 206

Alphen aan den Rijn, 68, 218–19, 223; noble landownership in, 36; bourgeois landownership in, 44, 46; social structure of, 63–64; population of, 93; farm size in, 128–30; fertilizer practices in, 151

Altena, Land van: landownership in, 36

Amersfoort: population of, 97; fertilizer trade of, 150

Amstel River, 64

Amstelveen (Nieuwer Amstel), 48; bourgeois landownership in, 46

Amsterdam, 86, 87, 90, 100, 161, 171, 191, 206; rural landownership of, 45–46; purchase of seigneurial rights by, 48; population of, 89; relative importance of, 99–100; migration to, 108–09; health conditions in, 110; burials in, 111; age at marriage in, 111; demographic characteristics of, 115; investors in, 124, 193; markets of, 133, 154, 199; entrepôt functions of, 166; trade with Germany, 166; cheese exports of, 167–68; grain trade of, 169, 172; grain prices in, 181–82; land of Burgerweeshuis in, 187–88; boatmen's guilds of, 207; vessels to Friesland, 208; trekvaart routes from, 208–09

Antwerp, 99; population of, 81–84; decline of, 108; real wages in, 182–83; as market for peat, 202

Arable farming: incidence of, 71, 144–46; techniques of, 71, 146; yields from, 152. *See also* Fertilizer; Grain

Arkel, Land van, 67

Arnhem: grain prices in, 182

Artois: population of, 82–83

Asperen: social structure of, 63, 65

Assendelft, Heer van, 39

Assendelft: bourgeois landownership in, 46; social structure of, 63, 65; population of, 92; arable land in, 145

Baarderadeel: farm size in, 58; arable land in, 145

Balk, 103

Baltic sea, 2; grain exports from, 71, 169; imports of Dutch products by, 166; volume of trade with, 170–71. *See also* Grain

Barradeel, 146–47, 217, 219; cultivated land in, 33; peasant landownership in, 51–52; landless population of, 57; farm size in, 59; herd size in, 138–39; arable land in, 145; crop yields in, 152, 154

Barsinghorn, 211; population of, 92

Bed ownership, 114, 217–18

Bedfordshire, 220

Bedsheets, 220–23; prices of, 223

Beemster polder, 132; herd size on, 140; cheese production on, 144, 160; coleseed production on, 153; rental values in, 188

Beets, 44; bourgeois landownership in, 45; peasant landownership in, 54; farm size in, 66; population of, 92; migration in, 112

Beklemrecht: as practiced in Groningen, 16. *See also* Tenurial customs

Benthuizen: social structure of, 65; herd size in, 70; population of, 93

Berg, 81

Bergen, 68

Bergum, 103

Berlikum: horticulture in, 154